Motherhood Online

Motherhood Online

Edited by

Michelle Moravec

CAMBRIDGE
SCHOLARS
PUBLISHING

Motherhood Online,
Edited by Michelle Moravec

This book first published 2011

Cambridge Scholars Publishing

12 Back Chapman Street, Newcastle upon Tyne, NE6 2XX, UK

British Library Cataloguing in Publication Data
A catalogue record for this book is available from the British Library

ISBN (10): 1-4438-2913-7, ISBN (13): 978-1-4438-2913-7

TABLE OF CONTENTS

Case Studies

Blogs and Community

PREFACE

HOW THE INTERNET SAVED MY SANITY AND OTHER WAYS LIFE ONLINE SHAPES MODERN MOTHERHOOD

MICHELLE MORAVEC

Sometime late in the nineties, I was seized by baby fever. In many ways it was all too predictable, last ditch effort to save a bad marriage, rapidly approaching thirty, stuck in a seemingly endless graduate school career, take your pick for the true underlying motivation. All I knew was I wanted a baby now and my then-husband just as adamantly did not. Girlfriends surrounded me with loving partners who seemed anxious to become fathers. Switching from briefs to boxers, check. Taking zinc supplements, sure. Abstaining for two days, timing intercourse to peak fertility, checking cervical mucous, whatever it took, these guys lined up eagerly.

I felt alone, ashamed and abysmal. I can't remember quite what internet-search query led me to BabyCenter.com, but there I found salvation in the form on an online bulletin board, as they were called back in the day, titled "ready to TTC, but my partner isn't." From the safety of my glassed-in sun porch I could vent my frustration, pour out my angst and in general spew in ways that my reticence and pride would never allow IRL.

Fast-forward some years. Ph.D. obtained, first husband lost, I found myself unexpectedly, but quite happily, pregnant. I quickly rejoined BabyCenter thinking 'MY TURN FINALLY." Sadly at six weeks that pregnancy ended in miscarriage, yet during that brief return to BabyCenter I became intrigued with the interaction of women online. When I again got that BFP, I joined yet another "pregnant for the first time" group within an hour of POAS.

Seven years have passed. I still post daily with some of the women I met during that first pregnancy. My children have worn their handmedowns. We exchange holiday cards and Secret Santa gifts. I cook their recipes and rely on their advice. I have traveled to meet many of them. When I weaned my first child, one talked me down from the sobbing as I hid in the basement while my husband put him to bed. During my son's difficulties in school, these women held my hand, virtually, as I anxiously awaited his daily behavior report.

The members of my online mommy group have become the single greatest influence on my parenting. I speak to my mother on a daily basis, and do not lack for IRL mommy friends, but still with these women online, I have shared intimate aspects of pregnancy, childbirth, and early motherhood that no other people are privy to. Along the way we have endured deployments, deaths, divorces, new jobs, houses and relationships. We have lost members and seen social networking supplement posting to the group, but still we continue.

Online I am a friend to people totally unlike my liberal, big-city, academic-feminist self. We have had our share of difficulties over politics, religion, economics, and parenting choices. Still I often liken the group to family, not to indicate the strength of the bonds, but rather the attitude we have towards one another. You know the saying, you can pick your friends but not your family? Actually, no, not in this case. My online mommy group shared an experience that will not be repeated, my first pregnancy and emerging motherhood. We may get on one another's nerves, each prefer specific members over others, and probably roll our eyes while reading more than any of us care to admit. Still we stay together because we cannot make new friends who share that singular experience. Having a community, albeit virtual, of women who know me in that way, women who not only shaped, but also understand me intimately as a mother is too precious to discard over annoyances.

I would be remiss if I did not thank my village, both virtual and in real life, which provided support over the long course of completing this manuscript. For invaluable assistance in editing I owe Melanie McBride a huge debt of gratitude. Cindy Kopp, Esther Mas, and Katrinka Somdahl-Sands offered extra hands and encouraging hearts. Most of all to my family, which motivates my writing about modern motherhood, you have made me a better scholar and person. This book would not exist without you.

Motherhood Online explores the thousands of mommy groups that populate the web. Whether centered on region, religion, race, or some other aspect of identity, these groups are creating a new space for mommy and allowing many women to maintain a grasp, however tenuous, on sanity in this crazy-making world of modern motherhood.

FOREWORD

THE TRUTH OF MOTHERHOOD ONLINE

ALEXANDRA SAMUEL

Eight days into my life as mother, I found myself sobbing my eyes out. My midwives had sent a breastfeeding counselor to my house, and she'd delivered heartbreaking news: I wasn't producing enough milk for my baby. While my husband drove across town to access a secret stash of pre-screened donor breast milk, I collapsed under the weight of exhaustion, guilt and disappointment. I had never felt so discouraged, nor so alone.

And then I logged in. BFAR – Breastfeeding After Reduction – was an online community I had discovered while preparing for my daughter's birth. I had long known that the breast reduction I'd had at age 18 could impact my later desire to breastfeed, but as an older friend had said to me at the time, "breastfeeding is less important to being a mother than feeling good about yourself". Now I was going to find out if she was right…and with all the expert advice on the medical and emotional benefits of nursing, I wasn't so sure. I had only been a mom for a week, and I was already failing.

As soon as I'd finished giving my daughter her first donated milk – from another, better mother – I sent my tearful update to the list:

> I thought I was prepared for this possibility but I had really hoped to have enough milk for the first few weeks...and while it is great to see my daughter finally satisfied after a feeding I feel so sad that our marathon feeding sessions of the past few days turn out to be a symptom of under-supply rather than just her bonding.

Minutes later, the responses started pouring in.

> I know how hard it is to have to supplement… Even if you're prepared for the possibility, and even think it's a probability that you'll have to supplement, it's hard to accept it at first.

> I know that feeling of total disappointment at having to supplement. But first of all, take heart in knowing that there have been many moms on this list who have had to supplement....And try not to feel like just because we've all gone through that heartbreaking feeling, we're used to it. With each new baby, many of us experience the same disappointment again when having to supplement -- believe me, I sympathize with you totally...It sounds like you're doing all the right things. Keep up the great work, and congratulations!
>
> With both of my babies, this was the worst moment in the entire post partum period. Even when I was more prepared for it the second time, it was still devastating. You just have to put it behind you as a fact of life.
>
> My baby was born in May and we started supplementing when he was almost a week old. I remember how much I cried that day. I know how disappointed you feel. Just hang in there. Pretty soon, supplementing will come easier.

And most important:

> You're not alone.

This book is a journey inside the many online worlds that have given mother after mother that same essential message: You're not alone. From general interest online communities held together by the common thread of a baby's birth month, to special interest online communities linked by the shared experience of in vitro fertilization, teen pregnancy or raising an autistic child, the Internet offers today's mothers new ways to connect; new ways to discover that however isolated they may feel, they are not alone.

That message is more than a lifeline: it's a revolution. As a friend of mine forewarned me when I was first expecting, "motherhood is both utterly overwhelming and completely under-stimulating". But in a culture that deifies the self-sacrificing mother, and vilifies the self-interested one, do you want to tell the mom next door that you're feeling overwhelmed and under-stimulated? Not when the price could be a permanent seat at the Bad Mommies' table.

But on the Internet, nobody knows you're a dog, which liberates you to be a bitch. Not a bitch to others – as many of these chapters recount, online mothers' groups are quick to sanction hostility – but the impatient, imperfect bitch of a mom who uses jarred babyfood, disposable diapers and a TV-as-sitter. The mom who takes off the halo and admits to imperfection, as Arnold recounts:

> I like that I can say things like things about sometimes disliking my kids, or being embarrassed by them, or whining about everyday minutiae, or even secrets about my marriage that I wouldn't want people in my social circles to know.

…or the mom who can pause to acknowledge the effort it requires to advocate for her autistic child, as quoted by Burgess:

> I trust that god knows what he is doing. . . . I will be a bit scuffed up, bruised up, worn out and somewhat out of breath due to being mom and challenging everyone who says "He cant" or "She wont" In the end Ill show them how wrong they all were.

…or the mom admits to the truth that teen motherhood is *not* a catastrophe, as Vinson reports in the case of a young mother sharing:

> …the joy I will feel thinking of that idiot social worker, how convinced he was I could not succeed in college, and how he almost convinced me as I fill out my law school application.

Online, as these stories show, you get to be the mother you actually are; the real mom you can't be in "real" life.

The idea that the Internet can support us as the mothers we actually are, rather than the mothers we're supposed to be, is doubly subversive. If we create spaces – even virtual ones -- where mothers can be accepted as they are, it breaks the paradigm that offers mothers a binary choice between self-sacrifice or self-recrimination. And if we acknowledge that the Internet can actually be a liberating and constructive part of parenting, rather than the demon that sees Mom texting her way through the family dinner, it breaks the paradigm that offers mothers a binary choice between unplugging and being a bad mom.

In challenging the increasingly popular narrative of the Internet as home-wrecker, this acknowledgement of mothering communities complicates the conversation about our online lives. For anyone grappling with the question of whether, how and how much the Internet transforms our social context, these chapters are a revelation. Forget the laundry lists that run through all the different ways the Internet has changed business, government or personal life. Instead, take a microscope to a single, foundational institution: motherhood.

Peer through this lens and your ability to make declarative statements about the Internet's social impact will quickly fall away. You'll meet mothers who use the Internet as an organizing tool, mothers who use it as a source of information, mothers who use it for social camaraderie. You'll encounter women who have come to see themselves as part of a community, and women who have been able to discover themselves as individuals. You'll meet Chinese bloggers, and American Facebookers.

And far from feeling like you've traversed the full landscape of motherhood, you'll simply awaken to its endless variety and find yourself hungry to discover even more of its online outposts.

In recognizing online motherhood in all its variety and complexity, this volume thoroughly breaks the narrative of The Internet vs. The Family. That is a tale that requires a monolithic Internet, and equally, a monolithic Motherhood. Break apart the mythology of a single mothering experience, and you lose the ability to make comprehensive claims about what the Internet is doing to that experience. The Internet is making mothers harried and distracted and amused and expressive and overwhelmed and nourished and victimized and empowered. In other words, it's doing what motherhood has *always* done: pushed women to the limits of their capacity and creativity, and in so doing, uncovered new capacities and new creation.

These chapters break another paradigm, too. By liberating us to tell the truth about our experience as mothers – the horrifying, hysterical, scatological, miraculous truth – the Internet has opened the door, just a crack, to a new way of being a mom. If you can write a blog post today about how you don't especially mind letting your baby cry herself to sleep, then maybe tomorrow you can tell your mother's group – in a whispered aside – that sometimes you let your baby cry a little. If you can post a Facebook update in which you complain about the culture of overscheduling, then maybe you'll find the strength to refuse the next extracurricular activity. If you can make a YouTube video in which you talk honestly about your fears for the world your daughter will one day inhabit, then maybe you can share those fears with her, too.

And when someone asks you where you learned to be that wide-open, courageous, *real* mom, you can say proudly: you learned it online.

THEORETICAL PERSPECTIVES

CHAPTER ONE

EXPECTANT MOTHERHOOD: HOW ONLINE COMMUNITIES SHAPE WOMEN'S EXPERIENCES OF PREGNANCY

> BABYCENTER® is the leading global resource for parents, reaching 78 percent of new and expectant moms online in the United States, and 16 million parents monthly across 21 markets worldwide. … As the voice of modern motherhood, BABYCENTER is the go-to resource for 21st Century Mom™ insights. Through its unique combination of content and community, BABYCENTER delivers award-winning stage-based content to parents via personalized home pages, e-mail newsletters, useful online and mobile tools, two popular parenting blogs (MomFormation™ and FameBaby®) and the BABYCENTER Community, the fastest growing parenting community on the Web (Company overview 2010).

BabyCenter.com, started in 1997, positions itself as a primary shaper of "modern motherhood," going so far as to trademark the phrase "21st Century Mom.™" The influence of BabyCenter has not gone unnoticed by scholars, particularly those interested in e-commerce. However, other academics, myself included, have turned a feminist lens on BabyCenter and the ways in which it attempts to shape modern motherhood.

In the summer of 2003 I presented research on the BabyCenter community at the National Women's Studies Association. Shortly thereafter I became pregnant again, and the project languished as I went through a difficult pregnancy including twelve weeks of bed rest, and a move to a new tenure track job the week after my son's birth. However, I remained interested in the topic of women's online communication, mostly because of the importance of my own BabyCenter birth group.

It was with some surprise then that I read Lisa Hammond Rashley's critique of BabyCenter in the Spring 2005 issue of NWSA Journal (Rashley 2005). While I found her analysis of the consumer forces at work on BabyCenter compelling, I had a profoundly different understanding of the BabyCenter community. As a long time participant on the BabyCenter bulletin boards, I believed that pregnant women online challenged in many way the expert-driven discourse about pregnancy, what one team of researchers has termed "the doublespeak of advice literature" (Michie and Cahn 1997, 2). I felt, both as an academic and a participant, vaguely insulted by her analysis of “gendered expectations” which seemed to imply that women were blind readers of the site. While the owner-provided content of BabyCenter, the parent company is the baby product leviathan Johnson and Johnson, certainly relies on both marketing and experts who at times reaffirm gender roles, the community section often provides a fascinating counterpoint in women’s own voices.

In this chapter, I revisit the arguments I made in 2003 about the role online groups play in shaping the “expectant mother” on BabyCenter. In a highly influential essay “Pregnant Embodiment: Subjectivity and Alienation” in 1984, Iris Marion Young noted that “the specific experience of women has been absent ” from the discourse on pregnancy (Young 1984, 46). Since that time, academics have theorized about pregnancy in many ways, often from the perspective of their own pregnancies (Mullins 2005, Hogan 2006) however as Saeten points out, despite Young’s call some twenty five years ago for scholars to attend to the women themselves, relatively few scholars take this approach (Saeten 2000).

My study is intended as a small contribution to that effort. I first focus on one online group, which I will call Babies to Be, that formed on the Pregnant for the First Time bulletin board of BabyCenter.com during the summer of 2002 and then look another BabyCenter group of first time mothers in 2010 in order to explore how a redesign of the site in 2009 to incorporate aspects of social networking may have influenced how pregnant women use the site.

Eavesdropping Online[1]

Over the past decade as I have chatted, and yes eavesdropped on the internet, I have heard echoes of earlier times in history when women controlled pregnancy and childbirth. Scholars have documented the precise shifts that moved female centered childbirth into the realm of medically controlled pregnancy and birth (Ginsburg and Rapp 1995, Rothman 2000, Inhorn 2007). This transformation has had a complex and mixed legacy for women. Judith Walzer Leavitt’s pioneering survey of reproductive practices in America reveals that nineteenth-century women often embraced new medical interventions in the hopes of a safer and less painful delivery (Leavitt 1986). By 1920, in large part due to women’s desire for a painless birth, the majority of women in the U.S. received care from obstetricians and gave birth in hospitals since only physicians had access to narcotics, although midwifery and home birth remained as part of the experience of some women, particularly those in rural location and among some immigrant and religious groups (Borst 1995, Danzi 1997, Fraser 1998, Barney 2000, Klassen 2001).

The shift in who attended births came with a concomitant shift in who produced knowledge about pregnancy and childbirth¸ away from women's experiences to the authoritative scientific knowledge of mostly male medical professionals (Jordan 1978, Oakley 1984, Martin 1987, Rothman 1991, Davis-Floyd 1992). The medical model views pregnancy and childbirth as aberrant conditions, as opposed to an older viewpoint that considers pregnancy and childbirth to be part of the functioning of women's bodies. Furthermore, under a medicalized model, technology becomes positioned the best way to offset the perceived risks that accompany the processes of reproduction (Lupton 1999a, 1999b, Rothman 2006, Jones 2007). Through non-invasive procedures such as ultrasound (Mitchell 2001, Taylor 2008) to the far more invasive constellation of genetic screening methods (Petchesky 1987, Rothman 1986, Rapp 2000), technology now provides almost complete surveillance of women during pregnancy. The potential problems that occur in pregnancy are seen as medically controllable and women are expected to produce the "perfect" baby with the aid of technology (Rothschild 2005). It is not hyperbole therefore to conclude that a pervasive discourse of risk surrounds pregnancy for many women and that the riskiness is reinforce throughout pregnancy by interaction with the various diagnostic procedures considered the standard of care.

In order to explore how pregnant women online challenge, affirm and in other way interact with medically dominated notions of pregnancy, I chose to focus on the first trimester of pregnancy. During those first twelve to fourteen weeks, depending on how you count, pregnant women have the least contact with the medical establishment. Estimates of pregnancy loss vary widely, but the vast majority occur in the first trimester with only 1-2% occurring in the second trimester (Atik, Hepworth-Jones and Doyle, 9). Since physicians can do nothing to prevent miscarriage, most obstetricians wait until the viability of the pregnancy has been established, with the first prenatal visit occurring at an average of nine weeks (Romano 2007). Thus in the earliest period of pregnancy, women are left on their own to grapple with their fears. How women's interaction shapes their reactions to the uncertainties inherent to early pregnancy is the major theme of my analysis.

minutest variations in their symptoms. Each woman has access to her own physical sensations, yet she is also surrounded by advice books, online sources, including the other sections of BabyCenter, and the omnipresent medical discourse of risk, which contextualize her understanding of the physical symptoms of pregnancy. Prior to the advent of highly sensitive home pregnancy tests, women were often unaware of their pregnancy during this waiting period. However, now that technology has advance to the point where women can determine pregnancy before her menstrual period is even late, the waiting stretches out for many women. The expectant woman is caught in a perpetual stage of uncertainty, during which time there is little she can do to influence the viability of her pregnancy or be certain of it.

During the first two months of Babies to Be, many women post to ask if cramping in the lower abdomen is "normal." These sensations are attributable to implantation cramping, uterine expansion, or round ligament pain. Cramping is such a common pregnancy phenomenon that posts regarding it became quite predictable, occurring on twenty-one days during the first two months of Babies to Be. On the second day of posting, before the group has even coalesced, the first symptom mentioned is a query about cramping. Very quickly, four women from other monthly due date groups, who are further along in their pregnancies, respond to confirm the normalcy of this symptom. These answers not only reassure the women who posted the original inquiry, but also another mom-to-be who had the same symptoms, but was "too frightened to ask anyone about it." This pattern of fear then reassurance continues for the next two months as many of the newly pregnant women who feel cramping post to discover if these feelings are normal.

During the first trimester, the members of Babies to Be provide an important resource for one another, which becomes clear when closely examining the patterns in response to queries about cramping. Some members first sought information from other Babies to Be about individual physical sensations of cramping. They then sought confirmation from medical authorities. In other words, they asked pregnant women online if they felt the same thing, and then asked their doctor to confirm the normalcy of the sensation as well. Conversely, another women first refers to pregnancy advice literature before reading online that other women felt the same thing. In this case, she still expresses relief to find additional confirmation from other women online "I read in a book that [cramping] was normal" but "hearing that others have experience the same thing is great!" Still other members of the group seem to have skipped the doctors and books completely in favor of the group's collective knowledge.

Does Anybody Else Feel This Way?

Babies to Be formed in the summer of 2002 in a typical fashio BabyCenter. One woman posts looking "to start a group to help u share what's going on in our bodies." A member from another monthly date group welcomes her to the "pregnant for the first time board" encourages her to keep posting until other women who share her due d month begin to join. The involvement by members of an existing group indicative of the supportive culture on the Pregnant for the First Tin bulletin board, which is reinforced in two ways. First, women bo respond to questions and pose questions to other groups' discussion threads. This practice not only expands the sharing of information among women, but also creates a larger community in which each woman is implicitly responsible for helping other members. Secondly, because women often read the discussions of other groups, particularly those of the due dates a month or two before their own, they become acculturated to the practices of BabyCenter, particularly the style of and rules for discussion.

Eventually, about sixty women become regular participants in Babies to Be.[2] Each day a member of the group would start a thread with that day's date, and all members respond to that thread. Posts typically consist on extensive "personals" which are comments directed to specific individuals who have already posted. Individuals offer updates about themselves, pose questions, or converse about a variety of pregnancy related topics. My analysis is based on over eight hundred separate messages posted during the first trimester.[3] I wanted to understand the complex ways women online both create and share information about pregnancy. I found that while they often began by seeking embodied knowledge, the information derived from direct experience of physical sensations, they quickly moved to offering support and providing solace to one another. The participants employ a sort of syllogistic logic; if what I am feeling is like what you are feeling and your pregnancy is fine, then mine must be too. Their logic based on their own bodily experiences provides these women with reassurance during a period defined by uncertainty.

Not surprisingly, during the first trimester, how pregnancy feels preoccupies the Babies to Be. Physical symptoms can be either a source of reassurance, as they provide tangible "proof" that a woman's body is changing, or a source of anxiety, as they may be interpreted as indication that something is amiss. During these first weeks, the women attempt to prognosticate about the viability of their pregnancies by attending to the

One woman responds to yet another query about cramping by writing "judging by the other posts I have read it is probably just the round ligaments stretching."

Many scholars have noted the supportive function of online pregnancy and mothering groups.[4] However, this close reading of the Babies to Be reveals additional information about this support occurs. Information about what causes the cramping could be found online, in a book or from a medical professional, but the support offered along with and implied by the embodied knowledge can come only from other pregnant women. In no instance did a member of Babies to Be provide information without explicit emotional support in an attempt to assuage the fears of their group member.

During that expectant period, the combination of sharing information plus emotional support provided by the online group is central to its value. One woman thanks the group for the “encouragement” while noting the reassurance she derives from knowing “that others are feeling the same things." Another woman explains "It really helps to ease your worries when you hear other people at your stage in pregnancy are also feeling." The worries to which this member refers derive from the fear that cramping is not only a symptom of normal pregnancy but also an indication of miscarriage. One woman complains that "Any time I have a minor cramp, I run to the bathroom to check for spotting. I've had a tiny bit, but probably not enough to worry about. Am I paranoid? I'm just so scared that something will happen." Sadly, she miscarries the following week.

This last example helps to explain why the participants of Babies to Be need the embodied knowledge of other pregnant women to provide reassurances beyond that available in pregnancy advice literature or even from medical professionals. As one woman notes “I have lots of questions and am reading books but sometimes the answers just aren't there.” For women to whom cramping is a frightening indicator that something is potentially amiss in her pregnancy, the knowledge and support of a community of women are invaluable. While a physician or a book may offer women an explanation of the physiological changes, the other pregnant women provide support in addition to information. As one member explains "It really helps to ease your worries when you hear other people at your stage in pregnancy are also feeling."

Additionally, I would argue that the responses they seek could not be found by any other means than access to another pregnant woman. The Babies to Be want to know what pregnancy is supposed to feel like. Even more, they want to know what it is not supposed to feel like. So they ask what may seem like an incredibly insensitive series of question to the woman who has just undergone a miscarriage. What did it feel like? How did it differ from other sensations during pregnancy? Did the woman have any other symptoms or clues that pregnancy loss was imminent? While these queries may seem intrusive to outsiders, the member is not offended. She understands the desire to hear from another woman with embodied knowledge and responds with both reassurances as well as the requested information about her symptoms and sensations.

However, not all aspects of pregnancy can be addressed through shared information and emotional support, which becomes quickly apparent for the Babies to Be. Discussion of human chorionic gonadotropin (hCG) levels provides a stark contrast to the conversations that occurred about cramping. hCG is produced by the placenta and is the substance detected by pregnancy tests. Some physicians routinely test for increasing hCG levels, while other practices only use this testing in cases of prior infertility or pregnancy loss.

The relationship between hCG levels and a successful pregnancy complicated. Increasing hCG levels are only indicative of a healthy pregnancy for the moment and cannot predict the future outcome of the pregnancy. Furthermore, levels of hCG are subject to medical interpretation. For example, extremely high levels of hCG early in pregnancy may indicate multiple fetuses or a molar pregnancy, two extremely different outcomes.

Most members of Babies to Be believe that higher levels of hCG cause increased morning sickness, which is interpreted as a positive symptom of a healthy pregnancy. As early as the first week of the group, a member of Babies to Be expresses concern about her lack of morning sickness. That fear resonates with other members of the group. One woman responds that she too has heard that morning sickness is a sign of healthy pregnancies, although she hastens to add that she is sure that you can have a healthy baby without being sick lest she alarm other members of the group. At this point a third group member chimes in to offer further evidence that she has gathered, not from medical authorities or from advice literature, but from other new mothers who have told her that they experienced no morning sickness and delivered healthy babies. As in the case of uterine cramping, hearing about first hand knowledge from actual pregnant women who have had successful pregnancy outcomes seems to provide some comfort.

However, this comfort is short lived as some women begin to share their hCG levels. About a week after the first discussion of the potential role of hCG in morning sickness, the issues arises again when a member's physician orders a repeat hCG test. It appears her doctor has not adequately explained the reason for the testing and she is concerned enough to share her fears with the group. While an initial hCG test is used to confirm pregnancy, hCG levels are only useful in pairs as it is the rate of increase that indicates a viable pregnancy. At this point, members of the group are able to provide the missing medical information. While one woman offers information based on medical authority, she is a lab technician; another woman provides information from her own pregnancy. This second woman also offers additional information in the form of a website that she has found that lists normal hCG values by duration of pregnancy.

This usage of the internet to provide medical knowledge occurs throughout the women's pregnancies, with uneven results. One woman, whose hCG levels are on the low end of the normal range for her gestational period is upset when she sees the chart on the internet. The original poster also remains anxious. When her hCG levels increase, she is pleased, but then learns that some of here group members have higher levels, which causes her to become concerned again. A group member offers reassurance pointing out that at similar estimated due dates other group members had similar hCG levels. The original poster finds this comforting and thanks her group mate for her reassurances specifically noting the value of the first hand knowledge about hCG levels.

While the original poster may feel better, other women are now concerned. Not all physicians routinely perform hCG testing as there is no medical intervention for declining hCG levels. This lack of medical technology in their pregnancy becomes an issue for some woman. One group member wonders how she will know if something is wrong with her pregnancy if her hCG levels are not medically monitored. Ironically, the discussion on the board has increased her desire for medical confirmation of the health of her pregnancy and illustrates that at times participation in Babies to Be exacerbates anxiety for its members. In the case of hCG testing, shared information and emotional support falter in the face of a medical intervention over which the women have no control.

However, the combination of sharing and support does help dispel other sort of anxieties. What is particularly unexpected for the Babies to Be is the way that uncertainty in early pregnancy pervades all aspects of their life. For example, an anticipated happy moment in pregnancy, "the telling" to friends and family of the expected new arrival, becomes a hotly debated issue. Discussions about who to tell, when to tell and how to do it occur on twenty-three days in the first trimester. The participants in Babies to Be share their plans for surprise announcements, time the big news to coincide with happy occasions, such as birthdays or family events, or concoct unique gifts that break the news, such as a sonogram image in a grandparents photo frame. The Babies to Be weigh carefully the possibility of having to inform people of a miscarriage should it occur against their pressing desire to share their excitement immediately. Some members feel that it is acceptable to communicate the news of the pregnancy with anyone on whom a woman would rely for emotional support during a miscarriage, while others prefer to avoid the possibility of having to reveal bad news after sharing the happy news. In fact one of the earliest reasons sited for finding the group was a desire to talk about pregnancy among women who have not shared the news with people in real life.

As the women begin to tell, the responses they receive to their revelations vary widely. While some of the women received the ideal response, described by one member as “priceless”, for other women, the reactions to their big news were far from the expected. One woman’s mother reacted by telling her it was “too early” to share the news, which caused the pregnant woman to feel "let down" by her reaction. To early, by which her mother meant still in that first trimester frame in which most pregnancy losses occur reinforces for all participants who read the post the idea of riskiness in early pregnancy.

This riskiness increasingly pervades the participants’ pregnancies and confounds their prior expectations. One woman finds herself inexplicably “nervous about something being wrong, but so far I have nothing to justify this” and wonders if she is “just being paranoid?” Other women chime in to confirm that they too feel that way, implicitly offering reassurance that she is not being paranoid. In this fashion, the group not only functions to reassure women that their physical sensations of pregnancy are normal, but their emotional reaction is as well. Over time, Babies to Be becomes a place to express ambivalent feelings that women may not feel comfortable sharing with people in their face-to-face life.

This function is made even more important by the lack of preparation among the women for their ambivalent feelings. For women who happily anticipated their first pregnancies, the negative aspects were quite unexpected. One woman laments "I didn't think pregnancy especially the first trimester would be so stressful.” In addition to the fears of pregnancy loss, changes wrought by pregnancy also create negative feelings. Another woman asks "is anyone else starting to really become afraid? Just afraid of the changes, the first weeks after the baby is born, etc? I'm trying not to let it get to me but sometimes it brings me down.” Interestingly for this woman, it is the preparation for becoming a mother, she watched a video about infant care, that has caused her to develop self doubt. She becomes “sort of nervous about my abilities and what I've gotten myself in to."

The emotional impact of being pregnant also catches some women off guard. "Is anyone else experiencing significant mood swings?" queries one woman. While another responds "I feel very emotional too,” she complains. “No one mentioned that but I feel like I could cry at the drop of a hat." For still other participants, it is their changed status as pregnant a woman that causes them difficulty. One woman complains of "feelings of being able to do nothing when I have always been independent." For some women the pregnancy seems to alter their self-perception. One woman apologizes for the depressing tone of her message on the prior day. "Before I got pregnant people use to view me as someone who is high on life. Now I'm sure everyone I work with probably thinks I'm hell on earth. It's just been really hard for me. Pregnancy and I haven’t got along very well."

The women react to these feelings in a variety of ways. Some women apologize for burdening the others with their complaints. Another woman, who has experienced extreme morning sickness starts "to get really angry about this. It certainly takes the joy out of pregnancy." Other women begin to experience “guilt about day care and I haven't even birthed yet!” She asks “is anyone else worrying about this issue. DH [Dear Husband, a common BBC abbreviation] told me last night I should have thought about this before I wanted a baby so badly (that was really helpful).” These changed relationships with family are unanticipated for most women. In particular, the women lament their partners’ inability to understand them. Sometimes the women blame perceived gendered differences, such as lack of men’s emotionality, for their partner’s inability to provide the support they need. For other women, it is the physical experience of pregnancy, that causes them to conclude, “he can’t understand what I’m going through.” Again, their responses to the perceived failures of their partners differ, ranging from “hurt” to “annoyed” and outright anger and frustration.

The perceived riskiness of pregnancy and the varying levels of support women receive during this crucial early phase of pregnancy help to explain yet another value that Babies to Be provides for members. For some of these women, their pregnancy has become the central concern of their life, and they want to talk about it extensively, or as one woman put it “to just dream” about the infinite details and decisions. These women worry that they are boring workmates or overwhelming their spouses. Thus, in addition to support, sharing and a normalizing framework for their emotional responses to pregnancy, the group of pregnant women online provides a space where the women can discuss their pregnancy as much as they want with women who are not going to tell them that they should not be thinking so much about it, or should keep the news to themselves, or are going to react in judgmental ways.

Not surprisingly, given the multiple needs that the online group fulfills, despite the anxiety that participation may at times create, the participants overwhelmingly describe it in positive ways. Women find it "comforting" "helpful" "exciting" to participate in Babies to Be. Specifically they value the ability to "compare notes" "ease your worries" or "find someone who understands." They seek "support" a place to "vent" and simply other women with whom to "share the experience with." Yet clearly more than that occurs.

Over the course of nine months, a group of relative strangers forges a close-knit community and shares a complex and important life event. Careful reading of the posts reveals that the ties between the women move beyond simply posting to one another about details of their pregnancies. They share personal information about themselves, their careers, where they are located, and their partners. Some women who live in geographic proximity meet in person. The group also begins to coalesce and self-define. Presence on the board becomes so expected for habitual posters that other members note absences. Some members even post in advance if they will be gone, or post explanatory apologies for their absences. The group begins to take concrete form as one member compiles a roster of members that she updates and posts frequently. It includes the screen name of participants, estimated due date and in a separate section note upcoming doctor's appointments. Despite the delineation of group members, the Babies to Be remain open to new members, welcome lurkers when they come out and happily respond to the women more advanced in their pregnancies that check in on the newly pregnant women. After childbirth some members continue on the "new mommies" board of BabyCenter. Eventually, the group becomes private, and eight years later, a subset of the original Babies to Be continues as a online group.

Eight Years Later

In 2007 BabyCenter bought Mayasmom, a social networking site, for its underlying technology. In early 2008 a beta site that integrated new capacities was opened to existing BabyCenter members, and thus the oldest boards on the current BabyCenter website date to March 2008. That summer the new site went live to the public. A press release touted the ways "BabyCenter's new community enables parents to connect and share with each other using many new features and tools including:

- Create public and private groups around any topic
- Share photos and video among friends by uploading to Profiles and Journals
- Distribute a personal blog feed from other blogging platforms into a BabyCenter® Journal
- Pass Notes to other members, post Shout-Outs, comment on Journals
- Match with people who share common interests, locations, childrens' ages and more
- Publish "kid-isms," the hilarious things kids say
- Tag photos and profile (Babycenter Launches 2008)

Thus, in addition to posting to specific groups as occurred in earlier incarnation of the BabyCenter site, BabyCenter 2.0 includes multiple ways for participants to share information and communicate with one another. A profile page exists for all users who may create unique avatars. Each profile page has suggested entries categorized under "milestones the moments that matter in your pregnancy and your baby's development," "tidbits - details about yourself" in the form of fill in responses to preset questions, and "kiddims" funny quotes from your kid. Ways to communicate between users have also proliferated including passing notes via an internal email system, sharing journals, via a blog hosted BabyCenter and Shoutouts, open messages from other members that appear on a user's profile page. Aspects of social networking have also been incorporated, such as friending, and a Facebook-like status update that appears below the avatar and user name. Even posting to boards has changed with users now able to create elaborate signatures with embedded links such as fertility charts, or "tags" to popular topics.

The new site design of BabyCenter.com comes with vastly increased involvement by site administrators of the BabyCenter community. "Birth club" boards are created by BabyCenter employees called "hosts." The involvement of host-created boards has transformed the function of the community groups. BabyCenter hosts start the monthly birth clubs far in advance of conception, so that an entire calendar year is present on the site. There are two immediate results of this change. The first is that women trying to conceive constitute the earliest posts in these hoped for due date months. This shift effectively combines what used to be a separate board with the birth club boards and pushes the conversations in the due date months from expectancy back to the period of conception.

On the positive side, women who do conceive are able to share the earliest aspect of pregnancy, that period of waiting between ovulation to conception. However, inevitably some women will not become pregnant that month, and leave the group, making for a far more fluid membership in these earliest months and inflating the initial membership numbers. As a response to the huge number of women who join each monthly birth club, which can quickly rise to the thousands, participants within these monthly boards create their own subgroups Typically there are three ten-day estimate due date groups, in addition to many thematic groups based on other aspects of identity, regional location, profession, or number of pregnancies.

BabyCenter 2.0 eliminated the "pregnant for the first time" board. However, sometimes groups for women who are pregnant for the first time, "first timers," form, as offshoots of monthly due date boards. Babies to Be II formed much as its predecessor did. In a post titled "first time moms?" a woman hopes to find "other first timers" in order to compare "how everyone is feeling" and to discuss "how husbands are" reacting. She is aware of the practice of starting first time mom groups, but jokes that it is "too much responsibility for me- lol." Her post attracts other first time moms, who chat away about the expected, comparing symptoms, complaining about spouses, deciding if grandparents to be should be let in on the big news yet. Five days later, another woman does start a group.

However, rather than creating a sub-group on the larger monthly due date board, she chooses a new option, a user initiated group. She makes the group public so that anyone can join, but because the group is not linked to the much larger monthly due date board it gets lost in the literally thousands on groups on BabyCenter. When two days later another poster starts a thread for first pregnancy on the same board, unlike BabyCenter in 2003, there is no continual first time mom culture to direct her to the emerging first time mom group. Her post is not ignored. A woman much further along in her pregnancy does offer reassurance about her cramping, which motivated her post looking for other first time pregnant women, but the knowledge of other groups, that was present in the prior incarnation of BabyCenter is lost in the vastness of boards on the newer site.

Within ten days of starting Babies to Be II, sixty women have joined, presumably by following the link from the larger due date board. Eventually around one hundred women regularly participate in Babies to Be II during the first trimester, posting over four thousand messages to over five hundred threads over a period of ninety-three days.[5] This dramatic increase over the original group (864 comments to sixty-one posts over ninety-one days) reflects several changes in BabyCenter culture. Rather than simply replying to a daily conversation, the participants start many daily conversations centered on specific topics. The average number of conversations started each day is five for Babies to Be II. While this approach makes it easier for participants to find exactly the information sought, it lessens the communal interaction that one continual daily conversation created. 80% of post received twelve or fewer responses and 50% received six or fewer as compared to the daily threads of the 2003 group, which routinely reached over a hundred per day.

Not surprisingly, the content of the messages, how pregnancy feels both emotionally and physically, preoccupies the Babies to Be II much as it had in 2003. Pregnancy is still pregnancy. Posts in fact could have come verbatim from the board eight years earlier. Conversations on the now predictable subjects of cramping, hCG level, emotional reactions to pregnancy and transformed relationship with friends and family all emerge. Again, sharing and support occurs, albeit in a more fragmented form dispersed across multiple conversations.

For the remainder of this chapter, I want to explore the ways that participants of Babies to Be II utilize the BabyCenter 2.0 social networking functions. Because members join a group and are listed as members, it is possible to quantify lurkers, since members can anonymously join the board without responding to threads or posting to the "roll call." Despite the existence of an official group membership of over 300, only about 100 women actively participate. Still even fewer members respond to two "roll call" posts that request users provide specific information about themselves. The initial roll call occurred in the first month of the first trimester and the second in the last moth of the first trimester. I combined those lists to garner thirty-two women who responded to both and examined their profiles in depth. Of that group eighteen, slightly over half have publically accessible profiles.

The most frequently utilized new function is the ability to share photos, with 83% posting at least one. Sixty-six percent have been friended with the average number of friends just under seven, although two members who have thirty-three and forty-four friends respectively heavily skew that number. Only three women write journals and only two, the group owners, have received a "shout out" from anyone other than BabyCenter staff who maintain the community. Thus despite the many new ways of interacting, other than sharing photos, it is seems that most Babies to Be II do not avail themselves of them. The participants seem to want, as the original group did, conversation with other pregnant women.

Because the groups to which a member belongs are listed on their open profiles, it is possible to assess in greater depth how users participate in the larger BabyCenter community. Seven women belong to the officially associated "photo club" although some confusion may exist as an "unofficial" user-initiated group titled Babies to Be II Photo group also exists. All of the women belong to more than one group in addition to

Babies to Be II. The highest number of groups is twelve groups with the average number just under five. It seems possible that this proliferation of participation in multiple groups, a practice that was uncommon on the original Pregnant for the First Time board, may attenuate the communal bonds that form. Indeed, while the initial Babies to Be held a virtual baby shower in which they exchanged gifts and met up with members who lived in close geographic proximity, I have found no such evidence of extended ties in Babies to Be II.

However, I have found more extensive interaction across boards, which points to new ways of utilizing BabyCenter. In BabyCenter 2003, women further along in pregnancy would check in on the neophytes, and members of the prior year's monthly due date group popped in to wax nostalgic, but no formal relationships between women across groups existed. Ties across boards are far more common on the new BabyCenter. The members of Babies to Be II were offered the opportunity to participate in a user initiate project that began at least as far back as the fall of 2009 and has become part of BabyCenter culture. This "adopt a mommy" project paired women from the same monthly due date group in the prior year for advice-giving and friendship and involved 134 women. Further evidence for the cross board bonding appears in another aspect of board culture, "Find a BabyCenter Parent near you," a practice that dates back at least as far as the summer of 2009, and reappears intermittently. Although the Babies To Be II have not yet participated on their board, their larger due date month has, so it may jump to their board or they may sign up there.

Conclusion

In my own online mommy group I have seen the impact of social networking sites such as Facebook and Twitter, which pull people's attention away from the group, so the trends on BabyCenter do not come as a great surprise. I completely understand why BabyCenter site owners have attempted to incorporate as many aspects of internet communication into the site. Users equal dollars from advertising revenue. It seems from my admittedly small analysis, however, that BabyCenter members are not interested in using these functions. What they seek now, as in the past, is direct interaction with other pregnant women.

That these conversations are less sustained is puzzling. I am not sure why users shifted to multiple conversations as opposed to daily threads. From the inception of the new BabyCenter site, this practice has occurred on the more active boards. Searching the oldest groups for women pregnant or the first time, I see only multiple conversations occurring rather than a single daily thread. I suspect this transition had to do with volume of posts. With posts reaching over one hundred daily, the increased amount of participation would have made daily thread far too long. Then again, it may be that individuals have become more fluent in multitasking online as technology becomes ever more pervasive. Interacting via texting and social networks has joined online groups and email as ways of interacting. Holding multiple simultaneous conversations is a common feature of many women's lives.

In November 2010 as I finished this chapter, I noticed a change on BabyCenter The official hosts are now creating first time mother boards beginning with the year 2012, in addition to the monthly due date boards. I find this shift an interesting confirmation of my paper's analysis of the value of these boards as clearly BabyCenter community analysts have noticed that almost every monthly due date board ends up with at least one for women who are new to pregnancy. However, I also find the shift somewhat distressing. The benefit of my own first time mom group was its relatively small size. With these new 2012 boards I foresee an influx of women trying to conceive, which will result in a huge number of participants, many of who will not become pregnant and will therefore leave, but not before their inflation of the group membership may inhibit the formation of close ties.

In the end, I remain confident that BabyCenter community participants will come up with their own response, be it smaller monthly subsets of these first time mother boards, groups based on not first time motherhood combined with other aspects of identity, or the ultimate fall back, the user created group. Despite the changed patterns of interaction, and the lack of interest in web 2.0 functionality I found in the latter Babies to Be group, I remain convinced that for many women, online space provides a significant outlet during pregnancy. That need for support, shared reference points, and normalization of emotions has not changed even if the technology that facilitates it has.

Works Cited

Atik, Ruth Bender, Barbara E. Hepworth-Jones and Pat Doyle. 2010. "Risk factors for miscarriage," *Early Pregnancy,* edited by Roy G. Farquharson and Mary D. Stephenson. 9-18. Cambridge, UK: Cambridge University Press.

Babycenter Launches Social Network for Largest Parenting Community Online, 2008. Accessed December 17. http://www.jnj.com/connect/

NewsArchive/all-news-archive/20080714_120000

Bakardjieva, Maria and Andrew Feenberg. 2001. "Involving the Virtual Subject" *Ethics and Information Technology* 2(4):233 - 240

Barney, Sandra. 2000. *Authorized to Heal: Gender, Class, and the Transformation of Medicine in Appalachia, 1880-1930*. Chapel Hill, NC: University of North Carolina Press.

Borst, Charlotte. 1995. *Catching Babies: The Professionalization of Childbirth, 1870-1920*. Cambridge, MA:Harvard University Press.

Bylund, C. L. 2005. "Mothers' involvement in decision making during the birthing process: A quantitative analysis of women's online birth stories." *Health Communication* 18(1):23–39.

Cavanagh, Allison. 1999. "Behaviour in Public?: Ethics in Online Ethnography." Cybersociology Magazine 6. Accessed December 17. (http://www.cybersociology.com/issue_6_research_methodology_online/index.html).

"Company overview," accessed December 17. http://www.babycenter.com/help-about-company

Danzi, Angela D. 1997. *From Home to Hospital: Jewish and Italian American Women and Childbirth, 1920-1940*. Lanham, Md.: University Press of America.

Davis-Floyd, Robbie. 1992. *Birth as an American Rite of Passage*. Berkeley: University of California Press.

Dickerson, S. S. 2006. "Women's use of the Internet: What nurses need to know." *Journal of Obstetric, Gynecologic, and Neonatal Nursing*. 35(1):151–156.

Drentea, Patricia and Jennifer L. Moren-Cross. 2005. "Social capital and social support on the web: the case of an internet mother site." *Sociology of Health & Illness* 27(7):920-943.

Ess, C. 2002. *Ethical decision-making and Internet research accessed December 17*. http://aoir.org/reports/ethics.pdf.

Fraser, Gertrude. 1998. *African American Midwifery in the South: Dialogues of Birth, Race, and Memory*. Cambridge, MA: Harvard University Press.

Ginsburg, Faye and Rayna Rapp. 1995. *Conceiving the new World Order: The Global Politics of Reproduction*. Berkeley: University of California Press.

Herman, JoAnne, Kathryn Mock, Deborah Blackwell and Tara Hulsey. 2004. Use of a Pregnancy Support Web Site by Low-Income African American Women. *Journal of Obstetric, Gynecologic, & Neonatal Nursing*, 34(6):713-720.

Herring, Susan. 2004. Computer-mediated discourse analysis: An approach to researching online behavior. In: S. A. Barab, R. Kling, and J. H. Gray (Eds.), Designing for Virtual Communities in the Service of Learning (pp. 338-376). New York: Cambridge University Press, 338-376.

Hogan, Susan. *Conception Diary: Thinking about Pregnancy and Motherhood.* Sheffield, UK: Eilish Press.

Inhorn, Maria C. 2007. Reproductive Disruptions: Gender, Technology, and Biopolitics in the New Millennium. New York: Berghahn Books.

Jones, Dawn. 2007 "Fearing the worst, hoping for the best': the discursive construction of risk in pregnancy" in *Risks, Identities and the Everyday* Julie Scott Jones, and Jayne Raisborough, eds. Ashgate Publishing, Ltd., 37-50.

Jordan, Brigitte. 1978. *Birth in Four Cultures: A Crosscultural Investigation of Childbirth in Yucatan, Holland, Sweden, and the United States.* Montreal, Canada: Eden Press.

Kim, Hosu. 2007. "A Flickering Motherhood Korean Birthmothers' Internet Community." S&F Online 5:2.
http://www.barnard.edu/sfonline/blogs/kim_01.htm

Klassen, Pamela. 2001. *Blessed Events: Religion and Home Birth in America* Princeton University Press, 2001.

Koeber, Amy. 2001. "Postmodernism, Resistance, and Cyberspace: Making Rhetorical Spaces for Feminist Mothers on the Web." *Women's Studies in Communication* 24(2):218–40.

Lagan B, Sinclair M, Kernohan WG. 2006. "Pregnant women's use of the internet: a review of published and unpublished evidence." *Evidence Based Midwifery* 4(1): 17-23

Larsson, M. 2007. A descriptive study of the use of the Internet by women seeking pregnancy-related information. *Midwifery* 25(1):14-20

Leavitt, Judith Walzer. 1986. *Brought To Bed: Childbearing in America 1750-1950.* New York: Oxford University Press.

Lupton, Deborah. 1999. *Risk* New York: Routledge.

—. 1999a. "Risk and the ontology of pregnant embodiment" in *Risk and Sociocultural Theory: New Directions and Perspectives*, Cambridge University Press, 59-87.

Madge, Clare, and Henrietta O'Connor. 2005. "Mothers in the making? Exploring liminality in cyber/space" *Transactions of the Institute of British Geographers* 30(1):83-97.

Madge Clare, and Henrietta O'Connor. 2006. "Parenting gone wired: empowerment of new mothers on the internet?" *Social & Cultural Geography* 7(2) 2:199-220.

Martin, Emily. 1987. The woman in the body. Boston: Beacon.

Michie, Helena and Naomi R. Cahn. 1997. *Confinements : Fertility and Infertility in Contemporary Culture.* New Brunswick: Rutgers University Press

Mitchell, Lisa. 2001 *Baby's First Picture: Ultrasound and the Politics of Fetal Subjects.* University of Toronto Press.

Miyata, Kakuko. 2002. "Social support for Japanese mothers online and offline." Edited by Barry Wellman and Carolyn Haythornthwaite. *The Internet in Everyday Life,* 520–549. Oxford: Blackwell Publishing.

Mullins, Amy. 2005. *Reconceiving pregnancy and childcare: ethics, experience, and reproductive labor.* Cambridge, UK: Cambridge University Press.

Oakley, Ann. 1984. *The Captured Womb: A History of the Medical Care of Pregnant Women.* New York: Basil Blackwell Publisher Ltd., 1984.

O'Connor, Henrietta and Clare Madge. 2001. 'Cyber-Mothers: Online Synchronous Interviewing using Conferencing Software' *Sociological Research Online,* 5(4) accessed October 10, 2008 <http://www.socresonline.org.uk/5/4/o'connor.html>

O'Connor, Henrietta, & Clare Madge. 2004. "My mum's thirty years out of date:" The role of the Internet in the transition to motherhood. *Community, Work, and Family* 7(3):351–369.

Petchesky, R. 1987. "Foetal images: The power of visual culture in the politics of reproduction. *Feminist Studies*, 13, 263-292.

Rapp, Rayna. 2000. *Testing Women, Testing the Fetus: The Social Impact of Amniocentesis in America*. New York: Routledge.

Rashley, Lisa Hammond. 2005. " 'Work it out with your wife': Gendered Expectations and Parenting Rhetoric Online." *NWSA Journal* 17(1):58-92.

Romano, Amy M. 2007. "A Changing Landscape: Implications of Pregnant Women's Internet Use for Childbirth Educators' *Journal of Perinatal Education* 16(4): 18–24.

Rothman, Barbara Katz *1986. The Tentative Pregnancy: How Amniocentesis Changes the Experience of Motherhood.* New York: Viking Press.

—. *1991. In Labor: Women and Power in the Birthplace.* W.W. Norton and Company, 2nd ed.

Rothman, Barbara. 2000. Recreating Motherhood. Piscataway: Rutgers University Press.

Rothman, Barbara Katz. 2006 "Laboring Now: Current Cultural Constructions of Pregnancy, Birth and Mothering" in Laboring On: Birth in Transition in the United States, Barbara Katz Rothman, Wendy Simonds and Bari Meltzer Norman. CRC Press, 29-96.

Rothschild, Joan. 2005. *The Dream of the Perfect Child.* Bloomington: Indiana University Press.
Saetnan, Ann Rudinow. 2000. "Thirteen Women's Narratives of Pregnancy, Ultrasound, and Self" in *Ann Rudinow Saetnan*, Nelly Oudshoorn, and Marta Kirejcyk, eds. *Bodies of Technology*, 331-354, Columbus: Ohio States University Press.
Taylor, Janelle. 2008. *The Public Life of the Fetal Sonogram: Technology, Consumption, and the Politics of* Reproduction New Brunswick: Rutgers University Press.
Young, Iris Marion. 1984. rpt 2004. "Pregnant Embodiment: Subjectivity and Alienation" in *On Female Body Experience: Throwing like a Girl and Other* Essays New York: Oxford University Press, 46-61.

Notes

[1] Following the 2002 guidelines of the Members of the Association of Internet Researchers (Ess 2002), I determined that informed consent was not necessary since BabyCenter is a public site available to read without a password and that does not prohibit usage. The user faq required for registration states "Please remember that if you post any information in areas of our Sites that are generally accessible to users, such as chat rooms and message boards, it will be available to the public." While some researchers have rejected all use of online groups that does not involve explicit informed consent in advance (Bakardjieva and Feenberg. 2001) I do not believe that approach would be possible on a public site like BabyCenter where group membership is highly fluid. This difficulty, and more, are discussed by Cavanagh who suggests that the online group itself signals it public status in its reaction to "lurkers" (Cavanagh 1999). I would add to that in addition to the warm welcome given to women who unlurked, they also responded positively to members of other groups on the Pregnant for the First Time Board who periodically popped into their group to ask questions or offer unsolicited advice. Thus from their own responses, it seems clear that the Babies To Be do not regard their online discussions as a private conversation. My conclusion follows those of many other researchers using online groups (Koeber 2001, Bylund 2005, Drentea and Moren-Cross 2005, Rashley 2007). Because Babies to Be 2002 no longer exists in any form on the internet, I have quoted from these discussions. Babies to Be II is currently accessible online and thus I have chosen not to use direct quotes.

[2] Obviously given varying due dates with the shared month, my delineations of trimesters is only a rough division of the time covered in this paper. 129 individual users posted 864 separate messages to the bulletin board. 52.3% of the women posted only on one or two days. The second trimester posts occurred on ninety-eight days. Seventy-three individual users posted 2085 messages. 26% women posted on three or fewer days. The third trimester consisted of eighty-eight days of postings and 2457 separate posts.

[3] I draw on Susan Herring's idea of computer mediated discourse analysis (CDMA), (Herring 2004) which she defines as analysis of logs of verbal interaction (characters, words, utterances, messages, exchanges, threads, archives, etc)" (Herring 2004, 379). I combined the temporal and thematic approaches that Herring identifies as the two most useful methods of CDMA. I used the temporality of pregnancy to structure my analysis by using trimesters as dividing lines. I then hand coded posts into clusters under themes that related to my research question about interaction with and responses to medical technology and the potential for aspects of social pregnancy.

[4] Most studies of pregnant women's internet usage have been conducted by health science researchers (Herman et al 2004, Dickerson 2006, Lagan, Sinclair M, and Kernohan 2006, Larsson 2007). Far more studies have been done of mothers on the internet (Koeber 2001, Miyata 2002, O'Connor and Madge, 2001, O'Connor and Madge 2004, Madge and O'Connor 2005, Drentea and Moren-Cross 2005, Madge and O'Connor 2006, Kim 2007).

[5] Again, I considered participants to be active if they posted more than three times during the first trimester. There were almost an equal number who posted fewer than three times.

CHAPTER TWO

BEYOND DISCUSSION FORUMS: THE TRANSMEDIATED SUPPORT CULTURE OF AN ONLINE PREGNANCY AND MOTHERING GROUP

BARBARA L. LEY

In the fall of 2009 members of Coming up Roses, an online pregnancy and mothering support group, engaged in numerous discussions about declining participation on the site.[1] Tina, one of the site's members and administrators, expressed concern that Facebook contributed to this trend. She speculated that members who spent time on Facebook had less time to devote to the Coming up Roses website. To be sure, numerous members acknowledged that they spent an increasing amount of time on Facebook and that their Facebook time led to decreased participation on the group's website. Yet many of them argued that the time they spent on Facebook did not detract from interacting with other "Roses," as members affectionately called themselves. Due to increasing job, family, and other life responsibilities, they had less time to devote to online activities. Thus, they used Facebook to connect and interact with multiple social and familial networks at once, including their fellow Roses.

In the past fifteen years, hundreds of pregnancy and mothering groups have formed online. Various social and cultural factors account for the formation of such groups, including the integration of the Internet in everyday life (Hampton and Gupta 2008; Holloway and Valentine 2003; Wellman and Haythornthwaite 2001); increased lay participation in health care decision-making and the rise of citizen-based health social movements (Fox 2007; Layne 2003; Ley 2009); and the decline of women's offline familial and social networks, which have led women to recreate such networks online (Drentea and Moren-Cross 2005; Taylor, Layne, and Wozniak 2004). Whereas some of the earliest pregnancy and mothering groups formed via email list-servs, many—if not most—of them formed in web-based discussion forums that became popular in the late 1990s and early 2000s. A growing number of these online groups, however, are now expanding their technosocial boundaries by relying on a broad range of new digital technologies and platforms to stay connected. In this chapter, I develop the concept of "transmediated support" to explore the range of digital media that members of one pregnancy and mothering site—Coming up Roses—use to connect with one another and the group more generally. In doing so, I highlight the ways in which such transmedia connections influence the meaning, significance, and practice of online support and community for Coming up Roses' members.[2] I also touch upon the ways that individual members of the group negotiate the group's transmediated landscape in different and sometimes conflicting ways.

Transmediated Support

Coming up Roses was founded in November 2005 after splintering off from another pregnancy and mothering group Stork Talk. Most of the site's 200 registered members live in the United States, and the rest hail from Canada, the United Kingdom, France, and Jamaica. Coming up Roses is a non-commercial website, meaning that membership is free and its administrators make no money from running it. The site is also private; women who wish to join must be referred to the site by an existing member and be approved by one of the site's moderators. As evidenced by this referral system, some members knew one another before joining the site. Yet even members without preexisting connections have sent one another gifts through the mail, met up for dinner or drinks, and organized regional "Rose" parties.[3]

Since its inception, the Coming up Roses website has served as the focal point for its members. Members have interacted with one another in sixty forums devoted to topics such as trying to conceive, adoption, pregnancy, toddler care, breastfeeding, and childbirth methods. They have also participated in forums devoted to celebrity gossip, social and political debates, venting, relationships, health, and hobbies. To date, members have started more than 21,000 discussion threads and have posted more than 215,000 replies to these threads. In addition to participating in the forums, they have sometimes interacted with one another through the website's personal messaging system and, to a lesser extent, its chat room. The former has enabled the Roses to communicate asynchronously one-on-one in a private setting, and the latter has allowed two or more members to hold real-time discussions in a semi-private "room."

In recent years, the group's technosocial boundaries have expanded. Members log onto the website not only with their desktops and laptops but also increasingly with their iPod Touches, Blackberries, and other smartphones. Just as significantly, a growing number of members interact with one another on social networking sites (e.g., Facebook and MySpace), microblogging sites (e.g., Twitter), photo sharing sites (e.g., Flickr and Shutterfly), and personal blogs. As a result, the group's social interactions and support practices are now taking place via a wide range of communication technologies and Internet platforms. This communication expansion has both enhanced and challenged the centrality of the Coming up Roses website for individual members and for the broader group.

"Transmediated support" is a useful framework for conceptualizing the meaning and significance of the use of multiple communication channels by members of Coming up Roses to connect with one another and the group more generally. My notion of transmediated support builds on Christina Dena's notion of "transmedia practice" (Dena 2009). This umbrella concept relates to a range of transmedia approaches taken in various social and professional arenas, the design decisions that producers make when constructing transmedia projects, and the ways in which consumers engage with such projects. One facet of transmedia practice that is especially relevant to my project is "transmedia storytelling," a term that Henry Jenkins coined to describe a narrative approach embraced by the entertainment television and film industries in the Web 2.0 era. According to Jenkins (2006, 95-96), "a transmedia story unfolds across multiple media platforms with each new text making a distinctive and valuable contribution to the whole." NBC's *The Office*, now in its sixth season, provides an example of transmedia storytelling. During the show's run, NBC's website has featured personal blogs "written" by various characters; a series of mini episodes during the summer focusing on the work antics of several characters; a music video starring several characters; and games inspired by the show that users can download and play on their smartphones.

To begin with, storytelling is an important part of Coming up Roses' support culture and of support culture in general. The sharing of personal stories allows members of a support group to understand and process their experiences, communicate such experiences to their fellow members, and respond empathetically and sympathetically to one another (Høybye, Johansen, and Tjørnhøj-Thomsen 2005; Hsieh 2004; Orgad 2005). The process of sharing personal stories and experiences in a therapeutic context does not occur in a linear and straightforward manner, however—particularly when it happens online. Rather, it often takes place in a patchwork fashion over time, with bits and pieces of information emerging in different contexts and conversations (Orgad 2005). Coming up Roses' increasingly transmediated existence both enhances and is enhanced by the multifaceted and somewhat fragmented nature of the group's support culture. Specifically, members' engagement with new digital technologies and platforms provides them with new temporal, social, and spatial opportunities for connecting to their fellow Roses. Just as significantly, members use particular technologies and platforms in particular contexts to connect with one another in particular ways. As critic Jeff Gomez (Wikipedia 2010) observes, "Most of us flow naturally from one medium to the next. With transmedia, each part of story is unique and plays to the strengths of the medium. The result is a new kind of narrative where story flows across each platform forming a rich narrative tapestry."

My chapter contributes to the burgeoning conversation about transmedia storytelling and practice. To date, this research has primarily focused on the television industry, the film and cinema industry, gaming culture, and, to a lesser extent, social activism, journalism, advertising, and publishing (e.g., Aarseth 2005; Costanza-Chock 2010; Dena 2009; Hietanen and Turpeinen 2010; Jenkins 2006a, 2006b; Norrington 2010; Perez 2010; Srivastava 2009). Thus, my analysis extends this literature by highlighting its relevance to a new social context—online pregnancy and mothering support groups—and, in doing so, contributes a new perspective on the meaning and significance of transmediated narratives, engagements, and experiences.

This chapter also contributes to the body of research regarding online pregnancy and mothering groups. In recent years, scholars from various disciplines have written about the social, cultural, and therapeutic dimensions of such groups, especially those that meet in web-based discussion forums (e.g., Drentea and Moren-Cross 2005; Koerber 2001; Ley 2007; Nakamura 2008; O'Connor and Madge 2004; Rashley 2005). Although some of these studies have examined the ways in which the technical, social, and support dimensions of such forums co-construct one another (Ley 2007; Nakamura 2008), few, if any, studies have examined how the social and support culture of such forums are evolving due to members' increasing use of multiple communication technologies and platforms to stay connected to one another and to the broader group. To illustrate the transmediated dimensions of Coming up Roses, I focus on three types of digital media use by members: mobile devices (especially mobile phones), social networking sites, and blogs.

Mobile Devices

The use of mobile communication technologies in the United States devices has surged in the past decade. Such technologies include laptops (especially those with Wi-Fi) as well as handheld devices such as cell phones and smart phones. A 2009 Pew Research survey of U.S. residents found that 36 percent of respondents owned laptops and 79 percent owned cell phones. Of particular note was the finding that 39 percent of respondents were "motivated by mobility," relying heavily on mobile technologies and integrating them into their daily activities. Indeed, 66% of individuals in this category agreed that "it would be very hard to do without their cell phones" (Horrigan 2009).[4] Mobile technologies allow users to access the Internet as well as communicate with others via talk, text, email, and instant messaging. Users rely on them for connecting with friends and family, for work, for school, for entertainment, and for therapeutic purposes. For example, health professionals have incorporated cell phones into HIV/AIDS treatment plans and prevention efforts (Puccio, Belzer, and Olson 2006; Ybarra and Bull 2007), weight loss programs (Tufano and Karras 2005), smoking cessation programs (Obermayer et al. 2004), and alcoholism recovery support groups (Campbell and Kelly 2006, 2008).

Mobile technologies are also used for support related to pregnancy and mothering. Over the years, member of Coming up Roses have relied on laptops because they provide flexibility regarding when and where they can log onto the main website. Members have used laptops to sign on while working in coffee shops, while on vacation, and even while in the hospital before and after giving birth. The ability to log onto the site while away from home or work has enabled members to share important information as soon as they receive it. For example, women have used their laptops to announce the arrival of their new baby and post photos from their hospital bed. The ability to log on while on vacation or while out of town has also alleviated members' "Rose withdrawal" by allowing them to stay abreast of the daily happenings of other members and contribute to the group's ongoing conversations.

More recently, members have started using their smartphones to relay messages to the main website. The website was not originally designed for phone access, however, so it was difficult at first for members to log directly onto the site with their phones. Some could not access the site at all, whereas others could read messages but not post them. As a result, members who had information to share tended to use their phones to call or text another member, who then posted the information on the site for them. Melanie, a participant in the Trying to Conceive (TTC) forum, had been taking her temperature and posting it on FertilityFriend.com (FF), an ovulation tracker site. Because her signature on the Coming up Roses site linked to her FF page, her fellow Roses could easily access her FF chart. Eight days past ovulation, Melanie had a temperature dip, a potential indicator of implantation. She and other members were excited, anticipating the next day's temperature to see whether it would rise (a sign that implantation might have occurred) or drop (a sign that her period might be on the way). Unfortunately, Melanie had to leave for work early the next day and could not post her temperature on FertilityFriend.com or on the Coming up Roses website before leaving. Knowing that people were eager for the results, she asked whether she could email via her Blackberry her temperature to a fellow Rose, who could then post it on the website for other members to see. The plan worked, and women started discussing and analyzing her temperature change even before Melanie logged on later that day.

The website became more accessible to smartphones in early 2010 when Tina and her husband Robert developed a mobile version of it. Some of the push to make the site more accessible to phones stemmed from members' positive experiences with Facebook's mobile version. As Dena, one of the site's administrators, explains, "As more and more of us moved to Facebook and realized just how easy it is to stay in touch that way, we realized we wanted the Rose to function much that way." Dena also speculated that making Coming up Roses accessible might increase site participation: "[T]here are plenty of times that I'll be waiting for a meeting or something like that and I will mess around with FB. I would [want] post on the Rose but [couldn't]—so hopefully this will increase the site traffic."

Kara affirms Dena's perspective about the benefits of the site's mobile access. Although she primarily logs onto the Rose from home through her laptop and desktop computers, she finds her iPod Touch convenient for staying connected to the Rose when she is out and about town, especially when she is also toting around her baby and baby gear. On one occasion, she was reading her city's newspaper on her iPod Touch and found information regarding the fertility treatment that another Coming up Roses' member was about to undergo. Kara loved that she could immediately post a link to the article on the website for this member to read, as the latter woman had many questions and concerns about the treatment. Kara also finds the ability to log onto the website via her iPod Touch socially and emotionally comforting given her life with a new baby. She explains,

> The thing is, it can feel really isolating being out with the baby, waiting for appointments, sitting in tea shops while she sleeps, and if I can connect during the day, it makes me feel less isolated, less like I am missing the party.

The convenience and flexibility that smartphones provide with regard to accessing the site is similar to that of laptops if not better. Unlike laptops, iPhones and other 3G/4G phones allow members to access the site anytime and from anywhere because the phones are not dependent on the availability of Wi-Fi. Although iPod Touches require a Wi-Fi connection, they are still smaller and lighter than laptops. As Kara's experience highlights, these features make iPod Touches easier to bring along on errands, trips, and other outings, particularly if one also has a baby and baby gear in tow. At the same time, logging onto the site through a smartphone instead of a laptop changes the way in which members participate on the site. Some members find that their smartphone's small screen and keyboard lend themselves better to reading posts than to writing them, especially long ones. The posts that members do write on their phones tend to be on the short side. In this regard, smartphone users tend to read posts and wait until they have access to a laptop or desktop computer to post their own messages. The fact that smartphone users emphasize reading posts over writing them does not necessarily make their site participation less meaningful, however. As evidenced by Kara's desire "not to miss the party" and members' more general efforts to avoid or alleviate "Rose withdrawal," logging onto the site to stay updated on other members' lives can serve a valuable emotional and social function.[5]

In addition to using mobile phones to access the Coming up Roses website, members use them to connect with one another offsite. For example, such phones enable administrators to address site problems and logistics quickly and efficiently. Although they also use landline phones for these purposes, cell phones, particularly smart phones, allow them to deal with site issues on the spot while at work or in transit. As Dena further states,

> For me, being able to access the site from my phone helps me for admin stuff as well as just regular participation. I can access the Rose from work, but at work I have to, well, work! Being able to access from my phone means I can participate when I may have a few minutes downtime but not necessarily a computer—in between meetings, early in the morning when I first wake up, late at night when I lay in bed for a couple minutes before sleep. From an administration perspective, I can now update members, read emails, etc…and then act on it without having to wait until I get to a computer to fix a problem.

Another reason why members use mobile phones is to deepen their personal relationships with other Roses. They use them to coordinate offline dinner dates and play dates with Roses who live in their area or who are visiting the area from out of town. Members also use them to enhance the giving and receiving of support. Sometimes members who are going through tough times need sustained, one-on-one support from another member. Furthermore, cell phones have enabled numerous onsite relationships to transform into strong offline friendships. Two longtime members, Corinne and Pam, became best friends even though they live in different parts of the country. They have only met in person once and have relied heavily on cell phones for convenience and financial reasons to build and sustain their close friendship. As Corinne explains, "We have used land lines in the past but we are most accessible on [cell phones]. We both have AT&T so it saves us money to chat live/text that way." Pam adds,

> The timing lends itself better to cell phones. We tend to talk more during the day, which is when I am at work. Evenings are harder for both of us with dinner, bedtime, routines, etc. So, since during the day I'm usually at work and Corinne might either be home with the girls or out doing stuff, we know we can always reach each other on our cells. It allows that immediacy that best friends often need.

Social Networking Sites

Although the Coming up Roses website is still the primary Internet platform through which members stay connected, members also interact with one another on social networking sites. Facebook and MySpace have been especially popular among the Roses. Indeed, a majority of the group's members have a page on Facebook, Myspace, or both. Their use of these sites reflects the growing popularity of social networking sites in the United States and worldwide. Facebook, for example, boasts 400 million active users, with more than 70 percent of them from countries other than the United States (Facebook 2010). Its account holders use the site to connect with friends, families, co-workers, classmates, as well as to connect with individuals who share common interests. Challenging earlier claims that Internet use detracts from social capital (Putnam 2000; Wellman and Haythornthwaite 2001), recent studies have demonstrated that social networking sites such as Facebook have the potential to enhance friendships and other relationships (Ellison, Steinfield, and Lampe 2007), as well as enhance civic engagement (Pasek, more, and Romer 2009).

One way in which members of Coming up Roses connect with one another on social networking sites is through satellite support groups. In August 2006, a member created a MySpace group called "Coming up Roses." Twenty-eight members joined this group. Eighteen months later, two members created a private Facebook group called "Rosey Roses" in response to the site's growing popularity among the Roses. By January 2010, 49 members—some of whom were also members of the MySpace group—belonged to this group. Of the two groups, Rosey Roses has been the most active, with several dozen wall posts, several discussion threads, and several downloaded photos of members' children.[6]

In part, members use these groups as back-ups to the main website. The MySpace group was initially created for this purpose. Several times a year, the server that hosts the website goes down. Usually the problem lasts for no more than a few hours, but occasionally it lasts for a day or more. When the main site is not working for a sustained period of time, members not only post messages to the Facebook and Myspace groups asking when the site will be up again; they also use the groups for social and support purposes. In fall 2009, for example, Chelsea posted on the Coming up Roses website that she might be pregnant. Her period was late, and a series of home pregnancy tests were inconclusive. She was distressed by this possibility because she did not want another child. In fact, her husband had undergone a vasectomy the previous year. She took a few more tests the following morning with a different brand, but the site went down before she could post the negative results. Fortunately, she was able to post her results on the Facebook group, knowing that the Roses who belonged to this group would check in due to the website's inaccessibility. Moira's post in response illustrates the excitement over the results as well as over Chelsea's decision to post them on the Facebook group:

> Oh Thank goodness you posted here...I was getting frantic with the Rose down!! Anyway...I'm glad you got the result you wanted—it's just all so strange how you got sooo many false positives (unless it was a [chemical pregnancy]).[7] I think you need to get [Chelsea's husband] sperm tested though—you just never know!!

In addition to using these satellite groups as occasional back-up sites, members sometimes use them to touch base with one another with simple acts that reaffirm the Roses' group bond, trust, and identity outside of the context of the main website. On the Facebook group's wall, Diane wrote, "I love my Roses," and Anna said, "Hi Roses!" Beth from the United Kingdom posted, "Happy Thanksgiving my American Roses." A few members who do not visit the main website anymore due to their busy lives and changing support needs also joined the Facebook group. Doing so has allowed them to reconnect every now and then with their fellow Roses without having to become full participants of the website. As Amy wrote, "wow- i sorta forgot about rose over the last 2 years. I miss it! [By the way]—menopause SUCKS! (but I never have to worry about [her menstrual period] being late—haven't seen her since last September!"

Although they serve an important social and support function, such groups constitute a small portion of the interactions among the Roses on Facebook. The vast majority of these interactions take place through their personal home pages. Many members are "friends" with several dozen—if not more—other Roses. As Facebook friends, they comment on one another's status updates, wall posts, and photographs. Through the site, they also give one another Facebook gifts, "poke" one another, send one other quizzes, and play games together. One member, Charlotte, even created a Friends list just for the Roses, which she accesses by clicking on the "Chat" feature. She created this list because she likes "being able to see everyone's status updates and photos and whatnot," and the list allows her to "see at a glance who is online."

Interestingly, the fact that many members have found it difficult to access the Coming up Roses website through their mobile phones makes Facebook an especially convenient and attractive way to connect with fellow Roses. As Juliet, a working mother to three children, explains,

> I haven't been able to access the Rose from my work Blackberry or from my cell phone, but I do use my cell to get on Facebook now, and I am able to keep up with how lots of people are doing, including Roses!...I used to only get [Facebook] at night at home… and now I am on [Facebook] every single day and can update my status or comment on a Rose's status, etc. throughout my day…I love how technology has made us cyberbuddies grow even closer. I get to see updated pictures of Rose babies, and see videos of first steps, first giggles, etc. without having to take too much time out of my day by logging onto a computer.

Similarly, Lori, a mother to a young toddler, cannot access the Rose via her Blackberry; like Juliet, however, she can use it to connect with fellow Roses through Facebook. She writes,

> It's just nice to be able to jump on quickly and see how people are, stay updated, etc., when I am somewhere without access to a computer. It is especially nice when I am somewhere waiting (like Dr. Office) and need to kill time….I have used [Facebook] to check updates on some Roses and especially to look at pictures of their little ones.

By "friending" one another on Facebook, members of Coming up Roses interact with one another as they would other "friends" from their work, school, social circle, family, sports team, and neighborhood. The integration of members' onsite and offsite worlds on Facebook is significant for several reasons. First, members gain the opportunity to learn about and immerse themselves in the broader social landscapes and networks that constitute their fellow Roses' lives. This integration also illustrates how online friends such as members' fellow Roses are just as real and legitimate as their offline friends and contacts, in contrast to popular discourses and rhetoric that privilege the so-called physical world over the so-called virtual world. Holly joined Coming up Roses in 2009 at the suggestion of her offline friend Tanya, a long-time member of the site. She felt very welcomed and found much support during her difficult pregnancy. Holly explains,

> The girls were absolutely fantastic. I felt like I had more support from these girls I had never met than my own family that I have known since birth…So, I started to look some of them up on Facebook. I wanted to include my new friends in the rest of my everyday life too.

Holly's "everyday life," then, includes a diverse array of people whom she knows offline and online.

The integration of members' Facebook lives and Coming up Roses lives is further evident on the Coming up Roses website. Here, some Roses use an application that allows them to post in their signature their Facebook photo, current Facebook status update, and a link that says "Follow me on Facebook." In the Open Discussion forum—the place for posting matters that do not fit into the site's other sections—members also participate in an ongoing tongue-and-cheek thread called "My Real Facebook Status Update." Some members censor the content of their Facebook updates because they do not want to share certain information with particular friends, family members, or co-workers. The status update thread on Coming up Roses allows members to say what they really think about the topic at hand—topics that have included their feelings about their bodies and health, husbands, jobs, neighbors, and other family members.

The fact that members sometimes post more honest status updates on the Coming up Roses website indicates that some members feel "safer" (Mitra 2006) sharing certain feelings and personal information on the site than on Facebook. In certain respects, their feelings of safety may reflect the relative anonymity of the site; previous research has shown anonymity to increase openness and personal disclosure in online settings (e.g., Turner, Grube, and Meyers 2001, Walther and Boyd 2002). At the same time, it is important not to overstate the role of anonymity. After all, most members of Coming up Roses have shared not only personal details about their life but also their real names; the names of their family members; photos of themselves, family and homes; their geographic location; the name of their workplace or school; and their contact information. Moreover, many members have met in person—or are even offline friends with—at least one other member. In this regard, members' sense of safety reflects the trust and intimacy that they have built with one another over the years, both online and offline, due to the support and friendship that they have given and received. In contrast to Tina's original concern that Facebook draws attention away from the Coming up Roses website, members' use of Facebook may sometimes encourage participation on the Coming up Roses website because of the perceived safety differences between the two sites. As Charlotte notes, "Sometimes I will see a 'hint' of something important from a cryptic post on [Facebook], and I will know to come check in at the Peach to get the real scoop. So I think that overall [Facebook] is a nice complement to our site."

Blogs

A third facet of Coming up Roses' transmediated support culture relates to members' use of personal blogs. The emergence of blogging platforms in the early 2000s has sparked widespread discussion and debate regarding their capacity to make authorship and publishing accessible to the general public, create a more participatory news and media culture, and even promote democracy and civic engagement (e.g., Maynor 2007; Nardi et al. 2004; Wall 2005; Warschauer and Grimes 2008). One growing phenomenon in this context relates to so-called "mommy blogs." Over the past decade hundreds of women have created blogs to share their experiences with infertility, pregnancy, childbirth, adoption, parenting, their children, work/life balance issues, intimate relationships, health, and the cultural politics of mothering more generally. Whereas some of these blogs have relatively small audiences consisting primarily of friends and family members, other have garnered national and even international attention, with some well-know mommy bloggers writing books based on their blogs and appearing on talk shows to share their perspectives on parenting and family matters.[8] Many mommy blogs welcome comments from readers as well as provide links to other mommy blogs. In this regard, they often function—either individually or in tandem with other blogs—as support groups and online communities in their own right (Friedman and Calixte 2009; Lopez 2009).

In recent years, numerous members of Coming up Roses have maintained their own blogs related to their family, pregnancy, adoption, and infertility experiences. Although they often discuss the same topics on both the group's website and their blogs, they tend to use the platforms in different ways. In general, many members use the website forums to ask specific health questions, update members about their pregnancy or TTCing efforts, request (as well as provide) support, or chat about whatever topic comes to mind. They also discuss feelings and life details they might not share with their offsite family and friends. Roses who maintain a personal blog do so to document their experiences not only for themselves but also for their family, friends, and general readership. Some also use their blogs to process and sort through their feelings, especially if they are going through difficult times. Given that their blog audiences often consist of individuals other than their fellow Roses, however, they sometimes use a different writing voice or omit personal details that they do not feel comfortable sharing with a wider readership.

Consider the blogging experience of Lisette, a long-time member of the site who has been trying to start a family for more than five years. She started her blog several years ago and updates it at least once a week. When asked about why she blogs, she states:

> For me, it's about venting, and also I love putting a personal/humorous touch to [the blog]. It's more like storytelling, rather than giving [the Roses] the facts straight up. It's focused... whereas here on the Rose you can talk about anything you want, i.e. "off topic" stuff. I do do that occasionally [on the blog] but for the most part I stick to the fertility stuff. [Another] difference between the Rose and the Blog is that my entire family reads my blog...so it's more upbeat and positive...whereas I can really be honest [on the Rose]. Also, my family wants to know how I'm doing - and it's a good way to keep them apprised.

Lisette's comments highlight another difference between support groups forums and the blog—specifically, they tend to promote different writing styles. The forums on the Coming up Roses website are designed to foster ongoing interaction among many members, as opposed to extended personal narratives. Indeed, members of Coming up Roses often apologize when they write personal posts that that they consider too long. Some will even write "(LONG)" after the post's title as a sort of warning to other members. In contrast, the format of blogs encourages this type of extended personal narrative, which has historically been associated with diaries, journals, and, as Lisette put it, "storytelling" (see also Nardi et al. 2004). Thus, some members—especially those who enjoy the act of writing—find blogs a better platform for documenting and reflecting on their life experiences in detail than the website's discussion forums.

The fact that blogs may serve different purposes than the website for members of Coming up Roses, however, does not mean that the two communication platforms are separate. Rather, blog posts and Rose posts are often part of a transmediated storytelling and support culture "tapestry," to borrow the term used by media critic Jeff Gomez. For example, some members post a link to their blog in the signature of their Coming up Roses profile. This link shows up in every post that they write, and their fellow Roses can click on the link to be directed to their blog. As a result, Roses read and sometimes comment on one another's blogs in addition to interacting with them on the Coming up Roses site.

Given the topical and stylistic differences between blog posts and forum posts, reading one another's blogs provides members with a different—yet just as meaningful—understanding of their fellow Roses' experiences than the forum alone provides. In this regard, the blogs and forums complement one another by providing a multifaceted approach to storytelling and support participation. Moreover, the storytelling and support that takes place with regard to a particular member's website posts and blog posts are sometimes inextricably linked. Consider again the transmediated storytelling of Lisette. Occasionally, her posts on the Rose summarize what she wrote on her blog and direct members who want more details back to the blog. Additionally, members who read her blog sometimes refer back to her blog entries in their posts about her infertility and treatment situation on the Coming up Roses website. As a result, members who do not read Lisette blog's may miss out on important information about her infertility treatment experiences and find themselves at times unable to participate fully in her support threads on the group's website.

Transmediated Negotiations

The technosocial boundaries of Coming up Roses have expanded beyond the group's website as a result of members' increased use of new technologies and platforms to connect with one another. Yet it is also the case that individual members navigate the group's transmediated landscape to varying degrees and in different ways. These variations highlights the way in which the meaning and significance of digital technology are shaped just as much by the particular social contexts in which users engage it as much as they are by the technology's "inbuilt" values (e.g., Boczkowski 2006; Holloway and Valentine 2003; Ley 2007; Nakamura 2008).

Just because members have the option of connecting to the group via mobile phones, social networking sites, blogs, and other media doesn't mean that every member embraces all—or any—of these communication tools. Mobile devices, for instance, are not for everyone. Some members continue to run into glitches when trying to access the Coming up Roses website from their smartphones, which makes them wary of using them to log on. Other women prefer not to use their cell phones to participate on the site because the small screen and keyboard make it difficult to read or post long messages. Still other members prefer to use their home computers out of principle. Jillian, a busy stay-at-home-mother with six young children, likes to keep her online activities simple and contained. She recently closed her account on Facebook for this reason. Jillian explains, "We have one computer smack dab in the middle of all the chaos and I can jump on a minute or two at a time to check in. I would rather not be able to check any of these media things from my cell phone. Being connected is highly overrated."

Social networking sites also have their critics. Some Roses would rather interact with other members on the main website, as opposed to keeping up with them on MySpace or Facebook. Lena, for example, is Facebook friends with more than thirty Roses. Although she responds to their updates and posts from time to time, she prefers to use the site to keep in touch with family and to reconnect with old friends. When it comes to using Facebook to interact with other Roses, Lena states,

> I feel like [Facebook's] been a time waster for me, more than anything else. I find it very impersonal… People write short updates about themselves. Most times, it's very redundant information I did not need to know or cryptic things…I like the picture sharing aspect of [Facebook] but I feel privacy is an issue.

In this regard, Lena's view that the "cryptic" posts written by other Roses are a timewaster and "impersonal" contrasts Charlotte's earlier statement that such cryptic posts actually pique her interest and lead her to "get the real" scoop on the main website. Ultimately, Lena prefers a designated discussion forum in which to interact with her fellow Roses.

Conclusion

Coming up Roses is anchored in a web-based discussion forum, but the group is increasingly sustained through a set of transmediated engagements and practices. This transmediation shapes the frequency of members' participation in the group, their ability to communicate with one another, the nature of support that they give and receive, the knowledge that they have of each other's broader lives, and the "strong" ties (Putnam 2000)—both online and offline—that hold the group together. Moreover, each type of technology or platform provides a particular view into the lives of members and a particular way to interact with them. Mobile devices, especially cell phones and smartphones, allow members to connect frequently and quickly with the main site and with individual women. They also allow individual women to deepen their friendships with each other. Social networking sites such as Facebook provide members with another online space for group interaction and enable them to immerse themselves into the broader online and offline lives of their fellow Roses—an immersion that helps members develop a more holistic context for the giving and receiving support. Finally, blogs not only allow members to tell their fertility, pregnancy, and mothering stories in greater depth and with more nuance than they do on the main discussion board but also serve as a complement to their board participation. Despite concerns about declining participation on the main website due to Facebook, the assorted technical glitches faced by smartphones users, and some members' individual preferences for particular modes of communication, it is clear the group's support culture and community is shaping and being shaped by members' growing reliance on a wide array of digital technologies and platforms.

Looking beyond this one site, my preliminary research indicates that other online pregnancy and mothering websites and forums—from small, relatively closed, and non-commercial site such as Coming up Roses to large, public, and commercial ones such as FertilityFriend.com and BabyCenter.com—also function within transmediated environments. On Facebook, for example, members of FertilityFriend.com have created almost a dozen groups including "Fertility Friend Girls," "Fertility Friend 2005," and "Fertility Friend December 2008." FertilityFriend.com and BabyCenter.com, even have official fan pages. FertilityFriend.com's fan page has over 4,100 "Likes," and BabyCenter.com's page has over 133,000 "Likes." Site administrators use these fan pages to disseminate information about fertility, pregnancy, relationships, sex, babies, and mothering, to provide a technosocial space for women to interact and support one another, and to promote their website, as well as their other services and products. An example of this latter practice that further illustrates the transmediated terrain of online support groups is FertilityFriend.com's use of its fan page to promote free applications that enable members to chart their menstrual cycle and connect to the FF online community via their iPhones, iPod Touches, and iPads.

In sum, my research provides a new perspective on the transmedia concept by examining its relevance to the arena of online support culture. Doing so not only provides new examples of what transmedia storytelling, participation, and communication practices entail; it also demonstrates the extent to which digital media and Internet platforms have penetrated everyday life, including the world of online support. To be sure, my account only scratches the surface with regard to the transmediated support culture of online pregnancy and mothering groups. Thus, future research on the topic should examine the extent to which the broader terrain of online pregnancy and mothering support occurs within a transmediated context, the specific types of transmediated practices that such groups embrace, and the effects that such practices exert on the nature of online support and community as well as on women's lived experiences with regard to infertility, pregnancy, and mothering.

Acknowledgments

I would like to thank the members of Coming up Roses for their participation in this project. I would also like to thank Sarah Leavitt and Paul Brewer for their suggestions and feedback on the chapter, and Vicki Callaghan for recommending literature that helped to shape the chapter's transmedia framework. Finally, I thank Michelle Moravec for her guidance and feedback, and for including this chapter in the anthology.

Works Cited

Aarseth, Espen. 2005. Game studies: What is it good for? *The International Digital Media and Arts Association Journal* 1 (3): 3-7.

Beckerman, Tracy. 2008. *Rebel without a Minivan: Observations on Life in the 'Burbs*. Cold Tree Press (http://coldtreepress.com).

Boczkowski, Pablo J. 2006. *Digitizing the News: Innovation in Online Newspapers*. Cambridge, MA: MIT Press.

Campbell, Scott W., and Michael J. Kelly. 2006. Mobile phone use in AA networks: An exploratory study. *Journal of Applied Communication Research* 34 (2): 191-208.

—. 2008. Mobile phone use among Alcoholics Anonymous members: New sites for recovery. *New Media and Society* 10 (6): 915-933.

Costanzo-Chock, Sasha. 2010. *Se Ve, Se Siente*: Transmedia Mobilization in the Los Angeles Immigrant Rights Movement. PhD diss., University of Southern California.

Dena, Christy. 2009. Transmedia Practice: Theorizing the Practice of Expressing a Fictional World across Distinct Media and Environments. PhD diss., University of Sydney.

Drentea, Patricia, and Jennifer L. Moren-Cross. 2005. Social capital and support on the web: The case of an internet mother site. *Sociology of Health and Illness* 27 (7): 920-943.

Ellison, Nicole B., Charles Steinfield, and Cliff Lampe. 2007. The benefits of Facebook "friends": Social capital and college students' use of online social networking sites. *Journal of Computer-Mediated Communication* 12 (4): 1143-1168.

Facebook. 2010. "Press room: Statistics." http://facebook.com/#!/press/info.php?statistics. (accessed September 4, 2010).

Feldman, Beth, ed. 2009. *See Mom Run: Side Splitting Essays from the World's Most Harried Moms*. New York: Plainwhite Press.

Fox, Suzannah. *Health Information Online*. Pew Internet & American Life Project, May 17, 2005, http://www.pewinternet.org/Reports/2005/Health-Information-Online.aspx.

Friedman, May, and Shana L. Calixte, eds. 2009. *Mothering and Blogging: The Radical Act of the Mommyblog*. Bradford, Ontario: Demeter Press.

Hampton, Keith, and Neeti Gupta. 2008. Community and social interaction in the wireless city: Wi-fi use in public and semi-public spaces. *New Media and Society* 10 (6): 831-850.

Hietanen, Herrko A., and Marko Turpeinen. 2010. The changing dynamics of television advertising. *Proceedings of the 8th International Interactive Conference on Interactive TV&Video*, 237-245.

Holloway, Sarah, and Gill Valentine. 2003. *Cyberkids: Children in the Information Age*. London: Routledge/Falmers.

Høybye, Mette T., Christoffer Johansen, and Tine Tjørnhøj-Thomsen. 2005. Online interaction: Effects of storytelling in an Internet breast cancer support group. *Psycho-Oncology* 14 (3): 211-220.

Horrigan, John A. *The Mobile Difference: Wireless Connectivity Has Drawn Users More Deeply into Digital Life.* Pew Internet & American Life Project, March 29, 2009, http://www.pewinternet.org/Reports/2009/5-The-Mobile-Difference--Typology.

Hsieh, Elaine. 2004. Stories in action and the dialogic management of identities: Storytelling in transplant support group meetings. *Research on Language and Social Interaction* 37 (1): 39-70.

Jenkins, Henry. 2006a. *Convergence Culture*. New York: NYU Press.

—. 2006b. *Fans, Bloggers, and Gamers: Exploring Participatory Culture*. New York: NYU Press.

Koerber, Amy. 2001. Postmodernism, resistance, and cyberspace: Making rhetorical spaces for feminist mothers on the web. *Women's Studies in Communication* 24 (2): 218-240.

Layne, Linda L. 2003. *Motherhood Lost: A Feminist Account of Pregnancy Loss in America*. New York: Routledge.

Ley, Barbara L. 2007. "Vive les Roses!": The architecture of commitment in an online pregnancy and mothering group. *Journal of Computer-Mediated Communication* 12 (4): 1388-1408.

—. 2009. *From Pink to Green: Disease Prevention and the Environmental Breast Cancer Movement*. New Brunswick, NJ: Rutgers University Press.

Lopez, Lori K. 2009. The radical act of mommy blogging: Redefining mothering through the blogosphere. *New Media and Society* 11 (5): 729-747.

Maynor, John W. 2007. Blogging for democracy: Deliberation, autonomy, and reasonableness in the blogosphere. *Critical Review of International Social and Political Philosophy* 12 (3): 443-468.

Mitra, Ananda. 2006. Towards finding a cybernetic safe place: Illustrations from people of Indian origin. *New Media and Society* 8 (2): 251-268.

Nakamura, Lisa. 2008. *Digitizing Race: Visual Cultures of the Internet*. Minneapolis, MN: University of Minnesota Press.

Nardi, Bonnie A., Diane J. Schiano, Michelle Gumbrecht, and Luke Swartz. 2004. Why we blog. *Communications of the ACM* 47 (12): 41-46.

Norrington, Alison. 2010. Harnessing "e" in storyworlds: Engage, enhance, experience, entertain. *Publishing Research Quarterly* 26 (2): 96-105.

Obermayer, Jami L., William T. Riley, Ofer Asif, and Jersino Jean-Mary. 2004. College smoking-cessation using cell phone text messaging. *Journal of American College Health* 53 (2): 72-78.

O'Connor, Henrietta, and Clare Madge. 2004. "My mum's thirty years out of date": The role of the Internet in the transition to motherhood. *Community, Work, and Family* 7 (3): 351-369.

Orgad, Shani. 2005. *Storytelling Online: Talking Breast Cancer on the Internet*. London: Peter Lang.

Pasek, Josh, eian more, and Daniel Romer. 2009. Realizing the social Internet? Social networking meets offline civic engagement. *Journal of Information Technology and Politics* 6: 197-215.

Perez, Carlos Elias. 2010. The future of journalism in the online public sphere: Where journalistic sources become mass media in their own right. *Estudios sobre el Mensaje Periodístico* 16: 45-58.

Puccio, Joseph A., Marvin Belzer, and Johanna Olson. 2006. The use of cell phone reminder calls for assisting HIV-infected adolescents and young adults to adhere to highly active antiretroviral therapy: A pilot study. *AIDS Patient Care and STDs* 20 (6): 438-444.

Putnam, Robert. 2000. *Bowling Alone: The Collapse and Revival of American Community*. New York: Simon and Schuster.

Rashley, Lisa Hammond. 2005. "Work it out with your wife:" Gendered expectations and parenting rhetoric online. *NWSA Journal* 17 (1): 58-92.

Sorkin, Andrew Ross. 2010. "Facebook makes headway around the world." *DealBook*. http://dealbook.blogs.nytimes.com/2010/07/08/facebook-makes-headway-around-the-world (accessed July 8, 2010).

Srivastava, Lina. 2009. "Transmedia activism: Telling your story across media platforms to create effective social change." Media Rights, http://www.mediarights.org/news/Transmedia_Activism_Telling_Your_Story_Across_Media_Platforms_to_Create_Eff (accessed July 8, 2010).

Taylor, Janelle S., Linda L. Layne, and Danielle F. Wozniak, eds. 2004. *Consuming Motherhood*. New Brunswick, NJ: Rutgers University Press.

Tufano, Jamesa T., and Bryan T. Karras. 2005. Mobile eHealth interventions for obesity: A timely opportunity to leverage convergence trends. *Journal of Medical Internet Research* 7 (5): e58.

Turner, Jeanine W., Jean A. Grube, and Jennifer Meyers. 2001. Developing an optimal match within online communities: An exploration of CMC support communities. *Journal of Communication* 51 (2): 231-251.

van Dijk, Jose. 2009. Users like you? Theorizing agency in user-generated content. *Media, Culture, & Society* 31 (1): 41-58.

Wall, Melissa. 2005. "Blogs of war": Weblogs as news. *Journalism* 6 (2): 153-172.

Walther, Joseph B., and Shawn Boyd. 2002. Attraction to computer-mediated computer support. In *Computer Technology and Society: Audience Adoption and Users*, ed. C.A. Lin and D. Atkin,153-188. Cresskill, NJ: Hampton Press.

Warschauer, Mark, and Douglas Grimes. 2008. Audience, authorship, and artifact: The emergent semiotics of Web 2.0. *Annual Review of Applied Linguistics* 27: 1-23.

Wellman, Barry, and Caroline Haythornthwaite, eds. 2001. *The Internet in Everyday Life*. London: Blackwell.

Wikipedia, 2010. "Transmedia storytelling." http://en.wikipedia.org/wiki/Transmedia_storytelling.

Ybarra, Michele, and Shaena Bull. 2007. Current trends in Internet-and cell phone-based HIV prevention and intervention programs. *Current HIV/Reports,* 4 (4): 201-207.

Notes

[1] Coming up Roses is a pseudonym, as are the names that I give site members.

[2] This chapter is based on ethnographic research that I conducted between August 2009 and January 2011. As a member of Coming up Roses since January 2005, I observed and participated in the group. Much of my research took place on the Coming up Roses website, yet I also studied the ways in which members of Coming up Roses have connected on Facebook, MySpace, and several personal blogs. In addition to my ethnographic research, I conducted numerous interviews through email and the site's personal messaging system. Finally, I posted questions on the site itself that generated several threads of discussion among over a dozen of the most active site members about the topics at hand. Whereas the ethnographic research provided me with a broad sense of the group's transmediated dynamics, the interviews and discussion threads gave me a deeper understanding of their meaning and significance for individual members.

[3] For a more detailed account of the history of Coming up Roses, see Ley (2007).

[4] The results of the Pew project are based on two surveys, both of which were conducted in December 2007. The first survey polled 2,054 U.S. residents through telephone interviews (both landline and cellphone). The survey population constituted a nationally representative sample. The second survey consisted of a callback survey of 1,499 interviewees from a 2006 Pew survey of Internet communication technology users. Participants in both surveys were asked the same questions.

[5] The growing phenomenon of online "participatory culture" (Jenkins 2006a, 2006b) in the context of Web 2.0 technologies and platforms has led to discussions regarding the various types of user practices and engagements that constitute online "participation." For an especially nuanced analysis of the term's different meanings, see van Dijk (2009),

[6] The trend of moving from Myspace to Facebook among members of Coming up Roses reflects a broader global trend (Sorkin 2010).

[7] A chemical pregnancy is a very early miscarriage, often occurring within a week or two after implantation. It is called a chemical pregnancy because the miscarriage takes place before an ultrasound could have detected the gestational sac.

[8] One such book, *See Mom Run: Side-Splitting Essays from the World's Most Harried Moms* (2009), is a collection of personal essays written by more than a dozen "mommy bloggers." Blogger Beth Feldman edited the book. Also, Tracy Beckerman, author of the popular syndicated blog, "Lost in Suburbia," has made dozens of media appearances and wrote the 2008 book *Rebel without a Minivan: Observations on Life in the 'Burbs.*

CHAPTER THREE

ONLINE MOTHERHOOD: A COMMUNITY OF MOTHERS REVISITED

PATRICIA DRENTEA
AND JENNIFER MOREN-CROSS

This chapter examines how mothering websites have evolved and grown exponentially over the past decade by revisiting one such large mothering board, and then examining a private mothering website. Themes of increased sophistication of the websites, social support, and social capital are considered.

In 2005, we published an article entitled "Social Capital and Social Support on the Web: The Case of an Internet Mother Site" in a leading sociology journal (Drentea and Moren-Cross 2005). The article examined how a website for new mothers created an atmosphere for sharing information and social support. We found that virtual communities of mothering offered a new way for mothers to connect, in an era of changing motherhood. In this chapter we discuss the social trends and ideas behind the first article and how the internet has become a new place for communication among mothers. We then we discuss how mothering websites have grown and changed since the early 2000s. We also examine a private mothering website in detail.

A number of websites are now devoted to creating virtual communities. A virtual community is a group of people who get together and exchange ideas and information--online. In the case of a mothering website, it is a prime place for sharing emotions as well. It is a space where anyone who has access to the internet can join, from anywhere in the world, and participate asynchronously, meaning any time of the day or night. Generally people join virtual communities when they have similar interests to share. Some have argued that while we may not spend as much time meeting one another face-to-face, we can spend time meeting on the internet, and still fulfill social needs such as companionship, socializing and social support (Wellman and Haythornethwaite 2001). Of course, there is also much concern with social life occurring over the internet, to the detriment of tangible social interactions. Some fear that without face-to-face interactions where we can monitor body language, get away from our computers and offer physical affection-such as a hug to a friend experiencing trouble, true friendships cannot be realized.

Virtual communities are much different than our local neighborhood community because our "neighbors" on the internet may be much more diverse and geographically scattered than those who live near us. As such, the network is often more heterogeneous in nature, and can be far larger. In instances of unusual or rare interests, being able to meet those with similar interests across the world can increase the network broadly. One can reach those around the globe instantly.

Virtual communities exist for an unlimited number of purposes; they can be for dog-breed aficionados, such as a borzoi dog rescue community--or for health purposes, such as those with a specific type of cancer. In this chapter, we discuss mothering virtual communities in which mothers congregate on discussion boards to talk about pregnancy, childbirth and raising children.

There are several key reasons so many women become involved in mothering websites, such as being isolated from both family as well as the desire to have intimate, frequent interactions with other mothers. The biography of the first author (Drentea) highlights and expands on such reasons. Our original study began in 2000, when Drentea learned she was going to have a baby, and realized that she barely knew anyone who was pregnant or had kids. This is not an uncommon situation for highly-educated women who have relocated to areas of the country in which they have no connections. As a female professor, and as one of the only women in an almost all-male sociology department, she knew that she needed to learn a lot, and she would not learn it from those she interacted with the most on a day-to-day basis—her work colleagues. She knew few in the same situation also because of her own small family. As is typical of many Americans, she is the daughter of immigrants, (about 12% of the U.S. population is foreign born) (U.S. Bureau of the Census 2003) and she has only one sibling. Almost 20% of American women (18% of women age 40-44 to be exact) don't have any children (U.S. Bureau of the Census 2003). This was the case for her one sister, thus she couldn't turn to her for help. Also, as is typical of women with Ph.D.s, she waited longer than average to have her first child (the average in the U.S. is 25.1 years old) (MMWR 2005), and she was 33. Thus, her family, who historically would have been the source of support and information, could provide her little information. Her cousins, aunts and uncles lived in another country and spoke a different language. Also, with so many years between when her mother was pregnant to her own pregnancy, a lot had changed in the advice and beliefs regarding having and raising a baby. It also meant that her mother had forgotten much of the early days with a newborn. Finally, as is typical in many American neighborhoods, the women down the street who had children were mostly working also, so they didn't have endless hours to be around one another.

Discussing how the first author began looking online for parenting advice exemplifies the larger trends of how women's networks and lives have changed dramatically over the past 50 years. It is also explains the path to how she found the on-line mothering board. Women still enter pregnancy and child rearing with many questions, but unlike before, many do not have a strong network of women available to them at home or work, or even in their own families to help them through all the new mysteries. There are not as many siblings to draw upon, women have children later in life, and they are having fewer children on average.

In the past, typically women received a lot of information and support from midwives, who are women who assist in the delivery of babies (Wertz and Wertz 1989). However, in the 20th century birth has been medicalized and professionalized, which moved childbirth from a natural experience, usually happening at home, with the assistance and support of women, to a medical event, often with male doctors, in a hospital (Wertz and Wertz 1989). While this change created much safer births, and infant mortality dropped, it also created a much more rigid, medical and isolating experience for women at a vulnerable time. For the most part, women have embraced the more scientific approach to childbearing and motherhood, but this also has moved all the general information from a circle of mothers to a circle of professionals (Litt 2000).

Review of How Mothering Websites Work: The Mechanics

Our 2005 article examined one of We Love Babies'[1] "birth boards." We Love Babies is a parenting network site, which launched in 1997, and its birth boards are devoted to bringing together women giving birth at the same time (i.e., have due dates during the same month). Women followed the web board from when they learned they were pregnant, possibly for many years later, as their children grew. The boards are organized so that each month of each year there is a birth board. For instance, if you learn you are pregnant with a due date of August in 2011, you would join the August 2011 birth board, and follow others within the same stage of pregnancy. The first author joined and then read her birth board daily for a period of about a year. The data in our study were the discussions that occurred on the website. Threads (i.e. a topic is posted, to which others reply), were analyzed, and basic patterns were identified on the web board. We maintained notes of themes in the data, and analyzed those threads that reflected typical topics or greater symbolic meaning. We looked for common recurring themes, and instances demonstrating the mechanics of a virtual community. We also discovered the length mothers would go through to support and maintain their birth board as a supportive environment (see Drentea and Moren-Cross 2005 for detailed information).

Resources Provided by Mothering Virtual Communities

We had several important findings. We learned that both social support and social capital were found on the internet website. We learned that mothers with young children are especially isolated due to social demographics and modern life, and we learned what women do to maintain their "safe place" in their online community. We will discuss each of these below, but begin with brief definitions of social support and social capital, which frame an understanding of a virtual community.

Social Support

Social support is defined as the reciprocal exchange of help between people to ameliorate a situation. Scholars often classify social support into three types. These include emotional, instrumental, and informational support (Wills 1985). Emotional support is the one we would be most familiar with. This includes caring for someone, being there for them and being willing to talk and/or comfort someone when they are upset. Instrumental support involves helping someone with day-to-day activities and needs by means of providing something tangible. Thus this may include driving someone to the store, helping them financially if they needed to borrow money for necessities such as food or medicine, or helping them with routine care needs. For instance, a daughter may help an elderly parent make breakfast and bathe. Or, as is more relevant in our study, a parent or friend may come over to a new mother's house, bring food and hold and care for the newborn while the mother takes her shower, gets dressed, or goes to a doctor appointment. Finally, informational support is providing information for someone to take care of a problem. For instance, a family member who has diabetes, and knows how to take care his/herself, may help a family member who was recently diagnosed with the disease. Social support during pregnancy helps the mother during that first hard year and has even been shown to lead to better health outcomes in children (Oakley 1992, Oakley 2005).

In the context of our study, we found that emotional support was the most common theme that emerged from these posts. Women commiserated about frustration and stress with pregnancy, children and family. They discussed many physical feelings and discomforts in pregnancy, wondering if it was normal or not, and they discussed all their emotions surrounding pregnancy and birth. They congratulated one another during the span of about one and a half months when all the babies were born (at the time about 500 women were on the board), so a lot of time and effort went into all the congratulating. Women asked for support when dealing with difficult situations with their husbands, other children, parents and in-laws. Quite a few times women wrote about controversial subjects such as one's husband having an affair with a minor (during the woman's pregnancy), or letting a baby cry for an extended amount of time to try to teach her to sleep. In both cases, plenty of women on the board felt the woman posting should have done something else, and it caused a lot of discussion. However, in both cases, there was a strong emphasis on preserving the website for support. That is, even if one does not believe in a woman/mother's choices, the web board was for *support,* thus your role on the board was to either say something nice or do not say anything at all. In addition, if someone did cause trouble by ridiculing or antagonizing someone, the moderator could remove them from the board. Sociologists call the ability to remove someone from a website as institutional power or institutional control to maintain the status quo. That is, the web moderator has legitimated power to control the content of the website--and for this web board the status quo and culture was one of support.

Social Capital

Social capital is a broad theoretical concept that is used in many arenas such as political science, health studies, sociology and psychology. For the purpose of this book on internet and mothering, we will focus on a definition that is pertinent to our topic. As such, we use the definition of social capital as "resources embedded in a social structure that are accessed and/or mobilized in purposive actions" (Lin 2001:29). In our case, the resources for mothers on an internet website is the information and social support exchanged, that is then translated into usable information regarding pregnancy, birth and child rearing.

We also found that the website was a source of social capital, meaning that the resources embedded in the discussion board included instrumental support—both formal and informal. Informal instrumental support included informal information sharing over issues such as pregnancy, breastfeeding, and colic. In these discussions, a topic may come up, usually asking if something is "normal," such as the number of times a day the baby nurses. Then, there could be a series of answers (usually between 2-10), on what others were experiencing with the same age child. This information sharing is thus a resource that can help a mother decide when a problem is serious enough to contact a physician. The women also shared instrumental support that was formal in nature. In this case, they would reference "official" outside sources to answer the topic. For instance, they might talk about the recommendations given by the American Academy of Pediatrics, or they would discuss the specific information from their own physicians, or from books on the subject.

Maintaining a Community

The website and discussion boards also were a site of community building and community protection. Women (mothers) want a place on the internet where they can share personal information, and discuss their triumphs, worries and concerns. As with the case of a website that included mothers of newborns, it is no surprise that the main discussions surrounded worries, concerns and complaints about pregnancy and being tired. However, as is also the case with a community of hundreds of women discussing childrearing, there were many different opinions and controversy did occur. A few times someone posted a message that attacked another woman and/or her childrearing techniques. When this happened, other women and even the moderator would step in to protect their virtual community from being unsupportive. As a result, women protected their interests, and kept the virtual community thriving and being supportive. In a similar paper examining the exodus of about 100 women to a private website due to frustration with the moderator, Ley (2009:1388) found that women share a high level of trust and commitment with one another. In the next part of the paper, we seek to examine the changes that have taken place over the years, namely the exponential growth in websites.

Update Since the Original Study

Explosion in Number of Sites

Since we published our original study on online mothering there has been an explosion in the number and level of sophistication of online virtual communities, including websites devoted exclusively to parenting and mothering. For instance, in our original study—at the height of membership on the birth board (which occurs during the birth month), there were approximately 629 members. By comparison, the current month's We Love Babies birth board as I am writing this (October 2009) has 5,650 members and already has 47,762 posts! And while there were originally a few specialized boards on the main site beyond the birth boards (e.g., fertility issues, loss and grieving), there are now countless additional groups. One can join a group on preschoolers, toddlers, baby names, cooking for your family, trick or treating, and shutterfly moms—to name only a few.

Beyond the mothering website we studied, an immeasurable number of other forums for parenting/mothering virtual communities have been developed in the past few years. Among the most well-known is Circle of Moms, which was launched in October of 2008 and is partnered with Facebook. It currently boasts 2,349,567 monthly active users (and their FAQ states they have over 6 million members)(September 4, 2009). Like the mothering site we originally studied, Circle of Moms allows one to post threads related to one of the particular sub-communities and topics, such as breastfeeding moms and working moms. With 9,000+ such topics available, one is bound to find a niche, and if not, may create one. Also, among your own Facebook female friends, you may identify women to be included in your own "Circle of Moms." Doing so alerts others in your circle about events happening with your children, such as their birthdays, and vice versa. Examples of other common mothering websites with discussion boards include www.mothering.com, http://parenting.ivillage .com, www.cafemom.com, www.llli.org, (La Leche League, an organization which promotes breastfeeding), www.fertilitycommunity.com, www. ParentsPlace.com, www.FamilyEducation.com, and Moms LikeMe.com—to name just a few.

The mothering virtual communities discussed so far are generally set up by an organization that may have (financial) sponsors. As discussed in our original study, such boards have rules concerning what topics may not be discussed (e.g., explicitly sexual in nature in a context not directly related to mothering, childbirth, etc; lewd language; acting malicious, etc.), and some of these rules may be imparted by companies that sponsor the website. Moderators are in place to enforce the rules, and reprimand or remove members if necessary. When the second author of this chapter (Cross) was pregnant and had her first baby in 2006, she witnessed numerous members of her birth board receive warnings or be removed for violating rules—most of the time for acting in a malicious manner (most commonly by issuing personal attacks with inappropriate language), though sometimes the offender was never given an explanation for the warning or exile.

Related to this, a whole other source of mothering virtual communities is private web boards. Such sites are created by individuals who, in turn, set the rules (if any) for their own boards. Such boards do not have direct sponsors, but have random ads placed on a portion of the screen. It is impossible to know how many of these sites have been created, but we know of several that have developed as offshoots of a single birth board, so there are likely hundreds, if not thousands. Cross has been a member of one such private board for over two years. The board was initiated by a member of her first child's birth board, and anyone from that birth board was initially welcome to join. Approximately 125 women joined at its inception, but it was several months before I (Cross) joined. I delayed joining because I was writing my dissertation and did not want to commit to any more virtual networks, as this private board generally does not allow lurking (which I was mostly doing on my We Love Babies birth board). Also, I did not immediately realize that most of the funny women had largely left the We Love Babies birth board and joined this private one—and I would much rather have some snarky advice and support to balance the seriousness with some humor! By the time I joined, however, there had been some large split (for reasons I am still not entirely clear) and about 75 members remained. Since then, we have had occasional members end their membership and a few voted off.

We affectionately call the private board "The Refuge," meaning it is a refuge from the main We Love Babies site from which we all originally met and shared pregnancy and birth experiences. Though a single woman created The Refuge, its operation is predominantly a democratic sphere. So, in contrast to a site like We Love Babies where a moderator may wield ultimate power, big decisions are taken by a vote among everyone on The Refuge. Because there are only about 75 members who have grown relatively close over the past couple of years, instances of significant strife have become quite rare. To grasp a picture of the involvement of women on The Refuge, some members have posted less than three- or four-thousand posts, while there are also several members who have in excess of 20,000 posts! Thus for a sizeable number of the members checking in with the board daily, if not several periods during the day, is common. If someone suddenly stops posting, members notice and state they miss them, or call or text-message to ensure everything is all right.

Increased Sophistication of Mothering Boards

In addition to the sheer number of websites and discussion boards available for interaction, the level of sophistication has increased over the years as well. The use of screen names continues on most of these websites today, but the nature of "signatures" has changed. When we originally studied We Love Babies, women may have "signed" the bottom with their real name, and perhaps the names and birthdates of their child(ren). Now, it is still common for women to sign with their real (first) name, as well as list their children's names and perhaps birthdates (using a digital signature that automatically appears at the bottom of every post), but in addition, one or two pictures are shown in the signature portion of the post (usually of the woman's child(ren). Some women use a third-party site to create a photo montage for their signature. Further, some may include a favorite quote and/or tickers (created by third-party websites), which are digital countdowns (towards the number of days left in a pregnancy, number of days until an event, number of pounds left wishing to lose, etc.). Most websites also feature member profile pages, where one can put personal information, such as an email address, spouse/children information, work information, and so on that is seen when someone clicks on your screen name. Also, almost all sites allow for a member to send a private message to another member, whether her email is publicly listed or not. This allows for private discussions the rest of a board cannot see. Moreover, using Facebook and text messaging as a way to *augment* online interactions has added an extra layer of sophistication to the meaning and use of virtual communities. That is, once members begin to know one another better, some may become friends via Facebook and/or get one another's cell phone numbers and exchange messages via those mediums. Thus within the mothering groups, we see an integration of internet and communication technologies.

Over time the once clearer distinctions of "online friends" (which makes one feel like a crazy person or total loser to say to others!) and "IRL—in real life" friends becomes rather blurred. This is even truer once people begin to meet-up in real life. There have been countless meet-ups among members of The Refuge over the years, as women meet with women who live near them, or whose personal or professional trips take them near another member. This past summer, about one-third of the members of The Refuge met up in New York City for a fun-filled weekend of putting live faces to virtual profiles we had interacted with for years. Thus we see a blur between real and virtual life, rather than one possibly replacing the other (Ley 2009, Miyata 2002).

Effects on Social Capital and Social Support

Despite the large growth in sites, and the sophistication of sites, the issues of social capital remain the same. It appears however that issues of social support have changed.

Emotional Support. In our original study we found that the most prevalent type of post was emotional support. This remains true on virtually every type of mothering site with which we are aware. Whether at the stage of pregnancy and determining how to tell one's place of employment about the pregnancy; or, in the labor and delivery room sending and receiving online or text messages about your progress—no joke!; or, in the post-partum phase physically recovering and adjusting to changing family dynamics; or, years down the road, trying to potty train and discipline your toddler, the boards fundamentally remain a principal source of emotional support.

In our experience and observations, there are several factors that enhance the quality of support given and received. Obviously, on extremely large boards the quantity of support may be enormous, with dozens of women at any given time offering a virtual hug or expression of empathy, but the quality of support matters as well. At times, however, an ocean of relatively anonymous women does not have the same feeling of warmth and love as a more intimate board, where members have shared countless experiences, binding them tighter. On a massive board, someone may offer a mother support and five minutes later carry on with her life having totally forgotten about the interaction. On a board like The Refuge, women not only offer support, but initiate follow-ups days or weeks later to see how things are going. And, contrary to research cited in our original study stating that "flaming" behavior (making rude remarks or ostracizing a member) is hardly found in women-dominated groups, it can become quite rampant on mothering boards today—particularly large ones. Such boards amass a heterogeneous, largely anonymous group of women and a feeding frenzy can begin if a controversial topic is raised. One infamous site for such conditions is the We Love Babies Searching for Deals board. As the name implies, it was intended as a board to discuss sales and shopping strategies (mostly on groceries and baby items), but eventually became the congregation site for thousands of We Love Babies members (presently 14,443).

Another factor that affects whether members of mothering boards seem more personalized is the use of digital photos. We have already mentioned how many women have one or two photos in their signatures. Women often also post a series of photos from daily life or an event to share with other members, and such visualizations allow one to put actual faces with names.

The Refuge uses a visible, actually measurable, tool to give a high-five or offer support to another member—salt and pepper shakers. One may click on another member's salt shaker (exalt) or pepper shaker (smite… o.k., this is not very supportive). The technical act is anonymous, but often a member will state, "Giving you salt for xxxx!" It is a fun way to show support. Generally, one's salt levels are commensurate with her overall number of posts (that is, level of participation and offering of support to others), but this is not always the case. Smites are apparently rare, and almost never does someone admit to specifically giving them. Thus, with the boards, technology and graphics enhance the friendships.

Finally, we would like to stress that, unless one is insensitive to the norms of friendship, and is oblivious to others, the quantity and quality of social support is based on *mutual* support. One cannot expect to join a board tomorrow and instantly feel deeply meaningful connections to others, as if they are old friends. Like friends offline, such friendships have to develop over time based on experiences of trust and mutual support.

Instrumental Support

In the form of advice exchanged among members, this is almost as ubiquitous as emotional support. Because, unfortunately, babies and children do not come with manuals, there are endless questions at every life stage on how to handle things. For instance, during pregnancy, women sought recommendations for how to ameliorate morning sickness. This was followed by a barrage of posts concerning how to soothe a crying baby and get them to sleep more consistently. Women then exchange ideas on what foods to prepare for a toddler and how to encourage them to try different ones, or how to potty train. It is helpful to hear a variety of tested ideas. Women may pass along more formal recommendations from their own child's pediatrician or another such professional on topics like whether to get a flu shot, how much medicine to give, and when to call a doctor. The type of information may extend beyond topics directly related to parenting as well. Members who know one another may point out jobs in an area. As another example, a member of The Refuge recently described issues she was having getting her car repaired and covered by the warranty. Another member pointed out that her husband is a mechanic and he thought the repair place was ripping her off, and gave the reasons why. In response to this exchange, another Refuge member stated, "People in the world just don't know what they're up against when they fuck with a refuge biotch,"[sic] meaning the collective knowledge and support available on the board is diverse and rich. Beyond information, tangible items may be sent to one another. On The Refuge, it is common for individual members to send gifts to a member who just had another baby; or we may take up a collection and send a basket to a member who lost a family member; or simply send cash to someone in dire need.

Community Building

Our original study determined that the We Love Babies birth board was *explicitly* focused on support, with moderators policing the site to ensure people did not leverage personal attacks. As described above, this has become more difficult to achieve when portions of a board become overwhelmed with a heterogeneous, anonymous group of women addressing a controversial issue or person. It can become a race to see how much flaming can occur before the thread is locked up and people are warned or exiled, all with hundreds or thousands of onlookers enjoying their virtual popcorn to watch the show. There have even been blogs developed for people to cut and paste the drama so that if it is removed by moderators, it exists elsewhere for anyone to see. So, the notion that women do not act rude or malicious on a web board—even one with a supposed purpose to give and get support—is simply not true (anymore). It is important to remember that eventually civility has to be restored and offenders have to be removed, not only so that women enjoy a supportive environment, but also so that the site has a modicum of decorum and sufficient numbers of women still participate—and become exposed to the advertisements displayed by sponsors. There is a corporate interest in maintaining a supportive board.

The Refuge has an *implicit* focus on being supportive. It is inherently what we seek to provide and gain when interacting. Because I joined after the sizeable exodus of members several months after the board was created, I can only imagine that there were heated exchanges and a group of women decided to form a separate group. Interestingly, I cannot remember an instance where a member acted maliciously and was then voted off. Rather, there have been several instances where a member flames someone, other members express why she is wrong, and she subsequently self-deletes (which carries a never allowed back in rule). So, wielding social control and pressure are means used more often to curb perpetrators than the power of a single member or moderator.

Trust is a key issue for community building. On a public board like We Love Babies, anyone around the world may view what is posted—which is why I chose to mostly lurk and never put pictures of my children up. After joining The Refuge, over time, my walls came down. Most members, myself included, have posted hundreds of pictures of our children and shared voluminous amounts of deeply personal information (ranging from issues at work; marital and family issues; biographical information, etc.). There is almost no tolerance on The Refuge for violating trust. One cannot break the rule of passing along information to ex-members, or the public at large. We have shared too much information, which could adversely affect professional and personal lives if it were known beyond our virtual walls. While it is usually left up to an individual member to self-delete if she has been (usually repeatedly and with multiple members) malicious, one will quickly find herself under a Refuge vote to be exiled if issues of trust are violated.

Conclusion

In this chapter, we examined two virtual communities for mothers on the internet. We examined previous research and findings from a large parenting website, and then examined how it has grown, almost 10 years later. We discussed the explosion of websites for mothers and parenting, and the proliferation of private websites for groups of mothers. We then examined one such website in detail: a smaller private website. We saw that websites for mothers are still a major source of emotional and instrumental support. However, women's online interactions may be quite unsupportive as well, and more apt to "attack" a view they don't like, rather than embracing the feminine stereotype of being feminine, kind and supportive. This may be due to the increasing number of women on these websites, leading to even more heterogeneous groups of women, or it may reflect a cultural change in women. It may also reflect the new cohort of mothers who have been on the internet since they were children--after all, many women become mothers in their early 20s, and it can be assumed that most are on the web in some fashion. Many of these women have grown up on the internet, and may lack some of the formality that older women still hold in internet interactions.

Finally, it should be noted that, as with our original study, and even with all the advances the internet and such websites have made over the years, they do not completely replace human face-to-face interaction. Sometimes, there is not substitute for a real—not virtual—hug, or to actually see, hear and touch a baby in a doctor's office to diagnose a problem. And, at times there may be misunderstandings and confusions in online interactions because we are bereft of visible body language, voice intonations, and so on. Future research should examine how effective is the support from websites, how women use websites, and whether there are age/cohort changes with users, that will also reflect changes in mothering.

Works Cited

Drentea, Patricia, and Jennifer Moren-Cross. 2005. Social Capital and Social Support on the Web: The Case of an Internet Mother Site. *Sociology of Health and Illness.* 27:920-43.

Ley, Barbara. 2009. Vive les Roses! The Architecture of Commitment in an Online Pregnancy and Mothering Group. *Journal of Computer-Mediated Communication.* 12:1388-1408.

Lin, Nan. 2001. *Social capital.* Cambridge: Cambridge University Press.

Litt, Jacquelyn S. 2000. *Medicalized Motherhood: Perspectives from the Lives of African-American and Jewish Women.* NJ: Rutgers University Press.

Miyata, Kakuko. 2002. Social Support for Japanese Mothers Online and Offline. *The Internet in Everyday Life*, edited by B. Wellman & C. Haythornthwaite. 520-549. Oxford, UK: Blackwell Publishing.

MMWR. 2005. "Average Age of Mothers at First Birth." *The National Center for Health Statistics*. 54:488. Accessed October 8, 2009. http://www.cdc.gov/mmwr/preview/mmwrhtml/mm5419a5.htm

Oakley, Ann. 1992. *Social Support and Motherhood: The Natural History of a Research Project.* Oxford: Blackwell Publishers.

—. 2005. *The Ann Oakley Reader*. Bristol, UK: The Policy Press.

U.S. Bureau of the Census. 2003. "Percentage of Childless Women 40-44 Years Old." *News Release from the U.S. Bureau of the Census.* http://www.census.gov/Press-Release/www/releases/archives/fertility/001491.html (accessed Oct. 8, 2009).

Wellman, Barry, and Caroline Haythornthwaite. 2001. *The Internet in Everyday Life*. Malden, MA: Blackwell Publishers.

Wills, Thomas A. 1985. Supportive Functions of Interpersonal

Relationships. *Social Support and Health,* edited by S. Cohen & L. Syme. Orlando, FL: Academic Press, Inc.

Wertz, Richard W., and Dorothy C. Wertz. 1989. *Lying-In: A History of Childbirth in America.* New Haven, CT: Yale University Press.

Notes

[1] The Refuge and We Love Babies are pseudonyms.

CHAPTER FOUR

THREADS OF DISSENT: CONFLICT IN AN ONLINE COMMUNITY

SARAH LEAVITT

In the fall of 2001, I discovered the internet. Not literally, of course, but at the time, the realization that there was such thing as an online community of women who were waiting by their computers to talk to me about my pregnancy was nothing short of revelatory. This was fairly early in the era of online bulletin boards, and nobody I knew IRL [in real life] had yet discovered such a community. The one I found was hosted by iVillage.com, then purporting to be "the internet for women." The group was open to the public and populated by pregnant women due to deliver in the same month. Our conversations began as surface connections between strangers, but over the next months and years, especially after several dozen of us started posting on a private site, the relationships grew considerably more meaningful. Many of us have now met in person, in gatherings large and small. Over time, writing back and forth to these women and learning their stories challenged my ideas about friendship, conflict, and community and their meanings in contemporary mothers' lives.

My online experience began simply enough; that is, I wanted people to talk to, and there they were. But I soon started seeing the board as a place where women were doing cultural work through their posts. This was a community of women who would never have met without the internet. This was a group of people who purposely sought each other out and challenged and supported each other every day for several years. It was a group of people with potentially polarizing views on everything from abortion to vaccinations, who nonetheless purposefully came together for advice and companionship. This was something interesting. In fact, it is in the reconciliation of the similarities with the differences that we can begin to understand the deeper role of this virtual community in the lives of its members.

Mothers' groups, of course, are nothing new. Certainly, women have long formed groups to both support each other and to foment social change. In America, the late nineteenth century was the height of participation in women's clubs, both social and political. Thousands of women met frequently with one another to learn as well as to accomplish specific goals such as temperance, the establishment of settlement houses, and woman suffrage. In the late twentieth century, women organized massive campaigns in favor of gun control and both for and against abortion rights. Less formal groups organized by and for mothers, such as the coffee klatches of the 1950s and the consciousness raising groups of the 1970s, provided outlets for women to share stories and advice. These groups were often homogenous in terms of demographics and political orientation. The internet, however, has created new kinds of communities that are not limited by neighborhood, workplace, education level, or income, and therefore must encompass people who vote, pray, and live differently.

Elective groups, that is, communities one chooses to join, can thrive on commonality and a shared sense of purpose. But they can also survive on shared outrage—often even outrage at each other. Online mothers' groups may be made up of unrelated people who do not necessarily live near each other. They may not share an interest in particular activities, books, or sports. In fact, they may disagree on most subjects of importance to them. Some of the more well-trodden debates, about circumcision, breast feeding, "crying it out," and co-sleeping, drive traffic daily through hundreds of public message boards. Though constantly rehashed, these discussions are new to each new generation of parents and clearly—judging by the sheer amount of time people devote to these conversations—serve an important and culturally significant purpose. Indeed, what is most illuminating about online boards is often the way in which these subjects energize and enable a community experience. This essay will use one online board as a lens with which to examine the role of internet friendships in 21st century motherhood, exploring a new way to understand the role of dissent—everything from mild disagreement to real, visceral anger—in community formation.

The internet is a relatively new site for the enacting traditional rituals of friendship and is often accused of fostering angry debate instead of connection. Website discussion boards for mothers abound: some, such as urbanbaby.com, have the reputation of fomenting revolution at every turn. Blogs such as Motherlode on *The New York Times'* website can carry on about subjects such as wives changing their last names, paid childcare, and playground politics through hundreds of detailed comments. The anonymity of public websites gives people license to say things they would never say in person and much of that dialogue is not particularly friendly. But community building can happen on online boards in ways that are simply impossible in other forms of life experience. "Technology," as internet anthropologist Emily Ignacio has argued, "affects the construction of national, racial, ethnic, and gendered identities. And…this technology can help create new coalitions" (Ignacio, 4). For many mothers, private online boards became a platform, situated in the first decade of the 21st century temporally between the advent of "mommy blogs" and Facebook, for making lifecycle friends. These friendships have a certain gravitas perhaps otherwise unwarranted by their cyber-origins, based on the vulnerable period of life—pregnancy and early motherhood—in which the friendships began. Online communities of mothers model a certain kind of voluntary, and often fragile, coalition, demonstrating how mothers with little else in common can find friendship.

The Junebugs: A Safe Haven

In the first decades of the 21st century, internet usage by women surpassed that of men, a flip of the technology's demographics during the 1990s. Websites such as iVillage.com welcomed these women and hosted publically accessible discussion boards. Many were geared specifically to mothers, from raising children with special needs to cloth diapering. There was a separate board for women due to give birth each month. A few hundred women signed on to the "June 2002" board during their pregnancies. The board remained active through the regular and irregular traumas and worries of pregnancy, childbirth, and early infancy. Women came to the iVillage board seeking a safe space to come and share personal details and learn from each other. Many might imagine a "feminine internet" as a place where women come to find support and form groups in accordance with their own belief systems. Indeed, in studies of internet communities, women's use of the internet is often described as part of their search for a safe, supportive, affirming space (Consolvo, et al). Internet communities of women such as theknot.com, a site specifically for those planning weddings, and the online community sponsored by Oprah Winfrey do exhibit some of these features, in that the women specifically gather at these sites to support and learn from each other (Nelson and Otnes, 89-95). Many message boards are in fact monitored and policed to ensure proper behavior.

In the spring of 2003, when the babies born to the "June 2002" iVillage group were almost a year old, two of the women split off from the public site and invited about 40 other members to join them on a private, password-protected message board called "Junebugs."[1] The two original founders of Junebugs had similar touch points in their lives, including teen pregnancy, children from two different marriages, and a different religious belief system from their parents. They handpicked the women they thought would make the most interesting community with the intent to create a supportive board of mothers, not to tackle religion or politics. One of the main reasons to start a private board was to create a "safe haven" where members—friends—could enrich their general discussions with personal information. On the private site people could feel free to use their real names and describe, in more detail, their real problems, concerns, and joys. Though it was conceived as a place where friends could come to support each other, over time, the inevitable coming of interpersonal conflict and political and religious disagreements also played a role in building the community.

The forty women had been chosen somewhat randomly and somewhat purposefully. The leaders left out the most contentious members of the public board, those who consistently looked to pick a fight about circumcision or constantly posted about their own personal good looks. Though the original "June 2002" board had several hundred members, there were only several dozen who posted on any consistent basis toward the end of the pregnancies. These women made up the core of the new board. They were from all over the United States with concentrations in the mid-Atlantic region, in the Pacific Northwest, and in Texas. Most hailed from small towns and suburbs with only a few city-dwellers. A few members joined from Canada. Most of the women were white and Christian, with a few exceptions that included an African American woman, a Hispanic woman and a few with Jewish ties. A little more than half had gone to college and about half started their parenting lives by working outside the home, though others joined the workforce once their children were in school and a few eventually left the workforce to stay home with their children. Several women were divorced and re-married, some helping to raise older children from previous relationships. Socioeconomically, the women spanned the range of the middle class, with a few using food stamps and facing unemployment, foreclosure, and the loss of health care for their children and others working professional jobs and earning significant salaries.

The Junebugs board was busy from the start, with hundreds of posts a day on subjects ranging from diaper brands to reality TV to sex. There was much to discuss. The members, who often felt unsure of their parenting choices and had no clear support systems in their daily lives, turned to each other for advice, reassurance, and camaraderie. The discussions were personal and dealt with problems at work, at home, with disciplining children, with ailing parents and with uncommunicative husbands. Within a few years, members had experienced divorce, extramarital affairs, deaths in the family, and miscarriages. Trust built upon years of shared communication allowed for personal conversations of every nature.

While to a large extent the desire for supportive friendships created the Junebugs board, its survival depended on the willingness of mothers to go beyond their "comfort zones" and find a new kind of comfort in safe debate. It became clear that ignoring political and ideological difference would be impossible. The community feeling they sought would be meaningless if the members only shared part of themselves. During the contentious elections of 2004 and 2008, politics and religion were, in fact, prime topics for discussion and disagreement for the Junebugs. Members, it was revealed in an early poll, were about evenly split between Republicans and Democrats. So how did these disparate women form a community? The importance of dissent in the formation of community has not been widely addressed. Though many ethnographic studies discuss conflict, it is not often treated as a fundamental part of the pattern of identity-building but as a hurdle to overcome.[2] Though community studies often include an anecdote of disagreement, few address the role that conflict has in causing members to forge bonds with each other that would not be the same had the community remained a tidy group of like-minded people. The Junebugs community originally formed because all members had motherhood and the age of one of their children in common. However, this similarity alone does not explain the community. This is a story that involves the specific interaction between commonality and clash.

Having established a safe space in which members posted intimate details and troubling personal stories along with anecdotes of family life, the board made room for difference within the context of the community. In fact, the Junebugs created a special part of the board specifically for discussions about politics and religion to separate those threads from the neutral parts of the board. Unused to political discussions among their friends, many members worried about the consequences if people were actually allowed to say what they thought—about child raising, about God, about the tax cuts. But mutual animosity can have a flipside: often, women can become strong self-advocates on the internet. For women, the board may be one place where dissent can be practiced within the context of harmony. That is, the comfort inherent in a support group can specifically allow for an openness to disagree. They can argue online, with time to compose their thoughts, rather than face to face with immediate pressure to respond. The internet may allow for a less confrontational way to experience conflict. In the context of a mothers' group in which they already feel safe, members can express themselves in ways that are not possible in other areas of their lives.

Introducing Conflict: The Salon

In the summer of 2003, soon after the private board was founded, pop singer Britney Spears kissed 1980s rock icon Madonna at the MTV awards, a television show geared toward a young "edgy" audience. The kiss was meant to spark discussion and create publicity. It certainly did that on the Junebugs board. In an otherwise light discussion of that kiss, one of the members nonchalantly opined that "homosexuality is repulsive." And that was the beginning of the Salon, a separate part of the board for potentially difficult discussions. The remark was made in the confident way people speak when they are talking amongst like-minded friends. After creating a firestorm, the original poster did apologize for starting the debate: "once and for all let me say I apologize for the way I worded my response concerning the Madonna/Britney kiss," though she pointed out that others might feel the same way yet be reluctant to post: "several here do disagree with homosexuality yet they choose not to discuss it here, which is probably a very good idea."[3] The board members were reluctant to invite such discussion into their peaceful realm. One proposed solution was to ban all controversial subjects from the board. However, after much discussion, a separate forum was proposed. In the spirit of discussion and friendship, the name for the new forum was inspired by women's gatherings in 17th century Paris.

For many women, boisterous and angry conversation—even if the anger is not directed at one another—presents difficulties. "OK, maybe I'm in the minority," wrote one member after a particularly heated discussion, "but there is a reason that I don't discuss religion and other controversial topics with my good friends…. Perhaps it is best this is not discussed here anymore. Unfortunately, the world…is full of hate, discrimination, bashing, etc. Why in the world would we want to bring that in here…our safe haven?"[4] At times, after the Salon became a busy section of the board, some felt that their beliefs were being attacked rather than tolerated, understood, or appreciated. For example, a heated discussion about vaginal births after c-section (VBAC) caused some members to regret their remarks and wonder about the efficacy of such discussion. One woman wrote about her own experience in which her obstetrician refused to even consider a VBAC. A flurry of comments ensued, with some members detailing similar experiences and others complaining about the prevalence of c-sections in America. Nobody attacked the original poster; in fact all members were supportive of her decision to seek another doctor, but upon returning to the board and seeing over a dozen posts about her VBAC, she shied away from posting further information on the subject: "from now on, I'll turn all controversial issues to [other places] rather than starting a ruckus here."[5] The idea that bringing up a personal subject and getting responses, most of which were in fact quite positive and affirming, caused "a ruckus" demonstrates the reticence these women had toward anything that inched away from superficial support into a deeper discussion.

For people who are accustomed to debate—who grew up in families where the dinner table was the venue for open discussions, participated on the debate team in high school, were challenged in college classes by professors—the act of arguing from a particular point of view is usually neither difficult nor scary. But for others, who do not have this experience in their lives, the act of dissent is a learned discipline. Members often post a caveat explaining that they are unused to this type of argument with a comment such as "this is why I don't debate much of anything."[6] The internet can work as a forum for learning to express views, in the context of the safe affirming space that many women seek. Because the internet is remote, confrontation can be easier than it would be in person. Many members have expressed their fear of antagonizing real life friends by presenting their views. "I do relate to online people much differently," wrote one member. "In real life, I'm petrified of confrontation! I almost never discuss anything remotely controversial and am terrified (terrified!) of rejection."[7] However, in the context of this internet community, she felt comfortable posting about her personal beliefs and her political views. She used her comfort level with the community to build a platform for exploring controversy.

To many of these women, the Salon conversations are the first time in their lives that they have discussed controversial topics with friends. The board is an intervention in their lives. It does not change their particular opinions, but rather changes the ways they express themselves. The Salon upsets these women but also empowers them, and makes them confront their beliefs in a way that is not always necessary in other aspects of their lives. "I only have a couple true IRL friends," wrote one woman, "We share very similar beliefs on just about everything."[8] Another noted that in her daily life "I have a few friends here that have been built on mutual life experiences—babies around the same age and in the time we do have together, we tend to discuss baby stuff, etc." And this was a common refrain: "We're married, have jobs, husbands and kids so we don't have a lot of free time to get all philosophical with each other about our stances on certain issues….I wish I could spend more time with my friends but in all reality, it's just not an option."[9]

These women have not been purposely disenfranchised. But their families and friends never particularly encouraged them to talk about politics or to vote. "I grew up in a small town. We watched thc 6 pm news and read the paper but honestly, I cannot remember a time when my parents openly had a discussion about anything controversial when my sister or I was in the room. Honestly, I doubt they ever did. They're just not the type," posted one woman. "I never really thought about it [being unusual], till now."[10] In a later post, she noted that religion has also long been a taboo subject for her: "I live with a husband who is on the verge of a complete atheist and though it bothers me, it's just a topic I'm not going to discuss with him because it's sensitive…I won't bring up religion in my own home with my husband," she noted, so it was difficult to imagine bring it up on the board. She did write, however, that it was interesting for her to read through others' discussions and that she was learning a lot from the board members about both religion and politics. "I'm still learning about politics. My parents never voted and pretty much ignored elections and election time. Growing up that way I just accepted it." In her understanding of America, this was "typical….honestly I don't think any of my friends' parents voted."[11] Another member agreed, "I don't discuss these things with my mom and dad, because they just aren't the type to care. I don't think they have passionate ideas about anything."[12] And so, having no role models, they just did not see participatory democracy as having any particular meaning to them. As one noted, "I tend not to criticize the government much….I guess my theory is if I can't do a better job of if I don't have any better ideas I don't say too much that's critical."[13]

Decades of research on the behavior of girls in school, such as Carol Gilligan's now classic book on the subject, have often pointed out the reticence girls have when posing a question, always prefacing it with a caveat (Gilligan). This behavior is seen all the time in the Salon. "I'm not one for political debates, because I'm not very good at expressing my thoughts on that subject, but here it is…"[14] or: "I don't know…you all know I suck at debate/discussions like this so I am doing my best."[15] Even having opinions on political issues of the day with which they are familiar, such as jobs going overseas or the No Child Left Behind bill, causes many members to claim ignorance as an excuse. "I'm not a politician...I don't debate well."[16] On another occasion a member apologized for her writing style: "I rambled…thoughts not very together today…sorry."[17]

One member tacked on the caveat "I rarely post here, because I am SO bad at backing up what I believe or feel,"[18] to her post about Spanish-speaking immigrants who did not learn English. Common in the Salon were posts that emphasized the member's reluctance to post at all. "Glad I ventured here today," wrote one member before joining a discussion about husbands who did not participate actively in the family's religion.[19] Using the word "venture" emphasized her trepidation in approaching such loaded subjects as religion and politics. Others remained relatively reluctant, posting only occasionally and then usually including a comment such as, "the rest I'm staying away from because my views are obviously very different than most of the rest of you and I would rather not get into something big about it."[20] For many members, it was enough of a stretch simply to post once, though usually after posting a few times they grew more comfortable with the idea and continued to participate.

With the Salon, the Junebugs board became less a superficial support board and more a real Salon, where ideas were challenged, corroborated, celebrated, dissected, and otherwise discussed. The notion of a forum for conflict, though previously anathema to these women, became fundamental to this community. Junebug members had to learn how to discuss controversy; that is, how to ask the questions, how to respond, how to discuss, debate, and learn without causing too much distress. The Salon became more a place to air and test out opinions and get to know each other than a place to build consensus.

However, the Salon was not universally celebrated on the board. For many, the forum exposed sides of people that precluded future friendship. Indeed, from the beginning, members worried that the Salon could spill to other regions of the board and affect the friendships negatively. One member noted "we share a lot of ourselves here and despite our efforts to 'keep the Salon in the Salon' or 'separate our opinions on issues from our opinions of each other' they do overlap."[21] She urged members to remember to be gracious to each other even in the midst of severe disagreements. Another poster concurred: "I don't think we should gag ourselves and not say anything controversial…But if we're going to do so, we should recognize that feelings are going to be hurt."[22] And many struggled with their feelings about the Salon, feeling that too much exposure to conflict would destroy the safe haven. "I'm just having such a hard time supporting the fact that we're doing this….Doesn't it in the end kind of make us judge one another? Doesn't it usually end up with hurt feelings? I can't speak for the rest of you, but I for one want to come to the board feeling support….I need this outlet. I don't want to come to the board feeling tense because maybe I said something and somebody is mad." She concluded by noting, "I'm just so confused as to whether I like this forum or not."[23]

The Junebugs discussed all sorts of controversial subjects without derailment: hell, abortion, gay rights, illegal immigration, vaccines, and health insurance. The election of 2008, however, brought some new challenges. A discussion of Sarah Palin's vice presidential campaign was particularly difficult because of the way that some members identified with her as a conservative mother. After years of disagreement, this election proved the last frontier for many members, and several left the board entirely. The original board founders proposed getting rid of the forum. Feelings had been hurt and wide differences had been exposed. To them, the act of dissent became frightening when they felt it would threaten the survival of the board, even though the board itself had been forged at least in part, not despite but because of earlier difficult discussions. One member wrote a note to everybody asking them to respect each others' differences. "Political conversations have come up….and yet I have never ever felt offended or hurt. I've had very blunt things said, and out of complete respect I know that is that person's opinion and take it as such and leave and walk away."[24] As someone who was initially reluctant to start the Salon in the first place, one member noted that "I honestly thought we agreed at some point that stuff posted here isn't meant to hurt and offend each other….I just don't understand how these things are getting so out of hand."[25]

***

In the end most members stayed to do the hard work of disagreeing. "We're in the Salon," wrote one member, "where anything and everything can be discussed….The last thing I want to do is hurt one of my beloved sisters, but I want to really be free to express our opinions. Wasn't that the point of the Salon to begin with??"[26] Together, the several dozen remaining women agreed that it was. "I've told myself several times that I should stay out of this forum completely," wrote one member, "and not even read, much less post, but it's so darn hard to do that…. I want to say that no matter what our differences I still want to be friends with everyone. If I wanted to be on a board exclusive to Christians I could do that, but I love being here with you guys."[27] What convinced most of the members of the importance of the Salon was the desire to learn from one another. Ultimately, the risk of losing the Salon forum forced members to reveal the ways in which the forum was meaningful to them, both in terms of their relationship with the board and in their own lives. "I adore this forum," wrote one, "I've learned so much from you all. Honestly, I have no idea what I believe in."[28] Another noted that she was sure that writing about her strong Christian beliefs would change her friendships with others on the board, who may not have known before where she stood on certain things. She indicated her trust that these relationships would change for the better. "I went to bed so upset last night at the thought that this outlet might not be here for us when I woke up," she wrote after a lengthy discussion about religion. "I really do learn a lot when I'm here. There is more to me than just a mom to my children…..I have thoughts and ideas and I rarely get to express them or even to challenge them….I am surrounded by Christians….Here, I get exposed to other ideas."[29]

In many ways, the Salon showed that an understanding of each others' political and religious differences could lead to a new kind of bond that simply was not possible while only discussing family life. "I can honestly say I've learned so much from so many of you here," wrote one member. "I think this board has helped me expand my horizons in many ways. I love the diversity here, love the fact we don't always agree but we do…still continue our friendships."[30] For the Junebugs, the creation of the Salon as a place to post controversial issues became a way to both allow and segregate discord. In the beginning, the board was simply a safe place for a particular group of mothers to share and learn from each other. By moving forward to discuss contentious subjects such as religion and politics, the members exploded the safe haven and ended up with something else. The discord, the participants' very exercise of dissent, became a fundamental part of sustaining the board and underscores—even explains—the important role that virtual communities can have in mothers' lives. By presenting a forum in which they feel comfortable, safe, and loved, the internet can conversely and simultaneously create a forum for them to be upset and angry, and to feel safe in having those emotions. It can open up previously closed discussions; can make debaters out of those who ordinarily do not argue; can give women a voice to which they ordinarily do not have access. Though it was often a messy process, the Salon forged an intense and challenging community out of what before had merely been a safe haven. The board became a community of people, with all of their complexities, rather than simply a group of women who had once been pregnant at the same time.

Works Cited

Ault, James R. Jr., Spirit *and Flesh: Life in a Fundamentalist Baptist Church*. (New York: Knopf, 2004).

Consalvo, Mia, et al., *Women and Everyday Use of the Internet: Agency & Identity* (Peter Lang Publishing, 2002).

Gilligan, Carol, *In a Different Voice: Psychological Theory and Women's Development*. (Harvard University Press, 1982).

Ignacio, Emily N. Building Diaspora: Filipino Cultural Community Formation on the Internet (Rutgers University Press, 2004), 4.

Nelson, Michelle R. and Cele C. Otnes, "Exploring Cross-Cultural Ambivalence: A Netnography of Intercultural Wedding Message Boards," *Journal of Business Research*, 58 (January 2005), 89-95.

Notes

[1] The name of the board has been changed to protect members' privacy.

[2] See Ault, for example.

[3] Junebugs Salon Notebook. Note on Sources: All quotations come directly from the Junebugs board. No names are used here to protect the members' privacy.

[4] Junebugs Salon Notebook

[5] May-June 2004 Junebugs notebook

[6] Sept-Oct 2004 Junebugs Notebook

[7] May-June 2004 Junebugs Notebook

[8] Junebugs Salon Notebook

[9] Junebugs Salon Notebook

[10] Junebugs Salon Notebook

[11] Junebugs, Salon Notebook

[12] Junebugs, Salon Notebook

[13] Junebugs Salon Notebook

[14] Junebugs Salon Notebook

[15] Junebugs Salon Notebook

[16] July-Aug 2004 Junebugs Notebook

[17] Sept-Oct 2004 Junebugs Notebook

[18] Junebugs Salon Notebook

[19] Junebugs Salon Notebook

[20] Junebugs Salon Notebook

[21] Junebugs Salon Notebook

[22] Salon Notebook

[23] Salon Notebook

[24] Junebugs Salon Notebook

[25] May-June 2004 Junebugs Notebook

[26] Junebugs Salon Notebook

[27] May-June 2004 Junebugs Notebook

[28] Junebugs Salon Notebook
[29] Junebugs Salon Notebook
[30] May-June 2004 Junebugs Notebook

CHAPTER FIVE

10 YEARS OUT: PRESENCE AND ABSENCE IN A LONG-TERM ONLINE MOTHERS' COMMUNITY

LORIN BASDEN ARNOLD

In the fall of 1997, I found myself pregnant with my fifth child, and far from my extended family and my friends. "Found myself" might seem like a particularly low-agency way of phrasing the situation, but it is how it felt at the time. Because I didn't know anyone in my immediate area very well, and my distant extended family and friends had not been very excited when I announced the 4th pregnancy, I felt a bit stranded and like I had no one to talk to about being pregnant. So, I started "surfing" the internet looking for pregnancy talk. When doing so, I came across a message board for pregnant women with the same due date month as I. I spent two or three weeks just reading, because I had never participated in an online forum before and was hesitant to begin. But, then someone asked a question and, having been through it four times already, I knew the answer. That got me; I had to reply. So, I opened an account, logged in, and posted an answer. This began a relationship that has lasted for over 12 years.

As a participant in an online messaging community, I am certainly not alone. Since the mid to late 1990s, use of online forums (also known as message boards or bulletin boards) has grown tremendously. Today, there are so many Internet based message groups that a true estimate of their number is almost impossible. Boards exist for topics as diverse as home cleaning, the Dalai Lama, and particle physics. Based on this wide array of bulletin board use, scholars have conducted a variety of studies of boards and board users in the last fifteen years (see for example Burrows, Nettleton, Pleace, Loader, and Muncer 2000; Copelton and Valle 2009; Coulson and Knibb 2007; Lieberman 2007; Lieberman and Goldstein 2006; Malik and Coulson 2008; McCabe 2009; Pandey 2000). Many such analyses have found evidence that online communities are an important venue of social support for users (Campbell and Wright 2002; Hurley, Sullivan, and McCarthy 2007; Sharer 2005; Whitlock, Powers, and Eckenrode 2006). Studies specifically related to pregnancy or mothering (Arnold 2003; Chan 2008; Drentea and Moren-Cross 2005; Hudson, Campbell-Grossman, Keating-Lefler, and Cline 2008; Madonna 1998a, 1998b; Zelzer 1995) and the Internet have noted the importance of such forums in creating social support for mothers. These findings are consistent with what I experienced during my initial time with the pregnancy bulletin board, and in the discourse of participants I interviewed for my first study of the community.

The Initial Study

Having participated in this pregnancy bulletin board, I had some ideas about what it had brought to my life. What I didn't know was why other people had joined or how they understood the experience, and I was intrigued about the intersections between this online community and the mothering role. It was for this reason that when the children were around a year old – I started a study of the board (Arnold 2003). Though this analysis, I hoped to determine why this group of women turned to an electronic forum, what kind of experience they had with the bulletin board, and how the experience affected them. Twenty-three women, between the ages of twenty-six and forty-one, participated in interviews/surveys (face-to-face, by phone, and online) for that study. All of the participants had belonged to the same "Expecting Club" bulletin board on a popular parenting website. I asked the participants about the factors that led them to be a part of the community, as well as the outcomes of participation. Following the gathering of discourse, I conducted a thematic analysis of their responses and found several common themes in the discourse. Based on this analysis, I concluded that the women felt empowered as mothers by the information and relational support they received through participation in the bulletin board.

The finding of the early 2000s study corresponded well to previous research and theory about women and empowerment, in which scholars argue that, particularly for women, empowerment is created through mutually empathetic and supportive relationships (Liang et al. 2002; Jordan, Kaplan, Miller, Stiver, and Surrey 1991; Rubenstein and Lawler 1990). Empowerment, defined by Surrey (1991a, 164) as "the motivation, freedom, and capacity to act purposefully, with the mobilization of the energies, resources, strengths, or powers of each person through a mutual relational process," should be seen as something that occurs within the processes of empowering relationships, including those in the community. Liang et al. (2002) and Surrey (1991b) argue that such community relationships, characterized by mutual empathy and validation of feeling states, create feelings of belonging, value, and congruency with others. This mutual process then provides the relational members with the energy and confidence ("zest" as stated by Surrey) to make life choices and take action. For the expecting board I participated in and studied in 2000-2001, the exchange of information and mutual supportive relationships that characterized the bulletin board provided a sense of personal empowerment. Such empowerment can be very important, scholars argue, during the period of pregnancy and early mothering, because the medical discourse that surrounds the birth experience is understood as taking control away from the mother and placing it in the hands of medical professionals (Bird 1994; Bordo 1993; Markens, Browner, and Press 1997; Parry 2008).

Based on my analysis of the participant responses, and the correspondent theory/research regarding social support and empowerment in pregnancy, it seems reasonable to conclude that a pregnancy bulletin board can offer important benefits to women. But, what remained unexamined in that study, and in much of the other material regarding online bulletin boards and pregnancy (or online bulletin boards in general) is what happens if/when the event or condition that initially brought the group together is over. What happens to a pregnancy bulletin board when the women are no longer pregnant and the "babies" are growing up?

The group that I studied in 1999-2000 presents an interesting opportunity for such an examination, because now, 10 years later, over ninety women remain together as part of an online bulletin board. This presents us with a somewhat unique opportunity for study, because most research regarding online communities is about communities that have an ongoing "focus point" for participation (i.e. diabetes, running, love of a certain band), rather than a discrete even like pregnancy that does have a bracketed beginning/end. Additionally, much study of online communities over time has been about communities that have ever changing membership, with new members joining and older members leaving throughout; however, for this board, the membership has been limited and relatively consistent. Thus, the current analysis represents a revisiting of the board, to ascertain how it has changed and developed in the ensuing decade, how its members understand that history, and what they anticipate for the future of the board.

The Current Study

Since the time that the original study was completed, the bulletin board community maintained by this group of women has undergone pragmatic changes. First, following the due date of the pregnancies (in summer 1998), the board was moved by host site (Parentsplace.com) from the "Expecting Clubs" area to the "Playgroups" area, where the new mothers continued to discuss their newborn infants and the challenges of mothering. A few mothers joined that group in the early months of caring for a newborn child, while others left the group, for a variety of reasons, typically unstated but likely including being busy with the demands of an infant and feeling that their need for the board had passed. In late 2002, the Parentsplace site was sold to a new entity, which altered the site format and added substantially more advertising to each page, finally initiating a fee system for use. In early 2003, a group of the most active members of the site formally moved to an alternate private (password protected) bulletin board, utilizing Network54.com as a host. Within one day, over 50 individuals had moved to the new site for the group and begun posting there. Over time, the group grew as additional members "defected" from the original host site to the new page, to a maximum of around 110 members. In the ensuing years, some members have left the site or become inactive (again, reasons often go unstated, though some individuals have left due to conflict with other members). At this time, more than 11 years after much of the group came together, there remain more than 95 members on the bulletin board. During 2009, monthly posts ranged from 2,600 to 6,200. Page views per month ranged from 55,000 to 95,000. It is clearly an active online forum.

For this analysis, following human subjects review and approval, I invited members of the current board to participate in an online focus group. Consent was provided via participation (posting) in the focus group thread. While the focus group thread remained active for two weeks, the majority of the responses (over 90%) were posted in the first 3 days. All responses were posted within the first ten days. Twenty-six members of the board participated in the focus group, generating 297 posts. Though I am a participant in the community, I did not participate in the discussion beyond asking the questions and providing a few statements of encouragement ("interesting").

It is important to note that, due to my own participation in this community, and my knowledge of member conversation outside of the focus group, I assured group members that my discussion of their comments/claims/experience would be limited to what they said in the focus group. While my personal knowledge of some group issues may go beyond what was stated in the group, I will not provide information regarding specific issues or individuals that goes beyond the focus group discourse. However, I will provide some general reflections regarding my own experience.

After the focus group period was over, I read each response multiple times and engaged in analysis via a process of thematic comparison (Rawlins and Holl 1987). In this process, the researcher(s) repeatedly experience the data in an attempt to identify similar words and phrases. In addition, the analyst(s) look for common concepts, that may be expressed with differing word choice, but represent the same meanings. Such thematic analysis is a common component of interpretive work in communication studies and is discussed in greater detail by Glaser and Strauss (1967), Meyer (1997), Owen (1994), and Langellier and Sullivan (1998).

Based on this analysis, I found a number of common themes expressed across the discourse, including support, friendship, acceptance, anonymity, and diversity. While these concepts are wide-ranging, I argue that the totality of them can be understood through the application of dialectical theory, with a focus on the dialectic of presence/absence. In order to address that claim, I will first briefly discuss the concepts of relational dialectics.

Relational Dialectics

Relational dialectics, as characterized by the work of scholars such as Leslie Baxter, Barbara Montgomery, and William Rawlins (Baxter 1988; Baxter and Montgomery 1996; Montgomery and Baxter 1998; Rawlins 1988; Rawlins 1992) focuses on the "messiness" and complexity of human relationships. The perspective, which has many parts, utilizes the concept of relational dialectics – "contradictory" pulls or tensions that are experienced by relational members. The two parts of a dialectic seem to be contradictory, yet they require each other for existence. For example, dark/light might be said to be a dialectic, because we can only understand dark as the absence of light, and we understand light to be the absence of dark. Similarly, in relationships, we desire things that may seem to be contradictory. In one example of a foundational dialectic identified by Montgomery and Baxter, connectedness/separateness, we want to be connected to and identified with our relational partner (the "we"), but at the same time, we want to remain individuals with our own identity (the "me"). From a dialectical perspective, we may attempt to manage these seemingly contradictory needs ("I'll spend Saturday night with you, but on Friday I'm going out with the guys."), but both poles remain. We cannot remove one or the other.

The dialectical perspective speaks to the complexity of the human experience because it suggests that our needs and desires are not simple; they contain multiple "parts" that may sometimes appear to contradict one another. However, that messiness and apparent contradiction is not something that is wrong; it is something that *is.* In my analysis of the focus group discourse, I identified a primary dialectic of presence/absence that is expressed across several dimensions of the group experience, including social support, relational identity, and group cohesion.

Presence and Absence in Social Support

As in the first study, the focus group participants continue to maintain that social/relational support is a primary function of this online community. While the participants in the first study expressed that support as being related specifically to pregnancy issues, at this point, the members see it as a more broadly-based friendship community that provides support to its members. As stated by Heidi[1], "*I sincerely care about our members here and their families. I absolutely see it as friendship and support.*" Teresa agrees that the focus of the group is "*support and friendship*" and states that she *"can't imagine a time without"* it.

Social support can generally be defined as communication that makes an individual feel valued, cared for, and assisted within a particular group or relationship (Cobb 1976). Scholars have identified a variety of types of support; those primarily discussed include instrumental support, emotional support, and informational support (House 1981). Because the members of this board are distant from one another, we would expect less instrumental (task based) support, such as shared childcare, and more support of other types. The discourse of the focus group suggests that is the case. Interestingly, however, the notions of geographical closeness and temporal coordination were invoked in somewhat unexpected ways that point to the dialectic of presence and absence in these social support relationships.

Geographical distance and cyber-togetherness

Generally speaking, those in our lives can offer a greater 'quantity" of support if they are geographically close than if they are more distant, because instrumental support (watching the children, helping with a move, etc.) is less likely when relational partners are separated by distance. In considering the social support forms that can be offered via an online forum, it might be expected that participants would reflect on the forms of support that are not available due to geographic distance, or not invoke distance at all. However, in the discourse presented during this focus group, the members addressed geographic distance as a positive factor of the bulletin board, indicating the utility of having a place for support that docs not involve "*people I have to see every day*" (Lily).

For some participants, the geographic distance from other board members served a useful purpose because it gave them a place to discuss issues they might find embarrassing to talk about face-face. For example, when discussing her mother and her "in real life" friends , Abbigail states: "*There are some things that I would be too embarrassed to discuss with them. But there is pretty much nothing that I wouldn't bring up on the board.*" Similarly, Mary Beth notes that she feels closer to the board than she does to her "in real life friends" because "*there is no hiding behind anything! I can say or think or feel whatever, and it's OK, because I don't have to live with the girls here.*"

While some members addressed primarily the emotional aspect of embarrassment as a reason for sharing information on the board that they would not share with those in physical proximity, other board members focused specifically on the social consequences of sharing life information with people in geographically close social circles. This framing was best expressed by Stacy, who said:

> I like that I can say things like things about sometimes disliking my kids, or being embarrassed by them, or whining about everyday minutiae, or even secrets about my marriage that I wouldn't want people in my social circles to know. This forum can serve as my own private confessional. I can get things off my chest, find support, and not have any consequences.
> ~ Stacy

Stacy's comment and similar statements from others suggest that communication on the board provides a particular type of social support, not *in spite of* geographical distance, but *because of* geographical distance. Not being in the same place on a day to day basis eliminates some of the social consequences of sharing personal information with the group. In discussing these issues, many of the members invoked the phrase "real life" to distinguish between the proximal social milieu and the online world of the board. The board allows members to access a group of supportive friends (presence) even in, and partly because of, their physical distance (absence). It provides a venue for discussing possibly embarrassing or "scandalous" information with no fear of social consequences in "real life." As such, the dialectic of presence and absence is invoked in board talk about geographic proximity and social support in a way that suggests that this online mothering community provides its members with a "location" where they can be supported by others who are simultaneously present and absent from their lives. Such a need may well be heightened for women/mothers, because, as many feminist scholars such as Bordo (1993) and Hesse-Biber (1997) argue, the standards for behavior, appearance, emotion, etc. for them are so stringent in Westernized culture. Similarly, the expectations of motherhood and who can be judged a "good mother" are similarly hard to meet (Douglas and Michaels 2004; Hays 1996; Peters, 1998) and admitting to problems in the mothering role – or the feminine role – is not easy (Choi et al. 2005). Having a place to be where support can be achieved without airing the "dirty laundry" of life to those in the immediate community, who may then engage in judgment about the performance of motherhood or womanhood, could be particularly useful for mothers and is expressed eloquently by Jenny when she says: *This is the place I can go to where no one in my real life knows I go.*

Temporal disjuncture and coordination

While geographical distance is one issue that can affect social support, the coordination of time is another. One of the commonly mentioned advantages of online communication is the asynchronous nature of bulletin boards, which allows users to carry on discussions across time zones and around their other obligations (Barnes 2003; Burrows et al. 2000; Finfgeld 2000; Walther 1996; Wright 1999). Users of this group, similarly, discussed the convenience of knowing that the board was available twenty-four hours a day. However, they also discussed the extent to which the asynchronicity of time allows for members to dissociate from the board, or prevents full participation due to the time required for reading/typing.

"I might have to wait a bit if I am desperate for info in the middle of the night, but if I ever really need something, support, info, etc. I know you all will come through." In this quote, Mary notes the fact that the board represents members working around a variety of time constraints (and even time zones), but its nature allows communication and support to continue within, and because of, that temporal situation. Such comments were common in this discursive sample. Thus, members specifically acknowledge both their temporal absence from one another and the continual presence of the board, in its entirety.

While addressing the positive factor of availability of support despite and because of time differences, board members also made a point to say that the temporal nature of the board allows members to withdraw their support when/if they need to, which may not be the case in more synchronous relationships. This is represented in the comments of Erica, Karen, and Sandi.

> The board is a vehicle where for the most part you can give or take as much as you want/need -- unlike real life friends who get pissy when you are studying for your orals and therefore have to blow off their holiday party or who expect you to return their calls in a timely manner.
> ~ Erica

> Lately, I've not been as active, and this forum allows me to be as active (or not) as I can be in any given period in my life.
> ~ Karen

> I don't have service at home right now because I am on the computer at work all the time. And when I am home I try to focus on the kids. But work gets in the way of my group participation too.
> ~Sandi

In these examples, we see members making points regarding both the availability of members to provide support at any time and the ability to withdraw one's own support when other life commitments impinge upon the time available. These are issues of temporal absence that the members experience as a positive aspect of bulletin board communication.

Time asychronicity is not always a positive, however. The very nature of an asynchronous communication form like this makes it more time consuming to engage in social support. As stated by Heidi, "*Time is a factor. Sometimes I get lazy and just do not feel like typing.*" Several members discussed this issue during the group, with the phrase "*time suck*" being invoked frequently to describe board participation.

For the members of this board, the characteristic of time asynchronicity (absence) is seen as a positive because it allows for a constant access to support (presence) through a 24-hour community. At the same time, within the constant presence of community, members feel more capable to engage in relational withdrawal (absence). Again, this dialectic may be heightened for women and mothers, because the expectations of the feminine role, and the mothering role, call upon the woman to be extremely relationally connected to her friends and family and to always be available for their needs (Becker, 2005; Medina and Magnuson 2009; Tannen, 1990). Such a socialized expectation may be revealing with regard to why participants also mentioned that the board is a "time suck." As women, they are accustomed to being relational experts – to "being there" for their relational partners – thus they feel a certain pull to respond to the posts of others and provide the social support called for by the group (and they feel this even in the face of other – more geographically "immediate" calls upon their time).

In both a geographical sense and a temporal sense, the participants in this focus group called upon the notions of presence and absence in their discussion of how the board functioned as a community of social support and their own roles in that function. A similar dialectic can be seen in the discourse related to the creation of a relational identity within this system.

Presence and Absence in Relational Identity

An important part of our social relationships is the creation of a "self" within the relationship. That self and its components are what the relational partners respond to and the interaction between those "selves," along with the process of creating them, defines the identity of the relationship. While this forum is an online community composed to a significant degree of people who have never/rarely interact with each other in face-to-face settings (although a variety of dyads, triads, etc. from the group have met, and most participants in the focus group have met at least one other member of the board), many members classify the group as friendship, or even family:

> You guys are my friends now as much as any [in real life] friend.
> ~ Nickie
>
> I wouldn't know what to do without this board. You are all like family now!
> ~ Sue
>
> Our friendship grew into more than just "moms" but "sisters."
> ~ Lisa

The creation of this group identity (family or friendship) is a result of the communication patterns and presentations of self experienced on the bulletin board. As members discussed, sharing of personal information was a key characteristic of the developing relationships.

Creating a personal self with limited non-verbal cues

> The more personal information we shared with each other (and the support we received), the more we bonded as friends.
> ~ Abbigail

> Over the years, people (including me) have shared far more about themselves than I ever thought would happen.
> ~ Karen

> We know each other for what's inside and not anything outward. That's the beauty of the internet. You truly get to know someone for their values and choices, whether good or bad.
> ~ Hyacinth

Abbigail, Hyacinth, and many other participants in the focus group, discussed the extent to which sharing personal information, about life, love, family, work, etc., was an important part of the evolution of the group from a bulletin board to a set of friends (or even sisters). Interestingly, some, like Hyacinth, suggested that the physical absence experienced by board members allows for a more thorough sharing of the self. This is consistent with past research on online communities, that suggests the absence of physicality can be beneficial to Internet users (Barnes 2003; Burrows et al. 2000; Finfgeld 2000; Walther 1996; Wright 1999) because physical characteristics take on less importance in interaction and other aspects of the individual may become heightened in importance for evaluation.

While the online community allows, and provides for, the opportunity to share personal information, and the lack of a physical self in interaction may make the creation of a relational self easier in some ways, users also noted that the absence of physical self can be a challenge when understanding others or presenting the self. Walther (1996) notes that, in the absence of some information available in face to face encounters, online interactants may find it difficult to develop their images of others. This is confirmed by Lily when she says:

> The written word can be misconstrued and there's no real computer replacement for voice intonation, tone, etc. I sometimes get the feeling that it's very hard to judge people's true personalities from their posts and know that they are different in person than online.

Similarly, Jen worries that, without tone of voice and context, her irreverence and humor might be perceived as being "*really bitchy and mean*."

The seeming contradictory statements (often from the same person), with regard to lack of physicality creating both an increased presence of self due to lack of nonverbal distractions and a felt absence of self due to lack of nonverbal channels, is particularly compelling in the framework of this particular community. Generally, claims made about the advantages of the missing physical self online are based upon the idea that physical appearance judgments related to attractiveness, weight, disability, race, age, sex, are eliminated online – which decreases stereotyped response based on the physical and allows for better presentation of the "inner" self. On this board, having been together for more than a decade, most members have met multiple others on the board, and all have posted numerous pictures of self and family. Physical factors such as those mentioned above are not unknown to other members. We might, therefore, think that the importance of eliminating physicality would no longer be an issue that would arise in member discourse. However, because all participants in the group are women, it seems likely that this may be an echoing of our generalized social expectation that women should always meet rigid appearance guidelines, and a belief that women are constantly engaged in judgment of one another with regard to appearance (Bordo 1993; Hesse-Bibber 1997). Removal of the physical from interaction may feel like an ongoing relief to women in relationships. At the same time, because women tend to be more observant of nonverbal interaction cues (Hall 1984)- or at least they think should be – (Ickes 1997), perhaps the lack of these cues is simultaneously felt as a relational void.

In this community, we find that both presence and absence in information sharing and physical self are factors that have been important in the evolution of the group and the relational identity of group members. In a related theme of identity, members discussed the notion of online anonymity, and its impact on the community.

Anonymity and accountability

As previously stated, this group began its time together on a very public server space. Membership was required to post, but not to read. When the board changed servers, and moved to Network54, the choice was made to password protect the forum, so that only members could read or post. While no independent verification of identity (beyond prior participation in the pregnancy/playgroup board) was required, this made members feel that there was less anonymity in the interaction – a clearer presence of self – which promotes feelings of safety and accountability. However, at the same time, members also argue that there is some anonymity that remains, due to the lack of in-person interaction. As Anna puts it, the group is "*an online social outlet, friendship but blessed by a touch of anonymity as well.*" This combination of presence and absence of self, as revealed in terms of anonymity claims, is an important aspect of the group culture for the participants.

Having password protection, from the perspective of the members, reduced the anonymity of interaction and allowed the women to feel more comfortable about sharing their lives, as is clear in these comments from Karen's Mom, Julie, and Mandy:

> I think many, if not all, of us loosened our tongues as soon as the password came on.
> ~ Karen's Mom

> I love that what I say here, belongs here without interlopers getting to see it. It's like a sacred space. . .my own little bar in Vegas if you will.
> ~ Julie

> The move to a private forum helped people to open up.
> ~ Mandy

The process of applying for and receiving permission to post/read on the group forum reduces the chance that there may be unknown individuals posting to, or reading on, the board. Participants note that this is reassuring to them because they know who they are sharing with, and know that the things they share (often related to family members, spouses, co-workers, or their local community) will not make their way back to the individuals discussed and create negative life repercussions.

An additional factor of reduced anonymity was a greater accountability for relational actions on the bulletin board. Online communities are often troubled by "flaming," name calling and other antagonistic behaviors designed to create conflict. These focus group participants noted that sometimes such behavior is perpetuated by "trolls" (non-community members who just come across the site and want to stir things up) and sometimes by community members who just feel like they can say whatever they want and there will be no consequence. The members of this group believe that the password protection has reduced that problem and forced members to be more accountable for what they say.

> The lack of anonymity means that you can't just go off on someone in one thread and then play nice with them in another. It makes things more truthful.
> ~ Heather

> It makes us be more accountable, which is very important in online relationships. We can't hide behind a fake identity and spew all over the board, we have to be who we are and take into consideration what we want to say.
> ~ Mary

While these posts suggest a greater sense of individual identity on the board, as the reduced anonymity provides safety and accountability, the members also note that there remains some level of anonymity that functions on the board (which relates back to the prior discussion of geography). Kristen indicates that this is a positive, saying, "*The relative anonymity (we don't see each other at PTA or [home owners' association] meetings) lends itself to deeper sharing.*" Anna, on the other hand, argues that the anonymity is a positive partially because it *prevents* more sharing when she states "*IRL (in real life), I tend to overshare, and I find that the bit of anonymity that comes from online interactions, even with people you know well, helps me limit myself in a healthy way.*" It appears that the anonymity that remains on the board functions positively for members, in ways both related to greater identity revelation and reduced personal sharing.

In discussing how the lack of anonymity – through the use of assigned usernames and passwords - prevents potential damage to relationships both on and off the board, the participants enact an expected feminine attention to relational health. Simultaneously, these board members also suggest that the degree of anonymity that remains in the online environment may be good for personal identity and health, as it allow some participants to express aspects of self they may repress in other social situations, while it helps others to set limits on the self and maintain autonomy.

It appears that the board members are experiencing simultaneously revelation of personal identity, via greater sharing and reduced anonymity (presence), and a concealment of personal identity, via lack of non-verbal information and sustained anonymity (absence). While these factors may seem contradictory, they occur simultaneously in this group and their co-presence appears to be fundamental to the culture that has been created.

Presence and Absence in Group Cohesion

In addition to the establishment of personal identity in relationships, our interactions in social groups require the creation and maintenance of group cohesion. However, for all groups, there is a simultaneous need/desire to maintain individuality and difference within the group. While this focus group strongly celebrated their diversity, they also noted a need to suppress divergent viewpoints in order to maintain group cohesion.

Presenting divergent viewpoints and managing "hot button" issues

> I love the way I can post a question..., and so many different perspectives are offered. I've learned a ton about lots of things.
> ~ Karen

> Because this group of people is so diverse, I get perspectives I'd never get in real life, where I am more often surrounded by people who feel much the same as I do about things.
> ~ Nickie

> I feel so much more informed and knowledgeable about life experiences and other points of view that I never could have gotten anywhere else.
> ~ Meridith

The comments of Karen, Nickie, and Meridith are very characteristic of board members expressed beliefs about the diversity of the board and what it has added to the community. Members expressed strongly the benefits of gathering information from diverse viewpoints. Some, like Nickie, noted clearly that "in real life" their social groups would be much less likely to contain such different members, because we tend to socialize with those who are like us. Group members argued that the diversity present on the board made it more interesting, helped them to grow as individuals, and even had a positive impact on their mothering by providing more potential parenting options.

While the group was relatively celebratory regarding diversity, some members expressed the need to manage diverse viewpoints or avoid issues that might call that diversity too strongly into interaction. Examples can be seen in the comments of Kristen and Erica:

> I think because we didn't become polarized on the breast/bottle, circ/not vaccinate/no vaccinate, WOHM/SAHM . . . we were more open to evolving into larger debates and discussions in the respectful and supportive way we do.
> ~ Kristen

> Occasionally there are issues when a post offends some members of the community and as a result I sometimes (but probably not as often as I should) feel the need to hedge what I say so as not to offend and avoid any sort of conflict.
> ~ Erica

So, while the group member were extremely celebratory about diversity in their explicit comments, there were statements made that suggest a need to stifle some sorts of diverse opinions (see more below regarding acceptance/judgment). It's important to note that, while the group was emphatic about diversity being a key element, virtually members are white, middle class, and college educated. The diversity being celebrated is somewhat limited in scope and intensity. Though the group initially had members from more countries, more races/ethnicities, and represented a larger socio-economic and educational spectrum, over time many of those "more diverse" members have left the group – creating an absence in diversity even in its presence.

For this group, diversity was seen as a positive part of the interaction, and something that could likely not be achieved in "IRL" relationships. However, members also pointed out a need to carefully manage diversity in interaction so as to not damage group cohesion. Again here, this may reflect the socialized avoidance of conflict which women are expected to practice in their friendship relationships (Gilligan 1982; Rawlins 1992). While members were pleased to interact with others who are "different" from them, they wanted to avoid those differences becoming a site of tension in the group. Some members specifically noted that there had been times when this was unsuccessful (one member, in particular, had left the group due to an escalating conflict), but that the group had done well with it overall. Thus, the members experienced a desire to both bring diversity into the forefront of their relationship and keep it in the background. In a similar vein, participant discourse suggested complexity with regard to issues of acceptance of differing viewpoints/behaviors.

Acceptance and judgment

The idea of being accepted was a prominent theme in this focus group interaction. Many comments were made (and seconded) about how accepting the group is and the lack of judgments made about life decisions. From the first question posed to the group to the last, acceptance was present in the themes of the discourse. Relating back to the notion of personal sharing, members indicated that they felt they could say or ask anything, even if it involved "TMI" (too much information) with no fear.

> I keep coming back is because if I have a question or concern, I can come here and know I will get a response without fear of being attacked.
> ~ Heather

> I feel confident asking questions relating to ANYTHING!! … without fear of judgment.
> ~ Mary Beth

Our cultural understanding of female friendship includes a belief that friendship should be characterized by communication and honesty (Rawlins, 1992), and we expect that women will be supportive and empathetic to others (Ickes, 1997). These characteristics seem to be supported explicitly in member comments regarding the presence of acceptance they feel from the group.

However, while the idea of acceptance was repeated across member comments, this too was not without an oppositional pull. As stated in the previous section, members sometimes believe that their divergent viewpoints will be heard poorly. Joleen wonders if her "*comments or posts and/or lifestyle offend others*" and Hyacinth states that *"the fear of being judged"* is one of the most difficult aspects of the bulletin board. In fact, the very members who noted the accepting nature of the board often also commented about concerns related to negative judgment. This is quite clearly seen in two comments from Stacy, who says that one of the best parts of the board is the "*unconditional, non-judgmental support,*" but agrees with Hyacinth about the fear of being evaluated poorly and states, "*I find several of the people here to be very judgmental.*"

This fear of judgment from other women may not be particularly surprising, even though it seems to contradict our ideas about female friendship in some ways, because there is also a cultural understanding of women as catty, competitive, and malicious with one another (Heim, Murphy, and Golant 2003; Tanenbaum 2002) from an early age – as expressed clearly in the media image of "mean girls." Culturally we have created an understanding of female friendship as simultaneously accepting and judgmental, nurturing and competitive, kind and aggressive.

For the women in this focus group, group cohesion is affected by the dialectic of presence and absence in diversity and acceptance. Members celebrate the diversity of the board, yet feel compelled to somewhat constrain that diversity in order to avoid conflict, in a manner that corresponds well to research related to the feminine socialized conflict style. Similarly, members believe that the cohesive nature of the board will lead to the presence of acceptance, but that there is a danger that acceptance will be absent when divergent viewpoints come to the surface. Again, this seems to be a reflection of our larger cultural understandings of – and beliefs about – female friendship.

Where Are We Now?

Ten years after my initial study of this group, I find them to have evolved and changed, while maintaining some ongoing threads. This is certainly consistent with my own feelings about the group over the years. In the initial study, I argued that the group was characterized by empowerment of pregnant women through information and social support. The importance of social support has not department from the group, and most of the members still state that as its function. However, while at first the group was primarily about pregnancy/motherhood, and only secondarily about friendship, now those positions have shifted. To the members, this is a group of friends, who all happen to be mothers of 11 year olds, and who share information and support with each other about various areas of life, including family and mothering. This has been reflected in my own behavior. At this point, I find that I rarely post about my son (with whom I was pregnant at the time of joining the group) on the board – in fact, I can go extended periods without posting specifically about my children at all.

As this group has evolved over time, it has become less topic/event based. This makes some intuitive sense given the initial event that brought the group together. Pregnancy is a "high focus" life event, which creates many questions and decision making situations. Early motherhood is similarly intense. However, as children grow, the issues faced by parents grow and change and, while certainly no less serious, become more individualized based on a variety of personal/interpersonal/cultural factors unique to each family, and the experience of mothering an older child is less completely time consuming than mothering an infant. When asked why they though the group had changed over time, the participants in this focus group indicated that the shift from caring for a baby to having an older child or children has partly been responsible. In addition, many of the participants were first time mothers when they started the group. A decade later, most have multiple children. These women may feel that they now have a clearer understanding of the expectations of motherhood, and thus need somewhat less affirmation and direction from the group in that role.

The changes seen here also resonate with much research on women's friendships, which tends to suggest that women generally develop friendships focused less on concrete events or tasks (instrumental friendship) and more on the emotions and obligations of the relationship (Rawlins 1992). These members noted that, as the group spent more time together, the relationships between members increased in emotionality and person-centeredness – though sharing of personal information and responsive relationships.

However, just because the group is not as specifically focused on mothering now as it was in the early days of their time together, it is important that we not assume that it has no utility or function in the lives of these mothers. As in the themes discussed here, I would argue that the group, overall, functions in terms of a presence/absence dialectic in terms of social conformity and resistance.

This online community provides members with an opportunity to engage in some degree of resistance to social expectations of women, and particularly mothers. In being a part of the group, which is geographically distant from IRL family and friends – and protected from their gaze by passwords, members carve out a "me" space. For mothers, in a culture of intensive motherhood that positions the children as central and the mother as only experiencing the world via their needs and wants (Douglas and Michaels 2004), this is a form of resistance. Similarly, unlike in most relationships women have, board participants feel able to give as much, or as little of themselves as they want. Additionally, as members of the board post about issues, events, and beliefs on the board that they would not reveal to others due to societal restrictions, they perform a resistance through voicing the parts of their lives that can often go unheard. In these ways, the board functions to allow for an increased presence of resistance (or a decreased presence of conformity).

However, even while the board operates to provide a space for resistance, the discourse of the members indicates that it simultaneously replicates and reinforces standard expectations of mothering and femininity. Members of the board are pleased when conflict can be avoided, and worried that they could say something that would spark a conflict. They are pleased that they have such an accepting relationship, but also fearful that they are being judged. Though members feel that they can withdraw from the board as desired, they also say that the board can be time consuming because of the feeling of responsibility to respond to posts. Characteristics such as this make the bulletin board a relatively close reflection of our beliefs about "real life" friendships between women, and reify some of the stereotypes we might hope to move against –providing a greater presence of sex-role expectations, and an absence of resistance.

My analysis here suggests that this board, and the dialectic of presence and absence that is experienced across a number of domains, offers its members a social experience that, while replicating our expectations of female friendship relationships in many ways, is unique to this space. Based on the discussion that occurred in the focus group, participation in this bulletin board, though a "time suck" is not a frivolous activity. The members themselves unanimously agreed that they planned to continue participation as long as the board was available, and argued that the board experience has impacted them positively as mothers, as well as in other parts of their lives, and continues to do so. As a participant, I certainly have no intention of stopping any time soon. As Jen puts it, *"I'm a better mother, wife, daughter, friend because of the people and experiences I have encountered here."* And, said Erica, to a resounding chorus of group agreement, *"It's cheaper than therapy."*

Works Cited

American College of Obstetricians and Gynecologists. *Encyclopedia of Women's Health and Wellness*. ACOG: Washington, 2000.

Arnold, Lorin B. "Delivering Empowerment: Women's Narratives about the Role of Pregnancy Bulletin Boards." *Qualitative Research Reports in Communication,* 4 (2003): 45-52.

Barnes, Susan. *Computer-Mediated Communication: Human-to-Human Communication across the Internet*. Boston, MA: Allyn and Bacon, 2003.

Baxter, Leslie A. "A Dialectical Perspective on Communication Strategies in Relationship Development." In *Handbook of Personal Relationships,* edited by Steve Duck, 257-273. Somerset, NJ: John Wiley and Sons, (1988).

Baxter, Leslie A., and Barbara M. Montgomery. *Relating: Dialogues and Dialectics*. New York: Guilford, 1996.

Becker, Dana. *The Myth of Empowerment: Women in the Therapeutic*

Culture in America. New York: New York University Press, 2005.

Bird, S. Elizabeth. "It's the Talking that's Important: Pregnancy Folklore as Women's Discourse." *Women's Studies in Communication,* 17 (1994): 45-68.

Bordo, Susan. *Unbearable Weight: Feminism, Western Culture, and the Body.* Berkeley: University of California Press, 1993.

Burrows, Roger, Sarah Nettleton, Nicholas Pleace, Brian Loader, and Steven Muncer. (2000). "Virtual Community Care?: Social Policy and the Emergence of Computer Mediated Social Support." *Information, Communication, and Society,* 3 (2000): 95-121.

Campbell, Kristen, and Kevin B. Wright. "On-Line Support Groups: An Investigation of Relationships among Source Credibility, Dimensions of Relational Communication, and Perceptions of Emotional Support." *Communication Research Reports,* 19 (2002): 183-193.

Chan, Annie H. "'Life in Happy Land': Using Virtual Space and Doing Motherhood in Hong Kong." *Gender, Place and Culture: A Journal of Feminist Geography,* 15 (2008): 169-188.

Choi, P., C. Henshaw, S. Baker, and J. Tree. "Supermum, Superwife, Supereverything: Performing Femininity in the Transition to Motherhood." *Journal of Reproductive and Infant Psychology*, 23, 167-180.

Cobb, Sidney. "Social Support as a Moderator of Life Stress." *Psychosomatic Medicine,* 5 (1976): 300-314.

Coulson, Neil S., and Rebecca C. Knibb. "Coping with Food Allergy: Exploring the Role of an Online Support Group." *CyberPsychology and Behavior,* 10 (2007): 145-148.

Copelton, Denise. A., and GiuseppinaValle. "'You Don't Need a Prescription to Go Gluten-Free': The Scientific Self-diagnosis of Celiac Disease." *Social Science and Medicine,* 69 (2009): 623-631.

Douglas, Susan J., and Meredith W. Michaels. *The Mommy Myth: The Idealization of Motherhood and how it has Undermined Women*. New York: Free Press, 2004.

Drentea, Patricia, and Jennifer Moren-Cross. "Social Capital and Social Support on the Web: The Case of an Internet Mother Site." *Sociology of Health and Illness, 27* (2005): 920-943.

Finfgeld, Deborah L. "Therapeutic Groups Online: The Good, the Bad, and the Unknown."
Issues in Mental Health Nursing, 21 (2000): 241-255.

Gilligan, Carol. *In a Different Voice: Psychological Theory and Women's Development*. Cambridge, MA: Harvard University Press, 1982.

Glaser, Barney G., and Anselm L. Strauss, A. L. *The Discovery of*

Grounded Theory: Strategies for Qualitative Research. Chicago: Aldine, 1967.

Hall, Judith A. *Nonverbal Sex Differences: Communication Accuracy and Expressive Style.* Baltimore: Johns Hopkins University Press, 1984.

Hays, Sharon (1996). *The Cultural Contradiction of Motherhood.* New Haven, CT: Yale University Press, 1996.

Heim, Pat, Susan Murphy, and Susan K. Golant. *In the Company of Women: Indirect Aggression Among Women – Why We Hurt Each Other.* New York; Tarcher/Putnam.

Hesse-Biber, Sharlene. *Am I Thin Enough Yet?: The Cult of Thinness and the Commercialization of Identity.* New York: Oxford University Press, 1997.

House, James S. *Work Stress and Social Support.* Reading, Mass: Addison-Wesley, 1981.

Hudson, Diane B., Christie Campbell-Grossman, Rebecca Keating-Lefler, and Peggy Cline. "New Mothers Network: The Development of an Internet-Based Social Support Intervention for African American Mothers." *Issues in Comprehensive Pediatric Nursing,* 31 (2008): 23-35.

Hurley, Anna. L., Paul Sullivan, and John McCarthy. "The Construction of Self in Online Support groups for Victims of Domestic Violence." *British Journal of Social Psychology,* 46 (2007): 859-874.

Ickes, William. *Empathic Accuracy.* New York: Guilford Press, 1997.

Jordan, Judith V., Alexandra G. Kaplan, Jean B. Miller, Irene P. Stiver, and Janet L. Surrey. *Women's Growth in Connection: Writings from the Stone Center.* New York: Guilford, 1991.

Langellier, Kristin M., and Claire F. Sullivan. "Breast Talk in Breast Cancer Narratives." *Qualitative Health Research,* 8 (1998): 76-95.

Liang, Belle, Allison Tracy, Catherine A. Taylor, Linda M. Williams, Judith V. Jordan, Jean Baker Miller. "The Relational Health Indices: A Study of Women's Relationships." *Psychology of Women Quarterly,* 26 (2002): 25-35.

Lieberman, Morton. "The Role of Insightful Disclosure in Outcomes for Women in Peer-Directed Breast Cancer Groups: A Replication Study." *Psycho-Oncology,* 16 (2007): 961-964.

Lieberman, Morton. "Not All Negative Emotions are Equal: The Role of Emotional Expression in Online Support Groups for Women with Breast Cancer." *Psycho-Oncology, 15* (2006): 160-168.

Markens, Susan, C. H. Browner, and Nancy Press. "Feeding the Fetus: On Interrogating the Notion of Maternal-Fetal Conflict. *Feminist Studies,* 23 (1997): 351-372.

Madonna, Debra. "The Internet: Birthing by E-mail." *The International Journal of Childbirth Education,* 13 (1998a): 40-41.

—. "The Internet: What We Already Know." *The International Journal of Childbirth Education,* 13 (1998b): 36-38.

Malik, Sumaira H., and Neil Coulson. "The Male Experience of Infertility: A Thematic Analysis of an Online Infertility Support Group Bulletin Board. *Journal of Reproductive and Infant Psychology,* 26 (2008): 18-30.

McCabe, Jessi. "Resisting Alienation: The Social Construction of Internet Communities Supporting Eating Disorders. *Communication Studies,* 60 (2009): 1-16.

Medina, Sondra and Sandy Magnuson. "Motherhood in the 21st Century: Implications for Counselors." *Journal of Counseling and Development,* 87 (2009): 90-96.

Montgomery, Barbara M. and Leslie A. Baxter. *Dialectical Approaches to Studying Personal Relationships.* Mahwah, NJ: Lawrence Erlbaum, 1998.

Owen, William F. "Interpretive Themes in Relational Communication." *Quarterly Journal of Speech,* 70 (1984): 274-287.

Pandey, Anjali. "Linguistic Power in Virtual Communities: The Ebonics Debate on the Internet." *World Englishes, 19* (2000): 21-38.

Peters, Joan K. *When Mothers Work: Loving our Children without Sacrificing our Selves.* Reading, MA: Perseus, 1998.

Parry, Diana C. "'We Wanted a Birth Experience, not a Medical Experience': Exploring Canadian Women's Use of Midwifery. *Health Care for Women International,* 29 (2008): 784-806.

Rawlins, William. K. "A Dialectical Analysis of the Tensions, Functions and Strategic Challenges of Communication in Young Adult Friendships. In *Communication Yearbook, 12,* edited by James A. Anderson, 157-189. Newbury, CA: Sage, 1988.

Rawlins, William K. *Friendship Matters: Communication, Dialectics, and the Life Course*. Hawthorne, NY: Aldine de Gruyter, 1992.

Rawlins, William K., and Melissa Holl, M. "The Communicative Achievement of Friendship during Adolescence: Predicaments of Trust and Violation." *Western Journal of Speech Communication,* 51 (1987): 345-363.

Rubenstein, Hiasaura, and Sharene K. Lawler. "Toward the Psychosocial Empowerment of Women." *Affilia: Journal of Women and Social Work,* 5 (1990): 27-38.

Sharer, Kathleen. "An Internet Discussion Board for Parents of Mentally Ill Young Children. *Journal of Child and Adolescent Psychiatric*

Nursing, 18 (2005): 17-25.

Surrey, Janet L. (1991a). "Relationship and Empowerment." In *Women's Growth in Connection: Writings from the Stone Center* edited by Judith V. Jordan, Alexandra G. Kaplan, Jean B. Miller, Irene P. Stiver, and Janet L. Surrey, 162-180. New York: Guilford, 1991a.

—. "The Self in Relation: A Theory of Women's Development." In *Women's Growth in Connection: Writings from the Stone Center* edited by Judith V. Jordan, Alexandra G. Kaplan, Jean B. Miller, Irene P. Stiver, and Janet L. Surrey, 51-66. New York: Guilford, 1991b.

Tannen, Deborah. *You Just Don't Understand: Women and Men in Conversation.* New York: Ballantine Books, 1990.

Tannenbaum, Leora. *Catfight: Women and Competition.* New York: Seven Stories.

Walther, Joseph. B. "Computer-Mediated Communication: Impersonal, Interpersonal, and Hyperpersonal Interaction." *Communication Research,* 23 (1996): 3-43.

Whitlock, Janis L., Jane L. Powers, and John Eckenrode. "The Virtual Cutting Edge: The Internet and Adolescent Self-Injury." *Developmental Psychology,* 42 (2006): 407-417.

Wright Kevin B. "Social Support within an Online Cancer Community: An Assessment of Emotional Support, Perceptions of Advantages and Disadvantages, and Motives for Using the Community." *Journal of Applied Communication Research, 30* (2002): 195-209.

Zeizer, Donna D. "Weaving a Web of Birth Information." *Midwifery Today and Childbirth Education,* 36 (1995): 42-43.

Notes

[1] Names used here are pseudonyms chosen by each participant during the study.

CASE STUDIES

CHAPTER SIX

MORE THAN JUST A WEBSITE FOR YOUNG MAMAS: GIRL-MOM MEMBERS' STRATEGIES FOR COUNTERING THE DOMINANT PERCEPTION OF TEEN MOTHERHOOD

JENNA VINSON

- "Teen mothers are less likely to complete the education necessary to qualify for a well-paying job"[1]
- "Two-thirds of families begun by a young unmarried mother are poor"
- "Some 52 percent of all mothers on welfare had their first child as a teenager"
- "The daughters of teen mothers are three times more likely to become teen mothers themselves"[2]
- "The sons of teenage mothers are two times more likely to end up in prison" [3]

—Bulleted Information from The National Campaign to Prevent Teen and Unplanned Pregnancy's "Why It Matters" fact sheets

> Teenage pregnancy is not a "crisis" or "epidemic," like so many people would like us to believe. The only true epidemic associated with teen pregnancy is the overwhelming and universal lack of support available to young mothers. The only true crisis is the denial of the fact that teenage girls can be, are, and always have been, both sexual and maternal beings, with the capacity to love, procreate, and nurture. We love our children fiercely. We protect and care for them like any mother, of any age, would. Through Girl-Mom, We hope to slowly show that to the world.

—Excerpt from the homepage of girl-mom.com

> "I shockingly realized that these single moms felt that they, too, had made their bed and had to lie in it, that they had made a 'mistake' that in turn made them ineligible to participate in the world. . . I could discern on their faces the same feeling that I had as a teen mom, the feeling that I had ruined my life"
>
> —Katherine Arnoldi, Girl-Mom member

In 2002, Kelly Rowland's R&B album, *Simply Deep*, featured a popular song called "Stole." Shortly after the album's release, the music video for "Stole" premiered on major music video stations. The song tells the story of three teenagers—two male and one female—whose lives are "stolen" too soon. The first young man, "a good boy" and "the brightest in school," is bullied by his peers until he eventually commits suicide. The second young man, a promising basketball player, is shot in a drive-by. The third character is Mary, a teen whose life is "stolen" when she becomes pregnant, a moment highlighted by dramatic camera shots of her seated in a doctor's office and later on a bathroom floor pounding the cupboards, mascara streaming down her face. In the final scene of the video, young Mary is shown pushing a stroller—the action dramatized in slow motion—toward a mural commemorating the dead boys. The camera shots alternate between the young baby sleeping in the stroller and Mary writing with a large Sharpie, "Think before you act," on the mural.

As a happy eighteen-year-old mother of a 1-year-old daughter, I was outraged when I first saw Rowland's video. I was (and I am still) shocked by the parallel drawn between suicide, homicide, and motherhood. Since 2002, I have studied the progression and circulation of rhetoric about teenagers and mothers. I understand, now, that this musician's vision is part of a larger cultural discourse that associates the context of a woman's pregnancy with her success in life. Although Rowland's music video could be considered a rather dated version of the teenage mother storyline, recent images and examples of "teen moms" in popular culture reflect similar assumptions about teenage pregnancy. I will discuss these depictions further below. In short, the dominant narrative of "teenage pregnancy" presents pregnancy and motherhood as the worst things that could happen to a young woman, her family, and the nation.[4] As the story goes, if a girl becomes pregnant, she eventually drops out to lead a devastating life as a poor, lonely woman raising a child who becomes a criminal, insane, or worse—another teen parent. These stories, typically told or packaged by those who are authorized with "expert" status in our society, have circulated for the last forty years and work to frame teenage mothers as a deviant incubators of innocent (but nonetheless doomed) children.[5]

As single-mother-activist Katherine Arnoldi states in the epigraph above, young women who find themselves pregnant before the age of twenty often feel like they have ruined their lives. Considering the emphasis of the statistics published by the National Campaign to Prevent Teen and Unplanned Pregnancy, these young mothers' feelings are quite understandable. The statistical information is conveyed in a way that repeatedly places blame on the "teen mother." Allison Crews—who wrote and worked as a teen mother advocate from the age of 15 to her untimely death at 22—explains that to young women "these weren't just statistics . . . but invariable truths."

With few places to turn for moral support and indications that they can succeed, some young mothers participate in online communities where they can share their experiences with motherhood and encourage each other. Girl-Mom is a website that intends to provide "support, community, and education for young mamas." It is within this cyberspace that we see young mothers struggling with the cultural construction of the "teen mother" as they post narratives about their experiences, participate in surveys and discussion forums about parenting and other issues, and work to support all girl-moms' pursuits. Created by a young single mother for teen mothers, Girl-Mom is an exciting website that effectively shifts (if only for a moment) who gets to tell the story of teenage motherhood. In this chapter, I examine the strategies that Girl-Mom members use to tell counter-narratives—or stories that challenge popular assumptions of who teenage mothers are and what they can accomplish. I review emblematic examples of the members' personal stories about their experiences with pregnancy, birth, and parenthood posted on the site. Specifically, this analysis explores how Girl-Mom members use radical characters, such as the expert-as-villain and the marginalized single mother-as-hero, to subvert "expert" discourse and emphasize the potentially positive and empowering life change that stems from finding self-esteem and avenues for self-assertion as a mothering teen. I argue that the exchange of counter-narratives on Girl-Mom helps to create a space for marginalized mothers to redefine the terms and values of their world view.

The Dominant Narrative

Ethnographer Wanda Pillow builds from her research on teenage pregnancy discourse and the lived conditions of teen mothers in public education to claim that "the teen pregnant girl as a subject is both silenced and over-produced in discourses (political, social, moral) of teen pregnancy" (Pillow 2003, 148). That is, we most often hear "experts" (or non-parenting, non-teens who have visible education, expertise, and/or authority in our culture) discuss this social issue, and we rarely hear from mothers themselves. When we do hear the voices of teen mothers, they are framed as dramas, testimonies, or lessons for others. Often, teen mothers' perspectives are followed by authoritative interpretations from official figures like psychologists or researchers.

Public uproar over the pregnancy of teen celebrity Jamie Lynn Spears in 2007, the alleged "Gloucester Pregnancy Pact" in 2008,[6] the pregnancy of conservative Republican vice presidential candidate Sara Palin's daughter Bristol in 2009, and the release of reports showing an increase in teen birth rates[7] illustrate that teenage pregnancy is still widely represented in political, social, and moral discourse. For decades historians, sociologists, public health, and educational scholars have been fervently resisting the mainstream conception of this so-called social issue by showing that the negative statistics fail to take into account the socioeconomic factors that affect all mothers' ability to access the resources needed for success.[8] Furthermore, many feminist scholars have illustrated that, if anything, it is often society's *response* to young motherhood that circumvents young women's happiness and/or progress in life.[9] Yet, unfortunately, this research has done little to change the public's overall reaction to teenage pregnancy; young mothers are still framed within negative or dramatic contexts (Kelly 1996, 421). The success and proliferation of shows about teenage pregnancies and motherhood such as E! Entertainment Television's dark special "Teenage Pregnancy Nightmares," the dramatic ABC Family series "The Secret Life of an American Teenager," MTV's reality-based "16 and Pregnant," and its subsequent spinoff series "Teen Mom" hint at the reason why teenage mothers remain the catch-all scapegoats for American problems—they are stock characters in entertaining, profitable, and rhetorically effective storylines.

Stories help to sustain particular worldviews by persuading groups of people to look at things in a particular way. Communication scholar Sonja Foss argues that narratives "allow us to interpret reality because they help us decide what a particular experience 'is about' and how the various elements of our experience are connected" (2004, 333). For example, the teen mother saga helps to sustain a worldview that suggests reproduction should only occur within the context of heterosexual marriage, situated within an economically self-sustaining household, and in accordance with a lifestyle that allows for the parents to keep the upbringing of the child private (i.e., separate from work, school, and other institutional obligations). Since many teen mothers' experiences stray from these conventions, telling stories about their hectic or troubled lives assists in normalizing the conditions of parenthood above.

What is at stake in these representations of teen mothers? When young single women discover that they are pregnant, they are called to see themselves as the women described by that discourse—dropouts, bad mothers, burdens on the economic system, etc. Expert commentary about teen pregnancy from doctors, scholars, and other officials invites little skepticism from both young mothers and the public who are brought up to trust expert opinion. Thus, to identify (or to be identified) as a teen mother is to recognize oneself (or to be recognized as) a character in this narrative.

In a culture that deems teen motherhood as abject, young mothers must either accept that definition and see their choice as a mistake and their life as a failure, or they must struggle to recognize that their experience does not accord with the popularized image. Feminist poststructuralist Chris Weedon reminds us that "as individuals we are not the mere objects of language but the sites of discursive struggle" (1997, 102). She explains, "The individual . . . may resist particular interpellations or produce new versions of meaning from the conflicts and contradictions between existing discourses" (1997, 102). Weedon's point is that the stories we tell about teenage pregnancy and motherhood are just that—stories. Although the ways in which we talk about the "issue" has material effects for young mothers, this language can be resisted, revised, or subverted by new ways of speaking. It is not surprising that many teen mothers *do* speak out against the dominant narrative that casts them as illegitimate mothers and burdens on society. Self-identified teen mothers voice their first-person stories in edited collections, such as *You Look Too Young to be a Mom: Teen Mothers Speak Out on Love, Learning, and Success* (2004), *Breeder: Real Life Stories from The New Generation of Mothers* (2001), the Association for Research on Mothering's recent special volume on "Young Mothers" (2007), and other venues that offer them space to critique.[10] Some critiques are welcomed as eye-opening for their audiences while others are easily incorporated into the popular representation of the teen mother through techniques I will discuss later on in the chapter. For the purpose of this collection, I focus on the counter-narratives posted on the website Girl-Mom, a space that creates an effective framework for purposeful, albeit temporary, subversion of the dominant narrative as well as creative re-construction of what it means to mother.

Subversive Discourse on Girl-Mom

Girl-Mom

Figure 1: Girl-Mom Image by artist Johnny 'Thief' Di Donna

Clicking on girl-mom.com, a viewer first sees Girl-Mom's emblem, a motorcycling mother—sketched in black and white—cruising along with her helmeted young child seated beside her in the motorcycle's side car. The image implies a sense of empowerment—the mother is still speeding purposefully along the road of life, her little one in tow. This image is the staple of all subsequent Girl-Mom pages. The background colors of the site are a cheery combination of pink and green, a transition from the plain blue background the site had when I first encountered it in 2006. A large pink box of text grabs viewers' attention on the first page and includes a mission statement, disclaimer, and/or manifesto of sorts (see partial excerpt at the start of this essay) which states, very clearly, the content and purpose of the webspace. The statement also discourages typical critiques of positive representations of young motherhood in the third paragraph, "Girl-Mom in no way encourages teen pregnancy, as some critics have implied. Girl-Mom encourages mothers," and then again in the fourth paragraph, "We do not encourage childless teens to follow our path; face it, it's a tough path. But we encourage all teens that wake to the call of 'mama!' before dawn breaks, to do all that they can to empower themselves and nurture their children." By carefully framing their site as a space for young mothers, the editors of the site attempt to deflect judgmental posts in the discussion boards and encourage members to accept the terms of their space: "Teenage pregnancy is not a 'crisis' or 'epidemic,' like so many people would like us to believe" (Girl-Mom).

The site functions primarily as a discussion board for young mothers and "allies" (childless women or older mothers) to discuss prompts initiated by "mods" or moderators. Moderators are young mothers who volunteer to moderate discussion forums and post prompts for girl-mom members to respond to. Most of the activity on Girl-Mom occurs within the exchanges in the discussion forum section, about topics and news items generated by community members such as "So Overwhelmed," "Having Your Own Identity," and "What Birth Control Method Are You Using?" The site also features articles authored by girl-moms that address various mothering-related political issues such as reproductive options, parenting students' rights under Title IX, steps for filing for child support, breastfeeding mothers' rights, and advice about affordable quality daycare. Members also have general discussions about other feminist issues such as the effects of globalism, racism, and sex work. Finally, there are members' personal testimonies of their experiences with teenage pregnancy—stories that pose a stark contrast to the common story represented in mainstream media.

Analyzing Girl-Mom Narratives

I was stunned when I first accessed the site in 2006 and clicked on Allison Crew's article, "When I Was Garbage" (linked to the opening page of the site). The narrative progressed much like a creative non-fiction story I wrote when I first began thinking that my experience as a 17-year-old mother conflicted with popular representations of the "social issue." While the content of our stories differed a bit (she considered adoption, I did not; she struggled with her parent's involvement while I had my single mother's full support), the introduction, scenes, characterizations, and overall plotline were startlingly similar. I began to wonder about strategies "outsiders" use to counter popular representations of who they are. I began to ponder whether the similarities between Crews' narrative and my own had anything to do with rhetorical strategies for subverting mainstream discourse. Then, after I researched problematic outcomes of teen mothers' attempts to change public opinions about them,[11] I wondered if there was something about the framework of the online community that allowed for these narratives to be so welcomed and influential.

So, I reviewed twelve teenage mothers' personal narratives about experiences with teenage pregnancy and parenthood posted in 2003.[12] I noticed more common strategies that the women (both teenagers who had recently had their babies and older women reflecting on their experience) used to tell their stories. Many testimonies dramatize the experience of discovering their pregnancy, transition to personal reflections on what it means to be a teenage mother in the United States (a strategy that sets up the critique of the dominant narrative on teenage pregnancy to come), document struggles to choose the appropriate course of action while dealing with many enemies—interestingly the "experts" we typically think of as there to help—and finally, conclude with a relatively happy ending that at once critiques the narrative of teenage pregnancy while also lending advice and encouragement for other girl-moms. Noting the similar plot structure and rhetorical purpose of the separately posted articles I began to code them using a method derived from communication scholar Ernest Bormann's symbolic convergence theory. This theory "provide[s] insights into the shared worldview of groups" by looking at how stories circulate amongst specific groups of people (Foss 2004, 109). Basically, I looked for similar characters, actions, and settings in each narrative in order to discover if a common "rhetorical vision" was circulating within the web-based community.

Yet before I share my analysis, I would like to emphasize that in writing and publishing this chapter I do not mean to suggest that I am an expert on these women's stories. As a teenage mother,[13] I am deeply invested in finding effective strategies that women use to subvert cultural constructions which render them voiceless. I am not an active member of Girl-Mom and, thus, do not focus my analysis on the conversations exchanged in the discussion forums. I feel comfortable highlighting the strategies the authors use in the articles, because they are posted within a "featured" public section of the site, under the banner that articulates the Girl-Mom rhetorical purpose of changing "the face of teen parenthood."

The Expert as Antagonist

One key pattern across many of the Girl-Mom feature stories is the way each narrative incorporates the dominant discourses about teenage pregnancy as a way to subvert them. The mothers cast the "experts"—such as doctors, social workers, principals, and faceless experts such as "the statistics," "society," "the sex education story line," and "rhetoric"—as antagonists. In the narratives, these "professionals" continually re-surface as obstacles to mothers' healthy sense of self. In their individual stories each member re-tells their painful experiences with the people who did not think they could succeed (people who are typically considered knowledgeable on the issue of teenage pregnancy), until the expert—within this discursive community—becomes simply the easily recognizable villain; he/she is only useful in pushing the mother to prove him/her wrong.

For example, in her narrative, Nina Packebush[14] explains that for her son's fifteenth birthday she plans on giving him his life story, including memories of the trials and tribulations she went through as an eighteen-year-old-mother. She says, "I will write about how they [people at the hospital where she gave birth] assigned me a social worker that tried to talk me into giving him up for adoption. I will write about how they would talk to his grandma and my aunt instead of me" (2003). Then, when she is certain her son is seriously ill and takes him to the doctor she explains "how none of the doctors believed me . . . how they ignored me because of my age" (2003). Finally, she writes that "all the 'professionals' told us that if we didn't put him on Ritalin he would end up in prison" and "they continually noted the fact that we had him at eighteen in his records" (2003). Packebush's experience with young motherhood is narrated as a series of confrontations with "professionals"—doctors and social workers—who question her credibility as a mother. Packebush recasts these experts as an ominous "they," a pronoun which may confuse an outsider to the group. Yet, "they" appear in many of the teen mothers' narratives, and we can sense a community of women nodding their heads in recognition of "those people" and how they treat young mothers.

Indeed, the expert-as-villain, whom the girls have to deal with on a regular basis, is often so familiar to narratives of this community of women that members need not fully explain this character. For example, one member writes of "the joy I will feel thinking of that idiot social worker, how convinced he was I could not succeed in college, and how he almost convinced me as I fill out my law school application" (DuChene 2003). This mother never pauses to fully explain the situation or characterize "that idiot social worker"; however, as a familiar character type on the website, members of the online community may still relate to her struggle with him. They will still know who he is and how he affected the young mother.

Another narrative element that is not fully explained for an outsider of the discursive community is the reference to a "look." For instance, Yvonne Fide notes, "Being a young mother I was used to the stares. I was used to the lectures from all aspects of the 'adult' world. I heard it from doctors and social service workers. I heard it from schools and family. I was treated like I couldn't possible [sic] take care of my children and I proved them wrong" (2003). The "lectures" and "stares" (or as young mother Allison Crews terms it, "the Teen Mom Look"), though not always fully explained, are something that this community of young mothers reiterate in their narratives and, thus, experience as a whole. Historian Joan Scott's observations on experience, discourse, and identity help to explain this phenomenon. She writes, "Subjects are constituted discursively and experience is a linguistic event (it does not happen outside established meanings), but neither is it confined to a fixed order of meaning. Since discourse is by definition shared, experience is often collective as well as individual" (1993, 409). In sharing their experiences within a discursive space dedicated to teen mothers' subjectivity, the mothers create a shared discourse about the experience of teenage pregnancy. The outcome of this process includes characters that rarely need to be justified or explained.

Unlikely Heroes

Since physicians, social workers, and educators continually assure the young mothers that they are doomed, these figures are *not* credible sources for the women on Girl-Mom. Instead, those who encourage teenage mothers and those who have already "survived teenage pregnancy"[15] become the most credible sources of information. For example, in Mary DuChene's story, it is the older women in her neighborhood who give her hope. She explains, "In my neighborhood, many girls survive abuse and neglect, sexual assault, poverty and violence during their teen years. . . . When I was a pregnant 19 year old, the older women in this neighborhood told me I could still be anything I wanted. They told me never to let society's opinion of me as a young mama change my plans and goals" (2003). DuChene goes on to finish her undergraduate college education and apply for law school, confident in the message the older women gave her. Again, "society's opinion" is refuted as useless to young mothers and in their narratives they continually fantasize about overcoming that opinion or "beating those statistics" (Fide 2003). Often the realization that the expert could be wrong is the turning point in the young mothers' narratives. The dominant representation of teenage pregnancy is debilitating and mothers need heroes, like the older women in the narrative above, to help them imagine a different ending. These heroes, in turn, help undermine an ideology that maintains that women, especially poor minoritized women (who are the largest representatives of teen motherhood) are not sources of strength or power.

Another example of a young mother casting a marginalized subject as a hero is Jaime Colboth's story of a "magical stripper." Colboth explains that once she became a mother she dropped out of school, thinking she couldn't possibly succeed as a mother and student. "Then along came a magical stripper. No, not a fairy, I said stripper. We'll call her Leanne. . . .Anyway, Leanne told me that I could do anything wanted. Anything! She said that if going back to school would make me happy then my daughter would be happy too" (2003). With the help of this "magical stripper" Colboth realizes that "motherhood had changed me," in a positive way. Colboth's creative use of a "magical stripper" as a character that shifts the plot development of her story in a positive way (and the acceptance and publication of her narrative on the site) illustrates a rhetorical strategy that borderlands rhetoric scholar Adela Licona identifies in her work. "[B]y rendering visible the previously invisible, indecent, invalid, and unacceptable" (2005, 119), within a subversive discursive framework, to an audience of fellow "invisible, indecent, invalid, and unacceptable" subjects, the young mothers have the power to recuperate any figure marginalized by dominant ideologies, as long as they adhere to the young mother's value system. Members of the online community are so familiar with traditional heroes (doctors, social workers) disappointing them that more unlikely heroes—characters who are often outsiders like themselves—make sense within their discourse. While in the dominant narrative of teenage pregnancy the realization that a teenager is pregnant is seen as the end of her life, or at least the end of her positive contribution to the world, these the women benefit from characters who assure them that their pregnancies are just another step in their life paths.

A New Teen Mother

Many of the narratives end by suggesting that the mothers become the heroic type valued in their stories. In other words, the mothers narrate aspects about themselves that resemble the characteristics that they value in their heroes. Most represent themselves as women who find strength and wisdom in their personal experiences and use these qualities to either work for social justice, promote community among other women, and/or assure new mothers that they can succeed in balancing mothering and sustaining personal growth. This narrative strategy counters the widely–accepted vision of teenage mothers as victims, failures, and/or burdens and creates new empowered visions of the teenage mother. For example, DuChene illustrates a newfound commitment to helping her community and working for social justice when she describes opening up her home as an after-school hangout for teenage girls in her impoverished neighborhood. In another example, Omy suggests mothering is a communal effort when she advises new mothers to, "accept all the help that is offered, and if none is offered (as I'm sure is the case for many women) make sure you go out of your way to do everything possible to create a community of support for yourself" (2003). In encouraging mothers to "create a community of support" this Girl-Mom member recognizes the value in spaces, like Girl-Mom, where people recognize and respond to the power of relationships and helping one another out. Furthermore, Omy's suggestion revises a critical component of teen mothers' experiences, the need for public assistance, from an emblem of shame (or evidence that she is a burden) to a necessary component of mothering in general. Finally, girl-mom Yvonne

Fide ends her narrative with a new vision of the teen mom as strong and intelligent when she calls out to the online community: "I know we (teenage mothers) can beat the statistics. I know we posses the strength and intelligence to foster the next generation of geniuses" (2003).

Although Fide's call invests mothers with profound responsibility of raising "geniuses," her confidence in teen mothers as "strong and intelligen[t]" helps to associate important values with the task of mothering. Furthermore, we must remember that Fide's vision of young women raising healthy, smart children is motivated by a desire to counter the dominant vision of teen mothers raising criminals (or worse) and is positioned within a rhetorical framework that values multiplicity. Thus, members who find Fide's call too much to handle or not applicable to their situation can turn to another narrative. For example, Lisa's "Resistance is Not Futile" is the story of a dropout welfare mama who finds empowerment in her position as such (2003). Thus, there is no support for a worldview that renders some mothers good and some mothers bad on this site.

Conclusion(s) About Narratives on Girl-Mom

The recurrence of these character types suggests that the teen mothers have not only countered the widely circulated stories of teenage pregnancy, but they have also shifted the values of the framework for those personal stories. The fact that the characters do not need full explanations suggests that they are accepted and well-known figures in this community. This is evidence that the expert (or anyone who suggests that the women cannot make choices for themselves, or succeed if they choose the "wrong" choice), has been subverted and marginalized female characters have been recuperated into positions of value—they are heroes. These new heroes are credible and knowledgeable because of their lived experience and their willingness to encourage others.

Furthermore, the lack of lengthy explanation also suggests that the terms and values of Girl-Mom have shifted from dominant discursive frameworks which rely on either the authority of the expert or the presentation of lengthy deductive reasoning to make their narratives believable. Communication theorist Walter Fisher calls this kind of (dominant) discursive framework a "rational world paradigm" which sanctions the "expert" as the only legitimate authority able to speak on a subject. This paradigm casts the public as a passive (relatively ignorant) crowd of observers (1984, 2). In contrast, a "narrative paradigm," like the framework on Girl-Mom, allows "the 'people' to formulate and to adopt new stories that better account for their lives or the mystery of life itself" (Fisher 1984, 9). In the narrative paradigm, "the proper role of the expert . . . is that of a counselor" who may share wisdom without foreclosing other interpretations (1984, 13). The teen mothers on Girl-Mom adopt this sense of the expert, as their heroes are "experts" who counsel them from the basis of their own lived experience. This sense of value for sharing knowledge based on experience and reciprocity carries on in the discussion forums of the site.

Finally, the casting of unlikely heroes suggests that these women, and the members of Girl-Mom, embrace ambiguity and plurality, something indicative of a "third space" or a space "between the authentic and the inauthentic, the legitimate and the illegitimate, the pure and the impure, and the proper and improper" (Licona 2005, 106). This framework devalues an either/or mentality and assumptions that there is a "right way" of being or of doing things. For example, there is no one vision of who a hero is. Indeed, the heroes in these narratives are credible sources because they suggest that the women can "do anything" and because they also inform other women that "society can be wrong"—a recognition coherent with Fisher's narrative paradigm that suggests expert narratives are just a narrative of many.

However, it is important to note that Girl-Mom is a privileged space in many ways. Only women with time, space, computer literacy, and access to the internet can experience this website. Critical Studies scholar Tara McPherson articulates an important reminder for those who find webspaces emancipatory for otherwise marginalized subjects:

> . . . it is imperative to remember that, according to the 2005 World Economic Forum, a mere 12% of the world is wired. To those with access, the web may offer exciting possibilities for transformation and change, letting us feel we can control our own movements and create our own spaces, shifting our roles from consumers to producers of meanings. . .but we'd do well to remember that this promise of transformation is also something the web (and electronic culture more generally) concertedly packages and sells to us. (2009, 383)

Furthermore, while the multiplicity and fluidity of the discussion forums and counter-narratives can be argued to be rhetorically effective in fostering a sense of community and empowerment, it is difficult to determine if this is so for teenage mothers across lines of difference. Communication scholar Nancy Baym points out, "Knowing the structure and purpose of a site . . . does not tell us how it will be used nor what it consequences will be for any of its users, let alone particular ones" (2009, 129). Teenage pregnancy is a highly complicated social issue. As historian Rickie Solinger aptly shows in her work *Wake Up Little Susie Single Pregnancy and Race Before Roe v. Wade*, responses to young, single mothers are highly racialized (2000). That is, African American and Latina women are often assumed to be inherently sexually deviant (and thus dismissed as naturally problematic reproducers) and white mothers are often represented as good girls gone bad. This analysis certainly prompts the question: Do mothers of all races and classes find websites like Girl-Mom accessible and effective?

Counter-Narratives Outside of Girl-Mom

> To speak as an act of resistance is quite different than ordinary talk, or the personal confession that has no relation to coming into political awareness, to developing critical consciousness (hooks 1989, 14)

Many feminist scholars working on deconstructing negative images of teen mothers have expressed an interest in having teen mothers publish their stories and join the "expert" debates over policies that affect young mother's lives. Yet, young mothers' stories are complicated by audience's interpretations of their narratives.[16] For example, Deirdre Kelly finds from her research of popular publications on teen motherhood that "we rarely hear from teen mothers themselves in the mass media, or if we do, their remarks have been selected and edited in ways that make them feel that their main message has been distorted" (1996, 438). Often, teen mother "success" stories are framed as exceptional cases in order to sustain the conception that *most* teenage mothers do not make good parents, students, and/or citizens. In her more recent ethnographic study of schools for teen mothers Kelly found that "teen mothers emphasized, and I observed, that they did tend to play a preventative role in their schools" (2000, 110). Indeed, teen mothers' stories are often welcomed as useful in preventing the sexual activity of other teenagers. For example, The National Campaign for Teenage and Unplanned Pregnancy website homepage features dramatic and depressing testimonies from teen parents in their *Too Young* video. Videos like these encourage sharing teenage mothers' stories in the name of prevention. In other words, teen mothers are often only visible or recognized publicly as examples of what not to do. Another recent example of this includes Bristol Palin's invitation to act as an ambassador "fighting against teenage pregnancy" for the Candies Foundation.

In contrast to these discursive forums, which ask young mothers to "confess" their stories within an experts' framework (that is, authoritative adults who will edit, arrange, and explain their stories for the audience), Girl-Mom creates a rhetorical situation in which young mothers can speak out about their own experiences with teenage motherhood to an audience of other young mothers without mediation[17] or tolerated critique. Indeed, it is a website that values the knowledge of those who have experienced the subjects they write about.[18] Telling their stories empowers Girl-Mom members to revise not only the narrative of the teenage mother, but the ideology that ties young women's reproductive choices to their personal growth and success in life. Licona explains "the effects of these shifting relationships to agency and authority are to create spaces where expert and authorized knowledges can be critically examined" (2005, 119). Indeed, this rhetorical effect is happening on Girl-Mom, a website originally meant to be a place for young mamas to find "community, support, and education," but a site that has become a framework for many types of counter-narratives and social critiques. It is a space where women compose new stories, better stories, juicier stories about mothering, sex, justice, and more. This website demonstrates rhetorical practices that assist a new generation of young mothers in finding avenues for success and spaces in which to voice both their experiences and their critiques of society.

Works Cited

Adair, Vivyan. 2008. "The Missing Story of Ourselves: Poverty and the Promise of Higher Education." *NWSAJ* 20.1: 1-19.

Arnoldi, Katherine. 2003. "How I Became a Cartoonist by Katherine Arnoldi." *Girl-Mom: Support, Community, and Education for Young Mamas*. http://www.girl-mom.com/ (accessed 11 Sept 2007).

Baym, Nancy. 2009. "Response: toward understanding the libratory potential of effective affinities online." In *Webbing Cyberfeminist Practice: Communities, Pedagogies, and Social Action*, eds. Kristine Blair, Radhika Gajjala, and Christine Tulley, 127-31. Cresskill, New Jersey: Hampton Press.

Breeder: Real Life Stories from The New Generation of Mothers. 2001. Eds. Ariel Gore and Bee Lavender. Seattle, WA: Seal Press.

Colboth, Jamie. 2003. "September 10th, 2001." *Girl-Mom: Support, Community, and Education for Young Mamas*. http://www.girl-mom.com/ (accessed 11 Sept 2007).

Crews, Allison. 2003. "When I Was Garbage." *Girl-Mom: Support, Community, and Education for Young Mamas*. http://www.girl-mom.com/ (accessed 11 Sept 2007).

Fide, Yvonne. 2003. "Beat the Statistics." *Girl-Mom: Support, Community, and Education for Young Mamas.* http://www.girl-mom.com/ (accessed 11 Sept 2007).

Fisher, Walter R. 1984. "Narration as a Human Communication Paradigm: The Case of Public Moral Argument." *Communication Monographs* 51.1: 1-22.

Foss, Sonja K. 2004 *Rhetorical Criticism: Exploration & Practice*, 3d ed. Prospect Heights, IL: Waveland.

Geronimus, Arline T. 2003. "On Teenage Childbearing and Neonatal Mortality in the United States" *Population and Development Review* 13.2: 245-79.

Hamilton, Brady E, Joyce A. Martin, and Stephanie J. Ventura. 2009. "Births: Preliminary Data for 2007." *National Vital Statistics Reports* 57.12: 1-23.

hooks, bell. 1989. *Talking Back: Thinking Feminist, Thinking Black.* Boston: South End.

Kelly, Deirdre M. 2000. *Pregnant with Meaning: Teen Mothers and the Politics of Inclusive Schooling*. New York: Peter Lang.

—. 1996. "Stigma Stories: Four Discourses About Teen Mothers, Welfare, and Poverty." *Youth and Society* 27.4: 421-49.

—. 1997. "Warning Labels: Stigma and the Popularizing of Teen Mothers' Stories." *Curriculum Inquiry* 27.2: 165-86.

Lesko, Nancy. 1990. "Curriculum Differentiation as Social Redemption: The Case of School-Aged Mothers." In *Curriculum Differentiation: Interpretive Studies in U.S. Secondary Schools*, eds. Reba Page and Linda Valli, 113-36. Albany: State University of New York Press.

Licona, Adela C. 2005. "(B)orderlands' Rhetorics and Representations: The Transformative Potential of Feminist Third-Space Scholarship and Zines." *NWSAJ* 17.2: 104-29.

Lindsay. 2003. "Motherhood as Inspiration." *Girl-Mom: Support, Community, and Education for Young Mamas.* http://www.girl-mom.com/ (accessed 11 Sept 2007).

Luker, Kristin. 1996. *Dubious Conceptions: The Politics of Teenage Pregnancy*. Cambridge: Harvard UP.

Maja. 2003. "Over It." *Girl-Mom: Support, Community, and Education for Young Mamas*. http://www.girl-mom.com/ (accessed 11 Sept 2007).

McPherson, Tara. 2009. "Response: 'Resisting' The Utopic-Dystopic Binary." In *Webbing Cyberfeminist Practice: Communities, Pedagogies, and Social Action*, eds. Kristine Blair, Radhika Gajjala, and Christine Tulley, 379-84. Cresskill, New Jersey: Hampton Press.

Nathanson, Constance. 1991. *Dangerous Passage: The Social Control of Sexuality in Women's Adolescence.* Philadelphia: Temple UP.

National Center for Health Statistics (NCHS). 2008. "NCHS Data on Teenage Pregnancy."
http://www.cdc.gov/nchs/data/infosheets/infosheet_teen_preg.pdf

Omy. 2003. "Growing Up With Him." *Girl-Mom: Support, Community, and Education for Young Mamas.*
http://www.girl-mom.com/ (accessed 11 Sept 2007).

Packebush, Nina. 2003. "Growing Up." *Girl-Mom: Support, Community, and Education for Young Mamas.*
http://www.girl-mom.com/ (accessed 11 Sept 2007).

Pillow, Wanda S. 2003. "'Bodies are Dangerous': Using Feminist Genealogy as Policy Studies Methodology." *Journal of Education Policy* 18.2: 145-59.

—. 2004. *Unfit Subjects: Educational Policy and the Teen Mother.* New York: RoutledgeFalmer.

Rowland, Kelly. 2002. "Stole." *Simply Deep.* Sony. Audio CD.

Scott, Joan W. 1993. "The Evidence of Experience." In *The Lesbian and Gay Studies Reader*, eds. Henry Abelove, Michele Aina Bariale, and David M. Halperin, 397-414. New York: Routledge.

Solinger, Rickie. 2000. *Wake Up Little Susie: Single Pregnancy and Race Before Roe v. Wade.* New York: Routledge.

Vinovskis, Maris. 1988. *.An "Epidemic" of Adolescent Pregnancy?: Some Historical and Policy Considerations.* New York: Oxford UP.

Weedon, Chris. 1997. *Feminist Practice & Poststructuralist Theory.* 2nd Ed. Cambridge: Blackwell.

You Look Too Young to be a Mom: Teen Mothers Speak Out on Love, Learning, and Success. 2004. Ed. Deborah Davis. New York: The Berkeley Publishing Group.

"Young Mothers." 2007. Ed. Andrea O'Reilly. *Journal of the Association for Research on Mothering* 9.1.

Notes

[1] "Linking Teen Pregnancy Prevention to Other Issues" (2010)
http://www.thenationalcampaign.org/why-it-matters/pdf/introduction.pdf

[2] "Teenage Pregnancy, Poverty, and Income Disparity" (2010)
http://www.thenationalcampaign.org/why-it-matters/pdf/poverty.pdf

[3] "Teenage Pregnancy and Overall Child Well-Being" (2010)
http://www.thenationalcampaign.org/why-it-matters/pdf/child_well-being.pdf

[4] The circulation of this dominant narrative has been documented by historians, sociologists, and educational scholars. See the work of Deirdre Kelly (2000),

Nancy Lesko (1990), Kristin Luker (1996), Constance Nathanson (1991) and Wanda Pillow (2004).

[5] Kristin Luker, author of *Dubious Conceptions: The Politics of Teen Motherhood* (1996), finds that teenage pregnancy officially became a public social issue in the 1970s, especially when as Congress debated the National School-Age Mother Act in 1975 (67; see also Vinovskis 1988, 22-46). During this time, Luker explains that advocates who "had argued that older women lacked access to contraception and abortion because they were poor . . . now claimed that teenagers were poor *because they lacked access to contraception and abortion*" (67, emphasis in original). Rhetorically, the argument worked to get minors access to contraceptives; however, this narrative has since been reiterated in a way that legitimizes public scrutiny over the timing of women's reproductive choices.

[6] *Time* magazine published an article in June 2008, "Pregnancy Boom at Gloucester High," claiming that 17 girls at Gloucester High School in Massachusetts made a pact to get pregnant together. Soon after the article was published the town mayor, school officials, and other investigators questioned the existence of a "pact."

[7] Reports showed a 3% increase in teen *births* (not pregnancies) between 2005and 2006 and an estimated 1% increase in 2007. See NCHS Data on Teenage Pregnancy (2008, 2).

[8] For example, see Luker's *Dubious Conceptions*, Constance Nathanson's *Dangerous Passage* (1991), the work of social scientist Arline T. Geronimus (2003), and sociologist and historian Rickie Solinger (2000).

[9] For example, the claims made about young mothers "dropping out" of school often cover up situations in which mothers are asked to leave or pressured to transfer from "regular" school to an alternative educational option (Pillow 2004, 32). Vivyan Adair also points to the effects of welfare-to-work reforms which forced low-income mothers away from educational pursuits and into low-wage jobs (2008).

[10] A recent post to Ariel Gore's zine *hipmama* is especially delightful as young mother Heather Joy Jackson critiques media attention on Bristol Palin http://www.hipmama.com/node/42339

[11] See accounts of audience's reactions to young mothers narratives about their experiences in Lesko's "Curriculum Differentiation as Social Redemption: The Case of School-Aged Mothers" (1990) and Kelly's "Warning Labels: Stigma and the Popularizing of Teen Mothers' Stories" (1997).

[12] I chose narratives that mentioned what it was like to be a "teen mother"—the experience of finding out, telling parents, going to the hospital, etc. Since 2003 new features have been posted ("Breeder I Am," "Untitled," and "Too Young to Question, Not Old Enough to be a Mom") which demonstrate many of the same patterns I identify in this chapter.

[13] In debating over whether to call myself, and the writers on this website, a "teen mother" I stumble upon the contested site of identity formation. I myself struggle to know whether I am still a teen mother, since my motherhood has not ceased, though my teen years have. In dropping the "teen" and claiming myself just a

"mother" I am concealing (or at least not making evident) the fact that I deviated from a conventional time frame for procreation. I yearn to identify as a teen mom because I hope to everyday, through my existence as a living, breathing, successful scholar and mother, contradict discourses on teen motherhood. Yet, in identifying as a teen mother am I not, are we not all, accepting the accusation that our motherhood is somehow deviant? That our age *does* somehow negatively affect the way we parent? This struggle, for me, illustrates historian Joan Scott's argument that "identity is a contested terrain, the site of multiple and conflicting claims" (1993, 406).

[14] In citing these mothers' stories I use the names published on the site. At times, this includes a first and last name; in other instances, there is no name at all.

[15] This phrase is used by Girl-Mom member Jaime Colboth. In using it I do not mean to reify a belief that teen motherhood is something to "survive" but instead to bring up another instance of a Girl-Mom member using aspects of the dominant narrative in order to challenge it—that is, using the term "survival" in a narrative that celebrates a girl-mom's life experience renders ridiculous a belief that a certain age deems an experience of mothering "survival" when clearly the fact that many young mothers must struggle points to problems with our social systems of support and larger national issues like poverty.

[16] Again, see the above cited work of Nancy Lesko, Deirdre Kelley, and Wanda Pillow who each share instances of young mothers narratives being "interpreted" in negative ways.

[17] This is not to suggest that no one will further interpret these women's experiences. As Scott explains in her argument against the uncritical use of experience as evidence, "Experience is at once always already an interpretation *and* something that needs to be interpreted" (1993, 412). I mean to point to the fact that the framework of the website itself does not leave room for (or even welcome) mediation or interpretation of their experiences.

[18] For example, in a feature article/rant entitled "over it" a Girl-Mom member and sex worker named maja defines "empowerment" as "telling our stories, not letting others do it for us" (2003).

CHAPTER SEVEN

CLOSING THE REFRIGERATOR: MATERNAL EMPOWERMENT AND THE MYSPACE AUTIE MOMMIES

DENISE BARNUM BURGESS

> A warrior mother is a mother who hears there is no hope for her child and, instead of retreating and mourning, breaks down walls, weaves her way through obstacles, follows her intuition even when people tell her she is crazy. She is a mother who believes in hope. A mother who believes in miracles and is able to carry on with strength and determination, even when her partner doubts her and offers no support. A mother who never gives up when she keeps hitting dead ends. These are the women who will continue to open the door so future generations of children don't have to suffer. These are the mothers with hearts of gold and shields made of the strongest armor. (McCarthy 2008).

In the fall of 2007, spurred by the release of actress and former playboy model Jenny McCarthy's best-selling book *Louder than Words: A Mother's Journey in Healing Autism*, women raising children with autism gained national attention. *The Oprah Winfrey Show*, *Larry King Live*, and *Nightline* devoted episodes to autism, featuring the stories of celebrity mothers like McCarthy and Holly Robinson Peete; however, these celebrity moms are not the only women facing the challenge of raising a child with autism. The mothers of 1 in every 91 American children will hear the words, "I'm sorry, your child has autism" (Kogan et al. 2009, 1395). A developmental disability marked by impairment in social interaction, impairment in communication, and repetitive patterns of behavior. Autism is better understood as a spectrum of related but discrete disorders, referred to as Autism Spectrum Disorders (ASDs), rather than a singular disorder. Although individuals on the spectrum can vary greatly from one another in terms of behavior and intelligence, people with ASDs typically have "unusual ways of learning, paying attention, or reacting to different sensations" (United States 2007). An autism diagnosis has a profound effect on the parents of the child. The research of J. Holroyd and D. McArthur, as well as the research of A. Donovan, indicates that parents of children with autism experience greater stress than parents of children with other disabilities ("Living" 2007). This stress often leads to marital difficulties; in fact, an estimated 80-85% of marriages end after a child is diagnosed with autism (DeFord 2007).

The example of McCarthy; however, demonstrates the power of a mother who, after her marriage to her son's father ended, boldly stood alone as her son's advocate. While McCarthy is an incredibly controversial figure in the autism community, loved by some and loathed by others for her stance on "curing" autism, she exemplifies the power a mother-hero figure can wield. When she learned her son, Evan, had autism, she threw herself into learning as much as she could about the disorder, earning for herself what she has called in her recent public appearances "a PhD in Google research." Based on her findings, McCarthy thwarted the traditional medical establishment and pursued a radical biomedical approach to Evan's treatment with dramatic results: McCarthy claims the treatments have "healed" Evan, who now communicates like a typical child (McCarthy 2007). Not only did she "rescue" her son, but she is also spear-heading a social movement to rescue thousands more children through such events as her July 2008 "Green Our Vaccines" march on Washington, DC.

McCarthy is emblematic of the power a mother of a child with autism can wield. But what about the millions of other mothers of children with autism, mothers who do not have the benefit of notoriety as an actress or as the girlfriend of Hollywood powerhouse Jim Carrey? Is it possible for other mothers of children with autism to find the same maternal empowerment that McCarthy has? In order to answer this question, I examine the simultaneous empowerment and repression in one community of mothers who have children with ASDs: the MySpace Autie Mommies. While there are many different communities of autism mothers each with their own sets of values (for instance, some communities value neurodiversity and celebrate their children's uniqueness), the women in the Autie Mommies community devote their MySpace profiles to battling their children's autism. The Autie Mommies are not an official group on MySpace, but they have developed a strong sense of community through friendships between individual users. It is difficult to determine the exact number of community members due to individual users' privacy settings; however, profile searches using keywords indicate that the number is in the thousands. I began tracking this community in 2007, shortly after my own sons were diagnosed with autism. All profiles I cite in this chapter were public when I conducted my research; if a mother subsequently changed her privacy settings to private, I replaced her screen name with a pseudonym out of respect for her desire to limit access to her personal information. I have also replaced the names of all children with pseudonyms.

Ernest Bormann's symbolic convergence theory provides a useful framework for exploring how the women within the online community moderate their use of power. Bormann argues that individual meanings for symbols can converge through a dynamic process of group fantasizing into a shared, community reality for participants. Fantasy themes, which include setting themes, character themes, and action themes, are the means through which the participants within a community form their interpretation of reality. Bormann asserts that these themes "chain out . . . [to] catch up large groups of people in a symbolic reality" or a "rhetorical vision" (Bormann 1972, 398). I argue that a patriarchal view of motherhood requiring women to sacrifice themselves for the sake of their children has been internalized by the Autie Mommies and has chained out through their online community. I argue that this rhetorical vision reveals the problematic nature of the powerful, heroic roles that some mothers of children with autism adopt in their online personas, for while they are using their power to benefit their children, they tend not to use their power to improve their own status and position. I will propose, however, that the concept of gynocentric mothering provides potentialities for women to simultaneously use their power to improve the lives of their children and continue the feminist project of improving the status of women.

The purpose of my essay is not to critique the mothers themselves, but rather to practice the sort of empathetic scholarship Mark Osteen advocates. Osteen's vision of empathetic scholarship is a "convergence of the personal and professional, [a] blend of experiential knowledge and scholarly rigor" (Osteen 2008, 297). My work blends the personal and professional, for while I am an academic using her scholarly tools of analysis, I am simultaneously a mother of two sons with autism. Because of this personal connection, I have nothing but respect for the mothers who embody an unshakeable commitment, both to their children and to other mothers in the autism community. I in no way wish for my analysis to be taken as a critique of these mothers, for two important reasons. First, the profiles I analyze are virtual identities. While these virtual personas are likely tied to the real-world experiences of the women who created them, it would be unfair to generalize about the women's lives based solely on their online personas in one particular virtual environment. Second, my purpose in examining the profiles is not to critique individual women, either their virtual personas or their real life identities. Instead, my essay is intended to be a critique of the cultural structures that limit the ways in which women can wield power.

The Cultural Context of Mothers' Power

Before examining the fantasy themes of MySpace Autie Mommies, it is important to understand the larger cultural context of power in which the mother of a child with autism operates. Historically, mothers have not been viewed as powerful advocates for and heroes to their children with autism; on the contrary, they have been denigrated as the cause of their children's developmental delays. From the late 1940s through the 1970s, it was commonly presumed by medical professionals that autism was caused by so-called "refrigerator mothers" whose lack of affection led to their children's developmental delays (Simpson et al. 2002). In fact, mothers often received counseling designed to help them uncover their latent hatred for their children and become better nurturers. Jane Taylor McDonnell, feminist author and mother of a child with autism, explains that through reading books on children with autism and other developmental disorders, she "discovered that the worst mother in twentieth-century psychological literature is quite possibly the mother of the autistic or schizophrenic child" (1998, 223).

While mothers are no longer blamed, overtly, for their children's developmental delays, their experiences are still often devalued. A user comment on an AutismVox blog posting about Jenny McCarthy's book reflects this minimization of mothers' experiences: "I find the whole notion of 'mother's journey' distasteful and entirely insulting. It's not the mother's journey, it is the child's journey. Period. It's.not.about. the.mother" (Long Day's Journey into Acceptance, Autism Vox, comment posted September 19, 2007).[1] This post reveals a presumption that a mother's experiences do not matter. While she may face divorce, depression, and bankruptcy as the parent of a child with autism, her suffering has little cultural value. Her experiences are not deemed important enough to voice.

Within this context, it is a radical step for mothers to create their own networks of support on MySpace. Rather than accepting the larger cultural narrative that their experiences do not matter, Autie Mommies exert their voices through their MySpace profiles. Not only do they exert their voices, but they exert power. But what is the nature of this power? Andrea O'Reilly contends that mothers encounter four different power relationships:

"power-over," the constraints and limitations that lead to women's oppression; "power-to," the means of women's agency and resistance; "power-with," the enabling of women to act as a group; and "transformative power," the use of power to transform a child into "a responsible and acceptable citizen of the society in which she/he lives" (2005, 7-8). Despite progressive revisions of mothering practices, the emphasis of maternal power is on serving the child rather than transforming the mother herself. This lack of emphasis on the mother herself, O'Reilly contends, perpetuates the patriarchal domination of motherhood. As the fantasy themes of the MySpace Autie Mommies indicate, these mothers are using their "power-with" and "transformative power" for the good of their children without using their power to transform their own cultural position, perpetuating a patriarchal domination of motherhood.

Narrative Constructions a Communal Reality: Applying Bormann's Fantasy Themes

While we cannot presume to make judgments about the "real" lives of the women who create profiles on MySpace, we can learn about the online Autie Mommy community's shared perceptions about how women can and cannot wield power. The key to uncovering this communal view of reality is examining the discourse of the community. Feminist theorist Erika Horwitz defines discourse "as a specific structure of statements, terms, and categories that are historically, socially, and institutionally specific. Like stories, they 'create a communal understanding of power in relationships and appropriate rules of conduct" (2004, 44). The communal story aspect that Horwitz highlights is what makes Bormann's model useful for examining the discourse of a community. Through the analysis of the narrative elements found within a discourse community, Bormann's fantasy theme analysis provides a means through which to uncover the social and cultural impact of a discourse. When applied to the MySpace Autie Mommies' discourse, Bormann's themes reveal that the mothers do portray themselves as asserting significant power and agency; however, this power is always wielded for the benefit of their children. Conforming to the rhetorical vision of the group, the users' setting themes, character themes, and action themes demonstrate that the women adopt self-representations that focus solely on their roles as mothers and minimize aspects of their lives unrelated to mothering.

Setting Themes

The setting themes revealed through the Autie Mommies' MySpace profiles are important to establishing the community's rhetorical vision. The setting themes demonstrate the mothers' power to manipulate the existing setting to achieve their own purposes. Yet, at the same time, the women's choices for how to manipulate the setting reveal a singular focus on using power for their children alone rather than using power to bolster their own status as well.

The setting of the Autie Mommies' community is not a shared physical setting; according to the demographic information posted on the women's profiles, their physical locations span across the United States and into Europe; however, the women all share the same virtual setting, shaped by the constraints created by MySpace itself. The architecture of MySpace provides a standardized format for each user's profile. A user fills in the blanks in the categories set up by MySpace when creating her page. Sections include the following:

- a headline box where a user enters her name, location, age, profile and picture
- an "About Me" box where a user enters general information about herself
- an "I'd Like to Meet" box where a user describes who she would to connect with on MySpace
- an interests section with categories including "general," "music," "movies," "television," "books," and "heroes"
- a "Background and Lifestyle" box where a user lists her marital status, sexual orientation, reason for being on MySpace, zodiac sign, children, education, and occupation

The ways in which Autie Mommies choose to respond to or ignore these prefabricated categories in the virtual setting demonstrate how these mothers use the power of their online personas for the benefit of their children alone, mitigating the importance of using that power to benefit themselves.

In many mothers' profiles, information unrelated to a user's maternal role is notably absent. One mother, Autism Families United,[2] chooses to leave blank several sections that might provide clues to who she is outside of her role as mother. For instance, in the "Interests" box, she declines to provide any information about her general interests, her favorite music, her movie and television preferences, or her book choices. She also declines to respond to the "Who I'd like to meet" prompt, instead filling the space with a slide show of her children. In other boxes, she does fill in the blanks, but she mitigates the importance of her non-maternal functions. An example is what she lists as her career: "FT Mom/PT Hairstylist." By placing her role as a mother before her paying job, she emphasizes that her primary function is mothering her children: anything outside that role is secondary.

Likewise, a mother named Karrie goes against the site's architecture in the way she responds to the categories. In the "Interests" box, for instance, she lists nothing about herself, but instead pastes in a guestbook for her visitors to sign. In other sections, she fills in the boxes with information about her family rather than about herself. Karrie's "About Me" and "Who I'd Like to Meet" boxes, for instance, contain pictures and slide shows of her children and husband, yet no information about herself. Elsewhere, Karrie fills in the blanks with autism-awareness graphics. In her "Movies" and "Television" categories, for instance, she declines to provide any information about her viewing preferences and instead provides graphics with slogans like "Proud Mom of Someone with Autism!"

The ways in which Autism Families United and Karrie manipulate the construction of the virtual setting through their content choices not only reveal each woman's power but also what she uses her power for. By challenging the construction of the site through their content, both women demonstrate their "power-to" as they subvert and resist the corporate vision for the site and instead provide what they think is suitable content. Their content, such as images and words related to their children and autism, reveals that they use this power for the sake of their children with autism. The structure of their pages is focused on advocacy for their children, sharing with the world the message that their children with autism are cherished and worthy of love. At the same time, these setting choices reveal that the women also choose to minimize other aspects of their lives that are not related to mothering as they construct their virtual personas, not even allowing themselves to voice the names of their favorite movies.

Character Themes

The setting themes within Autie Mommies' MySpace profiles are closely linked to character themes, for the construction of the setting is shaped primarily by the two predominant character types: mother and child. The mothers are portrayed as tirelessly devoted advocates, while the children are portrayed as innocent angels. In addition to these characters, the fantasy themes contain a villain as well: evil institutions seeking to destroy the innocent angels.

The mothers, the central characters in my analysis, tend not to talk about themselves, preferring to focus their conversations on autism and their children, but we can learn about them through their screen names, their pictures/avatars, and their "About Me" sections. All three reveal that the mothers tend to construct their identities around their children. While some mothers simply use their first names as a screen names, many use names that reflect their status as a mother of a child with an ASD, like Autism Connections and Victoria~Mom of an Amazing Child w/Autism. Likewise, the pictures members post on their profiles reveal an online identity built upon parenting. Few women in the community choose a picture of just themselves for their profile. Many select a picture in which they are with their children. In most of these pictures, the children take the foreground and the mothers drift into the background, emphasizing the predominance of the child's importance over the mother's. Others choose to erase themselves completely, posting photographs of their children or autism-related graphics for their profile pictures. By choosing such images as their face to the online world, mothers actively construct a persona with a singular focus: working for their children with autism.

While one might assume the women would reveal more about themselves through the narratives in their "About Me" sections, this is often not the case. Their children tend to be the focus of a section that should be, by its title, about the user herself. One mother, Autism Families United, writes, "About me, hmmm, thats kinda hard since its always about my kids.lol." She follows this opener with a long paragraph describing her three children, Mitch, Destiny, and Gavin,[3] yet she never even provides readers with her own name. She says her children, especially six-year-old Gavin who has autism, "are the world" to her, and she "will do whatever it takes for them to succeed and be happy. It is my job to." Her singular purpose is to work to secure her children's future, not to simultaneously secure a future for herself; however, Autie Mommies do not seem to be uneasy with having their online personas so tied to their children; in fact, they embrace the role. Heidi "Poeticmama"[4] writes in her "About Me" section, "I devote 110% to the love of my life: my son, Zane.[5] He is the man in my life and will always be my focal point!" Likewise, Christine writes, "I am first a mother before anything else. [My son] drives me to do all I can." Christine's words reaffirm the absolute predominance of motherhood above all other aspects of identity within the community.

The children to whom the mothers are so tirelessly committed comprise the second major character group. In American culture, children with autism are often wrongly perceived as "unruly kids who choose to misbehave" ("What is Autism?" 2005), the persistence of this belief reflected in radio host Michael Savage's recent on-air tirade: "I'll tell you what autism is. In 99 percent of the cases, it's a brat who hasn't been told to cut the act out. That's what autism is" (Savage 2008). In sharp contrast to the popular conception of children with autism as ill-behaved children who throw tantrums, the mothers on MySpace tend to describe their children as innocent angels incapable of doing wrong. Autism Families United refers to her boys as "arch angels" and calls all children with autism "little angels." Autism Community Resources calls her son "a miracle." Valerie 1.0 calls her son "the most wonderful little boy." These verbal depictions of wonderful, angelic children are reinforced with photographic depictions. Over the course of my research, I visited nearly two hundred profiles, and I never encountered a profile that didn't have at least one picture of the child with autism. In fact, most profiles have multiple pictures and even slide shows. The pictures of the children cuddled in their mother's arms or timidly venturing into the water during a visit to the beach reinforce the image of the children as innocent. And, as innocents, these children need to be protected from the evils of the world.

This portrayal of the children as angels functions within the rhetorical vision in three ways. First, it separates the child from the diagnosis. Whereas a child with autism may have atypical and even violent behavioral tendencies, describing the child as an angel serves to separate him or her from the behaviors caused by autism. Second, describing the children as angelic strengthens the position of the mothers. Horwitz explains that the current dominant discourse on mothering "suggests that mothers are solely responsible for the physical, spiritual, and psychological well being of their children and, therefore, are held responsible (i.e., blamed) for their children's difficulties" (2004, 44). If the rhetorical vision separates the innocent children from the abnormal behaviors caused by autism; however, the mothers have nothing to be blamed for. Instead, the disorder is at fault for the behavior. This leads into the third function of the angelic portrayal of children within the fantasy themes. If the mothers are blameless and the children are innocent, then the stage is set for a moral battle of good versus evil. The just mothers position themselves in opposition to the evil forces that threaten the well-being of their innocent children.

The evil forces threatening children with autism are revealed through the third character theme to be institutions. One such evil institution is the medical establishment. Many Autie Mommies are highly critical of medical practices, especially injecting children with a series of immunizations containing a mercury-based preservative called thimerosal, which some suspect may contribute to autism.[6] Autism Families United writes angrily on her page, "Mercury approved! Kid tested! ~ Available at a Circuit Court near you! ~ Who Calls The Shots? It's time to reclaim our American Rights! ~I'm about 2 go hand out Exemptions forms my damn self!" As this user's comments about the courts indicate, the medical establishment has a partner in crime: the government. Not only do mothers portray the government as evil because of its universal immunization mandate, but they are also highly critical of its management of programs for children with autism. Christine expresses this on her MySpace blog:

> [In my travels through MySpace] I keep reading about these children like my son in other parts of the country. What angers me is these children are not recieving or only begining to recieve services!!! . . . Do you know that services such as PT [physical therapy], OT [occupational therapy], Early intervention, Home ABA [Applied Behavioral Analysis] are all services provided by a state basis. Another words the federal goverment gives each state money, each state then decided how much will go to education, and how much to special education. Some states provide no early intervention services. How is this fair to the children? It's not!

As Christine's comment illustrates, the government is depicted as an inefficient, even negligent entity that fails to provide children with necessary services. This depiction contributes to the rhetorical vision of the community, reinforcing the heroism of the mothers in opposition to the wickedness of the governmental institutions.

The most evil of all institutions in the rhetorical vision are the school districts who are supposed to educate children with autism. Once a child reaches the age of three and leaves a state's early intervention program, the local school district takes over providing therapy and educational services for the child; however, the mothers' MySpace profiles indicate that the school districts often fail to provide adequate services for children with autism. Christine writes, "There are so many families lost out there and there is no one for them to turn to because the school district doesn't provide adequate programs. I'm angry and scared. [W]hat will become of these children, without proper services . . . how will these children ever reach their full potental? . . . [W]ithout change our children will suffer!!!" As Christine's analysis indicates, the school districts threaten to harm the angelic children and because she depicts the school districts as simply an enemy, she can present a clear call to action: mothers must stand up against the school districts or the "children will suffer!!!" It is the job of the heroic mother to intervene, to enact change so that the children will not get "lost out there" in the bureaucracy of educational institutions.

Action Themes

The predominant action theme is tied to the evil institutional forces against which the heroic mothers fight. Whenever a mother runs into a difficulty with an institution, other mothers join her to fight against the unjust institution. This often happens when a mother is struggling against a school district to get services for her child. The mother posts her problem either on her profile, in a blog, or in a bulletin, and other mothers respond by providing battle tactics. For instance, Autism Connections posted a blog on her MySpace page about her struggle to get classroom services for her preschooler with autism, and several women replied with information about her child's legal rights and ways to fight the school system to get her son the help he requires.

One of the more poignant examples of mothers joining together to slay institutional dragons is the recent outpouring of support for a mother named Catie from Kentucky. Catie is the mother of a six-year-old son with autism who was sued because he hit one of his aides at school. Autism Connections heard about the lawsuit on her local television news and began a grassroots effort to support Catie's family. Overnight Catie went from having a handful of MySpace friends to having over three hundred. Soon mothers of children with autism were flooding the Kentucky justice system as well as the family's school district with letters, phone calls, and emails. When the family went to court, the results were favorable. Catie writes on her MySpace page:

> We are elated to report that because of your support, action, and outrage, as well as the merit of our defense, the charge of assault 4th degree against our exceptional, wonderful child was dismissed outright by Judge Todd Walton in the Bracken County Juvenile Court this 25th day of Septemeber 2007. . . . We are so blessed to have met you all and will never forget that all care so much about all our extraordinary children. We will always fight with you to make sure another special family need never suffer such heartbreak, anguish, pain, and unease.

United, the MySpace mothers of children with autism, were able to find justice for a child and as Catie's closing demonstrates, the mothers will continue to work together to fight against unjust institutions. This resolve, and the changes it can motivate, demonstrates the power that mothers wield in their heroic role. Rather than accepting the dominant discourse that mothers are to blame for their children's struggles, the Autie Mommies subvert cultural structures by banding together to affect change.

In addition to slaying dragons, the community of mothers plays the role of herald, announcing the truth about autism to the world. The mothers' aim is to spread autism awareness outside of the autism community and convince others of the need to work toward a cure. Sharing information about what autism is and who their autistic children are is of ultimate import: as Heidi "Poeticmama" says of her son, "Zane is AMAZING and I will die trying to show that to the world!!!" Jane[7] also wants to spread autism awareness and asks other mothers in the community to join her effort: "Please help me and others to spread autism awareness throughout all states and especially in Georgia where I live. I'm working on making a change here and in my community. . . . Strength is in numbers and together we can make a difference!! Change is possible!" Jane's emphasis on change being possible highlights the activist aspect of the mothers' heralding role. The mothers not only want people to be more aware of what autism is but they want to share that knowledge in order to create social change.

The methods mothers use to raise autism awareness vary. Many mothers post bulletins about where moms can get free autism awareness bumper stickers. Other mothers voice their concerns about autism whenever they are near someone who has enough public clout to make a major impact. For instance, Autism Families United tells an emotional story on her MySpace page of when she met her favorite musician, Aaron Lewis. She was about to leave after getting his autograph when she realized she had an opportunity to speak for autism and turned back to her idol. "Can I ask you a favor?" she asked. "If your ever have an opportunity to be involved or support Autism awareness [would you] please do so? . . . My son has Autism and many others as well." Afterwards she "felt so happy" for having had a chance to speak for her son and his friends with autism, and in that happiness, she began to cry. "I cried to god," she writes, "I asked him to put me on whatever path Im suppose to be on cuz its obvious that he accomplished this meeting not me . . . God has a purose for me. To be the voice. To make some noise. I cried for so many reasons. I cried for our kids. They will be heard one way or another."

Like so many other mothers of children with autism, this mother sees it as her responsibility to speak for a child who cannot. In asking her hero to support autism awareness efforts, she took a bold stand, choosing to "make some noise" for her son's sake. She, like other mothers, has made it her mission that "one way or another" people within her local and global community will become more aware of what autism is and more understanding of those who have autism.

Strengths and Limitations of a Heroic Vision

The image of the mother of an autistic child serving as a heroic champion, challenging institutions and educating the world, certainly reflects empowerment. Holly Robinson Peete, actress and mother of an autistic child, asserts that mothers "have to be like a superhero [or] Foxy Brown and kick that wall down and make cracks in that wall to bring your child through" (Winfrey 2007). The women in the MySpace community have adopted this superhero persona, kicking down walls and working with all their might to rescue their children. This superhero role can be empowering to women, transforming mothering from a private act into a practice that holds powerful implications for the public sphere. Andrea O'Reilly asserts that mothering, as a feminist practice, becomes a public act "through maternal activism. Motherhood, in Western culture, is most often seen as a private, and more specifically, an apolitical exercise. In contrast, feminist mothers understand motherwork to have social and political import. . . . Mothers, through maternal activism, use their position as mothers to lobby for social and political change" (O'Reilly 2006, 15). Especially through the coalitions Autie Mommies create to challenge institutions, we see the community's rhetorical vision providing a space for women to become politically active and affect social change.

While the image of a superhero can be empowering, as maternal activism indicates, the singular nature of the mothers' mission holds problematic implications. The women's online identity constructions are grounded wholly in their role as mothers, undercutting other aspects of their lives. This places women in a position which requires them to sacrifice much. Autism Families United demonstrates her singular devotion to serving as her children's hero brings hardship and forces sacrifice; however, for her, doing her duty as a mother is well worth the hardships she faces. She explains:

> I dont look back, I just put [my son] and my daughter on my back and keep pressing forward. . . . Im drivin to make life somehow easier for my kids for the future, so Ill go through the daily struggles now, while I can. . . . Our children depend on it. If not us then who. I go thru daily struggles . . . but in truth I would not have it any other way. This is my journey that has been chosen for me. I dont question it, I just handle it. I trust that god knows what he is doing. . . . I will be a bit scuffed up, bruised up, worn out and somewhat out of breath due to being mom and challenging everyone who says "He cant" or "She wont" In the end Ill show them how wrong they all were.

She is willing to sacrifice herself, and the aspects of her personality unrelated to motherhood, in order to fight for her children. In fact, she embraces the role, saying, "I would not have it any other way." Despite the bruises and scars, she accepts her mission to mother a child with autism. While her devotion to her children is deeply admirable, from a feminist perspective, her need to sacrifice other aspects of her life in order to be a hero to her children is problematic. Such martyrdom underscores O'Reilly's critique of mothering practices that employ maternal power only to transform the child and not to transform the mother as well as perpetuate the patriarchal domination of motherhood. While the position of the child with autism may be forwarded, the status of the woman who wields power for the sake of the child is not.

The Potential of a Gynocentric Form of Empowered Mothering

The fact that mothers on MySpace adopt the perception that they must choose one or the other—empowering themselves as women or working for the betterment of their children—suggests an either/or dichotomy. A woman can be an individual or a mother, but not both. This aspect of the community's rhetorical vision is influenced by a dominant cultural discourse positing "that being a mother is all that a woman needs to feel fulfilled" (Horwitz 2004, 44). Such discourse is dangerous, for it reflects a patriarchal view of motherhood that not only limits women's experiences to the domestic sphere but is also "oppressive to women," forcing them to abdicate their claims to individuality (O'Reilly 2006, 15). Because this discourse places such limitations upon women, it is essential that scholars and activists look for ways to challenge it.

Feminist scholars provide a model through which to challenge the sacrificial discourse tied to mothering, envisioning the possibility of an empowered mother who uses her strength both for her child and herself. Drawing upon Adrienne Rich's distinction between motherhood, a patriarchal institution, and mothering, a practice that empowers women, feminists advocate a gynocentric, or mother-centered, form of mothering. O'Reilly writes, "[M]othering, freed from motherhood, could be experienced as a site of empowerment, a location of social change if, to use Rich's words, women became 'outlaws from the institution of motherhood" (2006, 11). This outlaw mothering would move women away from the maternal sacrifice model and would instead emphasize "the importance of mothers meeting their own needs" (2006, 17-18).

There are some communities of mothers with children diagnosed with ASDs that do not conform to the self-sacrificial patriarchal model of motherhood. For instance, "Bad" Autism Mothers, a Facebook group created in January 2010 boasts, "We aren't doing everything possible to 'cure' our autistic children and we are proud of it. We don't care how 'hot' we are and we are not looking for anyone to tell us how strong we are. We just want to share some experiences so that we can help like-minded mothers navigate this truly special journey." In the Autie Mommies community, threads of mothers moving toward a form of gynocentric mothering are also starting to emerge. Heidi "Poeticmama" provides an example of a mother becoming aware of the possibility of serving as a powerful hero yet still maintaining an identity outside of autism. She writes in her profile, "I'm just getting back to living life for myself as well as for [my son Zane]. Life is always busy and usually stressful . . . there seems to be little time to smile or laugh. I'm doing both Zane and myself an injustice by that. Don't get me wrong—Zane is still my EVERYTHING, but now I realize that I deserve a little happiness for myself as well." Heidi "Poeticmama" is learning about balance. Perhaps that is the key: maintaining empowerment while continuing to nourish all the other aspects that shaped a mother's identity before she encountered autism. Thus, Heidi "Poeticmama" took advantage of the MySpace architecture to be both a mother and an individual: she created an additional personal profile. In a bulletin post she writes:

> I started a new account . . . my own personal profile. I am going to dedicate my current myspace to my son in efforts of Autism Awareness—in addition to my family affected by autism, etc. Although autism always has a deep impact and often seems to control most everyday life . . . I wanted to have a different account so others can get to know my personality & character somewhat outside of that. Just add "Heidi" if you want to get to know me . . . not just as a proud parent of a son with Autism, but as an individual. I look forward to hearing from you . . .

Heidi's experiences reveal that mothers need not reject other aspects of their personalities in order to heroically fight for their children with autism. In creating an additional account, Heidi is taking a step toward becoming both, a mother of an autistic son and an individual.

As Bormann's theories indicate; however, rhetorical visions are powerful constructions that are very difficult to challenge, especially if one wants to remain a member of the community. While Heidi "Poeticmama" does take a step toward the gynocentric mothering envisioned by feminists, her claim that Zane is still her "EVERYTHING" demonstrates that she is still entrenched in her community's rhetorical vision. Her actions reflect a challenge to the dominant discourse that dictates women should sacrifice themselves for their children, yet she still places her role as a mother as higher priority than the other aspects of her life. The difficulty of attaining the ideal of gynocentric motherhood, even for a woman like Heidi who has become aware of the need to be an individual, highlights the importance for feminist scholars and advocates to continue supporting mothers within the autism community. Partnering with organizations that work with families affected by autism, like Autism Speaks and Talk about Autism Now, can provide fertile opportunities to support mothers and challenge the dominant discourse of mothering.

Challenging the powerful legacies of dominant discourses is never easy, yet the potential still exists for communities of women to change their rhetorical visions in order to adopt a gynocentric form of mothering that empowers without requiring women to martyr their hopes, dreams, and ambitions outside of mothering. In revisioning mothering as a mother-centered practice, women can claim positions of agency and authority and in doing so they will be stronger warriors for the children they love.

Works Cited

Autism Connections. 2007. Proud Autie Parent! *MySpace*. http://www.myspace.com/ autismgroup (Accessed September 25, 2007).

Autism Community Resources. 'Be Yourself Because the People Who Mind Don't Matter, and the People Who Matter Don't Mind' Dr. Seuss. *MySpace*. http://www.myspace.com/autismcommunityresources (Accessed October 7, 2007).

AutismVox blog. 2007. http://www.autismvox.com/jenny-mccarthy-autism-mother/#comment-267531 (Accessed January 17, 2010).

"Bad" Autism Mothers. 2010. *Facebook*. http://www.facebook.com/ group.php?gid= 153188229956 (Accessed January 17, 2010).

Bormann, Ernest G. 1972. Fantasy and the rhetorical vision: A theoretical criticism of social reality. *Quarterly Journal of Speech* 58: 396-407.

Catie. 2007. Autism is not a TRAGEDY, ignorance is the TRAGEDY. Whatever you FOCUS on will GROW. *MySpace*. http://www.myspace.com/catie7995 (Accessed September 25, 2007).

Christine. 2010. I'm Engaged! *MySpace*. http://profile.myspace.com/index.cfm?fuseaction=user.viewprofile&friendid=206414597 (Accessed January 17, 2010).

DeFord, Susan. 2007. No group discount for autism care. *Washington Post*, June 3, 2007. http://www.washingtonpost.com/wpdyn/content/

article/2007/06/02/AR2007060200627.html (Accessed April 20, 2008).

Autism Families United. 2007. I'll be the greatest fan of your life! *MySpace*. http://www.myspace.com/DesindShea (Accessed January 10, 2010).

Heidi "Poeticmama." 2007. Live life to the fullest . . . each day is a gift." *MySpace*. http://www.myspace.com/zbspoeticmama (Accessed September 24, 2007).

Horwitz, Erika. 2004. Resistance as a site of empowerment: The journey away from maternal sacrifice. In *Outlaw mothers: Theories and practices of empowered mothering*, ed. Andrea O'Reilly, 43-58. Toronto: Women's Press.

Jane. 2007. Proud autism advocate--support autism awareness!! Working to make a difference! http://www.myspace.com/intropaces (Accessed September 24, 2007).

Karrie. 2007. People who live in glass houses should not throw stones! *MySpace*. http://www.myspace.com/mjkkak (Accessed November 20, 2007).

Kogan, Michael D., Stephen J. Blumberg, Laura A. Schieve, Coleen A. Boyle, James M. Perrin, Reem M. Ghandour, Gopal K. Singh, Bonnie B. Strickland, Edwin Trevathan, and Peter C. van Dyck. 2009. Prevalence of parent-reported diagnosis of autism spectrum disorder among children in the US, 2007. *Pediatrics* 124.5: 1395-1403.

Living with autism: Stress on families. 2007. *Autism Society of America*. http://www.autism-society.org/site/PageServer?pagename=about_lwa_stress (Accessed November 19, 2007).

McCarthy, Jenny. 2007. Jenny McCarthy: The day I heard my son had autism. *CNN.com*. http://edition.cnn.com/2007/US/09/24/jenny.autism/ (Accessed December 1, 2007).

—. 2008. *Warrior mothers: A nation of parents healing autism against all odds*. New York: Dutton.

McDonnell, Jane Taylor. 1998. On being the 'bad' mother of an autistic child. In *"Bad" mothers: The politics of blame in twentieth-century America*, eds. Molly Ladd-Taylor and Lauri Umansky, 220-229. New York: New York University Press.

O'Reilly, Andrea. 2005. Introduction. In *Motherhood: Power and oppression*, eds. Andrea O'Reilly, Marie Porter, and Patricia Short, 1-24. Toronto: Women's Press.

—. 2006. *Rocking the cradle: Thoughts on feminism, motherhood and the possibility of empowered mothering*. Toronto: Demeter Press.

Osteen, Mark. 2008. Conclusions: Toward an empathetic scholarship. In

Autism and representation, ed. Mark Osteen, 297-302. New York: Routledge.

Savage, Michael. 2008. Savage on autism: "A fraud, a racket. . . In 99 percent of the cases, it's a brat who hasn't been told to cut the act out." *Media Matters*. http://mediamatters.org/items/200807170005?f=h_latest (Accessed January 10, 2010).

Simpson, David E., J.J. Hanley, and Gordon Quinn. 2002. Refrigerator mothers. *P.O.V.* PBS Online. http://www.pbs.org/pov/pov2002/refrigeratormothers/aboutautism.html (Accessed November 21, 2007).

Valerie 1.0. 2007. Carpe diem. *MySpace*. http://www.myspace.com/ve2000e (Accessed September 25, 2007).

Victoria~Mom of an Amazing Child w/Autism. 2007. Life is too short to be mean. *MySpace*. http://www.myspace.com/votevictoria (Accessed September 24, 2007).

What is Autism? 2005. *Tucson alliance for autism*. 2005. http://autism.web.arizona.edu/what_is_autism.shtml (Accessed November 20, 2007).

Winfrey, Oprah. 2007. Mothers battle autism. *Oprah.com*. 2007. http://www2.oprah.com/tows/slide/200709/20070918/slide_20070918_350_101.jhtml (Accessed September 20, 2007).

United States Department of Health and Human Services. 2007. Frequently asked questions.

Autism information center. Centers for Disease Control and Prevention. http://www.cdc.gov/ncbddd/autism/faq.htm (Accessed November 18, 2007).

Notes

[1] Here, and throughout the essay, I quote online posting verbatim without inserting [sic] for errors, which would significantly impede readability.

[2] Pseudonym.

[3] Pseudonyms.

[4] Pseudonym.

[5] Pseudonym.

[6] Whether immunizations are a factor in children developing autism is the subject of derisive debate within the autism community that is beyond the scope of this chapter. Suffice it to say, it should not be assumed that all mothers of children with autism share the perspective that immunizations are at fault for their children's autism. For an examination of debates within the autism community about vaccinations and whether or not autism is something that should be "cured," see Heilker, Paul, and Jason King (2010). The rhetorics of online autism advocacy: A case for rhetorical listening." *Rhetorics and technologies: New directions in*

writing and communication. Ed. Stuart A. Selber. Columbia: University of South Carolina Press. 113-133.

[7] Pseudonym.

CHAPTER EIGHT

ONLINE PARENTAL UNCERTAINTY IN THE EXPERIENCE OF A CHILD'S PORT WINE STAIN

LIESBETH WIERING

For the longest time, Joie Davidow felt like she was the only person in the world who looked the way she did. A disfiguring purple mark, covering nearly half her face, made her look and feel almost unbearably different from others. Her parents, convinced that nothing could be done, decided the best way to help Joie was to ignore the matter, and to "not make a Big Deal" (Davidow 2003, 247). Decades later, Davidow logged on to the Internet and ran a web search for *port wine stain*. It was then that she finally discovered that there were in fact numerous people who looked like her, and with whom she also shared the experience of a childhood filled with loneliness, embarrassment, and pain.

Today, parents who are confronted with uncertainty brought on by their child's port wine stain (PWS) diagnosis can search the Internet for people with whom they share common experiences, whom they can ask their PWS-related questions, and with whom they can exchange PWS-related information. They can pick from several birthmark-oriented websites, such as that of the Vascular Birthmarks Foundation (VBF), or Birthmarks.com, which is the website Joie Davidow (2003) visited on her first web search for *port wine stain*. Parents like Davidow's may have had no choice but to resign to their family doctor's diagnosis, but parents of children with PWS today are no longer limited to local doctors' levels of knowledge and expertise. Online, several vascular birthmark communities with contacts all over the world are ready to embrace members, eager to provide them with support, general information, and the latest know-how on medical developments. The Internet has provided sublime means to help overcome the type of isolation as described by Davidow. Recently, the parents of a 9-year old girl expressed gratitude to the Birthmarks.com newsgroup for the fact that their daughter, because of this online community, had known other people with PWS her whole life.

Despite the availability of Internet sources, the confrontation with a child's PWS diagnosis is still a confusing experience for many parents. Feelings of uncertainty, fear, and guilt may continue to plague parents as it remains unclear what the future will look like, how the child will respond to the condition and its possible treatment, and how the condition was brought on in the first place. Davidow's grandmother used to tell little Joie that her mother had caused the PWS by dreaming of "delicious wine" during her pregnancy (Davidow 2003). While many years have passed since, and doctors and medical researchers have continuously insisted that PWS is not caused by specific eating habits or activities during pregnancy, myths such as "food cravings are linked to birthmarks" still tend to resurface as credible explanations (Burgoon and Hall 1994, 103).

In this article, I explore the dialectic of uncertainty and support in the experience of a child's PWS. In addition, I examine how parents and people with PWS coexist in online communities, how gender differences are present in these groups among parents of children with PWS, what participants in the online groups get out of their online experiences, and how participation may bring either relief, or increased uncertainty.

Confronting Uncertainty in Illness

The role of uncertainty in illness has been extensively studied within the field of health communication (e.g., Babrow, Kasch, and Ford 1998; Brashers et al. 2000; Cohen 1993; Mishel 1988, 1990; Sheer and Cline 1995). Several studies have examined the communication of information and support in health-oriented online communities and on message boards (e.g., Galegher, Sproull, and Kiesler 1998; Lasker, Sogolow, and Sharim 2005; Macias, Lewis, and Smith 2005; Muthaseb and Wright 2005). Communication researchers have often claimed that the greatest motivator for people to communicate with others, especially with strangers, is to find relief from uncertainty (see Babrow 1998, 2001; Berger and Calabrese 1975; Gudykunst 1995). The uncertainty people experience when faced with an illness diagnosis may provoke a similar response, and a desire to gather information. Information on a medical condition may provide explanations about the specific illness situation and enable people to prepare for the future (see Meredith and Symonds 1996).

According to Cotten and Gupta (2004), internet-based support groups have been identified as one of the primary methods for online health information-seeking today. Many studies of online communities stress the benefits of the Internet in health issues (e.g., Calhoun 1998; Lasker, Sogolow, and Sharim 2005; Muthaseb and Wright 2005). People confronted with an acute or chronic disease or disorder may respond to their illness-related uncertainty by looking for information beyond the doctor (Dutta-Bergman 2005). However, today's better-than-ever-informed parents may also experience *more* uncertainty than Davidow's parents, as they can find themselves overloaded with information. Many parents of children with PWS may now know more about PWS than the average general practitioner. Thanks to the Internet, they are fully aware of possible complications, treatment options, and of the risk for related syndromes. Not all of this information will necessarily make them feel better. At the same time, however, Babrow et al. (1998) have claimed that some people may actually look for information to increase uncertainty, as it can provide a source of hope, and an escape from the certainty of a bad prognosis.

Also well-documented and closely related to the concept of information-gathering is the role of social support in the management of illness-related uncertainty. Brashers, Neidig and Goldsmith (2004) have stressed how supportive others can help with information-seeking and provide instrumental support (e.g., assistance with transportation and household tasks), help with the development of coping skills, and give validation and acceptance. Numerous studies on the experience of illness have also pointed out the importance of support from people who have been in a similar situation (e.g., Ainbinder et al. 1998; Brashers et al. 2002; Davison, Pennebaker, and Dickerson 2000; Klemm and Hardie 2002).

People confronted with the diagnosis of a relatively rare condition such as PWS may have difficulty finding similar others in their geographical area (see Lasker et al. 2005; Patsos 2001). The tendency to hide the condition from the public eye may also keep PWS parents from meeting similar others. Online support groups provide the exceptional ability to reach and connect people who are dealing with a health condition that is relatively rare (Lasker et al. 2005; Muthaseb and Wright 2005), complex (Patsos 2001), often misunderstood (Davison et al. 2000; Lasker et al.), and possibly experienced as embarrassing, socially stigmatizing or disfiguring (Davison et al.; Galegher et al. 1998; Muthaseb and Wright; Reeves 2000).

Thus, the expectation is that information and social support messages found on the Internet can facilitate coping by providing information that contributes to reaching a desired level of uncertainty, either by reducing, maintaining, or increasing it (see also Ford, Babrow, and Stohl, 1996).

Living With PWS, Living With Uncertainty

The diagnosis and subsequent decisions about the treatment of PWS are expected to be surrounded by uncertainty, not only because of its complexity and unpredictable development, but also because the condition is relatively rare, yet often very visible and experienced as disfiguring, with a potential to provoke severe psycho-social consequences. According to the National Organization of Vascular Anomalies, PWS are venous malformations, also called *naevus flammeus*, that occur in .3% of the US population (2004). They are part of the larger family of vascular birthmarks. PWS are usually present at birth and can vary in size and color, from tiny pale pink spots to dark purple stains covering more than half the body (Syed 1999). An overabundance of dilated blood vessels causes a locally increased blood flow and pooling of blood under the skin. The vast majority of PWS, approximately 83%, appear on the face. PWS generally start off flat and tend to darken, swell, and thicken over time, if left untreated (Vascular Birthmark Foundation). About two-thirds of all PWS are expected to develop complications such as *hypertrophy*, overgrowth of the affected area, varicose veins, cobbling of the skin, and *blebs*, nodules on the skin that bleed easily (Geronemus and Ashinoff 1991), although this generally does not happen until adulthood. PWS is often confused with the more common hemangioma. However, PWS is considered a lifetime condition, whereas hemangiomas are expected to *involute* (i.e. shrink) and disappear, with or without leaving scars, before the end of childhood.

PWS can be indicative of larger, serious congenital disorders such as Sturge-Weber syndrome (SWS) and Klippel-Trenaunay syndrome (KTS). SWS occurs in 8-15% of people with PWS, most often among people with facial PWS. The syndrome involves neurological abnormalities and calcifications in the brain, and is often associated with seizures and glaucoma, and in more rare cases, mental and physical retardation (Geronemus and Ashinoff 1991; Sturge-Weber Foundation). KTS, more rare than SWS, involves asymmetric progressive malformation (enlargement or atrophy) of soft tissue and bones in the affected body parts. Symptoms associated with Klippel-Trenaunay syndrome include blood clotting, pain, bleeding in the affected area, and internal organ involvement. In some cases, amputation is required.

Since the late eighties, the most common treatment of PWS is laser therapy, aimed at lightening the stains and preventing further development of common PWS-related complications. The prediction of the course of development of PWS is surrounded by uncertainty, as no two cases are the same. Most often it is impossible to foretell when, what will happen, which complicates the choice for the moment and type of treatment. Not all PWS respond well to laser treatment, which can be painful and often requires general anesthesia in children (Rozell-Shannon and Marshall 1997). The severity of disfigurement that people face and the overall consequences that living with PWS entails is unpredictable and generally discovered through the passing of time.

The chance of getting adequate treatment may further be complicated by insurance companies considering laser therapy as a purely cosmetic procedure and denying patients coverage (Burton 2003; McClean and Hanke 1997). This point of view not only tends to ignore the potential for medical complications but also disregards the possibility of psychological damage that PWS may cause. On this account, Troilius, Wrangsjö, and Ljunggren (1998) claimed that early treatment of PWS in children can prevent or diminish the severe psychosocial distress. In this maze of potential obstacles, parents of children with PWS may find comfort and benefit in finding similar others.

The PWS Support Groups

One of the easiest Internet sites to gain instant access to live discussions among vascular birthmark community members is the discussion forum of the VBF (*www.birthmark.org).* The VBF, founded in 1995 by its president Linda Rozell-Shannon, is "an international charitable organization that provides support and informational resources for individuals affected by hemangiomas, port wine stains, and other vascular birthmarks and tumors, sponsors relevant research and promotes physician education" (Vascular Birthmarks Foundation). There is no need to sign up to read the messages on the VBF discussion forum. The VBF forum is openly-accessible for everyone with an Internet connection, thus making its content very public. For people affected by PWS, a special message category, Port Wine Stain Help, offers a myriad of threads on various aspects of the condition.

A website often recommended to VBF visitors with questions about PWS is the website Birthmarks.com that was mentioned by Joie Davidow (2003). Birthmarks.com is a nonprofit organization calling itself "the premiere Internet resource site for information about vascular and pigmented birthmarks" (Birthmarks.com). People who subscribe to the Birthmarks.com newsgroup receive list messages per e-mail. Birthmarks. com was founded in 1995 by Michael Steffano, who has a PWS himself, as his "contribution to helping people with a need to gather information about this [PWS] condition and possibly seek treatment" (Birthmarks.

com). At the time of the research, Birthmarks.com counted close to a thousand registered members.

Participation in Online PWS Discussions

Because PWS shares similarities with medical conditions that are also rare, stigmatizing, unpredictable in their course, and for which there is no cure, the communication related to the condition as it takes place in online support groups may offer clues about how such a condition and the uncertainty related to it is experienced by the people whom it affects. Messages on online boards and forums can be considered "naturally occurring conversations" (Beach and Anderson 2003, 1), and as such offer especially attractive opportunities for research because the raw data are not affected by researcher interference. An analysis of the content of these online messages may provide an exceptional opportunity to help pinpoint essential elements in the uncertainty experiences of PWS-managers.

My request for permission to use conversation data from the VBF website was enthusiastically received by founder Linda Rozell-Shannon who welcomed the attention to the vascular birthmark community and its key issues (L. Rozell-Shannon, personal communication, March 19, 2006). She and Birthmarks.com founder Michael Steffano readily approved my proposal to analyze a sample of messages posted in their web groups.[1] Additionally, to ask visitors of the VBF discussion forum and members of the Birthmarks.com newsgroup more directly about their experiences, a plea for participation in an online anonymous, voluntary, self-report survey was posted on both websites. This would enable me to compare what I found through the content analysis with what people report when they are asked directly about their experiences. Also, since online messages tend to be read many more times than they are responded to (Galegher et al. 1998; Nonnecke and Preece 2001), and because registered members have no obligation to actually participate in the communication, this would give these non-posters or so-called *lurkers* an opportunity to anonymously react to their experiences with PWS and the PWS-related websites, and thus provide them with a voice without the need for exposure to the groups.

Expressions of Uncertainty

During the 6-month sampling period a total of 2647 messages were posted to the Birthmarks.com newsgroup and the VBF discussion forum on the topic of PWS. These messages were posted in 360 different threads, of which 300 originated on Birthmarks.com, and 60 on the VBF discussion forum. Thus, 360 so-called thread-starters were examined for elements of uncertainty.[2] Uncertainty expressions were much more frequent and present in the vast majority of the messages on the VBF forum as compared to those sent to the Birthmarks.com board.[3] One of the reasons why this may have been the case is that the VBF site, because of its public nature, is more easily accessible to newcomers who may have a need for a quick response to their uncertainty. Obvious newcomers almost always expressed uncertainty in their messages,[4] while established group members also started non-uncertainty related threads, e.g., to update the community on how a treatment was coming along. Interestingly, the uncertainty that people expressed was most often related to PWS treatment and complications, which may indicate that they have a distinct desire to know more than what they have been told by their doctors. A typical example: "Hi, I am new here and my 3-month old son was officially diagnosed with a PWS yesterday. The doctor insists that laser therapy would not be helpful at this point. Is this true?"

Both websites attracted both parents of children with a PWS and people who have a PWS themselves ("selves"), and neither website distinctly separated parents from selves. Birthmarks.com overall attracted more selves than parents, which may again have to do with the fact that parents who face the uncertainty of a recent diagnosis, often that of a newborn child, may not want to take the time to go through a more laborious registration process such as that of Birthmarks.com before being able to engage in contact. Also, since the messages on the VBF are public and can be read by anyone who surfs to the site, people easily gain an impression of its character without having to register first. In other words, its what-you-see-is-what-you-get factor is higher. No explicit signs were found in the messages that indicated if parents were specifically looking for parents. In fact, in some cases, messages of selves to parents offered important information to prepare parents for what the future may bring for them and their children, and sometimes selves would indicate that they responded to messages to help. As one member stated: "I can help parents prevent that they put their children through what I went through." Unsurprisingly, parents tended to express uncertainty in their thread-opening messages significantly more often than did selves.[5]

It seemed plausible that, after their first posting experience, Birthmarks.com suits selves better as a support group, while the VBF board serves as the preferred community for parents. Among both established and novice community members, there appeared to be a discrepancy in the preference for posting to either website.[6] This may have to do with the fact that the amount of similar others (as in: other parents or other selves) may be higher on either board, and community members are more likely to look for people whose situation matched their own situation most closely. At the same time, selves may be seen as expressing concerns that are somewhat more personal, as they reveal intimate details about themselves rather than a child, and thus find the increased privacy offered by Birthmarks.com to be more attractive for sharing their experiences. In this respect, Birthmarks.com appeared to attract many proactive people who are currently involved in PWS laser treatment, either for themselves of for their child. This may account for the fact that, among presumed return visitors, slightly more than half of the thread starters on Birthmarks.com did not express uncertainty in the message. Many of these messages included updates of treatment, e.g., "Hi Everyone!! I have been busy healing up from the zapping!! I had some scabbing but I am noticing fading, too!! I am so excited!! I could not wish for a better birthday present!!"

Gender Differences

The discussions on both the VBF discussion forum and the Birthmarks.com message board are heavily female-dominated. Most of the time, gender of the author of a message was easy to determine, either by mention of it in the post (e.g., "I am the mother of a 2-year old daughter"), or based on the signing with a first name with an unambiguous gender association (e.g., Michaels were coded as male, Natashas as female).

Interestingly, gender was unknown almost twice as often in the VBF group than in the Birthmarks.com group.[7] This may indicate that when people start a thread on the VBF PWS forum, they feel less compelled than posters on Birthmarks.com to disclose more personal details to about themselves or to personalize their message by, for instance, signing with a first name or informing others about their specific relationship to the child. This may have to do with the fact that, since the VBF forum has no access restrictions, people who chose the VBF forum to ask their question may also make an effort to protect their identity. Especially newcomers who have not yet found a place in the online community, may want to test the waters first or simply want an answer to their question and not be bothered with self-disclosure for the sake of relation-building. In contrast, people who register to join Birthmarks.com are invited and encouraged to post an introductory message to the group with some details about their personal PWS situation and their relation to the PWS community, and the importance of becoming a community member seems to have more emphasis.

In both online PWS web groups more than five times as many women started threads than did men,[8] even though the occurrence of PWS is the same among men and women. By itself, this finding may not come as a surprise, as studies have consistently shown that when it comes to health issues, women seem to be much more active online than are men. For instance, women appear to be more inclined to do health-related web searches than are men, especially when concerned with a specific disease or medical problem (e.g., Cotten and Gupta, 2004; Fox and Fallows, 2003). In a recent study on two online cancer communities, Ginossar (2008) found that females were responsible for 75% of the messages posted within these support groups, a finding that was consistent with other such studies.

In the PWS web groups, gender differences became even more pronounced when selves were compared to parents. Among selves, females still posted much more often than did men. However, the parents in the sample were women 99% of the time. Of the 349 messages that were posted, only one of them was posted by an obvious father,[9] which, makes the group of parents who seek to connect with similar others on either of the PWS-related websites one that almost exclusively consists of mothers. This extremely large discrepancy in the proportion of male and female parents obviously raises many questions. For instance, when it comes to a child's PWS, is its management largely the responsibility of the mother? Are mothers of children with PWS more worried than fathers? Are mothers of children with PWS more available than fathers? Are mothers of a children with PWS more in need of support? Are women in general more interested in finding support online than are men?

When the thread starters were examined for gender differences related to the content of the messages, men's messages fell into the non-uncertainty category significantly more often than did women's. In fact, the majority of men's messages did not express uncertainty, while the majority of women's messages did.[10] These findings are consistent with widely-accepted ideas that men are typically less inclined to ask for help or directions than are women (Sachs 2007), and that men use communication more often as a means to supply information, while women use it predominantly to obtain information and to connect with others (see Tannen 1990). To answer several important questions that remained about the online PWS communities, I conducted an open survey over a two month period.

The PWS Uncertainty Survey

One of the main aspects I hoped the PWS uncertainty survey would reveal was whether visitors of the VBF forum and Birthmarks.com, when asked, would report experiences on their uncertainty and online connection that differed from the findings of the content analysis. Also, I wanted to know what characterized visitors, what they gained from posting and if they ever experienced that their uncertainty became more burdensome to them because of messages on either discussion board.

During the period that my plea for participation in the online survey was up on both websites, 98 people took the survey. The large majority of them linked to the survey through Birthmarks.com, which closely reflected the discrepancy in the amount of thread starters posted to each site in the content analysis sample period.[11] There are several possible explanations that may all somewhat contribute to the impression that among people affected by PWS, those who visit Birthmarks.com seem to be more proactive. Birthmarks.com is almost exclusively devoted to connecting with people with PWS, even though the welcome words on its homepage don't explicitly state this. The VBF does not seem to have a dominant connection to one particular type of birthmark, but it has different forums that are divided by type of birthmark. Its public character may make the community on the VBF forum more ephemeral, with more people popping in and out of the community and the possibility that its visitors' overall sense of community and commitment is perceived less strongly as it is by Birthmarks.com members. This perceived sense of community may also affect people's feelings of responsibility and position in the overall illness population, which may make established community members more inclined to seize an opportunity to contribute to a research effort that may benefit their community.

Half of the survey respondents were parents, and half were selves, thus giving the impression that both populations were roughly equally interested in contributing to my research. As expected, most of the respondents were women,[12] and most of the parents were mothers. Only two of the 98 respondents were fathers. Survey respondents' ethnicity was most often Caucasian, while their level of education was generally at the college level or above.[13] These findings strongly mirror the findings from other studies that have looked at such demographic data, which have repeatedly reported that people who use the Internet for health-related purposes are predominantly female, white, and well-educated (see Cotton and Gupta 2004; Fox and Fallows 2003). The idea that women, more so than men, are interested in using verbal communication to connect with others, and that white people's economic advantage over other ethnicities may make them more likely to both afford and know how to use electronic media, seems a very plausible explanation for this phenomenon.

Similar Others

In line with this assumption, survey respondents most often mentioned access to similar others as the main reason why they had been attracted to either website. The fact that the majority of visitors not only share a relationship to PWS, but that they are also knowledgeable women of similar skin color gives this group even more to bond over, and may thus create somewhat of a self-perpetuating phenomenon. This idea makes it even less surprising that the second most mentioned reason to visit PWS-related websites was to acquire more PWS information. Many respondents valued this information higher than the information they received from their doctors.[14] They were particularly interested in keeping up with new developments, and expressed this by saying, for instance, that they were "always looking for new information," "keeping up with technology," and interested in the "latest laser technology," "accurate, current information," "updated medical information," and "new scientific research." As one mother reinforced: "I just want to make sure that we are doing everything we can."

For almost a quarter of the survey respondents, the PWS web groups on the Internet also formed their most valuable source of support. One person stated: "I have had little or no support, until I discovered Birthmarks.com." While for six of the respondents, the day they took the survey was actually the first day that they had ever visited a PWS-related website, one in five respondents claimed they visited a PWS-related site every day, and most people replied that they visited once or twice a week.

In answer to my question if there had ever been a time that they did not want information, most people indicated that they had consistently wanted to receive information. Only few reported that at some point, they had wanted to stop reading the messages.[15] This question was asked to investigate if at some point information had in fact caused more uncertainty and/or discomfort as opposed to relief (e.g., by phenomena such as *information overload*). I wanted to see if the information ever pushed them to a level where they felt they needed to stop acquiring more information (see Brashers et al. 2000). One mother reported: "I sometimes feel overwhelmed by the information.... From time to time I take a break from the issue." Some claimed to "get tired of reading the same stuff over and over," while others reported that they had experienced periods of "denial."

As one respondent, a self with a PWS, wrote: "As a teenager, I just didn't want to deal with it." This sentiment was also voiced by someone else: "During adolescence I did as if the issue did not exist at all." Another two people indicated that they took a break from information during their early twenties. Some people were actively kept away from information by others. One mother reported about her PWS experience with her baby that "when she was first born and wrongly diagnosed I was scared and told not to read the Internet."

While many people denied that they had ever wanted to *not* receive information, several of them also reported that they had experienced discomfort through information. "There were times when I found what I was reading on the Internet was distressing," wrote one respondent. About half of the respondents reported that the online PWS messages had at times made them feel confused. However, the vast majority claimed that online PWS-related messages had also helped them to feel less uncertain. As one respondent noted: "Sometimes messages are helpful to hear and other times [they] can be a little bit confusing or depressing. You have to learn to weed out the negative and look to the positive." But for many, the importance of staying informed outweighed the disadvantages, as one mother described: "At first it was all overwhelming and I didn't want to hear the sad stories. But now I know that to be well informed is a way to advocate for my child and [in] his best interest."

Parents and Selves

The fact that the PWS online community represents one of the few online health communities that includes both parents of children with a health condition and adults who have the condition themselves makes it a particularly fascinating place to examine parenthood online. In the PWS survey, like in the content analysis, no explicit designations of either parents or selves to keep a separate segment within the online PWS community were found, nor did parents or selves indicate that they had made specific efforts to avoid each other. Only one parent claimed that some community members who had a PWS themselves had "not liked us moms of PWS for a while." It is not unthinkable that this particular parent felt that PWS adults accused today's parents of overreacting in their worries and concerns about the management of their particular PWS situations. This may have to do with the fact that the state of today's care and treatment options for PWS children has much improved over the last two decades.

More often, parents indicated that they were interested in hearing from selves about their life experiences, and welcomed the opportunity to get information that could help them better predict and understand what may await their children. Several selves in the survey found comfort in giving support and information to others, including parents. As one woman indicated, "I've been able to reassure parents that it's not the end of the world." Another wanted to "offer any advise as a 49 year old woman who has dealt with PWS, maybe give encouragement to others who may not have it as easy as I did growing up with PWS." One person explicitly commented to have "shared [his] surgery experience for the benefit of others."

Not everyone looking for similar others seemed to be interested in communicating with them. Some people for whom access to similar others was the most appealing feature of PWS websites had actually never posted messages to them.[16] Several people explicitly mentioned to find fulfillment in "knowing that I am not alone." Other interests in similar others that did not specifically include communicating with others were reading about other people's experiences and looking at pictures of others with PWS. As one mother explained: "My son likes to see pictures of other people with PWS since he doesn't know anyone [else] in real life with one." "It helps me to see other people going thru the same thing," commented another respondent. Others voiced that they were helped by peers through "Opinions and thoughts of other people with PWS or the thoughts of the parents with PWS-affected kids," "Finally in my life feeling like one of the crowd," and "Understanding what we are dealing with . . . how to best help my daughter live with this."

Turning Points

Several respondents, when asked, described having experienced a turning point through reading posts from others in the PWS support groups. "To find the site at all was a *critical incident*" wrote one person, a sentiment that was voiced by several. To gain awareness of the physical complications involved with PWS was an important revelation that many people described, such as when reading about "possible complications that I didn't know about. It was tough, but I am glad I know."

Another important discovery of this study was that some participants described that they considered the medical information communicated through the online support groups as more truthful and realistic compared to what doctors had told them. One person reported to have found out that "we can have a say in our choices for healthcare treatment. We don't have to take one doctor's word for fact, but can do our own research." Another testified: "Pediatrician advised us to wait to start laser treatment. At VBF website learned of importance of early treatment and sought it immediately," while another mother described reading a post that stated "any girl with PWS should not take the contraceptive pill because of the clotting factor, I had been thinking this made sense but my doc didn't. Our new specialist agrees!!!"

For some, this medical information provided new hope, as in this testimony "I looked at pictures of kids who had received laser treatment and I felt relief knowing there was hope for my child." For others, however, it created the exact opposite. One respondent noted that reading posts in the PWS community made her aware of the fact that "it's a probability that PWS will return." For yet another person, participation in the online community resulted in discouragement as well: "My feelings about treatment changed when I learned that maintenance treatments are required to keep the PWS from darkening again. Now I'm not sure if I want to treat it again." In contrast, others experienced a turning point by realizing the relativity of their own PWS situation, as one person noted: "it put things in perspective." This sentiment was also voiced by remarks such as "I realized that there are so many others who have a PWS . . . I am learning to count our blessings, " "Seeing people with far worse PWS then myself, it reminded me how minor my birthmark is," and "knowing that others had birthmarks and were going through the same things has enabled me to walk with my head high.... I actually feel special."

Conclusion

Similar to all people encountering health problems, parents receiving a child's port wine stain (PWS) diagnosis are expected to experience uncertainty as they try to understand how the condition will affect their child's as well as their own lives. Both the examined messages and the survey responses confirmed the idea that uncertainty functions as an important motivator for communication participation. Findings from both the PWS survey and the content analysis confirmed the suspicion that PWS-managers are particularly unsettled by the difficulty they have in their search for coherent medical information. Perceived disenchantment with medical doctors and loss of confidence in doctors' expertise reflected the idea that the PWS community suffers from a flawed supply of qualitatively sound medical information through the regular, traditional vessels such as family doctors and specialists. This involved messages sent by frantic parents not knowing whether they should seek treatment for their newborn baby or not, as well as selves faced with swelling and blistering after laser treatment, worried about scarring and not knowing how to best treat their laser wounds.

Parent posters worried more often about their PWS situation than did selves, who, in turn, were slightly more dominantly present. Obviously, selves in general have had more time to get used to the PWS diagnosis and get to know their individual situation. However, it was clear that parents and selves typically worry most often about the same sort of things: elements of the PWS experience that relate to physical complications and treatment. The online PWS survey made clear that the people who post messages to PWS web groups do not fully represent the whole online PWS community, as more than a third of the survey respondents claimed that they had never actually posted any messages According to Preece, Nonnecke, and Andrews (2004), these so-called *lurkers* are still considered community members (Preece et al.), and in the PWS survey they explicitly expressed that they value their online community experience, and take advantage of the offered information and support.

In her memoir, Davidow described the isolation she experienced in the small town where she grew up. Only once did she see someone with a facial mark similar to hers, and he was "a scary man" (Davidow 2003, 24). Her main drive to search the Internet, decades later, was motivated by a desire to read about others like herself. In my study, relief from isolation was mentioned more often as the main attraction to visit PWS-related websites than relief from uncertainty. This finding corresponds with claims from Galegher et al. (1998) that the exchange of online messages gives rise to group identity and a sense of community. A respondent's "Finally . . . feeling like one of the crowd" may thus be perceived as an independent, valuable aspect of joining an online group, in addition to the available support and information. This is also a feature that people can take advantage of without having to actively participate in the online communication. "Just knowing that you're not alone," as one respondent reported, can be enough.

The communication on the VBF PWS forum was dominated by parents more often than by selves, while the Birthmarks.com group counted more selves than parents. A common scenario seemed to be that a parent with a child who has recently been diagnosed with PWS, does a web search and finds immediate access to messages from similar others on the VBF website. The parent posts a message expressing acute uncertainty about the individual situation. Responses follow, along with a referral to Birthmarks.com or a different PWS-oriented support group. A self may do the same thing, but, when less acutely uncertain, may initially be more interested in lurking for a while. They may have a preference for reading the more intimate posts from people in a private group, which also features photographs of potentially similar others.

Overall, more than five times as many women were present among both posters and survey respondents than were men. Women in the PWS online community are even more overrepresented than those in other researched online communities such as cancer support groups (Ginossar 2008; Wright 2002). An explanation for this finding may be that about half of the survey respondents and thread-starting posters were parents, who were almost all mothers. This raises the suspicion that when online health searches involve the health of children, the discrepancy in presence between males and females may be significantly higher than the general male-female discrepancy as reported by Fox and Fallows (2003). Explanations for this phenomenon may be found in the fact that men, and thus fathers, are thought to be less likely than women and mothers to initiate communication with the purpose to gather information or to connect with people who are in a similar situation.

Not many people will deny the importance of support from friends, family, and similar others in the experience of illness in general, and the experience of PWS in particular, even without the results from this study. The current report has aimed to show that for parents of children with PWS, as an example parents of children with a medical condition that is relatively rare, complex, often misunderstood, often disfiguring and stigmatizing, and having the potential to cause loneliness and isolation, participation in online illness-specific web groups can bring important benefits. Similar others found online can provide informational clarity that doctors are unable to provide, despite the fact that an often heard concern about gathering medical information on the Internet is its lack of obvious reliability (Brann and Anderson 2002). Arguably, many PWS-parents have had no more reason to trust their medical doctors. At the same time, when information is distressing, or when it becomes obvious that the desired information is not available or non-existent, similar others also form a supportive environment in which the unavoidable PWS-related uncertainty is easier to bear. Recognition of the role of support in the light of insufficient, complex, or distressing medical information is key to this idea.

With many thanks to Patricia Geist-Martin, Linda Rozell-Shannon, and Michael Steffano.

Works Cited

Ainbinder, Judith G., Lynn W. Blanchard, George H. S. Singer, Mary Ellen Sullivan, Laurie K. Powers, Janet G. Marquis, Betsy Santelli, and the Consortium to Evaluate Parent to Parent. 1998. A qualitative study of Parent to Parent support for parents of children with special needs. *Journal of Pediatric Psychology* 23(2):99-109.

Babrow, Austin S. 2001. Introduction to the special issue on uncertainty, evaluation, and communication. *Journal of Communication* 51(3):453-455.

Babrow, Austin S., Stephen C. Hines, and Chris R. Kasch. 2000. Managing uncertainty in illness explanation: An application of problematic integration theory. In *Explaining illness: Research, theory, and strategies*, ed. Bryan B. Whaley, 41-67. Hillsdale, NJ: Erlbaum.

Babrow, Austin S., Chris R. Kasch, Leigh A. Ford. 1998. The many meanings of "uncertainty" in illness: Toward a systematic accounting. *Health Communication* 10(1):1-23.

Berger, Charles R., and Richard J. Calabrese. 1975. Some explorations in initial interactions and beyond: Toward a developmental theory of interpersonal communication. *Human Communication Research* 1(2):99-112.

Birthmarks.com. About us – The Birthmarks.com community. http://www.birthmarks.com/Index.cfm?Page=59 (accessed February 16, 2007).

Brann, Maria. and Anderson, James. 2002. E-medicine and health care consumers: Recognizing current problems and possible resolutions for a safer environment. *Health Care Analysis* 10(4):403-415.

Brashers, Dale E., Daena J. Goldsmith and Elaine Hsieh. 2002. Information seeking and avoiding in health contexts. *Human Communication Research* 28(2):258-271.

Brashers, Dale E., Judith L. Neidig, and Daena J. Goldsmith. 2004. Social support and the management of uncertainty for people living with HIV or AIDS. *Health Communication* 16(3):305-331.

Brashers, Dale E., Judith L. Neidig, Stephen M. Haas, Linda K. Dobbs, Linda W. Cardillo, and Jane A. Russell. 2000. Communication in the management of uncertainty: The case of persons living with HIV or AIDS. *Communication Monographs* 67(1):63-84.

Burgoon, Michael, and John R. Hall. 1994. Myths as health belief systems: The language of salves, sorcery, and science. *Health Communication* 6(2):97-115.

Burton, Claude S. 2003. *Answers to commonly asked questions about laser treatment of vascular lesions.* http://dukederm.duke.edu/modules/clinical_services/index.php?id=2 (accessed March 20, 2007)

Calhoun, Roberta D. 1998. Practice guidelines for patients with rare cancers. *Cancer Practice* 6(4):247-250.

Cohen, Marsha H. 1993. The unknown and the unknowable – Managing sustained uncertainty. *Western Journal of Nursing Research* 15(1):77-96.

Cotten, Sheila R., and Sipi R. Gupta. 2004. Characteristics of online and offline health information seekers and factors that discriminate between them. *Social Science & Medicine* 59(9):1795-1806.

Davidow, Joie. 2003. *Marked for life: A memoir.* New York: Harmony.

Davison, Kathryn P., James W. Pennebaker, and Sally S. Dickerson. 2000. Who talks? The social psychology of illness support groups. *American Psychologist* 5(2):205-217.

Dickerson, Suzanne S. Marcia Boehmke, Carolann Ogle, and Jean K. Brown. 2006. Seeking and managing hope: Patients' experiences using the Internet for cancer care. *Oncology Nursing Forum* 33, no. 1 (January). http://www.ons.org/publications/journals/ONF/volume33/issue1/330138.asp (accessed March 6, 2006).

Dutta-Bergman, Mohan J. 2005. Developing a profile of consumer intention to seek out additional information beyond a doctor: The role of communicative and motivation variables. *Health Communication* 17(1):1-16.

Ford, Leigh A., Austin S. Babrow, and Cynthia Stohl. 1996. Social support messages and the management of uncertainty in the experience of breast cancer: An application of problematic integration theory. *Communication Monographs* 63(3):189-207.

Fox, Susannah, and Deborah Fallows. 2003. Internet health resources: Health searches and email have become more commonplace, but there is room for improvement in searches and overall Internet access. http://www.pewInternet.org/report_display.asp?r=95 (accessed May 13, 2006).

Galegher, Jolene, Lee Sproull, and Sara Kiesler. 1998. Legitimacy, authority, and community in electronic support groups. *Written Communication* 15(4):493-530.

Geronemus, Roy G., and Robin Ashinoff. 1991. The medical necessity of evaluation and treatment of port-wine stains. *The Journal of Dermatologic Surgery and Oncology* 17:76-79.

Ginossar, Tamar. 2008. Online participation: A content analysis of differences in utilization of two online cancer communities by men and women, patients, and family members. *Health Communication* 23(1):1-12.

Gudykunst, William B. 1995. The uncertainty reduction and anxiety-uncertainty reduction theories of Berger, Gudykunst, and associates. In *Watershed research traditions in human communication theory*, ed. Donald P. Cushman and Branislav Kovacic, 67-100. Albany, NY: Suny Press.

Klemm, Paula, and Thomas Hardie. 2002. Depression in Internet and face-to-face cancer support groups: A pilot study. *Oncology Nursing Forum* 29, no. 4 (May). http://www.ons.org/publications/journals/ONF/Volume29/Issue4/290445.asp (accessed March 6, 2006).

Lasker, Judith N., Ellen D. Sogolow, and Rebecca R. Sharim. 2005. The role of an online community for people with a rare disease: Content analysis of messages posted on a primary biliary cirrhosis mailinglist. *Journal of Medical Internet Research* 7, no. 1 (March) http://www.jmir.org/2005/1/e10/Article e10. (accessed February 6, 2006).

Macias, Wendy, Liza Stavchansky Lewis, and Tenikka L. Smith. 2005. Health-related message boards/chat rooms on the web: discussion content and implications for pharmaceutical sponsorships. *Journal of Health Communication* 10(3):209-223.

McClean, Kelly, and Hanke, W. C. 1997. The medical necessity for treatment of port wine stains. *Dermatologic Surgery* 23:663-667.

Meredith, Catherine, and Symonds, Paul. 1996. Informational needs of cancer patients in west Scotland: Cross sectional survey of patients' views. *British Medical Journal* 313:724-727.

Mishel, Merle H. 1988. Uncertainty in illness. *Journal of Nursing Research* 20(4):225-232.

—. 1990. Reconceptualization of the uncertainty in illness theory. *Journal of Nursing Scholarship* 22(4):256-262.

—. 1997. Uncertainty in acute illness. *Annual Review of Nursing Research* 15:57-80.

Muthaseb, Ahlam, and Kevin Wright. 2005. Perceptions of support group advantages, types of support, and support providers within online support groups dealing with health-related issues. Paper presented at the annual meeting of the International Communication Association, New York, May 25.

National Organization of Vascular Anomalies. 2004. Hemangioma and vascular malformation information and assistance. http://www.novanews.org. (accessed April 9, 2006).

Patsos, Mary. 2001. The Internet and medicine: Building a community for patients with rare diseases. *Journal of the American Medical Association* 285(6):805.

Preece, Jenny, Blair Nonnecke, and Dorine Andrews. 2004. The top five reasons for lurking: Improving community experiences for everyone. *Computers in Human Behavior* 20(2):201-223.

Reeves, Patricia M. 2000. Coping in cyberspace: The impact of Internet use on the ability of HIV-positive individuals to deal with their illness. *Journal of Health Communication* 5(S1):47-59.

Shannon, Linda R., and Connie Marshall (with Milton Waner). 1997. *Birthmarks: A guide to hemangiomas and vascular malformations*. Minden, NV: Women's Health Publishing.

Sachs, Marilyn A. *Male/female communication styles.* http://ohioline.osu.edu/hyg-fact/5000/5280.html (accessed March 18, 2007).

Sheer, Vivian C, and Rebecca J. Cline. 1995. Testing a model of perceived information adequacy and uncertainty reduction in physician-patient interactions. *Journal of Applied Communication Research* 23(1):44-59.

Sturge-Weber Foundation. Newly diagnosed with SWS. www.sturge-weber.com/newly%20diagnosed.htm (accessed February 10, 2007).

Syed, S. (1999). Vascular birthmarks: Update on presentation and management. *Current Paediatrics* 9:20-26.

Tannen, Deborah. (1990). *You just don't understand.* New York: Ballantine Books.

Troilius, A., B. Wrangsjö, , and B. Ljunggren. 1998. Potential psychological benefits from early treatment of port-wine in children. *British Journal of Dermatology* 139(1):59-65.

Vascular Birthmarks Foundation. Birthmarks. http://www.birthmark.org/node/2 (accessed February 18, 2006).

—. History of the VBF. http://www.birthmark.org/node/18 (accessed February 8, 2006).

Wiering, Elisabeth. 2007. "It's just a birthmark": Communicating uncertainty, support and information in Internet-based port wine stain communities. Master's thesis, San Diego State University, San Diego, CA.

Wright, Kevin. 2002. Social support within an online cancer community: An assessment of emotional support, perceptions of advantages and disadvantages, and motives for using the community from a communication perspective. *Journal of Applied Communication* 30(3):195-209.

Notes

[1] Interestingly, despite their consent, the Institutional Review Board (IRB) of San Diego State University initially declined permission for content analysis because "people who post to such forums do not reasonably expect that their messages will be used for research purposes" (Wiering, 2007). Eventually the IRB gave permission after ensuring that no identifying information would be present in any of the data files.

[2] Messages were coded on expressions of uncertainty related to illness complexity; treatment/complications; finding/discussing a doctor; make-up/looks; insurance/ finances; probability of illness course; integratio/acceptance.

[3] 88% of the VBF messages contained uncertainty expressions, versus 57% on Birthmarks.com, $\chi^2(1, N = 360) = 20.88, p < .01$

[4] 96%, $\chi^2(1, N=360) = 44.16, p < .01$.

[5] Seventy percent of overall parents' thread starters contained uncertainty elements, whereas this was only the case for 60% of the selves, $\chi^2(1, N = 319) = 3.47, p = .04$.

[6] among the presumably more established thread-starting community members, the majority (59%) on Birthmarks.com were selves, while on the VBF PWS forum the majority (54%) were parents, $\chi^2(2, N = 274) = 27.11, p < .01$.

[7] 13% versus 7%, respectively ($\chi^2(2, N = 360) = 6.12, p = .05$)

[8] 84% of thread starters were posted by women ($n = 277$), 16% by men ($n = 55$)

[9] This finding was significant, $\chi^2(2, N = 336) = 50.68, p < .01$.

[10] Fully 56% of messages authored by men did not express uncertainty, versus 38% of those sent by women, $\chi^2(1, N = 332) = 6.46, p = .01$.

[11] 82% of survey respondents and 80% of the thread starters came from Birthmarks.com

[12] 87% of the respondents indicated they were female, while 13% were male.

[13] 91% were white. Fully 72% of respondents had a college degree or higher ($n = 60$).

[14] 63% of the survey respondents indicated that the Internet was their most valuable source of PWS information, versus 16% who mentioned their doctor as the most valuable source

[15] 71% of respondents had never not wanted to receive information, whereas 18% indicated they had periodically turned away from it

[16] 35% of survey respondents reported that they had never posted a message to either web group

CHAPTER NINE

"MOMMIES KNOW BEST!": EXAMINING SOCIAL SUPPORT AND CONSTRUCTIONS OF GENDER ON A PARENTING DISCUSSION BOARD

ELLEN BRADY

For most parents, the experience of parenthood is a positive one. However, the period following the arrival of the new family member is often marked by increased conflict and negativity within family relationships, as evidenced by a decrease in marital satisfaction for some mothers and fathers (Lavee, Sharlin and Katz 1996) and, in about 10-15% of cases, as clinical levels of depression for both women and men (Ballard and Davis 1996; O'Hara and Swain 1996). This has additional consequences for the quality of parenting, and the subsequent well-being of the child. Parenting stress affects the mother's ability to assess infant cues and to appropriately provide care and comfort (Pridham, Egan, Chang and Hansen 1986; Tessier, Piche, Tarabulsy and Muckle, 1992). In addition, higher parental stress during infancy is associated with less positive father-child interactions when the child is 1 year old (Darke and Goldberg 1994), while mothers who report more stress in the parenting role are also more likely to view their infants as difficult to care for (Mulsow et al. 2002). In order to explore the support networks available to parents experiencing stress and conflict in the parenting role, the present study aims to investigate how participants in online discussion groups experience support via the Internet, with a specific focus on the gendered experiences of users.

The Irish parenting website on which this study is based contained articles written by professionals and a classifieds section, along with an active forum, consisting of 68 separate discussion boards. The forum is publicly accessible, though an account is needed to post. The boards covered parenting related issues, like pregnancy, childbirth and childrearing, and specific aspects of parenting, such as raising children with special needs, along with more general boards for discussion of varied issues. The website also contained a new mothers' board, with a section for each of the preceding nine months, so that expectant parents could communicate with others at the same stage of pregnancy, and a 'new babies' board, which had a similar function for the years and months after the birth.

This study used a qualitative approach, where the experiences of the parents using online support was examined. The participants in this research were the users of the parenting discussion boards of an Irish parenting website during a two-week period in late 2007. All active threads during the period were downloaded and analysed. In addition, participants were invited to take part in a further qualitative interview. Two female forum users consented to take part in the final interviews.

Due to time constraints, only the boards that were considered to be primarily related to parenting were included in the analysis. Boards were chosen by their content rather than their topic. For example, a board discussing holidays and travel dealt with child friendly holidays, and was considered to be primarily parenting related, while another board focusing on family relationships discussed relationships with family members other than children, and thus excluded from the analysis.

For the analysis of the forum data, the threads were coded into categories defined by the content of the posts that made up each thread. After all threads were coded, and the frequency of each theme calculated, the forum data and the interview data were reviewed, and several overarching themes were noted.[1]

A total of 89% (n = 676) of the analysed threads were parenting related, discussing topics specifically related to pregnancy, childbirth, or raising a child. Of the 87 threads unrelated to parenting matters, half were located on boards discussing health or nutrition, while the remainder were dispersed across the rest of the boards.

In reviewing the forum data and the transcripts of the two interviews, a number of overarching themes were identified. These were topics that reflected patterns in the data rather than just discrete responses. In particular, many of these themes related to gender and the construction of gender in parenthood, both in the posters' depictions of their day to day lives, and in the interactions on the forum itself. In addition to themes outlining the gender differences present on the forum, themes examining the recognition of the expertise of mothers and the myth of motherhood were also seen to reflect gender roles.

Gender differences

Gender differences were apparent on the website in several ways. Firstly, it was apparently that the forum was predominately accessed by females, with just one of the 68 boards accessible on the forum targeted at fathers. While it is possible that the gender of posters may have been judged incorrectly due to the anonymity provided by the Internet, the assessment of the website as having a majority of female users was based on posters' descriptions of parenthood and the content of their posts. This suggests that while there were a small number of visible male users, it is possible that there may have been an indeterminate number of men accessing the boards, but they were not active members.

Secondly, the difference in parenting styles between males and females was often mentioned across different boards. One forum member advised a poster who was concerned about the lack of involvement from her partner during pregnancy that *"babies don't become real to most men till they actually hold them for the first time,"* adding that she was aware that her view might appear *"very sexist and condescending."* Similarly, a female poster commended a male forum member for being so involved in his children's lives, while adding, *"I hate to congratulate men on being fathers because I believed they should be just as involved as mothers, but… I do admire men who take time for their kids."*

In other incidences, the forum was used to address gender disparities in parenthood. For example, a disproportionate distribution of childcare, particularly soon after birth, was mentioned by posters (*They think just because you are breast feeding that you are solely in charge of the baby*). This was often extended to other areas of life, with one mother complaining that her husband would not help her with the housework because he had to work. Many female posters reported that they felt under appreciated by their partners (*DH [dear husband] doesn't understand how exhausted I am - he thinks he works and I sit here watching TV all day long*), who did not appear to recognise the work encompassed by motherhood (*Just do a quick tot of how much it would cost him if you dropped dead. Childcare, live in cook…Then have a look at what you are worth!*).

Interestingly, fathers were often seen as an inadequate source of support. A forum member, responding to a poster whose partner had left her midway through her pregnancy, said, *"Don't worry about going through pregnancy as most of us with partners don't get that much support anyway,"* while another poster added, *"Honestly male support is over-rated when it comes to having a baby!"* This was not limited to partners; users reported that families frequently failed to be supportive (*I just feel like I got no support in any of this, from family etc*). However, there was a subtle acknowledgment of the superiority of mothers as child-rearers, *"Mommies know best!"* As one mother of a son with autism commented, *"I think I am the one person who really understands my little man – no disrespect to DH [dear husband], I could write a book on him at this stage."*

Finally, gender differences were also common on the forum itself. As highlighted previously, the forum was predominately used by female posters, and much of the discussion focused on motherhood. There were occasions where men were a visible presence on the boards, however, these occasions were often associated with conflict. In particular, threads on the Single Parents board proved controversial. Various references were made to the Mars/Venus divide (*Mars & Venus, so the sparks fly*), along with a *"them and us"* mentality.

In addition, a male poster was seen as violating the supportive norm of the site on one thread, *"a place you could talk and not be judged or attacked,"* when he criticised two female posters for engaging in chatter, saying, *"Jaysus girls, is there not another thread for some chat about this, or do you need two threads to chat with each other and empathise!"* This norm was illustrated on another thread concerning infertility, where two female forum members posted several times during the one day, with one commenting, *"Thanks for being around and chatting today, didn't realise how much I needed it and have enjoyed your responses today. Really appreciate it xxx."* In contrast with the previous male reaction to 'chatter', other female posters praised the interaction, saying, *"It's nice to see you are all chatting,"* thus acknowledging the support that can be received from social interaction.

A male poster attributed the conflict to different approaches to the forum, saying, *"Men also tend to post objectively i.e. detached. Women tend to get involved and empathise. Neither view is wrong, just different,"* while many female posters were more vociferous in their views, commenting, for example, *"Certain posters trawl certain boards and posts waiting for someone to say something derogatory (as they see it, in their minds...) about men - and then they attack."* The same poster described many of the male forum members as *"jumping on the 'up with single dads'/'down with interfering single mothers' bandwagon,"* adding that *"This is what so many men do, in real life, attack rather than look at themselves for a change. It's quite ironic really that they imitate real life on these boards."*

One interviewee commented that she didn't see many men on the website, *"Maybe one or two."* The forum seems to be an almost exclusively female domain, where the work done by women throughout childbirth and rearing is acknowledged, *"Us Mums should be cherished for the wonderful jobs we are doing."* Men who did not recognise the importance of the work undertaken, such as those who left their partners during pregnancy, were pitied, as seen in the following quote; *"He knows not what he does... I can see...a future for him that is sad, while I have a beautiful baby."*

It could be considered that the intensely female nature of the forum, despite its description as a parenting website rather than a mothering website, appears to have led to the exclusion of male posters, as evidenced by the conflict on boards relevant to the two genders, such as a board for single parents. As outlined, men were often seen as violating the supportive norm of the site. While there have been suggestions that men are reluctant to use online support groups (Lieberman 2008; Wood and Wood 2009), Seale, Ziebland and Charteris-Black (2006) reported that roughly equal numbers of male and female cancer sufferers had accessed an online support group or forum in relation to their illness, indicating that males are not unwilling to use Internet forums. While men were more likely to seek information and women to seek social support, males were still willing to discuss intimate and personal details of their illness. This may be an attempt to develop a frame of reference, which Drentea and Moren-Cross (2005) described as a type of instrumental support.

Looking specifically at fathers, Shaw and Gant (2002) have suggested that online systems could be used to counter the dearth of information aimed at fathers, as males make more frequent use of the Internet and use it for seeking information more often than females. However, little research has been conducted into the use of online supports by fathers. Despite this, there is evidence that specific father directed online support may be a solution to some of the problems experienced by modern fathers. Erera and Baum (2009) analysed postings in a chat room for divorced fathers, and found that the site enabled an outpouring of emotion from participants, which allowed their voices to be heard, both online and in the context of the research, while Fletcher et al. (2007) found that fathers evaluated tailored parenting information delivered via the Internet in a positive manner, and felt that it would have an effect on their parenting. This suggests that fathers may be willing to use the Internet as a social support network, and that it may offer benefits similar to those experienced by the female users of an Irish parenting website, as described in this study.

Recognition of Parents' Expertise

Another important overarching theme that reflected gender was related to the role of the site in recognising parents' own expertise and knowledge. Many posters felt that medical decisions relating to pregnancy were based on more on the needs of the hospital or doctor, rather than the parents; one forum member commented, *"I hate to say this but sometimes I feel that certain programmes are pushed because they are of benefit to the consultants and the hospital rather than the individual."*

It was also noted that information was provided on the forum that had not been mentioned by medical professionals (*After reading some of your posts I wanted to start on [name of drug] as soon as I could, they have never mentioned it, found out about it here*). As a result, forum members wanted to hear from other parents to get a more realistic perspective. One mother commented, *"This is why I come to this discussion board, get help from other parents stuck in the same situation. I have enough lofty theories in the books on the shelf."* Questions were also asked on the board that posters felt uncomfortable asking their doctors (*I'd like to know in 'real' people talk and not a male doctor talk*).

However, the importance of the medical profession was not completely dismissed. In one example on the site, a mother posted about her daughter's health problem, and asked the forum for advice on whether or not to bring her to a doctor saying, *"I have made an appointment with [the] doctor for tomorrow, but it means she will miss Montessori (which she loves) and also 65 euro if there's nothing wrong. Girls, if it was one of you, would you bring her tomorrow or wait and see?"* Posters unanimously urged her to bring her daughter to the doctor, and offered advice for relieving her symptoms. One interviewee commented that she found very little misinformation on Internet forums, despite the predictions of doctors.

However, in many ways, medical expertise was contrasted with the expertise of mothers. This occurred most often during the period of pregnancy. In one case, a mother worried about the consistency of care from her doctor during pregnancy was advised, *"You should have a fantastic birth experience BECAUSE of your caregiver, but sometimes, you need to find a way to have a fantastic birth experience DESPITE your caregivers."* While it was acknowledged, *"when a medical situation does arise...unfortunately you have to trust the doc/midwife,"* the mother was viewed as the one who, ultimately, should be in control of the birth process, *"It's your body, baby and choice."*

By recognising and confirming the expertise of parents, the forum members may be consolidating themselves against the medical establishment. However this recognition of mothers' expertise can serve to reaffirm gender inequality and enhance the imbalances in the division of childcare. O'Connor and Madge (2004) reported that the interactions in cyberspace were broadly replicating traditional gender expectations, roles, and stereotypes, with the implicit view of childcare as a predominately female role. Gender inequalities risk being sustained via the Internet, but also may become exaggerated, as the signals of gender are more limited and thus more likely to be simplified (Malina and Nutt 2000).

This suggests that, rather than parenting forums providing empowerment for mothers, they may further relegate them to their societal position as primary care giver. Considering the role of fathers on the forum, it could also be considered that the prevalence of female posters on the boards and the conflicts associated with male users not only confines the mother in the role of main carer but also excludes the father from participating in the carer role, or its associated duties.

The Myth of Motherhood

A final related theme with a gendered dimension involved attempts to dispel the 'myth of motherhood', by highlighting the positive and negative aspects of parenting. Though there was recognition of the overwhelmingly upbeat experience of parenthood, for example, *"This baby will change your life, make you a stronger person, and bring you the most happiness you will ever experience,"* less positive aspects were also discussed. One forum member confessed how she found adjusting to the *"new role"* of motherhood *"exceptionally difficult,"* while another poster reassured a member who was having difficulty breastfeeding that;

> Motherhood is not the romantic, all happy, coochy coo experience that some people might think it is or lead you to believe. Don't get me wrong, it's fantastic and I wouldn't change it for the world and I love my two kiddies, but by God it's hard sometimes and it can feel that there is no end to it.

Mothers using the site often expressed feelings of anxiety and despair about their parenting skills, both seriously (*I feel like such a crap mammy that let this happen to my poor baby*) and tongue-in-cheek (*"My name is [forum username], and I'm a bad mother!"*). The role of the website in allowing this vent was noted by forum members, as one user added, *"Thank you all so much for allowing me to have a space to rant and moan. Truly a lifesaver,"* and posters were assured that they were not alone in their feelings of hopelessness (*I quite often feel like a crap mammy too and other posters have their moments as well but just sit it out and it will pass*).

A key issue discussed in relation to this myth of motherhood was the awareness of the lack of rules for parenthood. One single mother commented, "*If anyone who has any experience with this let me know, this 90% 10% parental responsibility split doesn't come with a handbook!*" while a mother expecting twins added, "*Motherhood's such a steep learning curve!*" This feeling was not limited to traditional parenting, with feelings of doubt and uncertainty present in threads on adoption (*It was the hardest decision we ever made…We have no way of knowing what is right or wrong*) and infertility (*We all have to go through things in our own way and cope as best we can*).

By attempting to dispel the myths associated with motherhood, the forum members strengthen the sense of community on the website. Removing the secrecy surrounding parenthood creates a safe environment of self-disclosure and reciprocity, from which participants can receive support from peers and form judgements about appropriate parenting practices. O'Connor and Madge (2004) described how virtual social support and the 'shared experience' it provided was vital in the transition of identity to motherhood, offering an additional source of advice and information, which increases mothers' sense of empowerment during a challenging time. Parenting sites also supply a captive audience with shared, narrowly defined interests, replicating the post birth situation described by Oakley (1979), in which ' everyone is in the same boat' (p. 130).

Recommendations

In addition to the general implications for Internet-based support, a number of issues were interpreted as potential suggestions for future research or consideration. Notably, the effect of gender segregation on parenting web sites needs to be studied. To ensure that both the genders benefit from online parenting support, it may be necessary to create separate forums for males and females. The conflict on the website even with the presence of a board targeted specifically at fathers indicates that the layout of the discussion board is not currently fulfilling that necessity. Though the current layout of the forum appears to be imperfect, due to the levels of conflict, it may be that creating a separate space for males as parents may further enhance the perception of women as the primary care givers, thus confirming the gender inequality that many posters cited as a source of stress and exhaustion. In addition, it should be noted that the fathers' board was not included in the analysis of the forum data, as the content was not primarily parenting related, suggesting that fathers may be less willing to discuss parenting than mothers.

Overall, this study indicated that participants in online parenting discussion boards viewed them as a safe, supportive environment, in which the expertise of parents as caregivers was recognised, providing empowerment against the medical establishment. Posts that violated the supportive norm of the site were heavily criticised. The results suggest that parenting websites could provide a viable solution to the decreasing social networks created by modern society and help establish supportive communities that extend into offline life. In addition, the construction of gendered parenthood within parenting forums, and the possible implications for offline parenting practices should be considered.

Works Cited

Ballard, Clive and R. Davis. 1996. Postnatal depression in fathers. *International Review of Psychiatry* 8: 65-71.

Braun, Virginia and Victoria Clarke. 2006. Using thematic analysis in psychology. *Qualitative Research in Psychology* 3(2): 77 – 101.

Clarke, Valerie, Barbara Hanna, Colleen Rolls, A. Grant, Elizabeth Bethune, R. Horne and M. Ching. 1995. *Evaluation of group sessions for first-time mothers provided by the Victorian Maternal and Child Health Service*. Geelong: Deakin University.

Darke, Peter R. and Susan Goldberg. 1994. Father – infant interaction and parent stress with healthy and medically compromised infants. *Infant Behaviour and Development* 17: 3 – 14.

Drentea, Patricia and Jennifer L. Moren-Cross. 2005. "Social capital and social support on the web: the case of an internet mother site." *Sociology of Health & Illness* 27(7):920 – 943.

Erera, Pauline Irit and Nehami Baum. 2009. Chat room voices of divorced non-resident fathers. *Journal of Sociology and Social Welfare* 36: 63-83.

Fletcher, Richard, Graham Vimpani, G. Russell and Diana Keatinge. 2007. The evaluation of tailored and web-based information for new fathers. *Child: Care, Health and Development* 34: 439 – 446.

Guerin, Suzanne and Eilis Hennessy. 2002. Pupils' definitions of bullying. *European Journal of Psychology of Education* 17(3): 249 – 262.

Lavee, Yoav, Shlomo Sharlin and Ruth Katz. 1996. The effect of parenting stress on marital quality: An integrated mother-father model. *Journal of Family Issues* 17: 114 - 135.

Lieberman, Morton A. 2008. Gender and online cancer support groups: Issues facing male cancer patients. *Journal of Cancer Education* 23: 167-171.

Malina, Danusia and Diane Nutt. 2000. Grey literature is a feminist issue: Women's knowledge and the net. *International Journal on Grey Literature* 1: 18 – 27.

Moran, Caroline Farbman, Victoria Holt and Diane Martin. 1997. What do women want to know after childbirth? *Birth* 24:27 – 34.

Mulsow, Miriam, Yvonne M. Caldera, Marta Pursley, Alan Reifman and Aletha C. Huston. 2002. Multilevel factors influencing maternal stress during the first three years. *Journal of Marriage and Family* 64(4): 944 – 956.

Oakley, Ann. 1979. *Becoming a mother.* Oxford: Martin Robertson.

O'Connor, Henrietta and Clare Madge. 2004. "My mum's thirty years out of date:" The role of the Internet in the transition to motherhood. *Community, Work, and Family* 7(3):351 – 369.

O'Hara, Michael & Annettee Swain. 1996. Rates and risk of postpartum depression: A meta-analysis. *International Review of Psychiatry* 8: 37 – 54.

Pridham, Karen F., Kathleen Batato Egan, Audrey S. Chang and Marc F. Hansen. 1986. Life with a new baby: Stressors, supports, and maternal experience. *Public Health Nursing* 3(4): 225 – 239.

Seale, Clive, Sue Ziebland and Jonathan Charteris-Black. 2006. Gender, cancer experience and Internet use: A comparative keyword analysis of interviews and online cancer support groups. *Social Science and Medicine* 62: 2577 – 2590.

Shaw, Lindsay H. and Larry M. 2002. In defence of the internet: The relationship between internet communication and depression, loneliness, self esteem, and perceived social support. *CyberPsychology and Behavior* 5(2): 157 – 171.

Tessier, Rejean, Christiane Piche, George M. Tarabulsy and Gina Muckle. 1992. Mothers' experiences of stress following the birth of a first child: Identification of stressors and coping resources. *Journal of Applied Social Psychology* 22(17): 1319 – 1339.

Wood, Richard T.A and Sabrina Wood. 2010. An evaluation of two UK online support forums designed to help people with gambling issues. *Journal of Gambling Issues* 23: 5 – 30.

Notes

[1] Initially, the owner of the site was contacted, in order to request permission for the participation of the website in the research. Once this was granted, all threads active on the discussion boards during the two-week period were collected. Forums users were then invited to take part in the further aspect of the study, the semi-structured interview, through a message posted on the two most active discussion boards on the website, both of which dealt with general discussions.

Readers were informed that the interviews would be conducted either online, using instant messaging, or by telephone, at their convenience. Potential participants responded to the message through email or the private message function on the website, and were emailed an information sheet with further details on the study. The two participants gave an emailed statement of consent to indicate that they agreed to take part in the interview process.

The two interviews were conducted by instant messaging and telephone, and involved questions about participants' use of the parenting website, and their experience of using the site and its discussion boards. They were also asked about suggestions they would make to the website and what they liked/disliked about it, in order to cover both positive and negative aspects of discussion boards.

For the analysis of the forum data, the threads were coded into categories defined by the content of the posts that made up each thread. The forum threads were examined to determine recurring themes, and sentences and paragraphs were coded into these themes (Guerin and Hennessey 2002). Once a large sample of the data had been coded, a consistency test was carried out, where two researchers identified and compared themes in a section of the text. Based on the discrepancies between these analyses, a more objective list of themes was developed, with various themes combined and some eliminated from the analysis.

The revised list was then applied to the forum data, and a further test of consistency was carried out. After all threads were coded, and the frequency of each theme calculated, the forum data and the interview data were reviewed using thematic analysis (Braun and Clarke 2006), and several overarching themes were noted.

For ethical reasons, any potential identifying information was removed from the interview transcripts. The usernames and actual names of participants were changed if it was necessary to refer them, and any personal information was removed from quotes used to illustrate themes. Similarly, the website was not referred to by name.

CHAPTER TEN

THE OTHER SIDE OF THE (GENDER) COIN: STAY-AT-HOME FATHERS' USE OF ONLINE DISCUSSION GROUPS

CURT LIVESAY

Estimates of the actual number of stay-at-home fathers (hereafter, "SAHFs") in this country range from less than 100,000, to somewhere around 300,000, to over 2 million (Dunham, 2003; Jayson, 2005; "Mr. mom nation reaches new peak," 2005; Nakamura, 1999; Tucker, 2005). According to Zimmerman's (2000) figures, SAHFs may comprise up to a full one-third of all stay-at-home parents. While sources tend to disagree about the exact number of stay-at-home fathers in this country, one thing that they do seem to agree on is the fact that SAHFs are a quickly growing demographic. Concurrently, the United States has seen a tremendous increase in the number of homes with computers and internet access. According to recent (2009) census data, approximately 18% of Americans had internet access in their homes in 1997. That number has increased exponentially, however, as 68-75% of Americans reported using the internet in their home in late 2009. In the following pages I examine the intersection of these two culturally important social phenomena—SAHFs' use of an online discussion forum.

I begin this chapter with a review of current literature on SAHF research. Next, I briefly discuss the results of a study that I conducted on SAHFs' use of an internet discussion forum. Finally, I attempt to situate these findings in light of the "bigger picture" of this book through a discussion of the nature of online communication. Ultimately, I argue that SAHFs' online communication offers scholars another metaphorical window through which to view the gendered struggles faced by both men and women and that computer mediated communication (CMC) is an outlet that both men and women may use to mitigate the negative effects associated with such a struggle.

Past research suggests that one of the major frustrations experienced and expressed by stay at home parents is the overwhelming feeling of isolation and loneliness (Doucet, 2006; Zimmerman, 2000), and Zimmerman (2000) argues that these feelings may actually be stronger in SAHFs than they are for stay at home mothers (SAHMs). While the purpose of this paper is not to compare the experiences of men and women in terms of which sex has it "worse," it is imperative to recognize that hegemonic masculinity (Connell, 2000) does not equip men to function in a traditionally feminized realm. As such, while SAHFs do not necessarily have it "worse" than their female counterparts the ways in which they experience many facets of stay at home parenting are certainly *different.*

Men who stay at home to raise children instead of fulfilling the traditional role of the "breadwinner" (Zuo, 2004) routinely struggle to find legitimation of their roles and identities on both interpersonal and institutional levels. They often face criticism from friends, family, strangers, and former co-workers and colleagues (Baylies and Toonkel, 2004; Carey, 2000; Drevitch, 2007; Elias, 2007; Marshall, 1998; Medina, 2004; Morris, Munoz, and Neering, 2002; Nakamura, 1999). They also endure ridicule, suspicion, and cynicism from employers and the legal system (Dunham, 2003; Gardner, 2003; Lawlor, 2004; Morris, Munoz, and Neering, 2002). Perhaps most important is the internal battle that these men face when they try to make sense of conflicting social discourses of what it means to be a "good father" (Lupton and Barclay, 1997) As a result of these struggles, many SAHFs turn to online discussion groups for companionship and to both seek and give support to one another. In the following section I will discuss a study that I conducted to learn more about these men and their use of online discussion forums.

Before examining the results of my study, it is important to understand the theoretical framework employed in order to help make sense of the findings. Doucet (2006) noted that "Fathers grappling with how to be 'a good man' while also recognizing the 'softening' that occurs while intimately involved in caregiving suggests the need to move beyond current theorizations on masculinities" (p. 237). Because past research suggests that contemporary images and portrayals of fatherhood are filled with contradiction (Marsigligo, Hutchinson, and Cohan, 2000) and that fathers' identities are constantly in flux and are "part of a reciprocal process negotiated by men, children, mothers, and other interested parties," (Marsiglio, Amato, Day, and Lamb, 2000, 1178) I chose to examine the online discourse between the SAHFs[1] through the lens of Relational Dialectics Theory (RDT) (Baxter and Montgomery, 1996). More specifically, I set out to answer the following research question:

RQ1:What dialectical tensions, if any, animate the discussions of the men in an online discussion group for stay –at-home fathers?

Baxter (2011) explains that RDT is a theory of meaning-making, and that "discourses are systems of meaning" (p. 55). RDT scholars focus on the interplay or the struggle between at least two, seemingly incompatible, competing social discourses. For example, in Baxter's early works, she discusses how many individuals who are in romantic relationships have competing desires as they relate to their romantic partner. On the one hand, is the social discourse of relational Connection. Many, if not all, individuals want to be connected to and associated with their partner. However, on the other hand is the competing discourse of Individuality or Autonomy. That is, they also want to have their own "space" and still maintain an identity as an individual person rather than just being seen as one half of a couple.

Baxter's more recent work (2011) has reframed RDT and has shifted the focus from the aforementioned individual desires to the interplay of the discourses themselves. Thus the dialectical struggles that are observed in any given interaction are no longer to be viewed at the level of competing individual desires but are better understood as a struggle between circulating discourses on the societal level. In other words, scholars who use the most recent iteration of the Relational Dialectics framework desire to understand the social discourses that individuals employ in their everyday interactions.

Results

The results of my study are consistent with past research that suggests that SAHFs struggle to make sense of their identities as fathers and most especially as men who are performing traditionally feminine labor (Baylies and Toonkel, 2004; Doucet 2004; 2006). In accord with RDT I analyzed this struggle between SAHFs as a dialectic that I labeled "Traditionally Masculine" masculinity – "Traditionally Feminine" masculinity. These SAHFs invoked discourses of a "Masculine" masculinity while acknowledging that their work was that of a more "Feminine" masculinity. These discourses were manifest in several ways, but for the purposes of this chapter I will focus on the overt and outright discussions of SAHFs' gendered identities.

Gendered Identity

The most obvious way that these men discussed their internal turmoil over this situation was through outright or explicit statements about their gendered identities. This was evident in the fathers' expressions of trying to do "what's best" for their children in terms of fulfilling the traditionally masculine role of financial provider while simultaneously struggling to fill the traditionally feminine role of taking care of the children at home.

Many men wrestled with how to live up to the social expectations for men by providing for their families financially, while also desiring to be at home with their children to "provide" for them in a more traditionally feminine way. One SAHF who was debating whether or not to go back to work when his wife's job forced the family to relocate stated, "We can make it fine on her income, so I am not real sure that I want to go back to that world. I have really enjoyed being with my son." This man's statement expresses an internal struggle with the idea of going back to work (i.e., "traditionally masculine" masculinity) versus staying at home to continue caring for his son (i.e., a new conception of masculinity that is more traditionally feminine).

Other fathers expressed similar sentiment. In a different thread a SAHF summed this up very well: "We have pressure to do the 'manly chores' and also the other chores as well. This creates a different pressure. The same pressure that says men shouldn't do 'womanly' chores." In response, another man claims, "I have to agree... The pressure at times can be enormous, social or otherwise, for any SAHF to find a job. Only now is society realizing fathers, as well as mothers, can be good homemakers." Another man said, "There is a lot of pressure (social norms) for SAHFs to work on the side, and most either work part time or are looking for work." Still another man stated, "Not being the bread winner is often a knock for our self esteem, and I think this is reflected by the number of fathers who are working part time or get back to work as soon as the children are in school."

In short, many SAHFs face a constant battle in the formation of their identities as "real men" who are also primary caregivers. Because the ultimate goal of being a "good father" is to do "what's best for the children" these men perpetually wrestle with performing the traditionally masculine role and performing the role of the "New Father," which is far more traditionally feminine (i.e., fathers as primary caregivers) (Edley and Wetherall, 1999) While the SAHFs wrestled with their gendered identity in other, more latent ways as well, I turn now to the medium in which they expressed this identity struggle, which really is the crux of this chapter.

The Nature of Online Communication

Thus far, this chapter has focused on the meaning-making process of the online communication between SAHFs. As such, at this point the reader may be starting to wonder what all of this has to do with a book called *Motherhood Online.* I believe that the answer to that question is twofold. First of all, despite what some pop psychologists have led our society to (mistakenly) believe, men and women are not really from different planets. There are differences to be sure, and sometimes it may *feel* like men and women are from different planets, but the simple reality is that men and women are far more similar than they are different. In fact, perhaps the most accurate description I have heard regarding differences between men and women comes from psychologist, Janet Hyde, when she quips, "Men are from North Dakota, women are from South Dakota."

How then does this similarity address the original question of how SAHFs fit into an anthology about motherhood and life online? The answer lies in the second half of this equation—*online*. When I conducted this study I did not set out to do a comparison of the lived experiences of SAHFs and SAHMs; I simply desired to learn more about these men and how they interacted online. As such, I didn't even collect data from SAHMs. However, past research on the nature of computer mediated communication (CMC) itself (e.g., an online discussion forum), coupled with what we know about the similarities between men and women suggests that perhaps even if I did have comparative data, it might not be that different.[2] I say this because in addition to the gender similarities, the medium of communication also influences the nature of interpersonal interaction. I will now turn my attention to what it is about online communication that is just so unique.

The Use of Computer Mediated Communication (CMC)

Computer mediated communication is an interesting and unique medium in which communication takes place between individuals and groups. Computer mediated communication provides individuals who use this method of communication greater anonymity than they would experience in face to face interaction. Consequently, both intuition and past research suggest that this may also lead to individuals feeling that CMC is a more "safe" medium in which they may express themselves more freely without fear of judgment or repercussion.[3]

The specific type of CMC that I looked at in my study was the online discussion group or "online community."[4] Matzat and de Vos (2000) define online communities as, "a group of users of a web-site who interact with each other by using the computer-mediated communication tools of this site. Interaction is centered on at least one topic that reflects the common interest(s) of the site users" (p. 45). These online discussion groups may exist for a number of reasons; however, the two most common types of discussion groups are social support networks and companionship networks.

According to the At-Home Dad Network's main page, the stated purpose of the discussion group is to serve as, "A forum for at-home fathers who want to discuss any activity to help connect at-home fathers. We are also here to discuss any issues concerning at-home fathers." Right off the bat one can see how the group blurs the lines between a "companionship network" and "a social support group." More specifically, the SAHFs in my study seemed to participate in this online community both for social connection as well as to give and receive support from one another, and it was almost impossible to place any single conversation into only one of those two boxes. At this point I would encourage the reader to also see Eileen Brady's chapter in this volume about Irish parents' use of a discussion forum for social support as an interesting point of comparison.

As discussed above, two of the primary frustrations that many SAHFs face are feelings of isolation and loneliness, frequently due to a lack of contact with other adults. While it is no secret that face-to-face interaction and CMC are fundamentally different in some ways, many SAHFs turn to online communication in order to supplement their general need for contact with other adults. Some of the conversations on this forum were simply chatting about how to best prepare a house for a new baby (i.e., "child-proofing" the house), which household products worked best and which ones to avoid, children getting braces, and how to deal with rude or offensive remarks about being a SAHF. Other discussions, however, really began to blur the line between simply interacting with other adults, and giving and receiving social support. One man mentioned this while giving advice to members who claimed to be "new" SAHFs looking for any information that they could find on the issue:

> Stay connected to this online chatter at at-home father network and begin looking into a local fathers playgroup with other stay-at-home fathers or fathers as primary caregivers in your area… Staying connected with others in your professional child rearing responsibilities on the 24/7 schedule will be an encouragement to you personally, whether you maintain contact online through this discussion group or in person at a local exchange on a regular basis (or both).

Postings like this were common throughout the forum, usually in the context of giving advice to a new member of the SAHF community. However, most of the time these responses were embedded in the context of a bigger posting on general advice for the new SAHF. There was one exception to this, however, as there was actually one entire thread devoted specifically to the topic of staying connected with other adults. The initial post (listed below) drew several similar responses (listed thereafter):

> I am a new stay at home father… My daughter is 7months old, obvously (sic) not talking yet, and with my wife at work I need some matured conversation for a few hours, any ideas?

> I too felt the need for more adult conversations sometimes I would find myself talking 'kid speak' ...very uncool (sic). when I did get to gether (sic) in an adult setting I would feel embarassed (sic) to hold conversations. I finallt (sic) started networking online and offline with other saty (sic) at home parents...huge difference...I feel like a normal persona agin (sic).

> I have not been able to maintani (sic) the "OLD contacts." They just don't feel like we have anything in common. That is part of the problem with the isolation that comes with being an at home father.

It should be clear by now that many of the postings regarding a need for social interaction can also be interpreted as social support in that these men were giving and receiving advice as well as just simply chatting with one another. Thus, my findings are consistent with VanLear, Sheehan, Withers, and Walker (2005) who argue that the distinction between "social support networks" and "companionship networks" may be somewhat misleading because "companionship networks often provide some of the most important forms of social support" (p. 7).

In short, it seems that this discussion forum acts as a sort of hub where these men can go to vent their daily frustrations, see how others have handled similar situations, and quite frankly, just chat with other men. Even though women would *very* occasionally post in these forums, I emphasize that these SAHFs were talking to other *men* because so much of their conversation featured a dialectical struggle to make sense of the identities *as men*, given that they were doing traditionally feminine work.

Given the nature of computer mediated communication and the types of things that these men talked about, I believe that my previous assertion about more similarities than differences between men and women in this situation seems reasonable. Stay-at-home mothers, just like SAHFs, surely experience the need and desire for more interaction and socialization with other adults. I would be willing to wager that in an online discussion group for SAHMs, they, too, would likely discuss things like best practices, dealing with everyday life issues, and they would also likely give and receive support—such is the nature of the online discussion group.

Participation in an online discussion group or community offers men and women alike many potential benefits. Wright (2000) argues that some of the advantages of participation in online communities include "lack of status, appearance, and social position cues... [along with] greater anonymity among interactants" (p. 102). Matzat and de Vos (2000) identified five major benefits of membership in a community: a) a sense of belonging, b) feelings of usefulness and being valued by other members of the group, c) feelings of mutual understanding, d) feelings of mutual trust, and e) feelings of fair or equal distribution of resources. Another important aspect of online communication that is particularly relevant to stay-at-home parents (both moms and dads alike) is that it is allows those who work from home to have more social contact with the outside world (Matzat and de Vos, 2000; Whittle, 1997) In short, it appears that CMC creates a more "level playing field" which allows interactants (be they male or female) to come together as anonymous equals to share with one another, both for fun and for social support.

Limitations

While I have argued for gender similarities my argument is admittedly based on theory and not on actual data. The nature of CMC does seem to suggest that men and women would surely experience similar things in a "virtual" world such as an online discussion group, but it is certainly possible that there are exceptions. Furthermore, we must not forget that even though the "traditional" gender roles as we know them are not that old in the grand scheme of human history, for the last 250 years or so women have been the primary caregivers of the children. As such, there are several generations of societal expectations, pressures, and norms that women have had to deal with that men have not. Thus, in some ways, the SAHFs are simply experiencing what women have had to deal with all along while in other ways, they are facing something entirely new by breaking the traditional norms.

Conclusion

These findings may have important implications for SAHFs, families with SAHFs, and for family communication scholars and counselors. First, the results of my study are certainly consistent with the findings of past research (Doucet, 2004; 2006), thus contributing to a growing body of research that may have very practical applicability for family counselors. An important contribution of this study, however, was the unique methodology. Unlike interviews with a researcher, my study examines the communication between SAHFs in a more naturalistic setting (i.e., CMC) in which the SAHFs are likely to feel "safer" and less likely to "edit" their comments for the many reasons discussed above.

Second, this study highlights the importance of the process of negotiation and communication in any marital relationship, but most especially in one where traditionally gendered normative behaviors are violated and/or reversed. Fortunately, the literature reviewed here suggests that the nature of certain online communities is one that can be quite supportive and may provide a very practical and accessible way for individuals (both men and women) to communicate with other individuals in similar situations. Hopefully, scholars will use this research as an impetus to gain a better understanding of this gender reversed family configuration so that family counselors will be better prepared to offer guidance on how to constructively deal with and manage these tensions. Encouraging individuals to actively participate in an online discussion forum may have potentially positive implications for clinical applications, though that possibility requires further and more extensive research before implementation.

Marsiglio et al. (2000) claim that "understanding how fathering roles are defined, negotiated, and expressed in diverse contexts and transitional periods [is becoming] increasingly important" (p. 1186) and the results of this study seem to offer credence to that assertion. The same could obviously be said for mothering. While my study focused on the online communication of SAHFs I believe that it also offers a window to the bigger picture of gendered socialization as well. If men who are performing a traditionally gendered role struggle to make sense of their identities as men and as fathers it is highly probably that working or career mothers surely experience similar frustrations. Additionally, past research has already documented the similarities in the feelings of isolation and loneliness experienced by stay at home parents, regardless of their sex. As such, future research would do well to examine the uses of computer mediated communication among these groups as well.

Works Cited

(2005, August). "Mr. mom nation reaches new peak." *USA Today, 134*, 12. Accessed October 1, 2007 from Academic Search Elite database.

Baxter, Leslie A. (2011). *Voicing relationships*. Thousand Oaks, CA: Sage.

Baxter, Leslie A. and Barbara M. Montgomery. (1996). *Relating: Dialogues and dialectics.* New York: Guilford.

Baylies, Peter and Jessica Toonkel. (2004). *The stay-at-home dad handbook.* Chicago: Chicago Review Press.

Bragadóttir's, Helga. (2008). "Computer-mediated support group intervention for parents." *Journal of Nursing Scholarship,* 40:32-38.

Braun, Virginia and Victoria Clarke. (2006). "Using thematic analysis in psychology." *Qualitative Research in Psychology,* 3:77-101.

Carey, Benedict. (2000, March). "The secret life of a stay-at-home dad." *Redbook,* 194:104-108.

Connell, R.W. (2000). *The men and the boys.* Berkeley: University of California Press.

Doucet, Andrea. (2004). "'It's almost like I have a job, but I don't get paid': Fathers at home reconfiguring work, care, and masculinity." *Fathering,* 2:277–303.

Doucet, Andrea. (2006). *Do men mother?* Toronto: University of Toronto Press.

Drevitch, Gary. (2007). "The new dad." *Working Mother,* 30:130-136.

Dunham, Kemba J. (2003, August 26). "Stay-at-home dads fight stigma: Men who parented full time say they get third degree at job interviews; 'Just weird.'" *Wall Street Journal,* p. B.1. Accessed September 20, 2007, from EBSCOhost database.

Edley, Nigel and Margaret Wetherall. (1999). "Imagined futures: Young men's talk about fatherhood and domestic life." *British Journal of Social Psychology,* 38:181-194.

Elias, Marilyn. (2007, August 22). "Don't call him Mr. Mom: Stay-at-home dads like the job, hate the label." *USA Today,* p. 7D. Accessed September 27, 2007, from EBSCOhost database.

Fernback, Jan. (2007). "Beyond the diluted community concept: A symbolic interactionist perspective on online social relations." *New Media Society,* 9:49-69.

Gardner, Marilyn. (2003, May 7). "Stay-at-home dads want more than laughs." *Christian Science Monitor, 95,* (113). Accessed September 20, 2007, from EBSCOhost database.

Jayson, Sharon. (2005, June 16). "Daddy's home to stay." *USA Today*, p. 1D. Accessed September 20,2007, from EBSCOhost database.

Jeong, Allan. (2006). "Gender interaction patterns and gender participation in computer-supported collaborative argumentation." *The American Journal of Distance Education,* 20:195-210.

Lawlor, Julia. (2004, August 1). "When stay-at-home fathers return to work [elsewhere]." *New York Times,* 153:1-3. Accessed October 1, 2007 from www.google.com

Lupton, Deborah and Barclay, Lesley. (1997). *Constructing fatherhood: Discourses and experiences.* Thousand Oaks, CA: Sage.

Marshall, Katherine. (1998, Spring). "Stay-at-home dads." *Statistics Canada,* 1-7. Accessed September 20, 2007, from EBSCOhost database.

Marsiglio, William, Amato, Paul, Day, Randal R., & Lamb, Michael. E. (2000). "Scholarship on fatherhood in the 1990s and beyond." *Journal of Marriage and the Family,* 62:1173-1191.

Marsigligo, William, Hutchinson, Sally, & Cohan, Mark. (2000). "Envisioning fatherhood: A social psychological perspective on young men without kids." *Family Relations,* 49:133-142.

Matzat, Uwe, & de Vos, Henk. (2000, June). *Online communities: Which conditions make them successful?* Unpublished research report. University of Groningen, The Netherlands. Accessed December 2, 2007, from http://www.ppsw.rug.nl/matzat/online-communities.pdf

Medina, Jennifer. (2004, December 22). "Stay-at-home fathers face isolation and a lingering stigma." *New York Times,* p. 1. Accessed October 1, 2007 from Newsbank database.

Morris, Betsy, Munoz, Lisa, & Neering, Patricia. (2002, October 14). "Trophy husbands." *Fortune,* 146:78-98. Accessed October 1, 2007, from Academic Search Elite database.

Nakamura, David. (1999, March 16). "Dads who rock the cradle." *Washington Post,* p. Z07. Accessed October 1, 2007, from www.fww.org/famnews/0316c.htm

Tucker, Patrick. (2005, September-October). "Stay-at-home dads: At-home dads can benefit children and mothers." *The Futurist,* 12-13. Accessed September 20, 2007, from EBSCOhost database.

U.S. Census Bureau. (2009). *Internet use in the United States: October 2009.* Accessed September 2, 2010, from http://www.census.gov.

VanLear, Arthur C., Megan Sheehan, Lesley Withers, and Robert A. Walker. (2005). "AA online: The enactment of supportive computer mediated communication." *Western Journal of Communication,* 69:5-26.

Walther, Joseph B. (1996). "Computer-mediated communication: Impersonal, interpersonal, and hyperpersonal interaction." *Communication Research,* 26:3-43.

Whittle, David B. (1997). *Cyberspace: The human dimension.* New York: W.H. Freeman and Company.

Wright, Kevin. (2000). "Computer-mediated social support, older adults, and coping." *Journal of Communication,* 50:100-118.

Zimmerman, Toni S. (2000). "Marital equality and satisfaction in stay-at-home mother and stay-at-home father families." *Contemporary Family Therapy,* 22:337-354.

Zuo, Jiping. (2004). "Shifting the breadwinner boundary: The role of men's breadwinner status and their gender ideologies." *Journal of Family Issues,* 25:811-832.

Notes

[1] Method: The messages chosen for analysis for this study were taken from all of the active threads of a Yahoo! online discussion community for stay-at-home fathers during the arbitrarily chosen month of October, 2007. During this month there were 23 active threads containing a total of 270 messages. After obtaining IRB approval for this study, I posted a message to the discussion forum informing the forum participants of my intent to observe their public discussions for one month. They were further informed that if they desired not to have their postings included in my observation then those messages would be excluded. No participants requested to have their messages removed.

All discussion threads were downloaded in their entirety to Microsoft Word documents. The messages were then examined for evidence of relational dialectics and thematically analyzed and coded. Braun and Clarke (2006) call this type of thematic analysis a "theoretical thematic analysis" in that the analysis is "driven by the researcher's theoretical or analytic interest in the area" (p. 84).

The forum members were also informed that they would be provided with the results of my study and that their feedback regarding my interpretation of their discussions was both welcomed and encouraged. Interestingly, only one SAHF responded to this information and upon reading my analysis remarked, "I will state that the document comes to some obvious conclusions for most of US. The information in it may come as a surprise to the REST of the world, though" (emphasis in original).

[2] For example, see Helga Bragadóttir's (2008) article on the gender similarities in response to a computer mediated support group intervention for parents of children with cancer and Jeong's (2006) examination of gender differences and similarities in CMC.

[3] See Walther, 1996, for a discussion of "hyperpersonal" CMC

[4] See Fernback, 2007, for debate over the semantic choice of the term, "online community."

CHAPTER ELEVEN

CONSTRUCTIONS OF GOOD MOTHERHOOD IN AN ONLINE FORUM FOR USERS OF PREIMPLANTATION GENETIC DIAGNOSIS

MICHELLE MCGOWAN

During the second half of the 20th century, genetic testing advanced rapidly into prenatal testing, newborn screening, and diagnostic and carrier testing for children and adults. Genetic testing first emerged in the context of assisted reproduction more than 20 years ago, through the application of preimplantation genetic diagnosis (IVF-PGD) (Handyside, Kontogianni, Hardy and Winston 1990). IVF-PGD combines the techniques of *in vitro* fertilization (IVF) and embryo micromanipulation with genetic testing to provide information about the genetic and chromosomal makeup of the embryo. The original users of this technique were couples with family histories of genetic disease, but IVF-PGD is now also available for individuals seeking infertility treatment, therapeutic tissue matching for an ill child, and non-medical sex selection (Baruch et al. 2008). Recent estimates suggest that PGD is available at 74% of fertility clinics surveyed in the United States (US), although this genetic test is only used in about 4% to 6% of IVF cases at those clinics, resulting in about 3000 IVF–PGD procedures conducted in the US in 2005 (Baruch et al. 2008). IVF-PGD provides an advantage over prenatal diagnosis in that genetic information is available before the embryo is transferred to a women's uterus and becomes an established pregnancy; however, the growing application of this technique has not been without controversy.

As the indications for the clinical use of IVF-PGD have grown, so too has public debate over the moral value of IVF embryos, prospective parents' reproductive autonomy, and individuals' and society's obligations to prospective offspring. Media depictions of IVF-PGD in the US have primarily focused on the use of this technology for creating "designer babies", sex selection, and screening for genetic markers associated with specific diseases, often representing IVF-PGD users as selfish, reckless, nurturing and/or altruistic (e.g. Johnson 2006, Kalb 2004, Tarkan 2005). These depictions raise the question as to how well media renderings map on to users' intents and experiences when using this technology to conceive and bear children. Unfortunately users' perspectives have been largely absent from media commentaries on the socially acceptable bounds of IVF-PGD's usage that have privileged the voices of scientists, clinicians, bioethicists, theologians, and policy experts. The impetus of this chapter is to broaden the scope of narratives of IVF-PGD by delving more deeply into women's self-representations of pursuing embryonic genetic testing to become mothers.

Utilizing an online bulletin board for IVF-PGD users as a primary data source, the central objectives of this chapter are to explore 1) the significance of an online bulletin board in users' experience of pursuing parenthood; 2) the construction of identities as IVF-PGD users and prospective mothers through participation the online bulletin board; and 3) the politics of inclusion and exclusion of the online forum. Positioned as they are at the front lines of the physical, emotional, and moral terrain of reproductive genetic technology, the women who use IVF-PGD play a crucial role in shaping the bounds of acceptable usage of the technique. Thus, their perspectives on IVF-PGD can provide a window on to the "intimate public sphere" (Berlant 1997, 5) of reproductive decision making, and provide insight into individual, familial and social implications of this technology that heretofore have been largely missing from the public domain.

Given the largely private terrain of reproductive decision-making in the contemporary US, I sought the perspectives of IVF-PGD users through a space designed to preserve users' anonymity: an online bulletin board. There are a variety of online bulletin boards and chat rooms for individuals seeking information and support regarding fertility treatments, but only one of the websites that I found broke out the threaded discussions by specific topic or technique (e.g. Donor Eggs, Surrogacy, IVF after age 45, Pregnant after IVF, etc.). It was in this online forum that I found a bulletin board specifically for IVF-PGD users, and which appeared to be one of a kind. The bulletin board was housed on a web application that described itself as a "support board" for individuals undergoing fertility treatments – there were over 150 bulletin boards on this website and more than 25,000 members. The IVF-PGD bulletin board was intended to provide a space for individuals considering and using IVF-PGD to share information about the reproductive difficulties that had led them to PGD and to support each other through the process of assessing and choosing to undergo the procedure. As of 2006, there were over 300 members of the online forum who had posted on the IVF-PGD bulletin board since it first went live in 2005. While a large number of those members had posted only a few times, others had posted hundreds of times to threads on a range of topics pertaining to achieving pregnancy via IVF-PGD.

In 2006 I posted a call for participants to the IVF-PGD bulletin board requesting permission from members to collect and analyze their postings to the board to learn how users of IVF-PGD and those contemplating using IVF-PGD were conceptualizing this technique.[1] Sixteen women gave me permission to gather and analyze their postings to the online bulletin board, and I collected their archived postings from February 2005 to July 2006.[2] In the eighteen months that I followed their postings, these sixteen women posted over 700 times to the bulletin board. This board consists of a number of simultaneous threads, and individual participation varied greatly, with participants posting between one and 360 times during this time period. Through threaded discussions of varying activity-levels these online posts documented the processes through which women contemplated and decided whether or not to try IVF-PGD as a reproductive intervention, and their experiences of undergoing the procedures of IVF, PGD and embryo transfer, and pregnancy. There was no evidence from postings to indicate that participants ever met offline in person. A cursory overview of a wider range of postings of the bulletin board gave the impression that the experiences and sentiments of the women who volunteered to participate in this research study represented the range of perspectives on PGD that appeared on the bulletin board as a whole during the time frame of the study.

Seeking Support in an Online Forum

The sixteen women who agreed to share their postings to the bulletin board for this study ranged in age from 29 to 43 and lived in ten states across the US. Of these women, four sought IVF-PGD to test their embryos for genetic mutations for cystic fibrosis or Charcot Marie Tooth disease. The other twelve participants were seeking fertility treatment. These women sought IVF-PGD to screen their embryos for chromosomal anomalies such as aneuploidy[3] or an unbalanced translocation,[4] or to try to determine why they had had multiple IVF failures or numerous miscarriages. None of the participants sought IVF-PGD for sex selection or therapeutic tissue matching.

As has been similarly documented in the literature on use of online bulletin boards in the context of infertility, pregnancy and mothering

(Arnold 2003, Drentea and Moren-Cross 2005, Malik and Coulson 2008, O'Connor and Madge 2004), the IVF-PGD bulletin board provided individuals trying to circumvent reproductive and genetic risk factors with a "virtual" space to seek support, vent frustrations and empathize with others in a similar situation. Given the gendered burden of undergoing IVF-PGD, it is not entirely surprising that the active participants on the bulletin board were almost exclusively women, and within this particular bulletin board married heterosexual partnership was assumed and normative. The gendered participation in the online forum may be best explained by the differential physical burdens that women and men experience in infertility treatments, as women's bodies are the site of the bulk of reproductive interventions (Thompson 2005). In addition to the gendering of responsibility for dealing with reproductive difficulties, Throsby (2004) has also suggested that women of reproductive age tend to be more accustomed to entering into conversations regarding their reproductive desires and intentions than men, and that women's propensity for "talking" about fertility may be a gendered form of problem-solving action around reproduction. Demonstrating the gendering of IVF-PGD and talking as a way to mediate reproductive difficulties, Megan[5] made the following comment on the bulletin board about her relationship with her husband:

> Although I know he loves and supports me, I know most of this he just simply doesn't 'get' and I've found much more support in talking to women like you who can really understand on a more personal level. I've found that it helpful at times to sit down with DH [dear husband] & explain to him that it's impossible for him to really get it because this is really a woman thing since it is our bodies going through this, our bodies carrying the pregnancy and ultimately us deciding how to proceed with that.

As women participating in the bulletin board considered whether or not to try IVF-PGD to alleviate their reproductive difficulties and genetic risk factors, they often characterized themselves as increasingly socially isolated in their fertility problems which is why an online forum appealed to them as an outlet seeking for social support. This feature of the IVF-PGD bulletin board has been consistently reported as a perceived benefit of online support groups for reproduction and parenting (Arnold 2003, Drentea and Moren-Cross 2005, Malik and Coulson 2008). For example, Jessica had an infertility support group in her local community, but all of the members had gone on to have children while she was still struggling to figure out why all of her pregnancies had ended in miscarriage. When her reproductive endocrinologist suggested that she try IVF-PGD to "help rule out problems with the embies,"[6] Jessica's moral and religious concerns led her to the IVF-PGD bulletin board for advice and support from others who might have had similar experiences with thawing frozen embryos for PGD and selecting embryos for gestation.

In addition to providing a virtual space to connect with others who might for advice and emotional support, the bulletin board served as a bastion of reproductive hope, which in the context of IVF-PGD required a great deal of perseverance and faith in both science and luck. For example, Lynn sent out this message of hope to the members of the online forum:

> My heart goes out to those of you who may get BFNs [Big Fat Negatives][7] today- but please stay hopeful. I went through 5 IVFs (2 with PGD- one with no "normals"[8] to transfer) before our 6th successful attempt. I know the pain of the BFN way too well, but the joy of success in the end makes you forget all of that. I even transferred a PGD normal before with a BFN and thought this could never work for me, and look where I am today. Please keep your chins up and know that it WILL work for you one day! Hugs, Lynn, [pregnant] 7 weeks 1 day with twins??!!

Lynn's statement linked perseverance with success with IVF-PGD – that if only one keeps a positive attitude and keeps trying, then eventually the treatment will work. Maintaining reproductive hope through postings of positive pregnancy test results was one of the most vibrant features of the bulletin board, and many women participating in the online forum indicated that it had a positive impact on them to continue with the emotional and physical trials of IVF-PGD.

In weighing the benefits and risks of doing IVF-PGD, one salient issue for bulletin board participants is how family members, friends, or eventually a child resulting from a IVF-PGD cycle might feel about the choice that a couple made to screen their embryos. Previous research has suggested that individuals seeking treatment for socially stigmatized conditions such as infertility might find more comfort and security seeking support online than in person (Kahlor and Mackert 2009), which was evident in the discourse of the IVF-PGD bulletin board. Threads on the bulletin board often characterized members' conflicted feelings of selfishness, guilt, and familial obligation towards their prospective children, relatives and friends related to using a controversial technique like IVF-PGD. As Melissa explained:

> I have struggled with a similar issue, worried about feeling very guilty about doing PGD (my husband has a genetic disease) and as if we are placing judgment on the value of someone's life by 'choosing' only the

> healthy ones. However, when a disease or in your situation with the miscarriages causes the 'life' (however you look at it) to end earlier (in your case prenatally) or in our case at a young age, to me it seems like a selfish choice to not do the PGD. My guilt isn't related to religious beliefs, however I think that adds an extra layer of 'guilt' or worry about making the 'right' choice…My in-laws are very religious and told us that if we do this, they don't want to know because they see it as very morally 'wrong'.

While there was not extensive discussion on the bulletin board regarding moral judgments on participants' decision to use IVF-PGD, it was clear that participants were acutely aware of the controversy surrounding its use. Some women expressed indignation that others would feel as though it was their right to judge them and their partners. As Megan, who had terminated two pregnancies that tested positive for cystic fibrosis described:

> I've noticed there are some women that have a very brief bout with infertility or whatever and then are past it and just don't get how deep this pain really runs. Nothing, nothing will ever bring me back the two children I lost...No one can ever understand the grief of that unless they have experienced it. Having to make that awful choice when you want a baby so badly is just heartbreaking. Not to mention how abortion and PGD are controversial political issues that every moron thinks he's entitled to an opinion on even though it doesn't affect them.

Both Melissa and Megan personalized their reproductive desires and decisions to use IVF-PGD, yet they recognized IVF-PGD as having social meanings outside of their own actions. The ambivalence that they expressed in regard to what IVF-PGD "means" – be it in terms of moral or religious values, what constitutes an abortion, evaluating prospective offspring based on limited genetic and chromosomal information, parental responsibility, or the grief of reproductive loss – engendered the isolation that many of these women felt as they negotiated the various risks and benefits of using a controversial technology to conceive. Similarly to research findings on online parenting communities (e.g. Drentea and Moren-Cross 2005, O'Connor and Madge 2004), the designated virtual space for IVF-PGD users was likely what lent appeal to this particular online forum for participants, in that turning to others who had experienced or were going through the same process, participants in protected space of the bulletin board could explore the tensions of the emotionally draining decision to use IVF-PGD without judgment from "the outside." This is not to say that this was a judgment-free zone or that participants in the online forum always agreed with one another, but there was a degree of expectation that the bulletin board was considered a safe space for discussion of ideas that might considered highly controversial in other contexts.

Differential Stakes in IVF-PGD

For the regular participants on the IVF-PGD board, there was no overt tension regarding the morality of their reasons for using IVF-PGD, yet their stakes in using IVF-PGD varied depending on their positionality. Analysis of postings to the bulletin board revealed that women seeking IVF-PGD to screen for a genetic marker for cystic fibrosis and Charcot Marie Tooth disease differentiated themselves from women seeking IVF-PGD for other reasons. For instance, women seeking IVF-PGD to screen for a heritable genetic condition were more likely to construe embryonic genetic testing as an obligation than as an active choice. Participants in the IVF-PGD board seeking IVF-PGD to screen for a specific genetic marker commonly referred to all of their reproductive options as choices, all of which had negative aspects so no one necessarily presented itself as the best option. They explained that they could choose to get pregnant naturally and later opt for prenatal testing knowing that there was a possibility that the fetus would carry a heritable condition. If they were to go this route then they knew they may be put into a position to decide whether or not to continue an affected pregnancy. The possibility of having to make the decision to choose to terminate a wanted pregnancy was conveyed by these participants as too heart wrenching for them. Another option would be for them to use IVF-PGD to screen for the genetic marker, so that they could have the assurance that any pregnancy that they began would not be affected by a gene linked to disease. To choose to use IVF-PGD was also fraught with difficulty though because of the emotional, physical and financial stressors of doing IVF. Thus, the bulletin board served as a venue for airing the women's ambivalence as to whether they should "take their chances" by conceiving naturally or use IVF-PGD to rule out the risk of passing along a debilitating genetic condition – the "choice" was not always clear as both options had significant negative drawbacks. By virtue of their participation in the IVF-PGD board though, it is plausible that most of these women felt that trying to conceive without IVF-PGD was not worth the risk of having to consider prenatal testing and a possible therapeutic termination later. These women also employed counter victim narratives to characterize their reproductive decisions, as they saw it as their personal responsibility not to pass along to a child a debilitating genetic condition that they know they have the ability to prevent. There was some acknowledgment that they saw it as an obligation to prevent future suffering it if was within their control, both suffering on the part of a child afflicted with a genetic disease and on the part of the parents who could have avoided passing along disease.

While I did not get the impression that women seeking genetic screening saw their reasons for seeking IVF-PGD as morally superior to others' reasons, they were more adamant that IVF-PGD was the *only* reproductive option for them other than getting pregnant naturally and then facing the possibility of a positive diagnosis through prenatal screening. Knowing their specific genetic risk factors made the option of conceiving "naturally" highly undesirable, particularly if the women had seen members of their families living with a heritable disease, or if they had suffered miscarriages or elected to terminate affected fetuses in earlier pregnancies. The women seeking IVF-PGD for genetic diagnosis did not have known fertility problems, and thus their pursuit of IVF and IVF-PGD was solely to avoid the risk of passing along single genes that would affect the health of their children.

For women seeking IVF-PGD for reasons tied more to fertility – to screen for "chromosomal risk factors" linked to their age, to try to figure out why they had had failed IVF cycles or multiple miscarriages, or to screen out embryos that would be likely to miscarry due to one partner's chromosomal translocation – their stakes in IVF-PGD were somewhat different. PGD was usually recommended to these women by a reproductive endocrinologist if they had already had a number of IVF failures or miscarriages or if they were over age 35 to check the chromosomal quality of their embryos prior to implantation. These women were not trying to remove a specific gene from their family tree, and the IVF-PGD testing for chromosomal rearrangements actually screened for nine to twelve common chromosomal anomalies instead of seeking out one specific gene. Hence, the language of reproductive choice tended to be more dominant amongst bulletin board participants seeking IVF-PGD for fertility reasons. These participants were more preoccupied with trying to find "strong embryos" that could help them to achieve healthy pregnancies. These women had suffered cumulative reproductive disappointments that finally led them to IVF-PGD; none had ever give birth prior to initiating treatment with IVF-PGD. For this group of women, IVF-PGD appeared to be one option of many that they might consider in hopes of increasing their chances of becoming pregnant. By having access to both chromosomal and morphological information about their embryos prior to implantation, reproductive endocrinologists and their patients hoped that they would be able to choose the "best" embryos to implant for gestation.

A topic on the board which highlighted these different stakes in IVF-PGD was the unknown impact of embryo biopsy. While debates on topics such as the impact of embryo biopsy appeared frequently on the bulletin board, the patients' different medical reasons for seeking IVF-PGD showed no evidence of creating adversarial "camps" of users on the bulletin board. Rather, these stakes highlighted subtle differences in the values and beliefs that users brought to their participation in the board. For instance, Erica claimed that:

> PGD does leave the embryos 'beat up,' as one of my doctors told me. Have you ever seen the video of PGD? It's on the web. Amazing. They basically have to wrestle with the embryo to get the freakin' cell off it. I'm the opinion that some labs (people) are better at it than others. No matter how you slice it, those are some sad looking embryos post-PGD. On the other hand, with PGD you know you're likely putting back a chromosomally sound embryo. Those factors supposedly cancel each other out, resulting in an overall benefit. Supposedly.

It is clear from Erica's skeptical tone that that she believed the risks of IVF-PGD harming or causing embryos to arrest would be canceled out by the "benefit" of knowing that the ones that survive the biopsy and chromosomal analysis were chromosomally sound. However, members of the bulletin board seeking IVF-PGD to screen for a specific genetic marker expressed more trust in the theory that the overall benefit of knowing the genetic makeup of the embryos outweighed the physical risks to the embryos. But women seeking IVF-PGD for fertility reasons who had had trouble producing large quantities of eggs for fertilization expressed more worry about any factors that could further reduce the numbers of embryos available for implantation. Fertility patients seemed more doubtful of the benefit that PGD promised given that their primary concern was to get pregnant – not to avoid passing along a specific genetic mutation. The comments on the IVF-PGD board suggested that some women were doubtful that PGD was really the best option for them in this regard if it lowered their chances of getting pregnant due to the heightened risk of losing embryos in the laboratory.

If the goal of IVF is to have a child and the goal of IVF-PGD is to prevent the birth of a child with genetic or chromosomal "abnormalities", there is a paradox for fertility patients seeking IVF-PGD. IVF-PGD was not necessarily their only reproductive option even if they were to continue fertility treatments without PGD, but it did offer informational benefits if it were successful. There was little conversation amongst fertility patients regarding what exactly they were "screening out" with

IVF-PGD, and a more pronounced preoccupation with trying to make sure that they would implant embryos with the best possibility of achieving a sustainable pregnancy. This raises the question of what normative state such IVF-PGD patients were trying to achieve. Were they more interested in using IVF-PGD to have a child without a genetic or chromosomal anomaly or simply having any genetic child at all?

IVF-PGD Online: Community-building and the Bounds of Acceptable Use

The bulletin board served as a site that both facilitated the growth of lay expertise on reproductive genetics and helped to alleviate feelings of isolation in facing reproductive risk. Ann Anagnost (2004, 146) has pointed out that participants in online bulletin boards need not have geographical proximity to build community. However, she has argued that these sorts of Internet forums are illustrative of Lauren Berlant's (1997) concept of the "intimate public sphere" in that they promise "universal access to participation in democratic debate but that may, in actuality, further segment the political in its solicitation of specific identities while also confining the political within the confines of private life."

Unlike the literature that has examined women's shared experiences online of pregnancy and transitioning to parenthood (e.g. Arnold 2003, O'Connor and Madge 2004) what made the IVF-PGD bulletin board unique was that rather than sharing parental experience or a medical diagnosis, the women on the board shared the experience of mediating reproductive and genetic risk on behalf of their prospective children. The women used a variety of techniques to share and grow their expertise on IVF-PGD as prospective parents trying to manage genetic and chromosomal risk factors. Their tactics included collecting statistics from one another on IVF-PGD cycles and compiling their success rates, comparing fertility drug protocols and clinic practices, and even sharing results of studies on IVF-PGD published in medical journals.

For instance, participants in the online forum engaged in debate over the best places to seek treatment even as they gave information to newcomers to the board about how the technique worked. A particularly lively topic of discussion was how to choose a clinic for treatment. Participants who were new to assisted reproductive treatment typically chose a clinic based on geographic proximity to their homes. However, as they delved deeper into the process, many of the women on the board debated getting a second opinion, and sought suggestions from their fellow board members regarding the best clinics for IVF-PGD. Some, like

Rebecca, took an authoritative tone in their recommendations to newcomers to the board writing:

> If I were in your shoes I would not bother with the local clinic... Truthfully, I wouldn't trust them... Usually what happens is the local clinic does the biopsy and overnights the cells. Most local clinics are not going to be that great at biopsy. I would avoid that at all costs. Look at my 4 embryos that arrested right after biopsy at PGD centers that do it all the time. It's too risky...Go directly to a clinic with a lot of experience with PGD. It is worth it.

It is not entirely clear how participants made their assessments of the "best" clinics, as there is currently no centrally compiled data source for PGD success rates in the US. However, many of the IVF-PGD board members expressed frustration with feeling isolated in using a technique that is performed relatively rarely and about which little centrally located information regarding success rates is available. Lee and Hawkins (2010) have argued that cancer patients with unmet informational and emotional needs are more likely to seek health-related information and emotional support online, thus it is plausible that IVF-PGD users turned to each other to pool and build up their knowledge and expertise on IVF-PGD for themselves rather than looking outward or taking an activist stance to change the social landscape around IVF-PGD.

While members of the IVF-PGD board shared their knowledge base and identified themselves in ways that accentuated their commonalities in terms of their reproductive struggles, genetic diagnoses, gender, heterosexuality and shared appreciation for the value of motherhood, other facets of their social identities which may have highlighted differences between them were largely marginalized or conspicuously absent from these conversations. For example, based on what the women wrote about themselves, there is little way of knowing how they self-identified in terms of racial/ethnic background and socioeconomic class unless these factor somehow into their PGD treatment plans. Despite their individualized approaches to IVF-PGD, there are transnational classed implications of a group of women using the Internet as a meeting ground for community building and developing lay expertise on embryonic genetic testing. Haagen et al. (2003) and Novas and Rose (2000) have argued that the demographics of users of reproductive technologies may be quite similar to the largest demographic of Internet users: relatively young, educated, affluent and living in the wealthiest nations in the world. Thus, while women who participated in the IVF-PGD bulletin board did not explicitly situate themselves within a transnational class structure, their positionalities as Internet users on the inside of the privatized US reproductive medical arena imply their ability to pay for services or that they have the social and material resources available to successfully appeal to a private insurance provider that IVF-PGD is "medically necessary." The growth of lay expertise on IVF-PGD may also point to transnational class implications of the growth of this technology, as those with the resources (e.g. time, financial, educational, access to and medical literacy to understand complex medical information) are best positioned to become self-educated about IVF-PGD and share their knowledge with others in a similar position. Then, to borrow from Shellee Colen (1995, 78) the "economy of desire" associated with IVF-PGD in the US continues to reinforce and reconstitute practices of stratified reproduction.

Further, the pervasive sentiment of women trying to provide the best chance for their embryos' survival may partially explain why women seeking IVF-PGD for non-medical sex selection may be un(der)represented on the bulletin board. On the rare occasion when queries regarding sex selection were raised to the board, the active bulletin board participants quickly dismissed the question as frivolous and discouraged further discussion of the topic. For example, in response to a newcomer's question as to whether IVF-PGD users take the sex of the embryo into consideration in choosing embryos for transfer, Megan replied "seems no one considers sex selection, although sometimes they [reproductive endocrinologists] tell you what they are putting back. Best idea is to put back best looking embies not based on sex."[9]

Even though some clinics in the US do offer IVF-PGD for non-medical sex selection, with estimates of up to 9% of IVF-PGD cases nationwide involving sex selection (Baruch et al. 2008), one would never know it from this Internet forum where the topic of sex selection was taboo. Lurking on the boards would alert any newcomer that threads with sex selection in the title were inactive – queries were typically silenced with a single curt response such as the one above. Sex-selection appeared to be an especially sensitive topic amongst the group of women for whom a healthy baby was of the utmost importance, and these women's concerns dominated the online forum. Only if a woman was seeking IVF-PGD to prevent passing along a sex-chromosome-linked condition was the use of IVF-PGD for sex-selection seen as morally acceptable.

On the other hand, women who discussed using IVF-PGD for a therapeutic tissue match for an ailing child were welcomed into the bulletin board with sympathy for the difficulty of their situations and for the mothers' desire to help the ailing child, but these participants were rare figures on the board and made up a very small minority of the board membership. The rarity of women seeking IVF-PGD for tissue typing may be linked to the fact very few patients seek IVF-PGD for this purpose in the US (Baruch et al. 2008). The distinctions that the bulletin board members made between themselves and women interested in IVF-PGD for "trivial" reasons established a form of gate keeping within the online community by defining moral boundaries of acceptable usage of this technology, and thus regulated the traffic and content on the message board. By welcoming in some women and their reasons for pursuing IVF-PGD while chastising others, the active IVF-PGD board members themselves were actively engaged in establishing what constitutes good and responsible "biosociality" (Rabinow 1996, 99) in relation to IVF-PGD.

Reproductive Hope and Maternal Responsibility

Postings to the IVF-PGD bulletin board revealed that women's attitudes about undergoing IVF-PGD were deeply entangled with their perceptions of motherhood. Themes that dominated the bulletin board included 1) an intense desire to have a healthy baby that is genetically related to its parents and 2) feelings of personal responsibility to take action to manage reproductive and genetic risks to achieve this goal despite its physical, emotional and financial burdens and socially controversial nature.

Feminist work on reproductive technologies has argued that the dominant cultural narrative that normative womanhood includes motherhood has nurtured and grown the "need" for reproductive technologies, especially for the white, upper- and middle-class, educated, married women who have been the primary constituency to use reproductive technologies in the US (Becker 2000, Inhorn and van Balen 2002, Thompson 2005). This phenomenon can be observed on the IVF-PGD bulletin board, where participants struggled openly with balancing their desire to achieve normative motherhood and the extraordinary technological means to which they subjected themselves in order to achieve this goal.

Feminists have also noted how fertility treatments do not lend themselves to a natural end point since it is difficult to discern when to give up trying as there are always new technological options or adjustments to drug protocols or new doctors that might yield different results (Becker 2000; Franklin 1997; Franklin and Roberts 2006; Sandelowski 1993; Thompson 2005; Throsby 2004). Throsby (2004) has argued that many women seeking fertility treatments feel the need to exhaust all of their options before they are willing to give up the possibility that IVF might not ever be successful for them, which is in contrast to Malik and Coulson's (2008, 28) finding that men participating in an online infertility support board expressed a "strong sense of helplessness" in the face of infertility. Reflecting this gendered differential response in the face of reproductive difficulty, on the IVF-PGD bulletin board users recounted the disappointments of failed IVF-PGD cycles, but usually turned around quickly to make adjustments for their next cycle. As Franklin and Roberts (2006, 177) have argued persuasively, "the pressure to undergo 'the PGD route,' then, is always relative: it is strongest ('our only choice,' 'not a choice') when the other options (such as adoption, fostering, gamete donation, 'trying naturally,' prenatal screening, or childlessness) are *least acceptable*" (authors' emphasis). Thus when women on the bulletin board expressed a preference for IVF-PGD over prenatal diagnosis and possibly terminating an affected pregnancy, it may be attributable to the timing. At the time that they were undergoing IVF-PGD knowing the genetic makeup of the embryo earlier than later was much more strongly desired than any other reproductive option.

Furthermore, the burden of personal responsibility that the women portrayed on the IVF-PGD board was intimately tied to their sense of what it meant to be a responsible mother. In this way, IVF-PGD users took up subject positions as responsible caregivers similarly to women who undergo strict prenatal self-care regimes and other forms of prenatal testing. Feminist theorists in the US and UK have noted how the need for various forms of prenatal testing have been constructed as choices within reproductive medicine, but also as obligatory as "the standard of care" for certain pregnant women (Lippman 1991; Press et al. 1998; Rapp 1999; Rothman 1994; Tremain 2006). Saukko (2004) argues that the various measures that women take during pregnancy in the name of prenatal "care" can be understood as a part of wider historically gendered regimes of care. In these ways, even from the earliest embryonic stages of human development, the gendering of genomic risk management within pregnancy can be seen as an extension of "women's traditional labour of love in an increasingly privatized world" (Saukko 2004, 314). As such, prenatal self-care and prenatal testing can be seen as part and parcel of gendered care-giving roles that women take on to provide the best for their children (Press et al. 1998, Rapp 1999; Saukko 2004).

In reviewing postings to the IVF-PGD bulletin board for a period of eighteen months it became clear that however strongly participants felt that IVF-PGD enabled maternal responsibility some participants' perceptions of the technique and the usefulness of the bulletin board shifted and changed over time. As one of the members indicated in giving permission to me to use her postings for the study, her opinion of PGD had changed considerably over the period of a few years of trying it unsuccessfully, and a number of participants' postings to the bulletin board expressed doubts that IVF-PGD was worth the risks to their embryos and to their own emotional well-being. While seven participants in the study ended up having at least one child with IVF-PGD, at least three participants ended up forgoing IVF-PGD in favor of "trying naturally" or using IVF without embryonic genetic testing. It is notable that the general preoccupation with the genetic and chromosomal health of embryos on the bulletin board would necessarily lessen in importance for individuals moving on to pregnancy without embryonic genetic testing. For a group of women who collectively emphasized the importance of having a genetic and gestational relationship with their children, it was somewhat surprising to find that at least three of the participants moved on to adoption, donor embryo or donor sperm to become parents. Women who considered or took up other routes to becoming parents engaged in what Thompson (2005, 145) has called "strategic naturalization" of their relationships with their potential children so that a genetic or gestational link with the children did not hold the same importance as it would have when they were pursuing IVF-PGD and engaged with the bulletin board. Thus, participants' attitudes towards reproductive options did not necessarily remain fixed, but were in a constant state of negotiation as the women encountered new stages in their reproductive journeys.

As for participation in the online forum, the participants in this study and their counterparts on the bulletin board came and went from the board as it suited their needs; when their time of considering or trying PGD has come to an end many moved on from the bulletin board as well. In the same umbrella network of fertility bulletin boards there was an online forum for "Graduates of PGD" (individuals who became pregnant via IVF-PGD) which allowed them to share their experiences with those who began their pregnancies under similar circumstances. Some participants moved on to use this online forum when they achieved pregnancy, however others dropped off of the online forums after becoming pregnant, after moving on to other family-building strategies, or for unknown reasons.

Conclusion

While it may be unwarranted to generalize the experience IVF-PGD users from a small set of participants from a single online forum, it is arguable that these women's perspectives are indicative of a particular set of views on IVF-PGD, namely those of individuals seeking IVF-PGD for genetic screening and for reasons related to impaired fertility and maternal age. Using an Internet bulletin board for data collection on users' perspectives provided an excellent source of foundational information regarding IVF-PGD users' understandings of the technique which will provide the groundwork for future research with individuals seeking IVF-PGD. However, the IVF-PGD bulletin board provided a window into a very specific and narrow timeframe in women's experiences with reproductive genetics. In focusing on the "present-tense" of PGD one can observe the emotionally charged experiences that women have as they go through the process of using IVF-PGD. At the same time, it is important to recognize that even as an online bulletin board captures and suspends their self-representations of their experiences in cyberspace, it can only provide a partial view into the totality of these women's reproductive journeys.

This analysis reveals that IVF-PGD users' self-characterizations are more complex than the way they are depicted in American print media. Sensationalist accounts of IVF-PGD users as either selfish or altruistic are reductionist, and do not represent the range of motivations and experiences of women who seek out this technology. In the setting of the IVF-PGD bulletin board, genes and biology are ultimately entangled with users' identities as would-be mothers, and a degree of gate keeping enables the women on the board to maintain their positionalities as morally upright users of IVF-PGD distinguishing themselves from more "frivolous" users seeking sex-selection. This particular online forum's strength was that it provided a venue for discussion of motivations, concerns, and experiences with IVF-PGD that would likely be unavailable in “everyday” life given the rarity of the technique's use, and for that the collective support provided by other would-be mothers undergoing of reproductive difficulty helped to make users' individual experiences feel less socially isolating. The intimate public sphere of the IVF-PGD online bulletin board provides a window on to the ways in which these prospective mothers define the bounds of good motherhood, and how they understand that controversial technology can be applied in responsible ways to achieve their goals of becoming mothers in ways which both confirm and diverge from the discourse on IVF-PGD that has been circulating in the public sphere since its inception.

Acknowledgements

Support for this research was provided by the Institute for Advanced Studies in Science, Technology Society in Graz, Austria and the Center for Genetic Research Ethics and Law (NHGRI grant P50-HG003390) at Case Western Reserve University. Special thanks to Michelle Moravec and my dissertation committee, Nancy J. Kenney, Judy Howard, Janelle S. Taylor, and Priti Ramamurthy, for their comments on earlier versions of this chapter and to Ruchi Sanghani for her editorial assistance.

Works Cited

Anagnost, Ann. 2004. "Maternal Labor in a Transnational Circuit." *Consuming Motherhood*, edited by J. S. Taylor, L. L. Layne and D. F. Wozniak, 139-167. New Brunswick, NJ: Rutgers University Press.

Arnold, Lorin Basden. 2003. "Delivering Empowerment: Women's Narratives about the Role of Pregnancy Bulletin Boards." *Qualitative Research Reports in Communication* 4: 45-52.

Baruch, Susannah, David Kaufman, and Kathy L. Hudson. 2008. "Genetic testing of embryos: practices and perspectives of US in vitro fertilization clinics." *Fertility and Sterility* 89(5): 1053-1058.

Becker, Gay. 2000. *The Elusive Embryo: How Women and Men Approach New Reproductive Technologies.* Berkeley and Los Angeles: University of California Press.

Berlant, Lauren. 1997. *The Queen of America Goes to Washington City: Essays on Sex and Citizenship*. Durham, NC: Duke University Press.

Colen, Shellee. 1995. "Like a Mother to Them: Stratified Reproduction and West Indian Childcare Workers and Employers in New York City." *Conceiving the New World Order: The Global Politics of Reproduction*, edited by F. Ginsburg and R. Rapp, 78-102. Berkeley: University of California Press.

Drentea, Patricia, and Jennifer L. Moren-Cross. 2005. "Social Capital and Social Support on the Web: The Case of an Internet Mother Site." *Sociology of Health and Illness*: 920-943.

Franklin, Sarah. 1997. *Embodied Progress: A Cultural Account of Assisted Conception*. London and New York: Routledge.

Franklin, Sarah and Celia Roberts. 2006. *Born and Made: An Ethnography of Preimplantation Genetic Diagnosis.* Princeton and Oxford: Princeton University Press.

Haagen, E. C., W. Tuil, J. Hendriks, R. P. J. de Bruijn, D. D. M. Braat, and J. A. M. Kremer. 2003. "Current Internet Use and Preferences of IVF and ICSI Patients." *Human Reproduction* 18(10): 2073-2078.

Handyside, A. H., E. H. Kontogianni, K. Hardy, and R. M. L. Minston. 1990. "Pregnancies from Biopsied Human Implantation Embryos Sexed by Y-Specific DNA Amplification." *Nature* 344: 768-770.

Inhorn, Marcia C., and Frank van Balen, eds. 2002. *Infertility Around the Globe: New Thinking on Childlessness, Gender, and Reproductive Technologies.* Berkeley: University of California Press.

Johnson, Clark K. 2006. "It's a boy! If you want a boy." *Chicago Tribune*, June 15, 6.

Kahlor, LeeAnn and Michael Mackert. 2009. "Perceptions of Infertility Information and Support Sources among Female Patients Who Access the Internet." *Fertility and Sterility* 91(1): 84-90.

Kalb, Claudia. 2004. "Brave New Babies." *Newsweek*, January 26. Accessed December 3, 2010. http://www.newsweek.com/2004/01/25/brave-new-babies.html

Lee, Sun Young, and Robert Hawkins. 2010. "Why Do Patients Seek an Alternative Channel? The Effects of Unmet Needs on Patients' Health-Related Internet Use." *Journal of Health Communication* 15(2): 152-166.

Lippman, Abby. 1991. "Prenatal Genetic Testing and Screening: Constructing Needs and Reinforcing Inequities." *American Journal of Law and Medicine* 17(1-2): 15-50.

Malik, Sumaira H., and Neil Coulson. 2008. "The Male Experience of Infertility: A Thematic Analysis of an Online Infertility Support Group Bulletin Board." *Journal of Reproductive and Infant Psychology* 26(1): 18-30.

Novas, Carlos, and Nikolas Rose. 2000. "Genetic Risk and the Birth of the Somatic Individual." *Economy and Society* 29(4): 485-513

O'Connor, Henrietta, and Clare Madge. 2004. "'My Mum's Thirty Years Out of Date': the Role of the Internet in the Transition to Motherhood." *Community, Work & Family* 7(3): 351-369.

Press, Nancy, Carole H. Browner, Diem Tram, Christine Morton, and Barbara Le Master. 1998. "Provisional Normalcy and 'Perfect Babies': Pregnant Women's Attitudes Toward Disability in the Context of Prenatal Testing." *Reproducing Reproduction: Kinship, Power, and Technological Innovation,* edited by S. Franklin and H. Ragone, 44-65. Philadelphia: University of Pennsylvania Press.

Rabinow, Paul. 1996. *Essays on the Anthropology of Reason*. Princeton: Princeton University Press.

Rapp, Rayna. 1999. *Testing Women, Testing the Fetus: The Social Impact of Amniocentesis*. New York: Routledge.

Rothman, Barbara Katz. 1994. *The Tentative Pregnancy: Amniocentesis and the Sexual Politics of Motherhood*. London: Pandora.

Sandelowski, Margarete. 1993. *With Child in Mind: Studies of the Personal Encounter with Infertility*. Philadelphia: University of Pennsylvania Press.

Saukko, Paula. 2004. "Genomic Susceptibility-Testing and Pregnancy: Something Old, Something New." *New Genetics and Society* 23(3): 313-325.

Tarkan, Laurie. 2005. Screening for Abnormal Embryos Offers Couples Hope After Heartbreak. *The New York Times*, November 22: F.1.

Thompson, Charis. 2005. *Making Parents: The Ontological Choreography of Reproductive Technologies*. Cambridge: MA: The MIT Press.

Throsby, Karen. 2004. *When IVF Fails: Feminism, Infertility and the Negotiation of Normality*. New York: Palgrave Macmillan.

Tremain, Shelley. 2006. Reproductive Freedom, Self-Regulation, and the Government of Impairment In Utero. *Hypatia* 21(1): 35-53.

Notes

[1] This study received the permission of the bulletin board's webmaster and the University of Washington Human Subjects IRB. The name and location of the bulletin board has been removed to preserve the privacy and anonymity of the individuals who participate in this Internet forum.

[2] Using inductive qualitative methods, I coded the postings with Atlas.ti software and analyzed how the bulletin board users' contemplated and experienced IVF-PGD and their characterizations of motherhood in relation to this technique.

[3] Aneuploidy is a condition in which either the egg or the sperm provide fewer or more chromosomes than typical. Higher rates of aneuploid embryos are associated with "advanced maternal age,"

[4] An unbalanced translocation is a chromosomal rearrangement in the DNA which predisposes a couple to generate a high percentage of chromosomally unbalanced embryos.

[5] Pseudonyms are used in place of the participants' actual names and screen names in order to preserve their anonymity.

[6] "Embies" is a common term used to refer to IVF embryos on the PGD bulletin board.

[7] On the PGD bulletin board a BFN is an acronym for Big Fat Negative, which means that a pregnancy test is negative. There is also the counterpart BFP – Big Fat Positive – when a pregnancy test is positive.

[8] Embryologists typically "grade" the quality of IVF embryos based on their appearance, color, clarity, shape and development to decide which embryos are

best-suited for transfer into the woman's uterus. Participants in the bulletin board saw PGD as adding a benefit of providing information about the chromosomal or genetic makeup of IVF embryos which would give embryologists a better sense of which embryos were genetically or chromosomally "normal" and the "best" to implant or should be rejected as "abnormal."

[9] The notion that embryos are chosen to be "put back" for gestation implies that embryos had been previously removed from the woman's body and are then returned for the duration of pregnancy. This language used by women on the online bulletin board who were undergoing IVF-PGD somehow slides past the issue that in fact embryos were cultivated in a laboratory and are only entering the woman's body for the first time when a fertilized embryo transfer is conducted in the clinic. But given that the women often conflate eggs and embryos, and eggs were removed from their bodies for IVF and PGD, this may explain why they see their embryos as being "put back." The language of "putting back" embryos could also signal ownership of reproductive material – that the embryos are the property of the prospective parents, thus they should be put back where they belong to be nurtured and grown.

CHAPTER TWELVE

"LATE", "EARLY", "NEVER": TIME, GENDER AND TECHNOLOGY IN ASSISTED REPRODUCTION

VENETIA KANSTA

When I started researching assisted reproduction my main interest was in how kinship relations are conceptualized and discussed. How, in other words, do new reproductive technologies change our ways of thinking about "what makes one a relative"/"what it means to be one's relative". In the meantime, almost all of my, until then childless, same-age friends became mothers. In astonishment, I watched one after the other get pregnant in the context of a long-term relationship, with a guy they had just met, with an old school mate or without a partner at all. Their explanations, "The biological clock was ticking", "Forty is the limit", "It was time for me to become a mother," all ideas which once would have caused a smirk, or have been uttered as irony, were stated now in earnest. The result was that I gradually became surrounded by babies, pampers and feeding bottles. It was in this context, my discussions with women who went through assisted reproduction, and the stories they narrated, began to take on new meaning. Their explanations focused in many cases—in some of them almost exclusively—on the idea of time.

The temporal dimension of assisted reproduction—a woman's age, interval between attempts, number of efforts—determine certain subjectivities which are subjected to counting, control, classification and categorization. Yet, drawing on research into a Greek internet forum related to medically assisted reproduction, I argue that the exchange of "miraculous" success stories, create the expectation for the "miracle" through the participation into the group. This notion of miraculous transcends the notions of controlled and controlling time and instead posits the possibility of escaping the constraints of reproductive time.

Time for motherhood

Motherhood is a persistent and recurrent topic in Greek ethnography. It was a main subject of interest for the first and second generation of Greek ethnographers during the 1970s and 1980s (du Boulay 1974 and 1986, Hirschon 1978, Dubisch 1983, Ruschton 1992), and it was implied in a number of works in the 1990s that focused on tourism, consumption, and ethnicity (Galani-Moutafi 1993 and 1994, Vlahoutsikou 1998, Agelopoulos 1994). The topic gained new life during the early years of the 21st century though the work of anthropologists interested in abortion, demographics, and population policies, and more recently in new reproductive technologies (Athanasiou 2003 and 2006, Paxson 2004, Georges 2008, Kantsa 2006 and 2010).

Why is motherhood so important? The reason may be that motherhood is to be counted among the anthropologist's own obsessions since, as David Schneider would have argued, "all anthropologists have mothers" (Schneider 1972). However, ethnographers of Greece have been eager to demonstrate that their preoccupation with motherhood is to be attributed to the specificities of Greek society. Greece has been largely described as a society where kinship and family relations play a crucial role in the definition of female and male identities, while full adult status for both women and men is obtained through marriage and parenthood (Loizos and Papataxiarchis 1991). Motherhood in Greece is a highly respected status, one might even say revered, and unintentional childlessness is the cause of many prayers, vows, and expenses. Meanwhile, medical practices, religious beliefs, law regulations, psychological and sociological judgments sustain and reinforce its significance.

In such a context, assisted reproduction is viewed as a means to facilitate the fulfillment of personal goals. It also provides an answer to nationalist concerns regarding low fertility and birth rate. It is a widely used technique in Greece. In 2006 there already existed —for a population of approximately eleven million— more than 50 assisted reproduction clinics and medical centers according to the European IVF-monitoring (EIM) Consortium for the European Society of Human Reproduction and Embryology (ESHRE) (de Mouzon et al. 2010: 1853). More than half are located in Athens and the remaining are divided among the major cities, i.e. Thessaloniki, Larissa, Patra, Ioannina, Aleksandroupoli, Volos, Chania and Heraklio. Ten of these centers belong to public hospitals (six to university hospitals) and the rest are private clinics and centers (Panagiotidou-Prapa and Prapas 2006: 236-239).

The legal context was first set in Law 3089/2002 on "Medical Assistance in Human Reproduction" followed by Law 3305/2005 on "Application of Medical Assisted Reproduction Methods". The 2002 Law tried to compensate for the previous legal vacuum and introduced amendments to the Civil Code on issues of kinship and inheritance; it defined kinship as a social-emotional relationship -where choice and the desire for child take priority over biological relationships-, and empowered with rights over reproductive technologies heterosexual married people and non-married couples, and single women alike. The subsequent 2005 Law focused on the applications of medical assisted reproduction and issues of "National Health." In contrast to the 2002 Law, where emphasis is placed on the definition of kinship relations and inheritance rights, the main principles of the 30 articles of the 2005 Law are:

> 1) the application of medical assisted reproduction methods in a way that secures respect of individual freedom, the right to personhood and satisfaction of the desire to acquire descendants based on the facts of medicine and biology and the principles of bioethics and 2) a concern that during the application of the aforementioned methods the interest of the child to be born be primarily considered [Law 2005, article 1].

Greek Law allows for preimplantation genetic diagnosis, embryo freezing, anonymous sperm donation, anonymous egg donation, embryo donation, surrogacy, research on genetic material (donated gametes and fertilized eggs), and the free transportation of genetic material and fertilized eggs from and to other European countries thus outlining one of the most "permissive" profiles among EU.

The permissive Greek Law and the large number of assisted reproduction clinics and medical centers can only be explained in relation to the cultural meanings of fertility and parenthood for Greek citizens. Athena Athanasiou writes that,

> In the face of a dwindling population, the *self-interest* of individual bodies join forces with the *social good* of the body politic in ways that tacitly bracket the internal differentiation of the national body as such (2006: 239).

Athanasiou draws on the work of Marilyn Strathern (1992) to argue that,

> What is imagined as a point of concentric confluence between the individual and the collective body is, indeed, their very condition of mortality instantiated in what is thought of as downward flow of time (2006: 246).

In a context where infertility is seen as the break of a future line—personal or national—assisted reproduction, "the cure for infertility", represents hope for one's individual future constituted through personhood and kinship relations and at the same time as a hope for the nation's future, a guarantee of its own existence and continuity. Meanwhile, ART depend heavily on the discourse of experts in reproduction—doctors, embryologists, genetists, lawyers, psychologists—who intervene and provide new definitions of kinship, decide who is eligible to become a parent and who is not, set limits on grounds of age, sexuality, chronic disease, the allowed number of attempts, and the anonymity of the donor (to name just a few). In order to do so, they draw on prevalent cultural notions of reproduction, fertility, kinship, parenthood, personhood, and continuity. These notions rely heavily on a persistent, recurrent, enduring discourse on motherhood as a state that is highly respected, one might even say revered, and that every effort towards its acquisition is worthwhile, regardless of physical, psychological, and economic cost.

The time of assisted reproduction

A close look at women's narratives in an online community reveals a more complex, fragmented, and inconsistent picture than implied by the expert discourses outlined above.

The ethnographic material that this paper draws on derives from a Greek internet forum on medically assisted reproduction of 700 members, the striking majority women. The forum is not commercial and does not collaborate with any state or private medical research centre or clinic on assisted reproduction. Therefore there is a striking contrast on grounds of aesthetics when compared to similar Greek internet sites so far as it lacks any visual marketing. The only visual interventions are the drawings or photos that accompany the name/ pseudonym of the user and the tickers that users have chosen at the end of each message in place of a signature. A ticker is a device which produces the tick-tack sound of the clock but in this case tickers are software programs provided for free on the internet. They count the passage of time during a certain period of time, for example, four months, two weeks and five days till the birth of a child, or, five months one week and two days from the date a woman got pregnant.

I have chosen to focus on about eighty accounts, or as they call them "life stories" about individual's experiences published on the site during a period of eighteen months from [23rd] November 2006 to [13th] May 2008. These stories were written by members of the forum who introduce themselves using pseudonyms and avatars. Many of these accounts contextualize reproduction within a broader story that relies on temporality.

In anthropology time is viewed

> as a symbolic process continually being produced in everyday practices. People are "in" a sociocultural time of multiple dimensions (sequencing, timing, past-present-future relations, etc.) that they are forming in their "projects". In any given instance, particular temporal dimensions may be foci of attention or only tacitly known. Either way, these dimensions are lived or apprehended concretely via the various meaningful connectivities among persons, objects and space continually being made in and through the everyday world (Munn 1992: 116).

In the stories I explore, time appears in multiple dimensions. Among them I discern four.

I. "*The time of narration*": I do not refer here to the online temporal dimension but to the specific moment members of the forum choose to narrate their own story. This occurs when the individual feels "ready" to do so and may happen several weeks, or even months, after subscribing to the forum. "Ready" may refer to the fact that a) they feel confident to tell their stories to others, b) they want to encourage and empower the rest of the participants, c) they just want to share their experience and thus "free" themselves. The moment of narration takes place in chosen time, has a coming-out effect, and usually evokes encouraging, admirable comments and/or consoling words, while in many cases it marks essential admittance to the forum.

II. "*The time of the relationship or 'life before assisted reproduction'*": A common motif in almost all stories is the narration of the current and in some cases even past relationships. Relationships are presented in a "linear", sequencing way, following a "logical" succession. Isolated mistakes, failed love stories, marriages and cohabitations do occur but they are remedied and the desire for a child usually follows or coincidences with the finding of the "right" guy. The linear narration of the relationship is interrelated with a parallel account of studies, professional choices, travels, and amusement. Even here the central motif is the element of "choice", "free will" and a sense of continuity. "We have met and decided to make it official. It coincided with the fact that I have found a job … Everything was fine till the moment we decided to expand our family". Or, "Till my thirties, I was foot loose and fancy free and had a very normal sexual life. … We met in September. After two months we decided to make it official". Intentionality and "free will" is the common motif even in cases which came out to be wrong: "I had other things to do", "I wanted to study", "We had to work first".

III. "*The time of the procedure*": The main characteristics of assisted reproduction are observing the menstrual cycle, measuring body temperature, counting sexual contact, classifying into "pure respondents" who will follow the "brief protocol" and those who will have to follow the "extended" one because are expected to respond better to treatment. During the treatment, one has to take hormones in form of injections at a certain time and on a daily basis, at least during the first nine days, and goes through blood tests and ovary ultrasound screening. It is a procedure that is based on the fragmentation and control of time. Through the procedure of controlling the woman's body, time has to be accelerated, decelerated, stopped, or frozen.

> Beginning of February, I had begun to take the drugs and started with the first injections on the 14th of February. The rest is more or less known. Almost daily I had to go through blood tests and ultrasound screenings. On the 25th of February they took the eggs from my ovaries. After one hour in the operating room the harvest was 47 eggs. I donated 12, 35 remained, and from them 21 were fertilized. On the 27th of February they placed into my womb 3 embryos, while the rest, 18 in total, were frozen. There followed one of the most difficult periods of my life, a long wait. ... And then the pregnancy set off with me lying in bed, bedridden ... from the second month.

The time of the procedure is very different from the time of the relationship. It is not linear, gradual, developmental, but rather its temporal dimension is one of permanent fragmentation and repetition.

In the chapter "Docile Bodies" of his book *Discipline and Punish: The Birth of the Prison*, Michel Foucault argues that the new element in the disciplinary control of time from the 18th century onwards does not refer so much to accuracy, assiduity, and regularity. These were fundamental qualities of the disciplinary system but they pre-existed. The new element refers, rather, to

> the disintegration of the act into its elements; for every movement is given a direction, a scale, a duration; the order of succession is determined. Time invades the body and, with it, all the thorough checks of power (Foucault [1976] 1989: 201).

Furthermore, the biopolitic discipline of time is not restricted to the planed occupation and the temporal regulation of action, to the exhaustive utilization and correlation between body and movement, body and object

(Foucault [1976] 1989: 198-206), but is intrinsically related to the notion of the "procedure". Therefore, as Kathrin Braun argues,

> The life that biopolitics targets has a supra-individual dimension, not just in a numeric but also in a temporal sense (Gerodetti 2005). Modern politics, as Foucault depicts it, consists of a set of government technologies which act upon a target, the biological processes in the population, within which individual life is just a transitory moment (2007: 11).

In assisted reproduction determinants of time such as "late", "early", "never" do not only refer to personal choices but also to procedures involving the medical environment —doctors, hospital, medical centers, and private clinics interested in success statistics that are closely related to the age of their "clients" and the degree of their ability to "respond"—, the legal context —laws that prescribe age limits for the recipients of assisted reproduction, egg donors, and egg receivers—, i.e., the economy of health. In the context of late capitalism, time has turned into a commodity that can be counted, exchanged, sold. Because of its commercialization and potentiality for control

> it can only be conceptualized in regard to power relations which are not confined just in cases time can be exchanged for money: rather they pervade "when", the right moment for action, the moment for interrelations, the tempus of natural and social procedures, the temporal frameworks according which life is being organized (Adam 1994: 515).

It is here that the transitional moment of Michel Foucault meets the "tyranny of the moment," of Thomas Eriksen. Eriksen argues that at the age of information the problem is not the dominance of a linear time because the latter has already been replaced by a "fragmented and precipitated notion of time" (2005: 217). Through a procedure of a perpetual fragmentation in increasingly smaller bits, "in sufficiently tiny units", time

> does not exist any more as duration but has been transformed into an unbreakable, maniac, incontrollable moment which changes ceaselessly and does not have any other future prospective except the very next moment (2005: 84).

Time during the procedure of assisted reproduction is there only to be replaced—the next moment, the next control, the next injection, the next effort. During this heavily controlled and controlling temporal dimension any references to husbands/partners, which were prominent during the temporal dimension of the relationship, are strikingly absent. Although it is the case that very often husbands and partners are responsible for childlessness, the painful and conflicted relationship with a fragmented time and with a "without an end" procedure involves mostly women who undertake the responsibility of failure, further reinforced by ideas which present them and their bodies as "unforeseen" and "irrational", thus justifying failed efforts and the need to "start all over again".

IV. (Fourth and last, but not least) "*The time of the 'miracle'*": Some times, rarely though it may be, there appear stories evoking wonderment. "Miraculous" stories about women who became mothers despite experiencing premature menopause and negative blood tests results, or hopeless medical diagnoses. Such stories "empower and encourage", "give joy and hope", "should be taken as a paradigm" and give good reason for constant encouragements among the members of the forum: "Don't give up!", "Keep trying!". The "miraculous", "exceptional" cases reinforce the belief in patience, perseverance, and endurance. This belief is further supported by the tickers underneath each message that enforce a different temporal dimension from the fragmented time of assisted reproduction, a future time which will allow for continuity and the wished for "happy end". The temporal dimension these women introduce is not the linear, logical time of the period of life "before" assisted reproduction, nor is it the fragmented time of the procedure. It is a dimension of time that gives hope, is a "sacred" time when "miracles" happen, is a time that subverts biomedical predictions and thus challenges biofuturity.

Postscript

The forum is aesthetically different from many other sites on assisted reproduction and is packed with thanks, sweet words, sketches, and drawings. It looks like a "girl's album" writes a member. The exchange of miraculous stories and reasons to hope for, the expectation of the "miracle" strengthened through the participation into the group creates a kind of biosociality, as examined by Paul Rabinow and Nicolas Rose. The latter adopts the characterization of Raynna Rapp (1991, 1999) "moral pioneers" in order to describe "new biosocial communities formed in the web and outside it", whose members act in the frames of a new biomedical citizenship. "They are pioneering of a new informed ethics of the self—a set of techniques for managing everyday life in relation to a condition, and in relation to expert knowledge" (Rose 2007: 146). I would argue that, in the above cases, the time "of the miracle" informs a new ethics of self who claims for a time that is not isolated and fragmented but progressive and accumulative in relation to one's expectations and, enables the establishment of close relations between non-related women that lie beyond the imperative to establish maternal ties.

Works Cited

Adam, Barbara. 1994. "Perceptions of time" in Tim Ingold, ed. *Companion Encyclopedia of Anthropology. Humanity, Culture and Social Life,* 503-526, London and New York: Routledge.

Agelopoulos Giorgos. 1994. "Mothers of the nation: Gender and ethnicity in rural Greek Macedonia", in Proceedings of the Conference *The Anthropology of Ethnicity: a Critical Review*, vol. 4: 1-16, Amsterdam.

Athanasiou, Athena. 2003. "I pitharheia tis sineheias. Chronos, soma kai viopolitiki sti sinhroni Ellada". *Sinhrona Themata* 82: 45-52.

—. 2006. "Bloodlines: Performing the Body of the 'Demos', Reckoning the Time of the 'Ethnos'". *Journal of Modern Greek Studies* 24: 229-256.

Braun, Kathrin. 2007. "Biopolitics and temporality in Arendt and Foucault". *Time & Society* 16(1): 5-23.

De Mouzon, J. et al. 2010. "Assisted reproductive technology in Europe, 2006: Results generated from European registers by ESHRE". *Human Reproduction* 25(8): 1851-1862.

Du Boulay, Juliet. 1974. *Portrait of a Greek Mountain Village*, Oxford: Clarendon Press.

—. 1986. "Women-images of their nature and destiny in rural Greece" in Gill Dubisch, ed. *Gender and Power in Rural Greece*, 139-168, Princeton: Princeton University Press.

Dubisch, Jill. 1983. "Greek women: Sacred or profane?". *Journal of Modern Greek Studies* 1(1): 185-202.

Eriksen, Thomas Hylland. 2001 [translation in Greek 2005]. *Tyranny of the Moment. Fast and Slow Time in Information Age*, London: Pluto Press.

Foucault, Michel. 1977 [translation in Greek 1985]. *Discipline and Punish. The Birth of the Prison*, New York: Random House.

Galani-Moutafi, Vasiliki. 1993. "From agriculture to tourism: Property, labor, gender, and kinship in a Greek island village" (Part One). *Journal of Modern Greek Studies* 11: 241-270.

—. 1994. "From Agriculture to tourism: Property, labor, gender, and kinship in a Greek island village" (Part Two). *Journal of Modern Greek Studies* 12: 113-131.

Georges, Eugenia. 2008. *Bodies of Knowledge The Medicalization of Reproduction in Greece*, Nashville: Vanderbilt University Press.

Halkias, Alexandra. 2004. *The Empty Craddle of Democracy. Sex, Abortion and Nationalism in Modern Greece*, Durham and London: Duke University Press.

Hirschon, Renee. 1978. "Open body/ closed space: The transformation of female sexuality" in Shirley Ardener, ed. *Defining Females*, 66-88, New York: John Wiley and Sons.

Kantsa, Venetia. 2006. "Family matters: Motherhood and same-sex relationships" in Evthymios Papataxiarchis, ed. *Peripeteies tis Eterotitas. I Paragogi tis Politismikis Diaforas sti Simerini Ellada* [Adventures of Otherness. The Production of Cultural Difference in Contemporary Greece], 355-381, Athens: Alexandria Publ.

—. 2010. "Expertise in hope: Assisted reproduction as investment for the future". 11th International Conference *EASA (European Association Social Anthropologists),* Workshop *The expert's voice: marketable discourses on choice and risk management* , organized by Alexandra Bakalaki and Venetia Kantsa, Maynooth Ireland, 24-27 August.

Loizos, Peter and Evthymios Papataxiarchis. 1991. "Gender and kinship in marriage and alternative contexts" in Peter Loizos and Evtymios Papataxiarchis, eds. *Contested Identities: Gender and Kinship in Modern Greece,* 3-25, Princeton: Princeton University Press.

Munn, Nancy D. 1992. "The cultural anthropology of time: A critical essay". *Annual Review of Anthropology* 21: 93-123.

Panagiotidou-Prapa Angelika and Nikos Prapas. 2006. *Odigos gonimotitas. I iatriki gnosi arogos stin elpida* [Guide to fertility. Medical knowledge aid to hope], Athens: Fereniki.

Paxson, Heather. 2004. *Making Modern Mothers: Ethics and Family Planning in Urban Greece*, Berkeley: University of California Press.

Rapp, Rayna. 1991. "Moral pioneers. Women, men and fetuses on a frontier of reproductive technology" in Michaela di Leonardo, ed. *Gender at the Crossroads of Knowledge: Feminist Anthropology in the Postmodern Era*, 383-395, Berkeley: University of California Press.

—. 1999. *Testing Women, Testing the Fetus: The Social Impact of Amniocentesis in America*, New York: Routledge.

Rose, Nicolas. 2007. *The Politics of Life Itself. Biomedicine, Power, and Subjectivity in the Twenty-First Century*, Princeton and Oxford: Princeton University Press.

Rushton, Lucy. 1992. "I mitrotita kai o simvolismos tou somatos" in Evtymios Papataxiarchis and Theodoros Paradelis, eds. *Tavtotites kai Filo sti sighroni Ellada* [Gender and Kinship in Modern Greece], 151-170, Athens: Kastaniotis Press.

Schneider David. 1972. "What is kinship all about?" in P. Reining ed.

Kinship Studies in the Morgan Centennial Years, 32-61, Anthropological Society of Washington,

Strathern, Marilyn. 1992. *After Nature: English Kinship in the Late Twentieth Century*, Cambridge: Cambridge University Press.

Vlahoutsikou, Christina. 1998. "I katanalosi: Metafora gia to monterno kai rogmi sti ginaikeia afaneia". *Sinhrona Themata* 66: 87-103.

CHAPTER THIRTEEN

CYBERSPACE AND CONTESTED MEANINGS OF ADOPTIVE PARENTHOOD: A CASE STUDY OF ADOPTIVE PARENTS OF FILIPINO CHILDREN

TODD LINDLEY

While adoptive parenting is not at all new, the way in which parents obtain information, formulate opinions, share insights, and interact with other adoptive parents has experienced a significant transformation owing to the advent of the Internet, email, and other instant modes of communication and information sharing. This chapter focuses on one specific set of adoptive parents (of children from the Philippines), institutions (governing rules and practices), child care agencies (in the Philippines), and adoption agencies (in the U.S.) to better understand how adoptive and potential adoptive parents use and are influenced by instant communication and the Internet. The study relies heavily upon virtual conversations and debates from one particular online forum created and utilized by potential adoptive parents (PAPs) and adoptive parents (APs) of Filipino children. The user group's name and address are withheld, and all study participants' names, children's names, and specific locations have been changed to ensure anonymity. Insight and empirical evidence in this chapter derive from fieldwork conducted in the Philippines during 2008 and 2009, from my own participation in the forum over the past few years, and from semi-structured interviews conducted with PAPs, APs, adoption professionals, and attorneys in the U.S. (2007-2009) and with child caring agencies (CCAs) and adoption professionals in the Philippines.

The forum began in November 2004 and by July 2010 contained 697 members who had posted 40,816 individual messages as part of 3,420 different topics. Inclusion in the group requires participants to submit personal information including their address and details about existing family members and prospective adoptive children. Messages post automatically to the forum, but may be removed at the discretion of the moderator. The moderator may also deny membership for any reason, so perhaps this community is not representative of all APs of Filipino children. Some members have participated regularly since 2004, but most engage in the forum only during key periods of time (e.g. the agency research period, the adoption application period, the waiting period, and during the first few months after adoption). Topics vary from the mundane details of application procedures to profound cries and confessions of the soul. Many participants become so emotionally attached to one another that they travel long distances to meet and spend time together in person. Some find regional culture camps where they encounter other APs and where adopted children, siblings, and other family members meet to talk about their shared experiences. Still others use the online group to obtain and share information about their child's orphanage, place of birth, or Philippine culture.

In general, adoptive parents from this study report that their participation in one or more online adoption communities helps them cope with stress associated with adoption and recent dramatic changes in intercountry adoption (ICA) – namely longer waiting times; more strict governmental and nongovernmental regulations; and changing restrictions placed by many source countries. For example, the Philippines recently enacted rules disallowing adoption by single parents, by those with certain medical histories, and by those with a body mass index higher than 35. Participants and informants from this study reported on their own use of Internet and email technology and how their membership in virtual communities changed their understandings of parenting adopted children both before and after adoption occurred.

Adoptive parents find their adoption paths in a number of ways. Most utilize the Internet as either a primary source for research, or they turn to the web to confirm and/or contest information they receive from agencies, friends, or other adoptive parents. PAPs also use the web to find maps, pictures, demographic information, and history about the Philippines before, during, and after their adoption experience. Most agencies don't inform parents about the available online forums (for reasons that become apparent later in this chapter). Instead, they learn about them from friends, other PAPs, or from a search engine. The forum that is the focus of this chapter is used in many different ways, but its utility can be categorized in general terms: first, as counsel/therapy; second, as a symbolic and/or literal connection to a world far away (in the Philippines); third, as a community space of negotiating meaning and proper behavior; fourth, as reconfiguration of the power relationship between adoptive parents and agencies. These four themes are explored more fully throughout this chapter to support the claim that engagement with and interactions within the Internet have a transformative effect in the reconfiguration and contestation of meanings associated with intercountry adoptive parenthood.

Online Community as Counsel and Therapy

As in many of the other chapters from this book, the most common way in which the Internet moderates and transforms the experiences of adoptive parents is through its ability to plug parents into in an informal network of communal and emotional support. Once parents make the decision to adopt, most often due to infertility or secondary infertility, PAPs from this study tend to bypass potential domestic options in favor of what they perceive to be the quicker, less intrusive, and less open option of intercountry adoption (Ishizawa et. al 2006, Lindley 2010). Those who choose the Philippines do so for three reasons. First and most importantly, they rely upon information from the Internet or guidance from nearby agencies specializing in Philippine adoption. Second, PAPs pragmatically select a country based upon health requirements, costs, travel requirements, waiting times, and/or personal preferences. Third, they may be influenced by friends or family members who have already adopted from that country or they may prefer to adopt a boy.[1] Prior to 2000 intercountry adoptions could be completed much more quickly and with younger children (infants) than was the case for domestic adoptions. In the decade following 2000, however, waiting times began to increase dramatically as the supply of adoptable young children was far outstripped by global demand of hopeful adopters (Lindley 2010, Selman 2006, Pertman 2009).

In the case of the Philippines, waiting times vary from 6 months (in rare cases) to 3 years with an average waiting time of just over 2 years, so it is not surprising that posts related to waiting appear most often in the forum and draw the largest number of responses from other members. PAPs typically recount the mundane details of their own waiting period and ask each other questions about paperwork, but more importantly their posts contain deeper articulations of alienation and powerlessness as expressed by this adoptive parent during our interview:

> Other parents don't understand. I mean. Well, with umm pregnancies, you have this definite window of time, and then it's over so other people can relate to that experience. But with adoption – especially now – you just don't know what to tell people. After awhile you kinda get tired of

> answering people's questions, and it makes you sad or angry but mostly just frustrated. The [online] group lets me talk to other moms who have gone through or who are going through the same thing. It lets me know that I'm not alone in feeling this way, and I also have a place to vent my frustrations with my mother-in-law, who was always asking about why everything takes so long! …and also the ones who have already been through the wait really can give good advice. It lets me know that there are others out there who have been through what I'm going through...and it helps me feel like I'm not all alone.

This mother also went on also to talk about how she bore more pressure from relatives regarding the adoption than did her husband. Although pregnancy is certainly rife with unpredictability, it also occurs within a predictable time period and physical body changes signal the progress of pregnancy both to the mother and to anyone with whom that mother comes into contact. Adoption waiting, however, doesn't invoke such physiological signals. So the stress of waiting is not accompanied by commiseration with strangers or the kind, knowing glances of other mothers. There are no places reserved at the front of the Walmart parking lot for waiting adoptive mothers as there are for pregnant ones. Nonetheless, the same feelings of anxiety, fear, weakness, and insecurity are experienced by waiting mothers in spite of the absence of any kind of physical marks upon her body that would signal "progress" for a pregnant woman. Relatives don't pressure pregnant women to give birth more quickly or to press their doctors to somehow shorten the delivery time. Nor do they ask why a child hasn't yet been born or suggest aborting a child, because the pregnancy has been too complicated or slow. Yet with expectant adoptive mothers, insinuations often arise regarding the mother and/or couple's choice of adoption agency, country, and adoption decisions in general. Perhaps because PAPs/clients have a choice of agencies or source countries and because the adoption transaction involves monetary exchange, relatives and friends more freely question such choices and critique the "gestation" period. Through the course of 64 interviews conducted for this study, women consistently reported that they had to field questions from in-laws, friends, neighbors, and relatives, while men most often escaped such close scrutiny. Such conversations would often turn to discussions of changing agencies or becoming more assertive or perhaps transferring the adoption application to another country program. Such pressures undoubtedly tend to fall unequally upon women. Yet both PAPs perceive such direct suggestions as a direct critique of their own parenting skills before proximate "parenting" has even begun.

The power of the Internet community in this case lies in its connective ability referred to by sociologist Anthony Giddens (1990) as 'time-space distanciation' whereby social relations are stretched across both time and space, allowing people across large distances to become engaged and meaningful actors in one another's lives. Adoptive parent support groups are by no means new, of course. However, the ability to connect simultaneously with lots and lots of other hopeful and adoptive parents from all different parts of North America, represents a brand new reality. People's social relations have long been stretching across greater and greater distances, but the ability and the willingness of individuals to make new connections with virtual strangers represents a paradigm shift in human society from one confined by communities, states, and countries to one better conceived as a "network society" (Castells 2000). Such is the case for PAPs in this adoptive forum where members resist the normative tensions existent in their traditional family and community networks and instead seek comfort, kinship, support, and affirmation from strangers who create a new kind of community connected only by virtual space and not by blood, geographic proximity, or time. One significant distinguishing characteristic of the online community is that its members are bound by common (though not shared) experiences rather than being constituted by the traditional connecters of geography, gender, language, ethnicity, citizenship, or class. As such, group members (92% women) view the online forum as a safe therapeutic space to vent frustration and to work through feelings of powerlessness as expressed by the following posts related directly to the emotional tolls of waiting for adoption referrals.

Post #1:
Can I just say that waiting is one of the most loathsome occupations known to humankind? And waiting with no knowledge of when the wait is going to come to an end, and no way whatsoever to make the wait go faster, is seriously a detestable business. Waiting makes people do crazy things.

Post #2:
Waiting for our referral was one of the hardest things I have ever done. There were days that I knew with my whole heart that my daughter was somewhere in the world, and that someday soon, I would be able to hold her... On some days I wondered why we had even started down this path.

Although such intimate expressions undoubtedly offer members therapeutic benefits in and of themselves. The online community responses serve the even more important role of comforting and counseling others. Unlike face-to-face encounters, however, discussions among this community defy both time and space. For example, online members spend hours reading through archived postings, many of which were written weeks, months, or years before. PAPs can actually connect with the most sacred and personal feelings of both current members and of those who are no longer even part of the community. Such connections to the deepest sentiments of others serve to empower parents with the knowledge that their emotional responses are not unordinary. This web group, then, represents a continuum of experience, knowledge, and emotion from both the past and the present.

Likewise, meaningful and long-lasting bonds form across long distances between people and families who likely will never meet in person. My interviews also revealed significant differences among forum members in terms of class, age, income, region, church affiliation, and residence (rural/urban/suburban), which suggests that the online forum facilitates interaction among those outside of the traditional circles of encounter. Catholics, Protestants, Jews, older women, multiple adopters, blended families, first-time mothers, Filipino-Americans, blue collar workers, white collar workers, Canadians, Australians, and residents of Papua New Guinea/England/Canada/New Zealand/The Philippines can all be found interacting and forming ties in this online forum. The online experience, then, serves to break down longstanding barriers to communication, kinship, and information-sharing pervasive in the material/physical world.

As evident in the expressions presented here, waiting times vary considerably among waiting PAPs. Yet, the unwritten rules of the 'community' oblige members to share the specifics of their cases (including exact wait times, dates, parents' age, medical conditions, and information about other siblings), so that others may benefit from communal/collective knowledge. A typical posting by Kim (below) illustrates how submissions to the online group operate simultaneously as calls for help and as contribution to communal knowledge.

Post 1:
Dear Group,

Could a few of you that are (or were) really long waiters for your referrals please send a few tips on how to make it to referral. I am usually very hopeful about it all. However, this week has been very difficult. We are getting close to 33 months after ICAB approval for a boy/girl sib group 0-6 years old (not counting the 8 months of paperwork and document gathering before approval). I will spare the details, but I just need to know how some of you who waited very long times got through, when it seemed like it would never happen. The blankets were knitted 2 years ago, the beds have been waiting empty, the dressers and closets stand full of various sized clothing (those clearance items we couldn't pass up), and scrapbooks have been started just waiting for their next entries- the referral. Other than pray and continue to enjoy our family at home, I don't know what else to do.

Several others quickly responded to this post by sharing their own stories of arduous waiting. Sheri, posted, "I know all about waiting ... as we waited for 24 months for our older son...I thought that the wait and not to mention the paperwork was too long and emotionally excruciating to be experienced again. But wouldn't you know it, within our son's first year at home, we decided to adopt--again." Others offered support by assuring Kim that the adoption would be worth the wait - such as the words offered by one mom who wrote, "I wish you and other waiting families the strength and fortitude to continue the wait and hang on just a little longer. Your beautiful child(dren) ARE making their way to you!" Still another poster added, "For those who have been waiting longer, please know that my heart goes out to each of you as I know that it has not been easy. Your time will come and it will be perfect."

Along with the 'encouragers' some posters also included their own details and waiting times, so that Kim would have some sort of measuring stick against which her own experiences might be measured. For example, another mother posted, "We were approved at the end of July 2009 and just received our referral mid last month (putting our wait time at less than 12 months)! We are very excited but I didn't post before today because I wanted to be sensitive to those who have been waiting much longer. But I suppose posting may also provide encouragement for others."

Such posts exemplify the frustrations and the potential triumphs associated with diligent waiting. But most posters tend to counsel others that their adoptions are 'destined' to happen, and that a proper mix of diligence and faith is most important to completing the adoption. While, a certain mix of fatalism, triumphalism, and helplessness accompany such postings, faith and belief in transcendental intervention are also clearly evident as exemplified by entries such as, "We are still trusting in Almighty God to have perfect timing. This week, however, I just need a little boost. Do any of you have a good poem, book suggestion, or testimony that will give encouragement to all of us (especially to some of us that are among the longest waiters at ICAB right now)?"

Such references to Divine involvement are not surprising given that the Philippines adoption system favors Christian adoptive families (Lindley 2010). Applicants are required to submit essays about the importance of God in their lives and also a letter of support from their own priest or minister as testament to their Christian values and practices. As such, members often use the Internet group to share testimonies of faith, cite the

Bible as a source of encouragement, and ask for prayer from other members. While references to faith and otherworldly intervention are certainly not new to online groups, sharing personal adoption miracles with others tends to encourage expressions of faith that perhaps would be shared more tenuously in face to face encounters. Community members of this forum, however, regularly share stories their own stories of miracles and Godly intervention. The word 'God' for example appears more than 5,000 times in the online postings, and the words 'miracle', 'faith', and 'Christian' emerge more than 4,000 times.

Besides its ability to link people together so quickly, the Internet also enables members to connect with others who share their own beliefs, faith, language, and values, such as the case with the adoptive parents in this study. Sociologist Manuel Castells (2000) suggests that the 21st century is best conceptualized as "The Network Society" whereby traditional categorizations of individuals according to nationality, citizenship, or geography give way to more narrowly defined "communities" of believers whose interests intersect in very narrow and self-defined but meaningful ways. Such is the case with PAPs from this study in that they interact with one another in deeply emotional ways based upon the intersections of faith, infertility, emotional distress, and connection to a country that is home to none but sacred to all because of their common unique adoption experiences.

Connecting with the Other Side

The second way in which online interaction transforms social relations and knowledge among adoptive parents relates to their connection to the other side – both symbolically and literally. In a symbolic sense, PAPs and adoptees (as they grow older) seek and grapple with understandings of birth culture, nationality, and ethnicity, and identity. In a more literal sense, PAPs utilize technology to communicate with and learn from intermediaries (government officials, adoption attorneys, and child-caring agencies) in the Philippines who without the Internet would be inaccessible.

Recent scholarship on adoption divulges the multiple ways in which adoptive parents and their children seek to make meaning out of their own multi-ethnic identities (Dorow 2006, Trenka et al. 2006, Volkman 2005). Parents frequently send their adopted Chinese and/or Guatemalan children to language classes, for example. Many families also form and participate in culture camps to learn about and maintain a sense of cultural heritage. Some also participate in homeland tours. Due to the ubiquitous nature of the Internet and email access, contemporary adoptive parents enjoy easy access to technology that could potentially allow them to form/maintain connections with their adopted children's birth country, with their child's orphanage, and even with biological relatives. Evidence from this study suggests that few adoptive parents or biological family members take advantage of technology to maintain or establish connections with blood relatives, however most PAPs do use the Internet to connect to the Philippines in other ways.

While one in five PAPs claim Philippine descent, most have never been to the Philippines – or any less developed country (LDC) for that matter. For them, encounters with structural poverty, with subsistence farming, with homelessness, with fish head soup, with squatter settlements, and with all the other sights, smells, and sounds of the global urban underclass are brand new and often unimaginable realities. As such, many turn to websites and forums to better help their children negotiate their own unique identities and to better understand the birthplace of their child(ren).

Some had traveled to the Philippines as tourists, as missionaries, or as members of the military, but most chose to adopt children from this country for more practical reasons. Whether they had previously visited the Philippines or not, PAPs and children use the Internet as a symbolic connection to a sacred place – one that is simply too far away or expensive or daunting to encounter in a material way. Adoptive families utilize the Internet and the user group to find recipes, shop for clothing, learn about cultural customs, learn Tagalog (although in many cases the adopted child would have spoken a different language entirely!), and to ponder/pose questions about culture, country, and meanings of Filipino identity. While pre-Internet adoptive parents relied on encyclopedias, friends, books, and/or their own conceptions of place and culture, online communities facilitate ongoing and fluid constructions of place, identity, and meaning through discussions, shared recipes, news accounts, and shared ideas about place.

Parents use the forum to share ways that they learn about and "teach" Philippine culture to their children, such as the sharing of books ("I read from our Philippine books every night - mostly tourist type picture books (and we learn a few Tagalog words) my daughter loves this, and it gives us a chance to talk about the Philippines everyday [sic]."). Others recount a sensory experience from the place of their adoption, such as this post from one parent, "we would hear young children walking up and down the streets as early as 5am, calling out, 'pan DE sal, pan De sal' always with the emphasis on the 'de'. The pan de sal we bought a few times were [sic] freshly-baked softish flour rolls. Although they were baked with 'sal', they also had a slightly sweet taste…" While seemingly benign, such posts serve the distinctive role of (re)creating a sense of place in the minds of adoptive parents whose information regarding the place might be otherwise limited to history books or travel guides. Other postings share information about holidays ("Oct 25 is a special non working holiday in the Philippines, due to local barangay (village) elections.") or recipes ("I have a recipe for purple yam pudding that looks good but haven't tried it yet. Let me know how your cake turns out and share the recipe if you have time. Good luck with the baking and waiting.") Many such posts, however, deal with local or regional markers of culture and represent special kinds of information that cannot so easily be obtained through typical accounts of countries available through encyclopedias or other traditional sources.

Other posts, however, address more explicitly the notions of identity negotiation, race, and 'otherness' as demonstrated in the following posts/conversations on race:

> **Post 1:**
> *I have 2 bio boys who are half Filipino, half white. They could care less. I was just talking to a friend who also has kids who are also half asian[sic]. His kids, especially his girl, seek out other kids who have a similar background. He informed me how this group refer[sic] to themselves, and I think it is pretty neat. They call themselves "Amasians". He said it so it sounds like he is saying something between am-Asians and amaze-ians. I would think that may[sic] of the children of people in this group would relate to this group, especially if they are Asians growing up in white families. Anyway, I thought I would put this out there for you all to think about, because, as I said, I think it is kind of neat.*
>
> **Post 2:**
> *I thought I'd add my two cents to this conversation on ethnicity/race/ and nationality. I hope I don't step on any toes, as that is not my intention, but I think there may be some confusion over the difference between the terms nationality and race. The term "white" isn't a nationality. "White" meaning "Caucasian" is a race.*
>
> **Post 3:**
> *At school yesterday, they asked us to check boxes for our kid's ethnicities. One category was Asian. A different category was Pacific Islander. Matt and I both were suddenly stumped. I think we checked both. But what is the real answer?*

While such online conversations may appear shallow to outsiders, those who are inside of the online community know that the ability to ask 'dumb questions' without scorn or judgment is invaluable. In spite of training on race sensitivity provided by their adoption agencies, parents interviewed for this study explain that they are not always well prepared for the subtle ways in which race, nationality, and ethnicity emerge in their everyday lives. The Internet forum provides a comfortable space where such questions can be posted and discussed without fears of appearing insensitive or unskilled in dealing with racial questions that are brand new to nearly all adoptive parents (80% of whom are white) living predominantly in homogeneous white neighborhoods, communities, and suburbs.

In a more literal sense, the Internet group also allows PAPs to connect to the Philippines to better understand the place and also to prepare for their visit to the country to pick up their adopted child(ren). In some cases, adoptive parents use the forum to re-connect with friends or caregivers of their adopted kids, such as the case with Madelyn, who recently posted, "An online friend of mine has been trying to track down the best friend of her adopted son. The kids are from RSCC in Quezon City and Julian was adopted sometime in 2009. The only info they have is that he possibly went to Austria." Other posts seek information about their adopted child's orphanage or about other children and/or caregivers that were present with their children. While Philippine and international rules prohibit communication between orphanages and prospective adoptive parents, many of them find ways around this rule and use the web to quickly find email addresses and other contact information for child caring centers in the Philippines. While some caregivers are reluctant to answer such inquiries, others embrace the long distance communication, and they establish long-term relationships with adoptive parents and adopted children.

Since most PAPs have never visited the Philippines before, many share certain anxieties about traveling to such an exotic place. Prior to the Internet, most parents would strictly follow the advice of their own adoption agency to arrange travel plans, reserve accommodations, etc. However, most of the parents I interviewed combine such advice with information gleaned from other parents or from the care-giving orphanage. Sometimes the advice puts parents' minds at ease about travel, but posters also tend to reinforce stereotypes and preconceived notions about the 'Third World' in posts such as one father who assessed his experience in Manila in this way, "They have a JolliBee which was our son's favorite. We also ate at the Shakeys Pizza, the Great American Steak, and Kenny Rogers Roasters. The food was alright, but they are stingy when it comes to napkins. There is not much around outside of the hotel and mall to do.

As a matter of fact, in my opinion it is dangerous to venture out onto the street." Another poster confirmed this assessment of the Philippines, adding, "The Philippines is still very third world as far as safety is concerned. There a [sic] guards everywhere. Be prepared for the pollution, smog, and poverty. I hope their new President pulls them up out of this."

The negative connotations apparent in such posts are not representative of the experiences of most parents. Rather, the vast majority of posts focus on positive elements of travel and of the Philippines as a place. The larger point, however, is that the unlimited capacity for opinions, experiences, and assessments of countries, cities, and neighborhoods made possible through online forums, increased bandwidths, and larger hard-drives are inextricably tied to the multifarious ways in which parents experience, conceive of, and reproduce notions of place. Although the web offers the possibility of homogenizing and normalizing the adoption experience, this particular adoption forum also sometimes polarizes it. In effect, users can search for nearly any opinion about the Philippines in this forum and find at least one piece of evidence to confirm or counteract that opinion. In essence, attempts by members of this group to reach out to and define 'the other side' often fall short, creating instead a fluid and dynamic set of seemingly disconnected realities from which PAPs may pick and choose, depending upon their own desires and/or predispositions. As with the effects of larger webs of connectivity associated with post-modernity, this particular forum simultaneously solidifies and segments its members through a complex set of ongoing contestations, interpretations, and reconfigurations of meaning.

Online Forum as Negotiation and Regulation

The third way in which online engagement alters adoptive parenthood has to do with the way in which online communities work to negotiate meanings and practices of parenthood both before and after adoption. Questions abound about proper behavior for adopted children, signs of attachment disorder, when to seek professional counseling, and whether or not a complaint should be leveled against an adoption agency. Such questions are posed by new and long-term members alike. While many post comments seeking solace or compassion, others negotiate 'proper' action or interpretations of a particular behavior or incident between parent and child or between parents and adoption agency. One particularly contentious case involved the way in which a mother should interpret and contend with behavior issues with her two adopted children and the framing of their birth mother. Her post and subsequent responses are included here in order to demonstrate the way in which such conversations often unfold in this adoption forum.

Posted by Helen:
Mario (adopted son) has a big problem with stealing and he hits a lot and has been teaching Max to steal too now, and I wanted him to know that Max isn't able to make decisions for himself and the last thing he needs is for his brother to be a bad role model.

We've been told by other parents who have adopted kids with it that he has most of the facial features [of fetal alcohol syndrome] (though some are hard to tell if it's just because he's Asian). But that would explain his severe learning delays a little better, and even for a filipino [sic] he seems likes[sic] he's really small.

...So what I'm asking basically is drinking a big cultural problem? Sure she could have drank no matter what most people do there. And also, the more and more we learn about the birth mom, the more awful she sounds. If we can confirm that he has FAS, can we stop with the sharade [sic] that "your birth mom loved you very much and just wanted was what best for you and she probably just couldn't provide for you so she placed you somewhere that you'd be taken care of"? I mean, she didn't place them there, they were taken from her because she left them home alone while she went to work, a 4 month old and a 5 year old. She was not a nice mother at all. I just have no positive feelings towards this woman. I mean, if she were in the US she's [sic] be in jail for what she's done to the boys.

Some community members such as Gabrielle (below) embrace Helen's frustrations and offer their own stories as hope for a positive resolution. Gabrielle empathizes with Helen's plight and suggests that the solution lies in finding ways to "escape" from the difficult situation by getting a manicure or some other relaxation techniques.

Posted by Gabrielle:
Hi Helen,

I remember going through that stage with my son too. He would hit and laugh (almost manically) too. This was during our first year but since he has turned three things have improved a lot. He hardly ever hits now, nothing like before and when he does, he often catches himself and says "gentle, gentle" and strokes the person he started to hit...This intense type of parenting is very hard on you so I also recommend that you take breaks, give yourself treats such as a new hairdo, manicure, catch up with girlfriends without the kids around, spend some time alone with your older daughter and so on. This is so you don't get too run down. I found that taking breaks helped me cope better during the rest of the time.

After several posts of support, however, many in the community intensified the discussion by accusing Helen of handling the situation inappropriately. One member, Mary, offered multiple suggestions that were routinely dismissed by Helen. Eventually, Mary posted the following.

Posted by Mary:
It is my deep and most sincere hope that Helen recognizes the unique needs of her adopted children and finds the professional, educated help that she and her family need, because I think she is failing to recognize the needs of her own children.

Later the same evening, Lynne supported Mary's criticism in a similar post suggesting that Helen was falling short as an adoptive parent.

Posted by Lynne:
Helen, ...without a clinical diagnoses this was really inappropriate especially considering you had previously said this little boy was diagnosed with RAD and the oldest boy had PTSD ...how much do you think Mario can handle. Stealing is an issue related to his own mental health.... It is a survival response he developed....I hope you have a great counselor to help both your children. It is all very sad...I wish you all the best.

A number of others then began to take sides, prompting Mary to add one final post the following day as follows:

Posted by Mary:
Susan mentioned my comments to Helen were unlike any I had made before and it surprised her. I did not make my comments lightly and had weigh [sic] the potential negative outcome against the chance of shedding some light on what I feel is a deteriorating situation. My comments were made because of a deep concern for what is going on. I could not, in good conscience, continue to act as though things were "ok" when I truly feel that they are not.

The discussion continued for a prolonged period of time during which several members suggested that Helen was uneducated and ill-informed as an adoptive mother and others (such as Ivonne below) argued that the mom "will always know what is best to do" – effectively rejecting the need for professional and/or community intervention.

Posted by Ivonne:
Sometimes we forget that people just need/want to vent and not receive a backlash of advice. I know that I once posted a thought and received way too much negative feedback that it makes me question posting again which is unfortunate as I think this site can be a great resource. Best wishes to Helen - as their mom you will know what is best to do!

While the community never reached unanimous agreement on this contestable issue, it became clear that many members were fully engaged in the discussion. Twenty-eight posts appeared on the topic during a 7 day period from 11 different authors (all of whose screen names appear to be women's). Perhaps more significantly, the times of posts varied widely from early morning (4:02am) to late in the evening (12:16am). While portions of the discussion occurred almost in real time, the majority of the discussion took place in different places (as indicated voluntarily by individual posters) and at different times. The topic ended with a more conciliatory tone, when a series of members suggested that the forum should allow for open and unfettered expression about adoption without fear of judgment of one's parenting ability/skills/decision-making. It is also interesting to note, however, that in Helen's subsequent posts (which were substantial) her tone and descriptions of her children seemed less harsh or accusatory suggesting that 'proper' or 'acceptable' ways of talking about adopted children were negotiated and 'settled' through the dialog within a particular online community that perhaps abides by different rules than those set in Helen's local community, neighborhood, family, or church.

Another example of negotiation among community members about 'correct' parenting is presented in the following case. Anna, a hopeful adoptive mother, received the disheartening news that her request for adoption of two children had been denied by officials in the Philippines, but that she could be approved to adopt just one child instead.

Posted by Anna:
All,
Our entire family has had a very stressful past few weeks. We were waiting for final approval and referral of our waiting children, a boy and a girl, when ICAB decided that they wanted more information on my husband's bipolar disorder and employment...

ICAB came back and told our agency liason[sic] Wednesday that we were officially approved for one child, not two, and would not be allowed to adopt the children. They will not give a reason, and said they do not have to give a reason - to us, or to the children, who HAVE ALREADY BEEN

TOLD they have a mommy and daddy waiting to come get them... We were preapproved by ICAB because of the medical conditions last April. And now this.

Their bedrooms are ready and waiting for them. Their pictures are all over the house. Please, somebody tell me what else I can do. If they say no, do we contact our senators? Representatives? WHAT DO WE DO TO GET THESE CHILDREN WE LOVE SO MUCH HOME WITH US? This is so wrong. I am devastated for us, and even more devastated for them. We have already offered to fly to the Philippines to meet with ICAB - DH, my parents, myself - the agency does not think they will accept that or want to see us. PLEASE tell me what to do now. I have been in constant prayer for weeks about this, and I don't know why God would do this to any of us. Please help!

Many responded out of sympathy for Anna, encouraging her to have faith and patience in the knowledge that the right decision would eventually be reached. Because of her request for advice, however, many began to weigh in on the right course of action. Some suggested harsh steps to be taken, such as those offered by Michelle:

Posted by Michelle:
If it were me there would be nothing stopping me from getting on a plane to beg them in person. Maybe that would be a waste, but there's nothing I wouldn't do for my kids.

However, the majority of members cautioned Anna not to take such drastic measures. After several rounds of advice, one member posted the following response to Anna's cries for help:

Posted by Alicia:
There are two things I want to say in reply:
1) going to ICAB to beg them in person might really, REALLY backfire (ICAB might be so offended and off-put that they would take Jennifer's ICAB-approval away), and
2) as agonizing and nightmarish as it is, as someone who has lived through what Anna is living through, they are NOT our kids until ICAB releases them to us when we travel. We have no rights until ICAB releases them to us.

After Alicia's post several others confirmed that they felt the same way, and they encouraged Anna not to take decisive action but rather to trust the system and the trained professional decision-makers handling the case. In the end, Anna took the advice and did not fly to the Philippines or file an official complaint. In a sense, the community 'talked her down' from her initial frantic state by convincing Anna that the best interests of her perceived 'own' children should trump any kind of dramatic action she might take to bring them home. In this way, the online group arrived at a virtual consensus about the 'proper' action a 'good' parent should take. Ironically, the group's advice to Anna was to 'relinquish' one child for the potential good of the other – the same impossible decision that birth mothers in the Philippines are forced to make – resulting in the global system of adoption in the first place!

Reconfigurations of Power between Agencies and Adoptive Parents

Until our adoption is finalized I am not going to mention the agency we went through because they may try to get me for slander, but for all out there looking for a good agency, I'd go for Wide Horizons or Bethany.

While the previous examples demonstrate the power of the Internet and instant electronic communications in shaping adoptive parents' experiences and actions, online communities and connections also have radically transformed power relationships among and between various stakeholders in intercountry adoption.

The ability to interact with other adoptive parents at any time of the day, regardless of their location, profession, social class, ethnicity, and/or gender fundamentally alters PAPs' access to information (and misinformation), knowledge and experiences in a way that empowers clients (PAPs and APs), but in some cases has the opposite effect upon adoption agency social workers in the U.S. who sometimes feel disempowered by the Internet. Likewise, some childcare agencies in the Philippines are better informed about those with whom they choose as adoptive parents for their children because of the Internet, email, and the adoption forum. Meanwhile, some U.S. adoption agencies view online groups as a potential threat to their own careful control of information and as a regular source of misinformation that spreads quickly from parent to parent based upon false/incomplete knowledge, unsubstantiated claims, or pure rumor.

One interview with Kim Johnson, an adoption specialist at a medium-sized agency in the Midwest, demonstrated her own conflicting views of the online interactions of parents as potentially damaging and empowering to PAPs and to her agency. Although she acknowledges that "it's good education" since previous adoptive parents are able to share lots of information with PAPs, she also calls it a “mixed blessing” in that “now everybody feels ENTITLED to know like every teeny thing” about the adoption process. Often PAPs now come to her with a list of questions that Kim can’t possibly answer regarding the medical condition of a particular child or the specific timeline during which a document in the Philippines will be processed. If she is unable to answer such questions, PAPs are much more likely to complain than in the past because they say that other adoptive parents in other parts of the world at other agencies are getting this information, so they feel entitled to it. Kim also argues that parents sometimes are so inundated with adoption information that they confuse the ‘good’ information that comes from her agency with the ‘untrustworthy’ information coming from the web. Such confusion makes her job more difficult, because she in some cases she has to re-educate potential adopters about the adoption process in addition to fielding far more email questions than ever before.

In spite of what Kim interprets as the somewhat negative effect of the Internet upon her own work relationship with PAPs, Kim also views increased global connections and communication across borders as an equalizing force when it comes to openness in adoption. For example, her communication with peers in the Philippines has evolved to become more transparent because of the ease of regular communication. When asked about other effects of the web on her clients, she also cites a “definite increase” in adopted children who seek to reconnect with birth countries and with biological relatives [including mothers].

While most who adopt internationally prefer not to interact with birth parents or relatives, Kim suggests that increased technology and connectivity will soon force parents to deal with the reality that their children will increasingly be able to find their birth parents, “ I mean, we already have DNA banks, and there’s gonna come a time, when these children are just gonna have to order a test tube online, scrape their cheek and put it in and send it off, and they will find out who their birth parents are. You know, that’s not science fiction.”

Although Kim foresees the possibility of more transparency in intercountry adoption (ICA) and predicts an increase in adoptees that reconnect with their birth countries and birth parents, she offers little evidence to indicate that adoptive families or adoptees are more or less likely to participate in such activities now than in the past. In Kim’s view, however, domestic and intercountry adoptions are on converging paths as a result of DNA technologies and increased participation in online parenting, which will lead to more transparency in adoption regardless of the location of the relinquishing parent(s).

Another long-time adoption professional, Vonda also perceives increased technology and greater communication across borders to be beneficial to all parties involved – PAPs, agencies, governments, and most of all adopted children, whose waiting times can be reduced due to more regular communication across long distances. She explains specifically that it is much easier and quicker now to match specific parents with specific children that would have been impossible before. She even cites a case of something that happened that very day as evidence:

> *For example, [our social worker] just got an email this morning about one of our families who forgot to include a document, and so we can know that and actually email it, where before that kind of communication would be impossible, so it's really incredible. Or for me to have a family come in out of the blue and call me and say can we come talk to you today and they say, we'd really like to adopt a boy between 9 and 11 years old and I call Imelda to see if they have any children on the special home finding list and the next day receive a match and the very next day them say yes, and the next day for them to start the application process – that whole thing would have taken months and months before.*

Vonda also credits the Internet with transforming relationships between agencies in the Philippines and those in the U.S. and also between PAPs and agencies. Social workers in all three agencies interviewed for this study claimed to be more transparent in their communication with PAPs because they know that parents are better informed due to their online communication with others. Agencies are also held more accountable because their clients are more willing to select an agency based upon recommendations from the online community rather than relying simply upon proximity. The most prolific adoption agency working with the Philippines, for example, is located in Boston but now services clients in 46 different states. While most agencies advertise online, certain agencies have earned reputations nation-wide as a result of information sharing in online communities such as the one featured in this study. As such, the relationship between adoptive parent and agency begins with a certain degree of trust facilitated almost entirely through communication of people across the world in which people that have never met are able to build trust and share information with one another. While adoptive parents previously relied upon the ability and proficiency of local agencies to guide them to parenthood, contemporary adopters utilize online community as a credible source of information that ultimately empowers them to make more informed choices about adoption and parenting.

PAPs also readily share information about specific agencies, which strengthens the position of some and weakens others. Some parents report that they used email to contact their children's orphanage directly in spite of directions from their agency not to do so. Given the fact that email addresses, phone numbers, names of social workers in the Philippines might be published online, parents sometimes take matters into their own hands, when they feel that their agency neglects its duty. One parent, for example, discovered that documents required for an adoption request had been lost by the adoption agency in the U.S., while the agency reported to the PAP that they were waiting on documents from the Philippines. Once the parent became involved more directly, the adoption proceeded as scheduled, but without direct intervention via email, the adoption very likely would have stalled indefinitely.

Although the effect of the Internet is perceived differently by different agencies, providers, child-caring agencies, government officials, and parents, the free flow of information has undoubtedly reconfigured relationships among all stakeholders. Overall, PAPs are more empowered as they have access to more information. Meanwhile, the role of agencies has changed dramatically as they understand that their clients may be armed with much more (mis)information than ever before.

Conclusion

This chapter has presented four ways in which adoptive and prospective adoptive parents of Filipino children utilize online groups and the Internet to perform and negotiate meanings of parenthood. The narratives provided here demonstrate that the online community is tightly woven and fulfills needs that are unmet by traditional support groups (community, church, family). Hopeful adoptive parents and those who have adopted before use the online community as a space of mutual emotional support, as a way to connect to the other side (both symbolically and literally), as a vehicle to negotiate meaning and 'proper' behavior/action of parents, and as a means to reconfigure power relationships between themselves and adoption agencies.

The evidence presented here suggest that the Internet has had a transformative effect upon adoptive parents who establish meaningful and sustained relationships online and upon adoption agencies that are better able to match adoptive parents with adoptable children. While the Internet provides a plethora of information to adoptive parents pertaining to countries, agencies, health concerns, costs, and other factors, participation in the online community profoundly transforms meanings of adoptive parenthood and the way in which that contemporary social role should or should not be performed. Intimate discussions about the most personal details of adoption, parenting, and discipline have traditionally been limited to family, friends, and professionals. In the 21st century, however, the community building aspect of online groups serves to reconfigure, renegotiate, and create new spaces of intimacy that defy traditional constraints of both time and place.

Works Cited

Castells, Manuel. 2000. *The Rise of the Network Society in the Information Age, 2nd ed.* Malden, MA: Blackwell Publishers.

Dorow, Sara K. 2006. *Transnational Adoption: A Cultural Economy of Race, Gender, and Kinship*. New York: New York University Press.

Giddens, Anthony. 1990. *The Consequences of Modernity*. Stanford, Calif.: Stanford University Press.

Ishizawa, H., et al. 2006. "Constructing Interracial Families through Intercountry Adoption." *Social Science Quarterly* 87(5):1207-24.

Lindley, Todd. 2010. "Intercountry Adoption in the Philippines and the United States: A Multi-Sited Migration Approach in an Era of Transnationalism." Dissertation. Indiana University.

Trenka, Jane Jeong, et al. 2006. *Outsiders Within: Writing on Transracial Adoption*. Cambridge, Mass: South End Press.

Volkman, Toby Alice. 2005. *Cultures of Transnational Adoption*. Durham: Duke University Press.

Notes

[1] Sixty-three percent of adoptees from the Philippines (1995-2006) were boys compared with adoptions from Korea, China, and other Asian source countries where the figure historically has been higher than 90%. Gender disparities are undergoing a rapid transformation, however, in many countries, where boys increasingly enter the adoption pool. Most are older boys who have special needs or did not become eligible for adoption until later in their childhood.

CHAPTER FOURTEEN

CYBER-COMMUNITIES AND MOTHERHOOD ONLINE: A REFLECTION ON TRANSNATIONAL ADOPTION

PETER BUZZI AND CLAUDIA MEGELE

Introduction

> The pupils of the first grade were discussing a photo of a family. In the picture, the hair of the youngest boy was of a different color than that of the rest of family. One of the boys in the class thought that the boy was adopted, to which a girl from the class said: 'I know everything about adoption because I am adopted.' 'What does adoption mean then?' the boy asked. 'It means', the girl answered, 'that a child does not grow in the mother's belly but in her heart.'" (translation from an online guestbook of a Finnish adoption website cited in McIlvenny and Raudaskoski, 2005:58)

The emotive sincerity and effusive innocence of above conversation reveals an ontological question of origin - where one comes from - and the fundamental need for belonging through narratives of rootedness. The fundamental continuity of one's personal narrative is contingent on the ability to locate one's self relationally with respect to significant others, family, relatives, friends, and the wider public, and to connect the where one came from to where one is and where one is going to. This connects the dots between one's origin, one's sense of present/here and now, and one's sense of purpose, life objectives, and 'destiny'.

For birthmothers, childbirth seals and completes the 'rite of passage' (Davis-Floyd, 1992) to motherhood, and establishes an indelible biological connection, a 'blood lineage' that embeds a narrative of continuity. Indeed, the knowledge of having come from "mummy's tummy" is an important assertion of continuity, belonging and connectedness. Such explanations of having come from "mummy's tummy" are often accompanied by narratives of how daddy and mummy met and how they loved each other, and then how much they and the entire family wanted the baby/child, and how s/he was born, and how delighted the family was, and so on. This offers the child an anchoring point of identity and belonging, a sense of 'natural' and 'taken-for-granted' continuity as the narrative of the child's beginning are interweaved with those of his/her parents.

Lifton (1994), herself an adoptee, suggests that such narratives are inseparable from the child's feeling of connection to his/her socio-cultural and moral rooting. She adds that such narratives secure the child's sense of belonging to the family lineage and define his/her identity.

Whereas, childbirth seals the rights of birthmothers and their narrative of connectedness, adoptive mothers are not accorded any such taken-for-granted narrative of belonging. In fact, the adoptive mothers and adoptive families' stories are quite different in nature. Whereas birthmothers' stories provide a sense of 'natural' continuation of and lineage, the adoptive families begin with a rupture, a discontinuity, or a 'disjuncture' (Appadurai, 1996). They begin with a presumption of its' 'unnaturalness' and a sense of 'not-belonging', of not being 'wanted', of rejection and relinquishment. Transnational adoptive mothers do not complete their 'rite of passage' to motherhood in familial places, and spaces of a hospital or a delivery room. Their transformative spaces to motherhood, are often 'non-places' of a hotel lobby, or a lawyer's office, or other non-familial places and spaces.

Narratives, Culture, Context, and Identity

People have a natural inclination toward structuring their reality in the form of stories and narratives that they tell others and themselves about their identities, lives, and experiences (Epston and White, 1989). This therefore, applies to parenthood and mothering given their particular importance and significance for individuals' sense of identity and behavior.

Kearney states that humans are story telling animals and that without a '...transition from nature to narrative, from time suffered to time enacted and enunciated, it is debatable whether a merely biological life (zoe) could ever be considered a truly human one (bios).' (Kearney, 2002: 3). While Hannah Arendt argues that 'The chief characteristic of the specifically human life... is that it is always full of events which ultimately can be told as a story.... It is of this life, bios, as distinguished from mere zoe, that Aristotle said that it "somehow is a kind of action (praxis)".' (Cited in

Kearney, 2002:3). Hence, narratives provide an explanation and meaning for actions and performance, and the temporal connection and continuity between past, present and future, and as such offer a sense of coherence and constitute our historicity.

Narratives both contextualize and locate identities and attribute meaning, they allow making sense of self and the 'other' and the relationship between the two in a dynamic process of meaning making, a sense of belonging and an anchoring point for both identities and relations/hierarchies. In fact, White (1980) suggests that social order is contingent on the capacity to narrativize events.

Our cognitions and cognitive structures lay the foundation of our identity, and cognitive theory recognizes narratives as structural foundations of self, consciousness, experience, and identity. In this sense narratives may be defined as 'integrative work, producing the continuity and coherence without which identity, experience and memory would not be possible' (Vasterling, 2007:79). Hence, Dennett (1992) argues that we confer identity based on tales we hear and tell throughout our lives. This appreciation of narrative is shared by hermeneutic phenomenology, with Ricoeur (1991a, 1991b) stating: 'We equate life with the stories that we tell about it.'

The sense of continuity in individual and collective narratives is an important element for anchoring of identities and cultures. Derrida argues that an unbroken narrative of identity offers 'a reassuring certitude.... And on the basis of this certitude anxiety can be mastered (1978:279, also see 1976). Broken stories, such as those of refugees, adoptees, immigrants and diasporic populations, create dissonance and incertitude and therefore, generate tension and anxiety.

Narratives convey meaning, hence, culture, or what is meaningful to people, can be considered as a collection of narrativised values, customs and norms. Indeed, in line with Geertz (1993) we may define culture as 'webs of significance' spun between people through narratives and their own social actions. Hence, we can say that cultural praxis is the interplay between signification and interpretation. Through this hermeneutic dynamic, identities, actions, practices, communities, subjects, and objects become cultural. Indeed, continuous cultural praxis both presupposes and creates more or less structured webs of significance – that is, interpretative communities (Fish, 1980), and this is the foundation of intersubjective understanding and cultural identity (Jansson, 2002:9).

Internet chat, tweeting, blogs, social networking and other forms of online interactions and exchange form a narrative discourse which constitute the self and the 'other' and the relation in between the two (Lawler,

2000:12-13). Islam drawing on Geertz defines the chat-room as 'a metasocial commentary… a story they tell themselves about themselves; that is, the chat-room can be … of the collective life of the group, a self-enacted story with its users as narrators.' (2006:82). In fact, we suggest that the same applies to online communities, social networks and blogs. Giddens (1991) argues that identity in late-modernity is a 'reflexive biographical project' as people dynamically filter incoming information and construct and re-negotiate their identities.

'Identity narratives provide a sense not only of rootedness, but also of exclusivity' (Yngvesson and Mahoney, 2000). As Featherstone (1995: 142-3) states: 'it is only possible to belong to one national genealogical tree'. We particularly wish to highlight the centrality of the desire for belonging and the subjectively experienced rootedness.

Ricoeur developed the concept of 'narrative identity' in his earlier work on Time and Narrative (in 3 volumes: 1984, 1985, 1988) with its focal point being the understanding of self-identity in terms of the interweaving of stories one tells about oneself, one's autobiography, with the stories of others, such that every identity is 'literally "entangled in stories"' (Ricoeur, 1996: 6; also 1991a). Such stories are rooted in the biographies of significant others, as well as in terms of narratives that invoke a collective and its past.

Cyber-space and the Liminality of Motherhood and 'Everyday Life'

Where not many years ago, one would have wondered if a community could exist online, today the question may be whether it can exist without cyber-space. However, there are certain aspects of online communities, websites, chat-rooms, blogs, and social networking that are either specific to internet and online transactions or particularly evident/important on cyber-space.

Although in earlier versions of social networking the trend was often to reconstruct a completely new online identity (Turkle, 1994), the liminality of 'everyday life' based on increasing integration of individuals' online and offline identities implies that cyber-space has become more 'identity-constraining' (Tufekci, 2008) as online identities, in many online interactions, are often rooted in individual's 'real-life' identity. Indeed, social networking sites 'constitute an extended social context in which to express one's actual personality characteristics' (Back et al, 2010).

The increasing interdependence and integration of online and offline activities, interactions, exchanges, and experiences have shrunk time and space, resulting in new proximities and have transformed the meaning of communication, connectivity, relationships, privacy, and so on, while the Googlization and hybridization of life and living, through integration of online and offline, have extended our consciousness and transformed our patterns of thinking as well as our experience of 'reality'. Therefore, on the one hand, 'everyday life' is substantially influenced, transformed and dependent on virtuality and virtual 'reality' (ranging from using one's mobile phone, to Googling the information one needs, to engaging in online networking and/or exchange), while on the other hand, cyber-space interactions and experiences bear residual impact of individuals' physical/offline/bodily 'reality' or corporeality (For instance, whether online or offline, our feelings, and our physical and mental states influence our reactions, judgement, thinking, mood, attitude, etc.).

Indeed, we can gain a better understanding of the nexus between agency and subjectivity through a phenomenological appreciation of the semiotic and hemeneutics of online communication (Lanigan, 1997). Acknowledgement of residual corporeality in our engagement in cyber-space, as stated by phenomenologist Merleau-Ponty '… that visceral body whose capacity for language and society is the foundation of all other institutions…' (O'Neill, 1989:3), and the methodology of semiotic phenomenology (Lanigan, 1988; 1992) offer us a theoretical framework to capture the reflexive expressions and (re)presentations of this liminality, straddling both corporeality and virtuality. In other words, Drawing on the works of Lanigan (1988, 1992) we can suggest that adoptive mothers' socially situated experiences in cyber-space form an ongoing event and process of transformation which accompany their corporeal experiences/'reality', which at times compete and conflict and at other times complement and reinforce their identities. Hence, the adoptive mothers' identity is a corporealized mix of their lived subjectivity experienced as a hybrid between virtuality and embodied/corporeal 'reality'. Indeed, O'Neill referring to Merleau-Ponty's 'visceral body' suggests that human body offers '… the bio-text upon which the principle social institutions inscribe themselves….'

Sherry Turkle (1995) reflects on the meaning of identity in the age of cyber-technology and suggests that 'identity' should be considered as a third dimension of analysis of public-private. Although technology, internet, and the context of our lives have significantly changed since then, the question of identity and identity (re)construction/maintenance remain important areas of reflection and research.

A Reflection on Transnational Adoption

Navigating and examining various adoption and adoption-related websites and cyber-networks is a journey in visual geographies of affect encapsulated in intertextuality of a visual culture, and complemented by narratives of pre-adoptive and adoptive mothers. However, the ease with which photographs of children, who Lisa Cartwright (2003) refers to as the 'waiting children', are circulated, and at times manipulated for economic return, in such cyber-spaces, can be equated to an exploitation of the children's affective value. These websites photo-listings offer search facilities for refining adoptive parent's search by children's sex, skin color, race, age, region, and ease of adoption. Cartwright (2003) suggests that these images function as 'lures to draw prospective clients into the adoption market'. In this sense, the affective value of the child is equated to commodity value of the child and aimed at facilitating the adoptive parents imaginings of 'their child' as 'a child' 'like these'. This engages the adoptive mothers/parents in a solipsistic imagining/absorption and introjection where the photograph of some of 'these children' become the image of the desired 'family photograph' of the adoptive parents, and where the adoptive mother's/parent's mind extends and shifts from 'what is' to 'what can be'. The adoptive mother's relational identity, therefore, undergoes a process of transformation that incorporates the fluid and evolving thoughts of what is possible, and as such, strengthens the idea/thought and attachment to 'solipsistic imaginings' of 'a child' of 'my own'. Adoptive mothers/parents rejoice the picture of 'the child' that is going to be 'their child' in the same manner that birthmothers/birthparents celebrate the ultrasound image of their child. Therefore, the impact and value of such visual parade of intertextuality for both the adoptive mothers/parents and the adoptee/adopted children, should not be underestimated.

The 'waiting children' images are also a tool for medical screening. Many adoption agencies offer adoptive parents photographs or video footage together with some medical details of the prospective adoptee child for evaluation and detection of possible pathologies by a handful of practitioners specializing in adoption medicine. For adoptive mothers such evaluations offer the equivalent of prenatal examinations for birthmothers (Cartwright, 2003).

The problematic nature of adoption system and the easy circulation and manipulation of images of 'waiting children' from some of the poorest countries as advertisement in global market of adoption based on its affective value has been subject of scrutiny and critical reflection for both policy and practice of adoption. Such problems have been accompanied by a number of other challenges and concerns including the potential for racial and ethnic discrimination due to image-based selection of children (ibid). Cartwright (2003) offers an excellent discussion and analysis of such image classification. Furthermore, separation from birthmothers/birthparents, although consensual on the part of such mothers/parents, can have serious effects and lasting emotional implications for children. Most importantly one of the biggest challenges inherent in all inter-racial/inter-cultural adoptions is a balanced approach for appropriately addressing racial, ethnic and cultural differences between the adoptive country and the adopted children's birth country. This is a question of identity and cultural dissonance.

Overall, the imaginings, narratives, and dynamics of identity, belonging, authenticity and legitimacy of race, ethnicity, gender, blood, and culture escape simplistic categorizations or fixed legislative responses, nor are they appropriately addressed by discourses and dichotomies of (post)colonization vis-à-vis benevolence/humanitarianisms.

In the meantime, in this changing and challenging context, adoptive mothers/parents and adoptee/adopted children continue their difficult and recurring struggle to overcome the dissonance, reconcile the difference, celebrate the diversity, seal the rupture, and heal the hurt/wound from which they suffer and/or have suffered for an enormity of reasons and causes ranging from reproductive and biological impairment/difficulties, to loss of a child, loss of father/mother or both parents, or just turn of events and circumstances beyond their control.

Clearly the right balance between cultural integration/assimilation and an appreciation and cultivation of cultural difference/diversity is as unique as each adoptee or adopted child and each adoptive parent or family.

Therefore, the adoptive mother/family 'of 21st century is caught between multiple worlds dominated by divergent policies, unbalanced economies, contrasting cultures, and divided communities, in a globalized and shrinking village of anomie' (Buzzi and Megele, 2011) faced with a paradigm of adoption defined by fusing and contrasting dualities of: rupture and continuity, separation and belonging; feeling at home and away; departing and returning; circulating and rejoining; and a sense of multi-belonging (Buzzi and Megele, 2011). As such, it seem to us that the adoptive mothers/parents, and adoptee/adopted children, embody the ideal-type of the management of a reflexive project of 'self' in a cyber-world of fluid liminality in eternal motion and evolution (Buzzi and Megele, 2011).

Works Cited

Appadurai, A. (1996) *Modernity at Large: Cultural Dimensions of Globalization*. Minneapolis, MN: University of Minnesota Press.

Buzzi, P. and Megele, C. (2011) 'Reflections on the 21st Century Migrant: Impact of Social Networking and Hyper-reality on the Lived Experience of Global Migration'. in German M. & Banerjee P. (eds.) *Migration, Technology and Transculturation: A Global Perspective*. Lindenwood University Press, Center for International and Global Studies, St. Charles, Missouri.

Cartwright, L. (2003). "Photographs of 'Waiting Children': The Transnational Adoption Market". *Social Text* – 74 Vol. 21(1) : 83-109.

Davis-Floyd, R.E. (1992) *Birth as an American Rite of Passage*. Berkeley: University of California Press.

Dennett, J. (1992). 'The self as the center of narrative gravity'. in F. Kessel, P. Cole, & D. Johnson (Eds.), *Self and consciousness: Multiple perspectives*. Hillsdale: Erlbaum.

Derrida, J. (1978) *Writing and Difference*. Chicago IL: University of Chicago Press.

Epston, D. & White, M. (1989). *Literate means to therapeutic ends.* Adelaide: Dulwich Centre Publications.

Featherstone, M. (1995) *Undoing Culture: Globalization, Postmodernism, and Identity*. London: Sage.

Fish, S. E. (1980), *Is There a Text in this Class? The Authority of Interpretative Communities*. Cambridge, MA: Harvard University Press.

Geertz, Clifford (1993[1973]) *The Interpretation of Cultures: Selected Essays*. London: Fontana Press.

Giddens A. (1991) *Modernity and Self- Identity*. Polity Press.

Islam, G. (2006) 'Virtual Speakers, Virtual Audiences: Agency, Audience and Constraint in an Online Chat Community', *Dialectical Anthroplology*. Vol. 30. pp. 71-889.

Jansson, A. (2002), 'The Mediatization of Consumption: Toward an Analytical Framework of Image Culture'. *Journal of Consumer Culture*, Vol. 2(1): 5-31.

Kearney, Richard (2002) *On Stories*. London: Routledge.

Lanigan, R. L. (1997) *'Communicology' in The Encyclopedia of Phenomenology*. General ed. Lester Embree. Boston: Kluwer Academic Publishers, 683-9.

—. (1992) *The Human Science of Communicology: A Phenomenology of Discourse in Foucault and Merleau-Ponty*. Pittsburgh: Duquesne University Press.

—. (1988) *Phenomenology of Communication: Merleau Ponty's Thematics in Communicology and Semiology*. Pittsburgh: Duquesne University Press.

Lawler, S. (2000) *Mother the Self: Mothers, Daughters, Subjects*. London and New York: Routledge.

Lifton, B. (1994) *Journey of the Adopted Self: A Quest for Wholeness*. New York: Basic Books.

McIlvenny, P & Raudaskoski, P. (2005). "Figuring the transnational 'child-to-be-adopted': The web as a virtual sociocultural contact zone for intercountry adoption". in Preisler B., Fabricius A., Haberland H., Kjaerbeck S., and Risager K. (eds.) *The Consequences of Mobility*, Roskilde: Roskilde University, Department of Language and Culture. p. 58-70.

O'Neill, J. (1989) *The Communicative Body: Studies in Communicative Philosophy, Politics, and Sociology*. Evanston: North Western University Press.

Ricoeur, P. (1996) 'Reflections on a new ethos for Europe', in R. Kearney (ed.), *Paul Ricoeur. The Hermeneutics of Action*. London: Sage.

—. (1991a) *Lectures*, 3 vols. Paris: Seuil.

—. (1991b) 'Narrative identity'. in D. Wood (Ed., Trans.), *On Paul Ricoeur. Narrative and interpretation*. New York: Routledge.

Ricoeur, Paul (1988) Time and Narrative, Vol. 3. *Trans. Kathleen Blamey and David Pellauer*. Chicago: University of Chicago Press.

—. (1984) 'The creativity of language', in Richard Kearney (ed.), *Dialogues with Contemporary Continental Thinkers*. Manchester: Manchester University Press.

Tufekci, Z. (2008). 'Can You See Me Now? Audience and Disclosure Regulation in Online Social Network Sites'. *Bulletin of Science Technology Society*, Feb 2008; vol. 28: pp. 20-36.

Turkle, S., (1995). *Life on the Screen: Identity in the age of the Internet.* New York: Simon & Schuster.

—. (1994). 'Multiple Subjectivity and Virtual Community at the End of the Freudian Century'. *Sociological Inquiry,* 67(1).

Vasterling, V. (2007) 'Cognitive Theory and Phenomenology in Arendt's and Nussbaum's Work on Narrative'. *Springer Science + Business Media, Hum Stud*, Vol.(30):79–95.

White, H. (1980) 'The Value of Narrativity in the Representation of Reality'. p. 1-23, in Mitchell W.J.J. (eds.) *On Narrative*, Chicago, IL: University of Chicago Press.

Yngvesson B. and Mahoney M. (2000) 'As One Should, Ought and Wants to Be: Belonging and Authenticity in Identity Narratives'. *Theory, Culture & Society*. Sage, London. Vol. 17(6): 77-110.

BLOGS AND COMMUNITY

CHAPTER FIFTEEN

MOMMY BLOGS: THE CENTRALITY OF COMMUNITY IN THE PERFORMANCE OF ONLINE MATERNITY

LYNNE M. WEBB AND BRITTNEY S. LEE

The chapter proposes an original theoretical model depicting the communities of mommy bloggers in the United States. The model describes how bloggers' identity, motivation, and blog content interrelate to sustain blog communities. Such communities facilitate the development of online relationships among mommy bloggers and the accompanying support they provide one another.

Blogging has been described as the offspring of personal webpages and user-generated content (Turkle). Personal webpages present original content, but are fairly static. In contrast, blogs feature new posts typically on a daily basis and allow readers to comment on each post, thus creating original, constantly changing content.

There are several genres of blogs, including the popular genre of mommy blogs. This chapter presents an original model, supported by previous research findings as well as the authors' ideas and arguments, depicting the U.S. mommy blogosphere. Our model describes how a mommy blogger's identity influences her blog content, and how content provides the basis for a sense of community among mommy bloggers--a community that leads to close relationships among mommy bloggers who provide mutual social support. The model also depicts symbiotic relationships among these factors such that mommy blog communities, in turn, influence mommy bloggers' identity and content.

History and Definition of Blogging

Blogging is a fairly new form of computer-mediated communication (CMC), as the term "blog" did not appear until 1997 (Jost and Hilpolit).

Because blogs are easy to create and maintain via software templates, and because various blogging services offer free blog space (e.g., wordpress.com, blogger.com, google.com; Rodzvilla), "anyone with access to a computer and the Internet to create and maintain a blog" (Stefanone and Jang 124). From 2000 to 2005, the number of blogs grew from 100,000 to more than 4 million (Woods). In 2009, more than 12 million adults maintained a blog (Schechter).

A weblog, or blog, is a webpage with regular posts that appear in reverse chronological order (Wei). Blogs contain information about a wide range of topics from personal life, to photography, to politics (Jost and Hipolit). Blogs typically have three main characteristics (Droge, Stanko, and Pollitte). (1) Blogs have original content in posts written by an author or authors. (2) Blogs usually link to other blogs. This list of links or "blogroll" enables blog authors to add others' blogs to their site, creating networks or communities of blogs called the "blogosphere" (van Doorn, van Zoonen and Wyatt 146). (3) Most blogs have an interactive component, allowing readers to comment on posts (Droge et al.).

Blogs are often categorized as either filter blogs or personal blogs (e.g., Herring and Paolillo; Wei). A filter blog "includes certain items while excluding others, often focused on news and political events" (Wei 533). Political blogs, for example, often link to the websites of traditional media sources, such as newspapers. In turn, traditional media outlets often quote political filter blogs (Tucker). Because filter blogs are typically written by men, quoting such blogs highlights the words of men versus women. Similarly, academic research on male blogs is more prevalent than on female blogs (Lopez).

In contrast, personal blogs are more journal-like and feature disclosures of events occurring in daily life and informal photographs (Jung, Vorderer and Song). While journal blogs are more private and personal in nature, they are written for a mass and ambiguous audience that may include family, friends, acquaintances, and strangers (Kleman). Such blogging can be characterized as a blend of interpersonal and mass communication. Bloggers write to communicate within relationships as well as to transmit messages to mass audiences. Therefore, blogging is the "epitome of masspersonal communication" (Kleman 2).

Mommy bloggers

Scholars have labeled one genre of personal blogs "mommy blogs." A mommy blogger, for purposes of this study, is defined as a woman whose blog content is predominantly about her family. A large number of mommy bloggers use BlogHer, a popular women's blog community that receives over 4 million unique visitors per month (BlogHer) and holds an annual off-line conference for bloggers. Mommy bloggers who attended the first BlogHer conference in 2005 reported feeling marginalized and disrespected by people who assumed they wrote only about mundane tasks such as changing diapers. In response, Alice Bradley of "Finslippy" (http://finslippy.typepad.com), described mommy blogging as a radical act that is redefining 21st century maternity (Lopez). BlogHer held a discussion session titled "MommyBlogging is a Radical Act!" at its 2006 conference (Camahort), providing credibility and validity to mommy bloggers. Thus began public recognition for the mommy blogosphere.

The title of mommy blogger

The mommy blog is a popular genre of personal blogs. The term "mommy blogger" brings over eighty thousand hits on Google, while "mother bloggers" only brings eight thousand (Friedman and Calixte). Some bloggers perceive "mommy blogger" as an appropriate label. On amommystory.blogspot.com, Christina wrote:

> I am a mommy, I am a blogger, and I write about my child and the experience of being a mother. So therefore I am a mommyblogger. I don't dislike the term at all. Instead, I embrace it with a sloppy, open-mouthed, toddler-style kiss. It is a part of who I am (McMenemy).

Another blogger, Karoli of "Odd Time Signatures" (drumsnwhistles. com) said:

> The value of the term mommyblogger is this: It identifies a very powerful and vocal demographic- a group of thinking, tech-savvy, engaged women. Women committed today to raising their kids, but also raising their kids in the context of what it means to live in today's world. . . . Moms committed to community, both virtual and 'real-life', to others, and to service. That's who you are, that's who *mommybloggers* are (Lowe).

However, other bloggers do not embrace the label "mommy bloggers," because the term comes with a "condescending pat on the head" (Rosenburg 263). Friedman and Calixte write "moms and mommies conjure up images of doting apron-clad sycophants smilingly paying homage to their tiny sovereigns" (25). Critics argue that labeling these women as "mommy bloggers" may disrespect other aspects of bloggers' identities including worker, wife, friend, and daughter. Author and blogger, Meagan Francis, responded to having the title on her press pass say "mommyblogger."

> I cringed, then I felt indignant. Mommy blogger? That's what I am? . . . I don't even like the word 'mommy'. . . it's always felt kind of smarmy and whiny to me, and it's more of an affectionate title used by young children than a descriptive term. Used in conjunction with 'blogger' – and written on the line that would usually indicate my credentials – it felt almost like an insult (Lowe).

Thus, while many identify with the act of mommy blogging and its community, the camp is split on what to call mommy bloggers. However, no one disagrees that there is money to be made.

Blogging motivation

Many advertisers view women as powerful consumers, because they typically make spending decisions for the family (Lopez). Following this line of reasoning, mommy bloggers have been called "a marketer's dream" (Thompson 6). Advertisers are "snatching up real estate" on popular mommy blogs to capitalize on the phenomenon. After hearing stories of mommy bloggers making $4,000 a month from ads, other types of bloggers start blogging to get rich (Quenqua). Some mommy bloggers sell their own brand of merchandise (Niedzviecki); others mass market for large corporations. BlogHer has an ad network of large corporate sponsors such as Google, GM, Dove, Disney and Kraft (BlogHer), supplying their blog network with multiple advertisements. The amount of money bloggers make on blog ads is often determined by readership, and no reliable statistics on money made from mommy blogs are publically available at this time.

Tucker explains that mothers write blogs "because they can, and because they hope to gain something from it" (2). In addition to financial gain, Kaye identified a variety of reasons for blogging, including a few reasons that seem especially relevant to mommy blogs, including convenience, personal fulfillment, expression, and affiliation.

Identity

In addition to affecting a woman's finances, blogging can impact identity. Here we use the term "identity" to reference a person's self-concept. Because identity is performed and enacted (Pearson), a blog functions as an "interactive extension" of identity (Tucker 6). Online environments, like blogs, take performance to another level by adding a public audience. Self-performance becomes a mix of public and private, of backstage and front stage behaviors. Events occur under the audience's gaze, while other events occur backstage and are not discussed on the blog. However, both arenas can impact a blogger's identity. "Maternal blogging can be construed as a performance of the self, a practice through which the mother recreates the setting and substance of her life through well-crafted lines of text" (Tucker 12). Writers of personal blogs seem especially engaged in the performance of gender (Hans, Selvidge, Tinker and Webb, 2011) and identity presentation as they disclose the details of their private lives on their blogs (Van Doorn et al.).

Blogging provides users with a forum to present their ideas, their creativity, and themselves—and to receive validation for such presentations (Kline and Burstein). Identity can be influenced by online associations, connections, community and relationships (Turkle). While a blogger potentially enacts identity on her blog, in turn, identity can be influenced by the performance itself—creating a mutually influential relationship between the blog and the blogger's identity. Merely writing about everyday life can impact identity, by prompting reflection and analysis; further, readers' posts can influence bloggers' identity.

While to some observers, journal blogs may seem like a rambling record of authors' mundane day, bloggers assign meaning to the stages and cycles of life that may otherwise be missed in their busy existence, if not chronicled. This is especially true for mothers who document, not only their lives, but the lives of their children.

Mothers also blog to enact and address their own personal struggles with their identities. Motherhood is typically viewed as a private and domestic matter (Lopez). By chronicling maternal events in the public realm, mothers can discuss and potentially redefine the meaning of motherhood. Mommy bloggers create their own motherhood identity, one that is often very different from the picture of motherhood presented in mainstream media. "Instead of the loving mother, we see women who are frazzled by the demands of their newborn baby, who have no clue what to do when their child gets sick, who suffer from postpartum depression and whose hormones rage uncontrollably" (Lopez 732). By embracing the reality of motherhood as they experience it, mommy bloggers create a new maternal identity.

Community

Because blogs typically limit their content to a specific and narrow focus, blogs lend themselves to community formation. We use the term community to reference a sense of cohesiveness, commonality, and propinquity among a group. Blogs form online communities around a specific theme, idea, industry activity, or other subject of the blog (Droge et al.). Some scholars trace the rise of blog communities to the loss of real life communities (Castells), arguing that users turn to virtual communities to fill the void left by the absence of real communities. Because many Americans live in close quarters, have their own corner grocery store, neighborhood school district, and smaller subdivided communities, they no longer have ready opportunities for a wider sense of community (Shirky). Because modern U.S. life has depleted "natural" community opportunities, community enactment now requires coordination. Enter blogs, where a "sense of community is developed through interactions with like-minded people" (Kaye 76). Through blogging, authors invite audience members to discuss, share, and support one another (Lopez). Community is formed through blogging by the talk between mommy bloggers and their audiences (Tucker), typically fellow mommy bloggers. This interactivity creates community.

Blanchard argues that blogs are virtual communities offering interactivity through comments and regular posting by the authors. Conversely, not every blog is a virtual settlement, or a place where community can grow. Blogs that fail to allow the reader and the author to communicate regularly do not serve as a village center for a virtual community. But most blog authors are writing to, and hearing from, their audience. Active, popular blogs fit the virtual settlement definition. Sustained readership and regular posters make most blogs a place in which virtual community happens.

As with any other online community, being able to communicate easily, frequently, and regularly about specific topics creates a sense of belonging and community, a place where users can talk to others and get feedback on their ideas. In a study of a community on LiveJournal, a blog hosting site, the establishment of connections among users created a community by allowing users to give advice and talk freely to one another (Kouper). The sharing of a common interest contributes to community formation (Hine). For instance, one mommy blogger community may be Southern mothers of young toddlers, while another might be moms who home school teens. The various communities form around common interests varying with the age of children, geography, activity (e.g. homeschooling, scrapbookers, mothers of multiples).

Mommy blogs were never developed to appeal to everyone but rather to fellow mothers in similar circumstances. Blog hosting websites require users to register and create a blog (although it can be an "empty" blog) to become part of their blogging community and thus to have ready access to multiple blogs for casual or focused reading. In sum, users with the most immediate access to mommy blogs are fellow bloggers.

Link sharing is another simple way that blog communities develop (Li and Chignell). Blogger A may list 10 blogs on her blogroll, thus connecting to those 10 people. As bloggers begin listing each other on their blogrolls, a community can form through association. Indeed, blogrolls typically reveal a blog's community. Unlike many other on-line communities, U.S. mommy bloggers are typically read by and commented upon by fellow mommy bloggers. The mommy bloggers are basically writing to each other and forming a specialized blogging community of blog authors who read and comment on each others' work.

In sum, mommy blogs, like other blog genres, are comprised of blog authors who usually also read other blogs. Bloggers use their blogrolls to link to other blogs they regularly read. Bloggers become connected by reading one another's posts, and through this familiarity, form blog communities.

Support

Because mommy bloggers read and comment upon each others' posts, they are positioned to provide and receive social support. By social support, we mean providing assistance and positive affirmation in times of need. One blogger said that the community of bloggers made blogging "worth the risk" (Niedzviecki 25). Having a group of seemingly strangers, who were now her blog friends, her community, rooting for her, facilitated her to self-disclose more information, so that she could receive further support. For mothers who are struggling, such as many new moms, this community can be quite meaningful. For example, Christina, from amommystory.blogspot.com, wrote that during her first year of motherhood she felt,

> isolated, lonely and confused. I guess I expected to join some secret society when I became a mom, but it wasn't there. . . I wanted help from someone who had been through this. . . I only wanted to know I wasn't alone – that there were others with babies who wouldn't nap, or it was OK to skip rice

> cereal and go straight to oatmeal ... Finding blogs helped me tremendously. I found moms … with similar issues (McMenemy).

Support is very important to the blogging community and previous researchers have conducted numerous, in-depth analysis of online social support (High and Solomon; Kouper; Turner, Grube, and Meyers). They documented that more women than men participate in online support groups (High and Solomon). Further, online support groups most frequently provide informational support and emotional support; they are especially helpful to people seeking to connect with others facing similar challenges, like new moms trying to connect with other new moms. Several types of online forums exist for supportive groups, including discussion boards, chat rooms, and social networks (High and Solomon). Blogs may provide more support than message boards because an individual's voice can be lost in a thread format. In contrast, a mother can articulate a distinct voice on her blog (McMenemy).

Thousands of moms turn to the Internet and to blogging to share experiences and, in turn, receive support and counsel from readers including largely fellow bloggers (Kline and Burstein). One primary reason for seeking support through blogging is to address unmet needs (Lee and Hawkins). A void in the face-to-face (FtF) support system may motivate an individual to turn to online sources. One mom described the support found on mommy blogs, saying:

> We share our lopsided, slightly hysterical, often exaggerated but more or less authentic experiences. If one bloggers writes about, say, her bad behavior at the doctor's office, then maybe at some point, some freaked-out new mother is going to read that and feel a little better – less stupid, less ridiculous about her own breakdown (Camahort).

Women who feel isolated or alone in the mothering process often turn to blogging to acquire social support. One mommy blogger, Ayelet Waldman of bad-mother.blogspot.com, described blog support saying, "The blogosphere is the perfect place for women to find advice and support, especially mothers" (Kline and Burstein 308). "It's a remarkable phenomenon to meet thousands of strangers who lend each other emotional support" (312).

Heather Armstrong, of dooce.com, a popular mommy blogger, received notoriety for losing her job after posting negative work-related comments on her blog (Rosenberg). After blogging about her sadness and anxiety after the birth of her child, she disclosed to her readers that she would be checking into a hospital psychiatric ward for treatment. After that post, she received a "flood of supportive emails" (262). She equated the support she received during that experience to stage diving at a concert – she took a leap in a moment of insanity, but was caught by the crowd of extending arms. She claims, "I believe my audience was part of what saved my life" (263).

Mommy bloggers receive support on issues beyond mothering. A blogger wrote about her husband's affair, and readers offered support. One commenter said, "If you need to come out to California to chill, our home is big, in the woods, and near the beach…you'll get your own bedroom, robe, a new toothbrush, and we'll go for spa treatments" (Tucker 9). Such an offer goes beyond informational and emotional support to instrumental support. To offer such instrumental support to a person known only through a blog demonstrates how blogging can facilitate the formation of close relationships between readers and writers.

Relationships

Supportive exchanges may lead to relationship formation online. We use the term "relationship" to reference volunteer adult associations of indefinite length. Tucker notes, "The emotional content of relationships made in the maternal blogosphere is undeniably real" (11). FtF networks may be less available than online support groups, especially for people who marry, have children, and become so busy, that they lose touch with past relationships (Bane, Cornish, Erspamer, and Kampman). In these cases, blogging can be used to strengthen existing friendships and to develop new friendships. Mommy bloggers write in journal style, posting personal information, in part to maintain relationships (Stefanone and Jang) with their readers, who are typically fellow bloggers. Because of the interactive nature of blogging, people can "talk" to one another, and, as they disclose, they grow to trust others who are like themselves (Jost and Hipolit), especially when offered positive feedback and/or social support.

CMC can facilitate relationship development (Bane et al.). The usual constraints found in FtF interactions are absent online, allowing relationships to form in ways that are not possible offline. For example, the asynchronous quality of CMC allows people to communicate at their convenience (Wellman and Hampton). While it is obvious that users can start romantic relationships (for example, through online dating websites) using CMC, certain online channels, such as mommy blogs, provide the platform for and facilitate the development of close friendships—due to the levels of self-disclosure and frequency of communication (Bane et al.). We use the term "friendship" to mean "a relationship involving voluntary or unconstrained interaction in which participants respond to one another personally" (Wright). In sum, when social support and interaction occur on blogs, the stage is set for relationship development, typically friendship development.

CMC relationships may take longer to develop than FtF relationships, because of the longer time it takes to transmit, decode and trust CMC messages; however, over time, CMC relationships can have the same, and sometimes more positive outcomes than FtF relationships (Ramirez and Zhang). Close CMC relationships form due to hyperpersonal communication or the extreme depth of interpersonal exchanges within CMC (Turner et al.). Bloggers often employ hyperpersonal communication, as they share very personal information that can facilitate successful relationships (Child, Pearson and Petronio). Furthermore, the longer the duration of a CMC relationship, the more it resembles a FtF relationship in terms of breadth, depth, understanding and commitment (Young).

Figure 1. A Path Model of the Mommy Blogosphere.

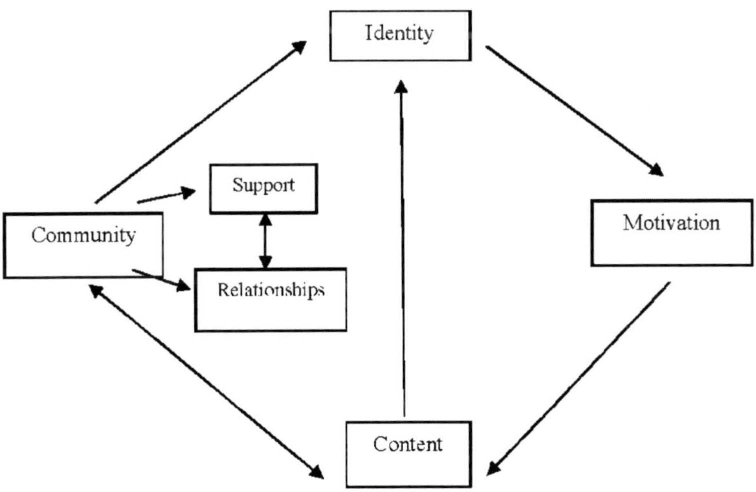

Our original path model

We assert that many characteristics of blogging discussed above appear interrelated (see Figure 1). As a woman is motivated to blog, she chooses her blog content based on her identity. Many mothers choose to blog about their families, and become labeled mommy bloggers. The specialized content and the interactivity among fellow bloggers as they post on her blog creates a blogging community, where members give and receive support, and, in turn, form friendships. The interactivity of these factors come full circle as a woman's identity is impacted by being a member of the blogging community and by having a space to share ideas and thoughts. As she blogs, she may discover additional things about herself that impact how she thinks about herself. These factors (community, support, relationships) impact a blogger's perception of self and in turn may serve as a stronger motivation to continue blogging, thus continuing the cycle of influence among identity, motivation, content, community, support, and relationships. While the above described variables and many of the relationships between them were identified in previous publications, our model is the first to connect this constellation of variables and display the relationships between them in one comprehensive array of connections.

Works Cited

Bane, Cynthia M. H., Marilyn Cornish, Nicole Erspamer, and Lia Kampman. "Self-disclosure Through Weblogs and Perceptions of Online and 'Real-Life' Friendships among Female Bloggers." *Cyberpsychology, Behavior, and Social Networking* 13.2 (2010): 131-139.

Blanchard, Anita. "Blogs as Virtual Communities: Identifying a Sense of Community in the Julie/Julia Project." *Into the Blogosphere: Rhetoric, Community, and Culture and Weblogs*. Edited by Laura Gurak, Smiljana Antonijevio, Laurie Johnson, Clancy Ratliff, and Jessica Reyman. Minneapolis, MN: University of Minnesota Library's Website, 2006. http://blog.lib.umn.edu/blogosphere/blogs_as_virtual.html

"BlogHer Network Joins Ranks of Top Women's Networks Online." *Media Report to Women* 35.4 (2007): 1-3.

Camahort, Elisa. "BlogHer '06 Session Discussion Mommyblogging is a Radical Act! On Day Two." *BlogHer Homepage*. BlogHer Publishing Network, 20 May 2006. http://blogher.org/node/5563

Castells, Manuel. *The Network Society: A Cross-Cultural Perspective*. Northampton, MA: Edward Elgar Publishing, 2004.

Child, Jeffrey T., Judy C. Pearson, and Sandra Petronio. "Blogging, Communication, and Privacy Management: Development of the Blogging Privacy Management Measure." *Journal of the American Society for Information Science and Technology* 60.10 (2009): 2079-2094.

Droge, Canelia, Michael A. Stanko, and Wesley A. Pollitte. "Lead Users and Early Adopters on the Web: The Role of New Technology Product Blogs." *Journal of Product Innovation Management* 27.1 (2010): 66-82.

Friedman, May and Shana L. Calixte. 2009. "Introduction." *Mothering and Blogging: The Radical Act of the Mommyblog*. Edited by May Friedman and Shana L. Calixte. 21-36. Toronto, Canada: Demeter Press.

Hans, Mark L., Brittney D, Selvidge, Katie A. Tinker, and Lynne M. Webb. 2011. "Online Performances of Gender: Blogs, Gender-bending, and Cybersex as Relational Exemplars," *Computer-Mediated Communication in Personal Relationships,* edited by Kevin B. Wright and Lynne M. Webb. 302-323. New York: Peter Lang Publishers.

Herring, Susan C., and John Paolillo (2006). "Gender and Genre Variation in Weblogs." *Journal of Sociolinguistics* 10.4 (2006): 439-459.

High, Andrew, and Denise Solomon. *Locating Computer-mediated Social Support within Online Communication Environments*. National Communication Association conference, San Diego, CA. November 2008.

Hine, Nick. 2004. "Stories and Blogs." *Proceedings of the Eleventh International Society for Augmentative and Alternative Communication Research Symosium*, October 2004, Brazil. Ed. Stephen von Tetzchner and M. de Jesus Goncalves. 193-197. ISAAC Press.

Jost, Kenneth, and Melissa J. Hipolit (2006). "Blog Explosion." *CQ Researcher* 16.22 (2006): 505-528.

Jung, Younbo, Peter Vorderer, and Hayeun Song. *Motivation and Consequences of Blogging in Social Life*. International Communication Association, San Francisco, CA. May 2007.

Kaye, Barbara K. "It's a Blog, Blog, Blog World: Users and Uses of Weblogs." *Atlantic Journal of Communication* 13.2 (2005): 73-95.

Kleman, Erin. *Journaling for the World (Wide Web) to See: A Proposed Model of Self-Disclosure Intimacy in Blogs*. National Communication Association Conference, Chicago. November 2007.

Kline, David, and Dan Burstein. *Blog! How the Newest Media Revolution Is Changing Politics, Business, and Culture*. New York: CDS Books, 2005.

Kouper, Inna. *The Pragmatics of Peer Advice Online: An Examination of a LiveJournal Community*. International Communication Association Conference, Chicago. May 2009.

Lee, Sun Young, and Hawkins, Robert. "Why Do Patients Seek an Alternative Channel? The Effects of Unmet Needs on Patients' Health-Related Internet Use." *Journal of Health Communication* 15.2 (2010): 152-166.

Li, Jamy, and Chignell, Mark. "Birds of a Feather: How Personality Influences Blog Writing and Reading." *International Journal of Human-Computer Studies* 68.9 (2010): 589-602.

Lopez, Lori K. "The Radical Act of 'Mommy Blogging': Redefining Motherhood through the Blogosphere." *New Media and Society* 11.5 (2009): 729-747.

Lowe, Shannon [Rocksinmydryer]. "What Do You Think of the Term 'Mommyblogger'?" BlogHer Homepage. *BlogHer Publishing Network*, 10 August 2008. Web. 1 October 2010.
http://www.blogher.com/what-do-you-think-term-mommyblogger

McMenemy, Christina. "Just Call Me a Mommyblogger." A Mommy Story (2006). *BlogHer Publishing Network*,
http://amommystory.blogspot.com/2006/08/just-call-me-mommyblogger.html

Niedzviecki, Hal. *The Peep Diaries: How We're Learning to Love Watching Ourselves and Our Neighbors*. San Francisco: City Light Books, 2009.

Pearson, Erika. "All the World Wide Web's a Stage: The Performance of Identity in Online Social Networks." *First Monday* 14.3 (2009): 1-7.

Quenqua, Douglass. "Blogs Falling In an Empty Forest." *The New York Times* 7 June 2009: ST1.

Ramirez, Artemio, and Zhang, Shuangyue. "When Online Meets Offline: The Effect of Modality Switching on Relational Communication." *Communication Monographs* 74.3 (2007): 287-310.

Rodzvilla, John, ed. *We've Got Blog: How Weblogs Are Changing Our Culture*. Cambridge, MA: Perseus Publishing, 2002.

Rosenberg, Scott. *Say Everything: How Blogging Began, What It's Becoming, and Why It Matters*. New York: Crown Publishers, 2009.

Schechter, Danny. "Credit Crisis: How Did We Miss It?" *British Journalism Review* 20.1 (2009): 19-26.

Shirky, Clay. *Here Comes Everybody: The Power of Organizing Without Organizations*. New York: Penguin Books, 2008.

Stefanone, Michael A., and Jang, Chyng-Yang. "Writing for Friends and Family: The Interpersonal Nature of Blogs." *Journal of Computer-Mediated Communication* 13.1 (2008): 123-140.

Thompson, Stephanie. "Mommy Blogs: A Marketer's Dream." *Advertising Age* 78.9 (2007): 6.

Tucker, Joan S. 2009. "Foreword." *Mothering and Blogging: The Radical Act of the Mommyblog*. Eds. May Friedman and Shana L. Calixte. 1-20. Toronto, Canada: Demeter Press.

Turkle, Shenay (1995). *Life on the Screen: Identity in the Age of the Internet*. New York: Simon and Schuster.

Turner, Jeanine W., Jean A. Grube, and Jennifer Meyers. "Developing an Optimal Match within Online Communities: An Exploration of CMC Support Communities and Traditional Support." *Journal of Communication* 51.2 (2001): 231-251.

Van Doorn, Niels, Liesbet Van Zoonen, and Sally Wyatt. "Writing From Experience." *European Journal of Women's Studies* 14.2 (2007): 143-159.

Wei, Lu. "Filter Blogs vs. Personal Journals: Understanding the Knowledge Production Gap on the Internet." *Journal of Computer-Mediated Communication* 14.3 (2009): 532-558.

Wellman, Barry, and Keith Hampton. "Living Networked On and Offline." *Contemporary Sociology* 28.6 (1999): 648-654.

Woods, Julie. "Digital Influencers: Business Communicators Dare Overlook the Power of Blogs?" *Communication World* 22.1 (2005): 26-30.

Wright, Paul H. "Self-referent Motivation and the Intrinsic Quality of Friendship." *Journal of Social and Personal Relationships* 1.1 (1984): 115-130.

Young, Stacey L. "A Comparison of Offline and Online Friendship Qualities at Different Stages of Relationship Development." *Journal of Social and Personal Relationships* 21.3 (2004): 305-320.

CHAPTER SIXTEEN

PARENTING CHILDREN WITH AUTISM ONLINE: CREATING COMMUNITY AND SUPPORT THROUGH BLOGGING

MARCELINE THOMPSON-HAYES

This chapter provides a case study of the blog "Adventures in Extreme Parenting." Although the stated purpose of the blog is to describe the author's experiences raising children with autism, analysis of the blog's content reveals the blog is situated within the larger community of persons touched by autism. Community is enacted through the blog via messages of empowerment and social support.

Parenting Children with Autism

"Adventures in Extreme Parenting" is a mommy blog which specifically addresses the experiences of mothers parenting children with autism. Currently, it is estimated that one out of every 110 children has an autism spectrum disorder (ASD), according to statistics from Centers for Disease Control and Prevention which makes the disorder more common than pediatric cancer, diabetes, and AIDS combined according to the non-profit organization Autism Speaks. While symptoms of autism vary from child to child and range in severity, ASD is characterized by unusual and/or repetitive behaviors, limited interests, limitations in social interaction, and communication deficits (Autism Speaks).

According to the Autism Society of America, parents of children with autism face unique stressors. For example, children with autism may have sleep disorders, limited food preferences, and may exhibit maladaptive behaviors such as the inability to sit still; the child is often confined to home, often at the expense of family outings. Parents of children with behavioral problems, such as parents of children with attention deficit hyperactivity disorder (ADHD) and developmental disorders, report more stress than parents of children with purely physical disorders (Autism Society of America; Gupta). These parents often experience physical and emotional exhaustion and thus seek forms of social support, including support from a relevant blog community.

The present essay will attempt to demonstrate how persons touched by autism create and maintain a sense of community online through blogging via a case analysis of one mother's blog dedicated to raising her children with autism. The blog, authored by Sunday Stilwell, is called "Adventures in Extreme Parenting (hereafter called "Adventures") and can be found at http://www.blogher.com/frame.php?url=http://domestic-superhero.blogspot.com.

Adventures in Extreme Parenting

There are many blogs focusing on raising children with autism. The first step in finding a suitable case study for the present analysis involved going to the BlogHer website and typing in the search terms "autism mom." BlogHer was chosen because it is large community featuring an array of blogs by women. This search terms led to many possible blogs. "Adventures" was chosen specifically to use as a case analysis because it met two criteria beyond focusing on raising children with autism: (1) the blog featured multiple original posts and (2) there were multiple comments on the original posts. Such criteria established the blog as being a community. The blog posts were read and reread to discover aspects of the blog that fostered a sense of bonding and community among members.

Description of "Adventures"

Through blogging, authors enact their identity by how they present themselves via the blog's content. However, the author's identity itself is impacted through the "performance" of how they present themselves (Tucker) and the reactions of others. In other words, identity is impacted through self-reflection as well as through feedback of others in the online community. Readers can post comments to the blog's author which can validate, offer support to, or even challenge the author's blog content.

Stillwell's author profile reveals aspects of her identity (i.e., a person "with a hectic life") that motivated her to blog ("to tell my tales of raising 2 boys on the severe end of the autism spectrum while attempting to laugh and blog about it"), that in turn determined the blog's content. Content impacts identity as blogging itself can prompt self-analysis and reflection. Stilwell's original intent may have been to tell her personal stories as a way to cope with the demands of mothering. However, her blog became a means of empowerment—a platform to advocate for autism. Thus, blogging allowed her to expand her identity to become a voice for those struggling with similar concerns in the larger autism community.

Stilwell's primary motivation (and original intent it seems) for writing "Adventures" was to document her life of raising children with autism. As stated in the author profile,

> Adventures in Extreme Parenthood is where I tell my tales of raising 2 boys on the severe end of the autism spectrum while attempting to laugh and blog about it. I began blogging in the winter of 2008 as a way of coping with life as a newly separated woman, navigating a divorce, working full time, and my boys' school and therapy schedules.

Such motivation is consistent with the notion that women blog to document their private lives (Li) and personal experiences (Haferkamp and Kramer). Stillwell employs a diary format and discusses personal experiences in terms of feelings rather than simply providing an objective account.

Many posts on "Adventures" do indeed describe personal experiences, feelings, and reflections that accompany raising children with autism, the stated motivation for the blog listed in the author's profile. For example, in a post entitled "Crispy," Stilwell stated:

> Lately I haven't been on the top of my game, feeling the love, pulling myself up by my bootstraps and all that crap we tell ourselves. What I have been feeling is crispy. Crispy is one step past burnt-out. Its worse because you're not just burnt, you're still actively burning. … Its the recognizing that you are past burnt-out but you can't do anything to change it at the moment and so you put your emotions and your life on a kind of auto-pilot.

Similarly, in a post entitled, "It's God's Hands That Are Holding You," she described the feeling of helplessness and sadness that can occur when children do not want to be touched, as happens with many children with autism. She wrote:

> But to be sure they do not want Mommy to pick them up and hold them, to comfort them and to remind them I will always be right there no matter what. They do not want my comfort. They simply can't stand it. And that breaks my heart.

Again, such content is consistent with the research documenting that women blog about personal experiences and feelings. However, another pattern emerged. In a post entitled "He screams, I scream, We All Scream for God Only Knows Why," Stilwell discussed her child's screaming as a form of communication. She wrote:

> He wakes up screaming and keeps it up for the first twenty to thirty minutes every morning. The most difficult part of the screaming is that I have no earthly idea what it is that turns my small child into a screeching banshee every morning at 5:00 a.m. All I have are guesses and assumptions because he can't tell me what is wrong.

Later in this same post she discussed nonverbal communication devices. She wrote:

> Clearly there are options for me to consider. While buying an assisted communication device is out of the budget, I do have the ability to use Noah's school's copy of Boardmaker Pro. Their resource room is open to parents and for a nominal fee I can print PECS cards, laminate them and then affix velcro stickers to create my own communication boards and schedules. My sincere hope is that when I begin using the PECS cards with Noah he will also begin using them with me and while I am sure it will not completely eradicate the screaming. I am hopeful that it will lessen it.

Although she was discussing her own situation, it appears she also attempted to provide others with helpful information. Another example of this dual focus occurred when she posted about the "communication breakdown" in social media scheduled to increase awareness of autism.

> This is why when the autism community goes radio silence on November 1st. I will still be tweeting, facebooking, and blogging about what autism really is and what it is not. I will educate with my words, and not my silence. I will change my boys' diapers, order in for dinner because going out is not possible, and I will be a voice for my sons until the day comes when they use their own. Because that day may never come. I urge my family, friends, and anyone who is not raising a child with autism or another special need to do something concrete on November 1st to make a difference in the life of a family struggling under the weight of parenting children like mine.

Further, she suggests ways readers can address autism. In her blog, she weaves personal experiences with a more public agenda, thus tying her blog to a larger autism community. Although the original intent of the blog was to document her experiences, it is clear that she feels part of a larger community of those touched by autism and wants to support such a community.

Community

"Adventures" has 278 blog followers. The latest post at the time of this writing garnered 26 comments within two days. Based solely on the number of comments, this blog appears to be is a site of potential community; that is, connection among members of a group centered around a common theme (Droge; Lopez). Further, Stillwell's blogroll of 47 blogs begins with the statement "This is a work in progress so if you don't see your website listed please be patient..." indicting that any reader who also blogs is likely a current or future member of the community surrounding her blog and thus entitled to a listing on her blogroll.

A sense of community can foster the development of relationships. In the blog community surrounding "Adventures," it appears that social support is at the heart of the relationships among bloggers. Indeed, many women turn to blogging for social support (Kline and Burstein), especially when women feel alone and isolated as mothers (McMenemy) as is often the case when raising children with special needs such as ASDs. Mothers of special needs children may be particularly susceptible to isolation, given that the time-consuming care of their children allows little free time to nurture tradition FtF relationships. In a recent post entitled "My Cup Runneth Over" the author writes:

5 years,
6 months,
29 days,
21 hours,
and 15 minutes.
May seem like a long time to wait...
because it is.
But, when its the length of time between your baby boy's birth and the moment he first signs "I love you"....You realize it was worth the wait.

Response to this post was emotional and supportive. Sample responses included: "Oh, I am so happy for you and for him…how awesome is that... ohhh torn between tears and dancing over here for you...," and "That, is by far, some of the best news I've had all day. Wonderful! :)," as well as "I may not know you but I am celebrating in your joy. Savor the moment and keep celebrating so it continues to evolve. Enjoy!" Thus, in the virtual space of this mommy blog, users connected and offered support. The level of emoting may be consistent with the hyperpersonal communication that occurs among online interactants (Turner et al.) and facilitates close relationships. It is also noteworthy that (a) many of the same usernames appear across posts and (b) posts often include links to the readers' blog or to specific sympathetic postings on their blogs, further demonstrating the connectedness and community among mommy bloggers.

A recent post entitled "Join the Special Needs Blog Hop" illustrates the sense of connectedness among bloggers by referencing 58 links to other blogs. Its many replies included: "Wow! All these blog hop blogs are amazing that I've seen so far. I'm going to have to spend some time on the weekend visiting them all more closely," and "Thanks for posting this :) I already follow your blog :)" Such exchanges demonstrate that bloggers identify themselves as part of a larger community. Additionally, in a post entitled "Back to Blogging, The Evolution of My Blog" the author reposted her very first blog with a humorous commentary (e.g., she wished she would have used a spell check) and invited readers to share their first blog. The post demonstrated that her identity as a blogger has grown over time as she was able to reflect back on her first post. She also recognized that the majority of her readers are fellow bloggers who form a mommy blogosphere—in this case a blogosphere of mothers with special needs children.

Finally, the post entitled "A Scary Successful Momz Share" documented a party held among bloggers, providing further evidence of a community of mommy bloggers. The post stated, "Saturday was our third Momz Share and it was held at the amazing home of blogging extraordinaire [name deleted for privacy reasons] [who] opened her home to over 70 influential women bloggers who noshed, networked, chatted, and cocktailed the night away." Such experiences may lead to stronger motivation to keep blogging, continuing the cycle of influence among identity, motivation, content, community, support, and relationships.

Conclusion

Raising special needs children, such as children with autism is difficult. Parents often feel exhausted, alone, and isolated. The case study of the mommy blog "Adventures" illustrates how one community of mommy bloggers functions to provide a sense of community among the author and blog followers by providing messages of social support to those whose lives have been touched by autism. In sum, the present case study demonstrates how interactants use blogs to form and maintain supportive relationships in an online community of mommy bloggers.

Works Cited

Autism Speaks, Inc. "What Is Autism?" *Autism Speaks* Website. 27 October 2010. [http://www.autismspeaks.org/whatisit/index.php]

Autism Society of America. "About Autism." Autism Society of America Website. 27 October 2010. [http://www.autism-society.org/site/PageServer?pagename=about_home]

Autism Society. "Living with Autism. Stress on Families."Autism Society Website. 27 October 2010. [http://www.autismsociety.org/site/PageServer?pagename=life_fam_stress]

Centers for Disease Control and Prevention. "Autism Spectrum Disorders." Centers for Disease Control and Prevention Website. 27 October 2010. [http://www.cdc.gov/ncbddd/autism/index.html]

Droge, Canelia, Michael A. Stanko, and Wesley A. Pollitte. "Lead Users and Early Adopters on the Web: The Role of New Technology Product Blogs." *Journal of Product Innovation Management* 27.1 (2010): 66-82. Web.

Haferkamp, Nina, and Nicole Krämer. *Entering the Blogosphere: Motives for Reading, Writing, and Commenting*. International Communication Association, Montreal, Canada. May 2008.

Gupta, Vidya B. "Comparison of Parenting Stress in Different Developmental Disabilities." Journal of Developmental Disabilities, 19, (2007): 417-425.

Kline, David, and Dan Burstein. *Blog! How the Newest Media Revolution Is Changing Politics, Business, and Culture.* New York: CDS Books, 2005. Print.

Kouper, Inna. *The Pragmatics of Peer Advice Online: An Examination of a LiveJournal Community*. International Communication Association Conference, Chicago. May 2009.

Li, Dan. *Why Do You Blog: A Uses-and-Gratifications Inquiry into Bloggers' Motivations*. International Communication Association Convention, San Francisco, CA. May 2007.

Lopez, Lori K. "The Radical Act of 'Mommy Blogging': Redefining Motherhood through the Blogosphere." *New Media and Society* 11.5 (2009): 729-747. Web.

McMenemy, Christina. "Just Call Me a Mommyblogger." *A Mommy Story* (2006). BlogHer Publishing Network, 2 December 2005. Web. 31

October 2010. [http://amommystory.blogspot.com/2006/08/just-call-me-mommyblogger.html]

Tucker, Joan S. "Foreword." *Mothering and Blogging: The Radical Act of the Mommyblog*. Eds. May Friedman and Shana L. Calixte. Toronto, Canada: Demeter Press, 2009. 1-20. Print.

CHAPTER SEVENTEEN

CONSTRAINED AGENCY: CHINESE MOTHERS BLOGGING THEIR CHILD REARING PRACTICES

YAHUI ZHANG

Introduction

Feminist thinkers have long been investigating the interaction between virtual and real, mind, and body (Haraway 1985; Hayles 1999). They have also been paying close attention to the interconnection between the virtual and the real spaces. Radhika Gajjala (2001) points out, "Online interactions, and the human subjects produced in interaction with the new mediating technologies, cannot be discussed in isolation from the cultural, social, political and economic contexts within which emerging technologies and new forms of communication operate" (113). It is important to investigate the connection between information and communication technologies (ICTs) and mind, body, and the subjectivity of the human subjects constituted in both the online and offline world. It is equally meaningful to explore motherhood in different cultural contexts as impacted and transformed by ICTs. Yet, no study has directly examined constrained agency of motherhood in China manifested in blogosphere, one important information and communication technology. This research explores the materiality of Chinese mother bloggers' existence as intelligible human beings, adding to our knowledge of the meaning of motherhood in China in blogosphere. More importantly, I highlight Chinese mother bloggers' constrained agency emerging in the artistry of blogging their childrearing with regard to new relationship, communal social bonding, and self continuity and improvement.

Data Collection

The data collection for this paper was conducted from June to August in 2010. The blogs that are pertinent to my study on Chinese mother bloggers' constrained agency are available at http://blog.baby.sina.com .cn/lm/baby/, one type of blog featured on www.sina.com.cn.

To gauge the popularity of this website, I searched for its ranking on www.alexa.com. "Alexa is a useful resource for people to discover information about websites. You can use Alexa to discover how popular a site is, to find new sites, to learn who owns a site and a lot more" (http://www.alexa.com/tour). According to Alexa, Sina website in China was ranked the 16th on its "Top Sites" list as of August 27, 2010. "Sina. com.cn has a three-month global Alexa traffic rank of 16. We estimate that 90% of visitors to the site come from China, where it has attained a traffic rank of 4" (http://www.alexa.com/siteinfo/sina.com.cn). Although it is difficult to get information on the popularity of the different genres of blogs at www.sina.com.cn, it seems reasonable to infer from the top rank of the website itself that bloggers in China have a higher chance of creating their blogosphere here. I read the posts almost daily especially in June and July in 2010 and copied and pasted the data into different categories to assist analysis. Primarily, I rely on observation and close readings of blogs focusing on parenting and raising quality children to examine how Chinese women's subjectivity is manifested in their act of blogging, a medium that builds new relationship, promotes social bonding with larger groups, and enhances the self.

To select the blogs for my analysis, I applied the following set of criteria:

1. The blogs were authored by Chinese mothers.
2. The bloggers were primarily based in China.
3. The bloggers keep blogs for their children.
4. The blogs were 'active', i.e. the blogger had blogged at least four times in the last two consecutive months.
5. The blogger had blogged for at least two months.
6. The blogs were written in Chinese intended for Chinese.

What is significant about blogs for the purpose of my study is that they are increasingly used by networks of middle class urban Chinese parents, most of whom are women. They gather together in the virtual communities for their shared love of their children; their desire to reflect on their parenting; and most important of all, to capture the memory of their children's growth. They use blogs, though not necessarily intentionally, as an emergent cultural form to engender "counter discourses, alternative and oppositional practices, or resistance" (Ginsburg and Rapp 1995, 11). In creating social networks, Chinese women have forged new lines of communications that are influencing, or have the capacity to influence, broader social conventions and practices (Hevern 2004; Hewitt 2005).

Theoretical Framework

Using feminist appropriation of Foucault's (1988) theory on the technologies of the self, I investigate "how agency and control are activated collectively and in context" as theorized by Morwenna Griffiths (1995, 79). Feminist thinkers like Margaret A. McLaren (2002) see the connection between Foucault's notion of technologies of the self and some contemporary feminist practices such as consciousness-raising, journal writing, and women's autobiography. She argues that they are practices or technologies of the self because all of these practices have social transformation as the aim. In a similar vein, and perhaps more succinctly, Karlyn Kohrs Campbell (2005), proposes that "agency (**1**) is communal and participatory, hence, both constituted and constrained by externals that are material and symbolic; (**2**) is 'invented' by authors who are points of articulation; (**3**) emerges in artistry or craft; (**4**) is effected through form; and (**5**) is perverse, that is, inherently protean, ambiguous, open to reversal" (1). What is important to elucidate here is, when Campbell contends that agency "emerges in artistry or craft," she does not only endorse "a canon of masterworks" (7). She emphasizes that "artistry … emerges equally in apt vernacular speech and everyday talk" (7). Blogs maintained by Chinese mothers belong to personal autobiographical memory journals using everyday talk to record their children's growth and their own recollections on the process of parenting.

In addition, extant literature on the purpose of autobiographical memory and of sharing memories with others suggests that they serve social, directive, and self functions. Autobiographical memory and reminiscence is social because using memories as a medium they build new relationships, nurture current relationships, and promote social bonding with larger groups (Alea and Bluck 2003; Bluck et al. 2005; Webster 2003). Sharing memories with others can also be used as a medium to teach, learn, and solve problems, fulfilling directive functions (Bluck et al. 2005; Pillemer 2003). Finally, keeping record of the past and reflecting on the past may serve the purpose of defining oneself. Self functions include the use of autobiographical memory for maintaining self-continuity (Bluck et al. 2005); for identity building (McLean 2005; Webster 2003); and for self-enhancement (Wilson and Ross 2003).

Building on feminist understanding of self-writing as a practice of the self, everyday talk and vernacular speech as artistry, and the autobiographical nature of blogs, I contend that blogging is the medium through which Chinese mother bloggers exercise their agency in regard to their relationship, community, and self.

The symbolic action of engaging in "everyday talk" anchored in their lived experiences in the form of blogs is made possible and intelligible because Chinese mother bloggers observe the unspoken, yet explicit, rule of "when it is considered appropriate for whom to say what" (Campbell 2005, 3). Their symbolic action in the blogosphere is the reiteration of what is appropriate and sensible to say about their children and their roles in the nurturance of the younger generation. However, more importantly, their blogging "is perverse, that is, inherently protean, ambiguous, open to reversal" (Campbell 2005, 1) to redefine the meanings of motherhood, parenting, and much more.

New Relationships

Chinese mother bloggers foster new relationships in the mediated space of the blogosphere characterized by more equal friend-like relationship between parents and their children. At the same time, their agency in the context of child-rearing promises a prospect of shared parenting, thus subverting the assumption that parenting is a sphere naturally associated with a specific gender. In addition, their attention to the uniqueness of their children in their blogs benefits the development of their children in tremendous ways.

Chinese culture, from a Western perspective, is high context, collectivistic, and has large power distance (Hall 1976; Hofstede 1980). The Confucian notions of harmony, face, and filial piety are still the main determinants of Chinese communication patterns and parent-child relationship (Chen and Starosta 1997; Gao and Ting-Toomey 1998; Jia 1997; Wu 1996). Traditional Chinese parents expect their children to respect and obey them. The relationship is usually characterized by an institutionalized hierarchy that gives parents more power over their children.

Cultural belief systems may also largely shape the functions of autobiographical memory and memory sharing (Kulkofsky, Wang, and Koh 2009; Wang and Ross 2007). Wang and Ross (2007) suggest that autobiographical memory and memory sharing is not as valued in East

Asian cultures as it is in Western cultures because East Asian cultures emphasize group identity and conformity. Their work confirms empirical research that showed Chinese middle-aged adults considered their autographical memories to be less personally important than did European American adults (Wang and Conway 2004). Enhancing relationships through the means of memory sharing may be less common in East Asian cultures than in North American context (Kulkolfsky, Wang, and Koh 2009). Studies on mother-child reminiscing have further shown that the main function of Chinese and Korean mothers' memory sharing is to instill proper behavioral conduct in the child, a directive function that has correction and discipline as its main purpose and the memory sharing is focused on social rule and behavioral expectations (Miller, Wiley, Fung, and Liang 1997; Wang, Leichtman, and Davies 2000).

Furthermore, in regard to child rearing, Chinese culture has endorsed the myth that women have been and are better at the day-to-day care of children, especially when the children are young. However, recent psychological and sociological studies cited in Diane Enrensaft's (1994) research reveal that men are as capable as women both physically and emotionally to parent. Parenting here does not only refer to the day-to-day care of children, but also the parent-child relationship.

Chinese mother bloggers treat their children as their equals. Many blog entries suggest that Chinese mothers regard their children as their friends and teachers. Seldom do they record how they use their blogs for the purpose of instilling proper behaviors. Instead, blogging is the medium through which Chinese mother bloggers understand their children, use age-appropriate parenting style, and establish and maintain intimacy between their children and themselves.

Chinese mother bloggers use their blogs to record their parenting practices with their husbands and extended families. Many blogs during my data collection feature children spending time with both parents and how happy they were when they were with their fathers. Many digital photos that Chinese mother bloggers included in the blogs show the intimacy and emotional bond between children and their fathers. During my data collection, I also run into men keeping blogs for their children. "Uttering Long Wheezing Cries in the Open Air" (http://blog.baby.sina.com.cn/s/blog_539853190100dfkl.html) has been actively keeping his blog entries for his daughter since March 1, 2006. He was one of the early adopters of blogs. His daughter was about five and a half then. Over the years, his blog entries ranged from his daughter's piano lesson, her school life, and life skills, to his take on politics and sports. "He Lu" (http://blog.baby.sina.com.cn/s/blog_5df54a910100ksyo.html) began to blog on his son and his role as a father since March 30, 2008 when his son was one-year, seven-month, and nine-day old. The early blogs were kept in a weekly regularity. More recent blogs in 2010 were daily publications.

More and more Chinese fathers are beginning to get involved in the day-to-day care of their children. By a few men sharing their child-rearing experiences and by many women sharing their husbands' involvement in parenting in their blogs, we see men removing themselves from the "patriarchal pedestal as the breadwinning but distant father, a position crucial to men's power in the traditional family" (Ehrensaft 1994, 436). At the same time, we see surfacing Chinese mother bloggers' other identities such as career women.

Blogging has brought changes to the culturally embedded understanding that parenting is a gender-specific realm that naturally belongs to women. It has also transformed the hierarchical parent-child relationship to more equal parent-child relationship. Simultaneously, blogging on parenting and child-rearing practices focuses on the child's own actions, preferences, and emotional, intellectual, and cognitive development, serving the social function of deepening the emotional bonds between the mother and child, while further helping the child to build a unique individual identity (Wang and Fivush 2005). Highlighting the individual uniqueness of one's child challenges the very cultural norms of group identity and conformity.

Reminiscing the uniqueness of one's child(ren) is one of the most salient characteristics of Chinese mothers' blogs about their children. "Twin Yilian's" mother recorded the inseparability of her twin daughters at http://blog.sina.com.cn/s/blog_4a0608fe0100iya3.html, using examples in her immediate world and tidbits of her daughters' everyday actions and reactions in different contexts to illustrate the point that there is a special connection and intuition between the twin sisters. "Angel's" mother has been recording "Angel's" insightful personal statements all the way from her childhood to the time of the research. One blog published at http://blog.sina.com.cn/s/blog_413ee0f10100k0nf.html recorded the critical thinking of Angel. She was not a student who took answers from her teachers indiscriminately. She asked her mother to double check the accuracy of her teacher's answer to a student's question online. Angel's mother has categorized her blogs into: Tidbits of Growth, Angel's Statements and Actions, Angel's Art Work Collection & Composition, etc. Many blogs feature conversations between "Angle" and her mother and how "Angel's" mother was amazed by "Angel's" intelligence, integrity, and humor.

Sigel and McGillicuddy-De Lisi (2002) have conducted an extensive review on how culturally shaped parental beliefs influence parenting practices, which in turn, impact children's developmental outcomes. Chinese mothers' blogging shows that memory sharing in the artistry of recording the growth of their children and their relationships with their children is personally important and bonds them with their children in meaningful ways beyond the hierarchical parent-child structure. Chinese mother bloggers, instead of maintaining and adhering to their authoritative positions as powerful parents, are ready to admit that parenting provides them a great opportunity to learn. Their children are their friends, teachers, and their most loved ones. A lot of times, parents think that they are always the smarter, the more rational, and the more far-sighted. They are used to their authoritative power as parents. It is refreshing and heartening to see Chinese mother bloggers willing to share how the everyday practice of parenting gives them chances to be attentive and self-reflexive.

Blogging and Connection

Equally important to the issue of agency is the fact that Chinese mothers form their own online community. By creating and maintaining a community of their own, Chinese mother bloggers break through the barriers to their voices being heard and carve out a space for themselves to articulate their distinctive interests in child rearing. They use the community to execute the technologies of the self by individual reflections and/or with the help of others. The impact of forming an online community for child-rearing is that Chinese women are able to use their own language, "apt vernacular speech and everyday talk," to affirm their experiences and exercise "textual agency" (Campbell 2005, 7). Also significant is the fact that online community entails the communal and participatory aspects of textual agency. It is in the connection with other women who have similar lived experiences that a Subaltern woman finds strength to claim her own subjectivity and agency (Spivak 1988; Jaggar 2000).

Chinese mother bloggers influence one another in their parenting in practical terms. They recommend and share recipes, books, and activities. "Laughter Brings Clear Sky" is a blogger who has blogged since May, 2007. In her blog titled "Small Scissors and Big Wisdom: The Multi-Functions of Scissors" available at http://blog.sina.com.cn/s/blog_4cfef25f0100khi5.html she used both text and digital photos to illustrate and summarize the educational function of the art of paper-cutting. There were 163 comments on this single post. Here is "Sunshine Bubble's" comment: "It is so exciting to be among the first to read your post. Mama is so good at educating your son. Usually, moms dare not let their children use scissors. You encourage your son and I should learn from you." Other comments to the same post reconfirm the educational value of paper-cutting and encourage moms to try it out. It is through the acts of reading one another's blogs and short comments like "yes, what you wrote was insightful;" "good job;" and "sofa" (meaning that the one who wrote the comment is the first in reading the blog) that they support, reaffirm, and learn from one another.

Chinese mother bloggers also impact one another in their parenting on deeper levels. Here is one excellent example at http://blog.baby.sina.com.cn/s/blog_5711289e0100kx48.html. This blog entry was written by the mother of "Chrishxiaoxi." She wrote, "All of a sudden I have the urge to reflect on why I blog. I guess the compliments from good friends on my day-to-day account are one of the main reasons." She recorded that she began journal writing for her daughter since her birth in a big notebook. It was a lot of hard work. However, the satisfaction from reading the journal made it worth it. It was not until she bumped into a mother community at www.qq.com and learned from some mothers there that www.sina.com.cn has a wonderful mother bloggers community that she began to blog on this platform. She continued:

> The closest of my friends are Flower Rain, Xiaobaozi, and Little Leaves. I have learned a lot from them. Because we have children about the same age, there are many areas that I can imitate them. I know I am ignorant and ill-informed....Later, while blogging, I also read other's blogs to see how they dress their daughters, what kind of books their children read, where they take their children to play, the challenges and problems in different stages of child development, and the solutions and lessons others share...

She made friends through blogging. When circumstances were appropriate, they exchanged personal contact information to have face-to-face interaction. Her assumption is that mother bloggers have a lot in common and they are trustworthy. She lamented the ridicule of those who could not share her devotion to blogging and who thought that she had too much time on her hand. She responded by saying that she had time to blog because she did not take naps, go shopping, or play games. She concluded her post with these statements, "I blog because blogosphere has a lot of parents like me. To record the growth of my child, listen to different voices, and be a responsible parent...."

This reflection on the value of blogging to Chinese mother bloggers in their parenting is a shared agreement. The mother of "Weiwei," posted at http://blog.baby.sina.com.cn/s/blog_49f66c840100kjon.html in regard to her journey with blogging for four years and thirty days. In it were recollections on blogosphere being the only comfort to her when she and her husband worked in Shenzhen (one of the most developed special economic zones in China) like fully wound clocks. Now she was a full-time mother taking care of her two-year-old daughter in Wuhan, paying attention to blogs on parenting. It was experts' opinion and many excellent mother bloggers' sharing that brought ease in her child rearing attitude and practices. She was emotionally attached to the community. Using her own words, "I can say that blogs and my life are inseparable" and she felt that "blogs communicate emotion, they also contain a lot of wisdom, opinions, and thought. To a certain degree, it is a new cultural phenomenon."

This new cultural phenomenon of blogging as memory sharing between parents and children and among bloggers in the community is both directive and social. It is directive in that by sharing and reading blogs parents teach and learn from one another. It is social because it is a medium to build new parent-child relationships, establish new friendships with like-minded parents, and promote social bonding with larger groups in the community. Blogging may assist textual agency, but it also has the capacity of serving as a medium for social bonding in real time.

This is the blog entry of "Sammitang1979" on August 3, 2010 at http://blog.baby.sina.com.cn/s/blog_4fe0c6390100kgi8.html. She wrote:

> I have blogged for two years and a half. Through blogging, I have made many friends. However, many are spread far and wide throughout the country. It is rare to make friends with bloggers who live in the same city. A few days ago, I got a notice from 'Luluo Flower Bloom' saying that 'Promise of Angel' was organizing the very first get-together for bloggers in Tianjing (one of the four municipalities in China). How happy I was to get the news.... From my conversations with two other mother bloggers, I know that many are looking for blogger friends living in the same city.

The rest of the blog post recorded that for the first get-together on July 31, 2010, ten families showed up and the fun they had, and the bonding among children and between adults. The texts and the pictures epitomize bonding among friends made through the medium of blogging as autobiographical writing and memory sharing.

In addition, blogging provides Chinese mother bloggers a medium through which they can create a language of their own to not only take pride in their mothering experience, but at the same time, grapple with the contradictions they see in their mothering practices.

Although the utterances of the hardships of motherhood are not often in the community, blogging in a community with like-minded people encourages disclosure of frustration and struggles. Quite a few bloggers express how tired they are as mothers. One blogger stated explicitly that

"Working as a full-time stay-at-home mother is more tiring than working a full-time job" at http://blog.baby.sina.com.cn/s/blog_6173cd5a0100ksg0.html. She detailed her schedule and how hard it was for her to have some time to herself. There were 20 comments to this post as of August 29, 2010.

Her expressing the hardships in her blogs did not incur criticism but received 20 responses showing understanding. Expressing appreciation for the toil mothers have to go through for the sake of their children is what runs through the responses. Although none of the responses challenges the biological determinism of motherhood and women, the supportive messages themselves are a comfort to the mother blogger. One comment suggested that "Kaka's" mom should take a nap at noon with her son to recuperate. Another comment showed understanding and also pointed out that even when women sacrifice so much their husbands may not necessarily appreciate it. This particular blog is not the only one that explicitly indicates the adversity of motherhood. There are many other blogs that align along the same dimension and share the hardship of being a mother. Having some blogger friends to understand what a mother blogger with a little child went through made the experience worthwhile.

On the one hand, Chinese mother bloggers are grateful that motherhood allows them to be "real women." On the other hand, they realize that motherhood is not only filled with happiness and blessings, but also sacrifices and hardships that are a lot of times gendered. It is through the technology of blogging their everyday practices of taking care of their children and sharing their blogs with parents in similar situations that they consciously reflect on their practices, conceptualize their experiences, and find a language to describe what is unique to them, exercising agency through memory sharing. They teach, support, understand, encourage, and learn from one another to construct and live out the meaning of motherhood. Through blogging they achieve communal agency and bonding.

Self-Building

In tandem, blogging offers Chinese mother bloggers a forum to engage in self-building and self-enhancement. However, it is important to bear in our mind that self to Chinese women is relational. In the blogosphere, there is ongoing reflection on their relational self not only as mothers, but also as wives, daughters, daughters-in-law, career women, and friends. Their coming to grips with the issues such as how much pressure is appropriate for their children in education, the relationships they should have with their children, and the kind of mothers they should become are just some examples of how their textual agency affords them the opportunities to discuss and reflect on their everyday practices of child-rearing. Equally important, their reflections on their relational selves are manifestations of their constrained agency within their life circumstances and their social relationships.

Research shows that talking about the past may serve the purpose of defining oneself, building identity, and enhancing self (Bluck et al. 2005; McLean 2005; Webster 2003; Wilson and Ross 2003). Blogging as autobiographical writing and memory may serve the function of self-building and enhancement. Chinese mothers usually categorize their blogs into Records of My Child's Growth, Personal Recollections or Rambling Talk or Miscellaneous Discussion, Photos & Videos, Statements of My Child, etc. Personal Recollections are seldom about the bloggers themselves. They are usually situated within a web of relations in a specific context, illustrating feminist understanding of relational self (Griffins 1995). It is through recollections on relations embedded in contexts and sometimes self-critique that Chinese mother bloggers demonstrate their identities.

The mother of "Sunshine Eva" shared her regret of getting lost in the sea of compliments and attention when her blogs and photos of her daughter began to garner a lot of online attention and traffic at http://blog.sina.com.cn/s/blog_49a7a2170100bn6h.html 12/2/08. For a period of time, she paid more attention to shooting sharp photos and updating readers on her daughter than to taking care of the emotional and practical needs of her then three-old daughter. Her blog was a self-revelatory critique, reminding herself that the most important thing is not attention but the day-to-day love relationship between her daughter and herself.

Self reflection is as important as self critique in self building and relationship maintenance. The mother of "Run Fast Lele" wrote on July 14, 2010 at http://blog.baby.sina.com.cn/s/blog_59404dab0100kkdh.html that she observed four changes in her husband since she began to blog: a heightened sense of crisis, less drinking, more exercise, and more reading. It is difficult to infer from the post the causal relationship between the husband's less drinking and doing more exercise with the wife's blogging. However, the first and the last changes seemed to have something to do with the wife's active blogging. Lele's mother shared that her husband told her one day that "I found that your life is richer, horizon wider, thoughts more progressive day by day after you began blogging. I can feel a sense of crisis in myself now." Maybe to keep pace with his wife and to fully understand his wife, the husband began to read books and magazines that interested his wife and was ready to discuss the content of the reading with his wife. By recording conversations between husband and wife, Chinese mother bloggers engage in self-explanations and self-evaluations, improving themselves and their relationships.

Further, in the act of autobiographical writing, Chinese mother bloggers enhance self-regard. Here are a few examples. The mother of Xuanwo shared in her blog on June 10, 2010 the many kinds of harvest that blogging brought to her at http://blog.baby.sina.com.cn/s/blog_617f32db0100i10a.html. Among them are better moods, valuable parenting experiences, a sense of achievement, and many pleasant surprises. Her sense of achievement was fulfilled because some of her blog entries were recommended onto the home page and were even published in parenting journals.

Similarly, the mother of "Twin Yilian" in her blog dated June 8, 2010 at http://blog.sina.com.cn/s/blog_4a0608fe0100iasb.html promoted her book that features 100 blog entries. She started her blog entry with her dream of publishing her own poem collection at the age of 18. She majored in Chinese at university in order to become a writer. However, she and publishers never seemed to have any click until she started blogging. Finally, in 2010 her book was published. She wrote that she appreciated her publisher for publishing her work of heart and blood of four years, keeping its original flavor. It is a comedy of the ups and downs of her mundane life after the birth of her twin daughters. It is a truthful record and her recollections of real life in regard to love, relationship, and friendship. The title of the book is "The Chaotic Parenting Life of a Twin Mother." She made it very clear that she was neither an expert nor a celebrity and she did not publish to cater to the taste of academic standard. In her blog, there were links to the online ordering of her book.

Through the act of blogging, many Chinese mothers see their intrinsic and immanent worth as individuals who have ideas and opinions that matter. The acknowledgement from other mother bloggers and the recognition in larger circles enhance their self-regard and encourage them to go beyond the scope of their own children and venture into other related topics and issues.

The mother of "Sunshine Eva" in her personal section wrote on the advantages and disadvantages of having a second child (http://blog.sina.com.cn/s/blog_49a7a2170100dqjm.html); love means respect to her sister who had a son labeled as at-risk (http://blog.sina.com.cn/s/blog_49a7a2170100cfev.html); and the responsibilities of a citizen in times of natural disaster like the earthquake in May, 2008 (http://blog.sina.com.

cn/s/blog_49a7a21701009frc.html). The mother of "Twin Yilian" lamented the fact that many Chinese parents had to rush their children into the rat race of sending their kids to all kinds of extracurricular trainings sessions so that they kids can go to key schools (http://blog.baby.sina.com.cn/u/1241909502). It is sad that quality education was such a rare commodity not readily accessible to all. The mother of "Bangni Princess" questioned and challenged the embedded cultural preference for son over daughter using stories she heard and was familiar with (http://blog.baby.sina.com.cn/s/blog_5f8faca50100krrc.html). The mother of "Happy Garden of Little Pig Beibei" asked herself on her birthday on August 6, 2010 (http://blog.baby.sina.com.cn/s/blog_4f4f3cc40100kx97.html) what women should do for themselves besides putting their children and husbands on the priority list. To her, economic independence and a rich and tranquil soul are the most important. The mother of "Fairy Tribe of Duoduo" shared the lessons she learned about the future educational path for her daughter and other children from her failure abroad and how unrealistic expectations on going abroad could bring negative consequences (http://blog.sina.com.cn/s/blog_6122258f0100ixpp.html). These examples show that Chinese mother bloggers use blogs as a tool for not only self-reflection for the purpose of self-building but also relational enhancement so that they become better mothers, wives, friends, and citizens.

They exercise their agency in interaction with others and they admit that motherhood is a process of becoming. They learn to be better mothers and better selves day by day with their children and their loved ones within the context of the one-child policy in China, highly competitive education, and the cultural preference for son over daughter. Autobiographical blogging, in the case of Chinese mothers, serves the purpose of defining oneself in relation to others.

Conclusion

I do agree with Karlyn Korh Campbell when she argues that textual agency "is related to generic conventions, to allusion, to the pleasures of alliteration and assonance, to the transformations effected by tropes" (2005, 7). The tropes of motherhood and meaningful childhood usher in new parenting practices that are shared, learned, and cherished. The blogging activity itself does grant agency to Chinese mother bloggers because it allows them to speak in their everyday language about the generic and new conventions of parenting. Chinese mother bloggers' love and respect for their children, whether their children are boys or girls, their emphasis on cultivating interest in their children and shared parenting, and a good balance between love and discipline, are definitely important in fostering new cultural practices of child-rearing. However, it is important to reiterate an equally important dimension of agency, the constituted and constrained agency.

Blogosphere provides Chinese mother bloggers with e-spaces to emerge as subjects wielding agency. However, as Radhika Gajjala argues (2001), "We would [also] need to open up issues for further consideration by problematizing some of the assumptions made in relation to women and the Internet" (122). She criticizes equating "women-centered e-spaces" as empowering to women. In the case of my research, it is imprudent if I only claim that we should celebrate the blogging of Chinese mother bloggers as empowering and Chinese mother bloggers as subjects participating in and embodying constrained agency. The cultural, social, political and economic contexts for the online embodiment of Chinese mother bloggers are still largely defined by a patriarchal discourse. At the same time, Chinese mother bloggers who inhabit the e-spaces are middle-class people with middle-class concerns engaging in symbolic actions that are recognizable and endorsed by the dominant discursive discourses of patriarchy, nationalism, modernity, globalization, and heterosexuality. Further, it takes time and efforts for the textual agency of Chinese mother bloggers to ripple its effects into the offline world.

Negotiating and redefining the meaning of motherhood using autobiographical memory and reminiscence sharing of blogging, Chinese mother bloggers forge new relationships with their significant others and their children, form communities that bond and affirm, and transform individual mother bloggers and the culture at large. Blogging is social, directive, and self-building, making it possible for Chinese mother bloggers to exercise constrained agency. They blog to record, improve, and transform.

Works Cited

Alea, Nicole, and Susan Bluck. 2003. "Why are You Telling Me That? A Conceptual Model of the Social function of autobiographical memory." *Memory* 11:165-178.

Bluck, Susan, Nicole Alea, Tilmann Habermas, and David C. Rubin. 2005. "A Tale of Three Functions: The Self Reported Use of Autobiographical Memory." *Social Cognition* 23(1):91-117.

Campbell, Karlyn Kohrs. 2005. "Agency: Promiscuous and Protean." *Communication and Critical/Cultural Studies* 2(1):1-19.

Chen, Guo-Ming, and William J. Starosta. 1997. "Chinese Conflict

Management and Resolution: Overview and Implications." *Intercultural Communication Studies* 7:1-16.

Ehrensaft, Diane. 1994. "When Women and Men Mother." In *Living with Contradictions: Controversies in Feminist Social Ethics,* edited by Alison.M. Jaggar, 432-442. Boulder: Westview Press.

Foucault, Michel. 1988. "Technologies of the Self." In *Technologies of the Self: A Seminar with Michel Foucault*, edited by Michel Foucault, Luther H. Martin, Huck Gutman, and Patrick H. Hutton, 16-49. Amherst: University of Massachusetts Press.

Gajjala, Radhika. 2001. "Studying Feminist E-spaces: Introducing Transnational/Post-colonial Concerns." In *Technospaces: Inside the New Media,* edited by Sally R. Munt, 113-125. New York: Continuum.

Gao, Ge, and Stella Ting-Toomey. 1998. *Communicating Effectively with the Chinese.* Thousand Oaks, CA: Sage.

Ginsburg, Faye, and Rayna Rapp. 1995. *Conceiving the New World Order: The Global Politics of Reproduction.* Berkeley: University of California Press.

Griffiths, Morwenna. 1995. *Feminism and the Self: The Web of Identity.* London: Routledge.

Hall, Edward T. 1976. *Beyond Culture*. New York: Anchor Press.

Haraway, Donna Jeanne. 1985. *Manifesto for Cyborgs: Science, Technology, and Socialist Feminism in the 1980s*. San Francisco: Center for Social Research and Education.

Hayles, N. Katherine. 1999. *How We Became Posthuman: Virtual Bodies in Cybernetics, Literature, and Informatics*. Chicago: University of Chicago Press.

Hevern, Vincent W. 2004. "Threaded Identity in Cyberspace: Weblogs & Positioning in the Dialogical Self." *Identity: An International Journal of Theory and Research* 4(4):321-335.

Hewitt, Hugh. 2005. *Blog: Understanding the Information Reformation That's Changing Your World.* New York: Nelson Books.

Hofstede, Geert. 1980. *Culture's Consequences: International Differences in Work-related Values*. Newbury Park, CA: Sage.

Kulkofsky, Sarah, Qi Wang, and Jessie Bee Kim Koh. 2009. "Functions of Memory Sharing and Mother-child Reminiscing Behaviors: Individual and Cultural Variations." *Journal of Cognition and Development* 10:92-114.

Jaggar. Alison M. 2000. "Globalizing Feminist Ethics." In *Decentering the Center: Philosophy for a Multicultural, Postcolonial, and Feminist World*, edited by Uma Narayan and Sandra Harding, 1-25. Bloomington, IN: Indiana University Press.

Jia, Wenshan. 1997. "Facework as a Chinese Conflict-Preventive Mechanism in Chinese Society: A Cultural/Discourse Analysis." *Intercultural Communication Studies* 7:43-61.

McLaren, Margaret A. 2002. *Feminism, Foucault, and Embodied Subjectivity.* Albany: State University of New York Press.

McLean, Kate C. 2005. "Late Adolescent Identity Development: Narrative Meaning Making and Memory Telling." *Developmental Psychology* 41(4):683–691.

Miller, Peggy J., Angela R. Wiley, Heidi Fung, and Chung-Hui Liang. 1997. "Personal Storytelling as a Medium of Socialization in Chinese and American Families." *Child Development* 68(3):557–568.

Pillemer, David B. 2003. "Directive Functions of Autobiographical Memory: The Guiding Power of the Specific Episode." *Memory* 11(2):193–202.

Sigel, Irving E., and Ann V. McGillicuddy-De Lisi. 2002. "Parent Beliefs are Cognitions: The Dynamic Belief Systems Model." In *Handbook of Parenting,* edited by Marc H. Bornstein, Vol. 3 of Being and Becoming a Parent, 485-508. Mahwah, NJ: Lawrence Erlbaum.

Spivak, Gayatri Chakravorty. 1988. "Can the Subaltern Speak?" In *Marxism and the Interpretation of Culture,* edited by Cary Nelson and Lawrence Grossberg, 271-313. Urbana: University of Illinois Press.

Wang, Qi, Michelle D. Leichtman, and Katharine I. Davies. 2000. "Sharing Memories and Telling Stories: American and Chinese Mothers and Their 3-Year-Olds." *Memory* 8(3):159–177.

Wang, Qi, and Martin A. Conway. 2004. "The Stories We Keep: Autobiographical Memory in American and Chinese Middle-aged Adults." *Journal of Personality* 72(5):911–938.

Wang, Qi, and Robyn Fivush. 2005. "Mother-Child Conversations of Emotionally Salient Events: Exploring the Functions of Emotional Reminiscing in European-American and Chinese Families." *Social Development* 14(3):473–495.

Wang, Qi, and Michael Ross. 2007. "Culture and Memory." In *Handbook of Cultural Psychology,* edited by Shinobu Kitayama and Dov Cohen, 645-667. New York: Guilford Press.

Webster, Jeffrey Dean. 2003. "The Reminiscence Circumplex and Autobiographical Memory Functions." *Memory* 11(2):203–215.

Wilson, Anne E., & Michael Ross. 2003. "The Identity Function of Autobiographical Memory: Time is on Our Side." *Memory* 11(2):137–149.

Wu, David Y. H. 1996. "Chinese Childhood Socialization." In *The Handbook of Chinese Psychology,* edited by Michael Harris Bond, 143-154. New York: Oxford University Press.

CHAPTER EIGHTEEN

TRANSNATIONAL SURROGACY, E-MOTHERHOOD, AND NATION BUILDING

SAYANTANI DASGUPTA
AND SHAMITA DAS DASGUPTA

In her re-examination of the Western feminist mantra "the personal is political," Cynthia Enloe, author of *Bananas, Beaches & Bases* (1990) asserted that the personal is, in fact, international, and conversely, the international is personal. Although written nearly two decades ago, Enloe's formulation interconnecting international politics and women's private lives has particular resonance for early twenty-first century. She wrote,

> …[I]t has become almost a cliché to say that the world is shrinking, that state boundaries are porous. We persist, nonetheless, in discussing personal power relationships as if they were contained by sovereign states. We treat ideas about violence against women without trying to figure out how the global trade in pornographic videos operates, or how companies offering sex tours and mail-order brides conduct their business across national borders. Similarly, we try to explain how women learn to be 'feminine' without unraveling the legacies of colonial officials who used Victorian ideals of feminine domesticity to sustain their empires… (1990, 196)

Enloe's description of porous postcolonial national boundaries frequented by human trafficking as well as ideological, technological, and commercial trade reflects the realities of the post-globalization era, where neoclassical economics and free trade of goods and services have come to predominantly define both real-life (RL) and online (OL) international relations, not only among states and nations, but also among individuals.

The phenomenon of transnational surrogacy, what has been sensationally called the Indian 'wombs for rent' industry, is one example of a commercial trade made possible by not only the permeable RL national boundaries of a globalized world, but also through porous cybernetic ones. The practice is marked by infertile women/ couples (intended parents - IPs) hiring the services of Indian surrogates who are then implanted with fertilized ova of the IPs' choice[1] and carry "their" fetuses to term. After delivery, the surrogates hand over the babies to the intended parents in exchange of money. The process is mediated by agencies and fertility clinics engaged in transnational reproductive commerce.

Through transnational surrogacy, cross-cultural constructions of gender, reproduction, motherhood, and family come into conversation with the shifting realities of a globalized, frequently on-line capitalist marketplace that reinforces colonial power hierarchies of the global North over South. Indeed, U.S. media headlines consistently compare Indian surrogacy to other forms of Indian 'tech support' (World Vision Report 2009).[2] Although this conflation of surrogacy with skilled labor – or 'tech support' – is vexed,[3] what is relevant here is the interplay of cyber-markets with the reproductive bodies of Indian women, and how such markets re-inscribe the gendered and racialized colonized subject.

This essay explores changes in the understanding of motherhood in both the global North and South as mediated by the growing use of artificial reproductive technologies (ARTs)[4] and online medical tourism. We emphasize in particular the practice of gestational surrogacy that is proliferating in the West with India as the service-provider. Although ART includes an array of technologies in the aid of reproduction, we are focusing primarily on gestational surrogacy to examine the development a new kind of motherhood in both India and the West. The few extant research studies (DasGupta and Dasgupta 2010, Markens 2007, Pande 2009a, 2009b, Rudrappa forthcoming) and newspaper reports (Bhatia 20 May 2009, Bhattacharya 12 January 2008a, Haworth August 2007, Mukherjee 12 February 2007, National Public Radio 15 June 2010, Nolen 13 February 2009, Thakur 21 March 2008, Wade 31 January 2009a, 31 January 2009b, Winfrey and Ling October 11 2007, Zakaria 25 June 2010) on the subject have converged on the surrogates' incentives, country conditions, as well as the industry's local contours. Simultaneously, they have drawn attention to the ethical and legal ambiguities entangled in such reproductive barter. In this chapter, we are approaching the topic from a different angle. Our goal here is to examine online communications among the female consumers of gestational surrogacy services (intended mothers, or IMs).[5]

Like the rest of the growing medical tourism industry, transnational surrogacy relies upon online brokers such as Planet Hospital (http://www.

planethospital.com/) and Surrogacy India (http://surrogacyindia.com/) to make the connections between Western IPs and Indian surrogates, usually engaged by Indian fertility clinics. In addition, email, skype, and other on-line modes of communication facilitate negotiations between Western IPs and Indian physicians, allows IPs to view ultrasounds and other screening tests, and mediate the IPs' relationships with both the surrogates and the fetuses they bear. Moreover, online communications including blogs and message boards help Western IPs connect with others like themselves, effectively creating a cross-border cybernetic 'nation' of surrogate clients.

For the purposes of this essay, we surveyed several blogs[6] and two message boards[7] explicitly focusing on transnational surrogacy interactions with Indian surrogates. We focused on blogs that were explicit about their Indian surrogacy experience (usually in their blog title). We also used the sidebar blogrolls of each site to track other bloggers when they commented, and discovered new sites. Since we were particularly interested in the online construction of intended motherhood, we focused on blogs of heterosexual couples. We did, however, survey a few blogs written by same-sex male couples,[8] who were active in the blogging community, appearing on the blogrolls of the other bloggers and commenting on their posts. In our searches, we found no blogs of lesbian couples or single women utilizing Indian surrogacy services, although these clearly might exist. Most of the primary (heterosexual) blogs were of couples who, from the photos they posted, appeared to be of white, Anglo-Saxon heritage, and all had a 'successful' surrogacy experience, meaning, they 'brought home' at least one healthy live baby.[9] The message boards we surveyed were almost entirely populated by individuals identifying as women, both Western surrogates and Western IMs. Except for those names we recognized from the Indian surrogacy blogosphere, or cases where message boarders posted a profile picture, the ethnicity of most message boarders was unknown to us.[10] In the end, we did not seek to be exhaustive in our search of Indian surrogacy related blogs and message boards; rather, we sampled some representative ones to help unpack the rhetoric of the Western IM 'nation'.

We have informed our reading of these blogs with studies of digital autobiographies and the blog as a form of cybernetic "diary writing." In the words of Laurie McNeil, "In their immediacy and accessibility, in their seemingly unmediated state, Web diaries blur the distinction between online and offline lives, "virtual reality" and "real life," "public" and "private," and most intriguingly for auto/biography studies, between the life and the text" (McNeil 2003, 25). As many scholars in the field of digital autobiographies have posited, one of the characteristics that distinguish Internet diaries from their RL counterparts is the ability of the blog to immediately engage the viewer, both entering into and creating communities of bloggers and readers.

Finally, as mothers ourselves,[11] we want to acknowledge the love and delight each of these bloggers seems to have for their child/children. The blogs we surveyed were resplendent with personal photographs and stories, day-to-day anecdotes about baby milestones, recipes, family gatherings, etc., which underscored the "public/private" nature of personal blogs (McNeil 2003). Drawing from these families' lives, we seek to critique the practice of transnational surrogacy broadly while recognizing how charged such a critique might be.

In our discussion, we argue that practices of 'othering' both Indian surrogates and India itself, as well as colonial/capitalist worldviews, are prominent and cohering factors of the emerging IM cyber-nation. We contend that these (intended) mothers express sentiments and use language that distinguish them as a 'nation' that manifest many of the features of the 19th century European colonizers. One of the critical tasks of this cybernetic 'nation' is to de-emphasize the relationship of IMs to surrogates, privileging instead the connections of Western IPs to one another, and ultimately 'naturalizing' the connections between an IM residing in Europe, Australia or the U.S. with 'her' fetus, residing within the womb of a gestating mother in India. We have placed our analysis on the backdrop of brief summary of globalized ART and gestational surrogacy in India. Ultimately, the essay highlights the nuances of a racialized (cyber) nation in the contexts of uneven economic, political, and informational powers among countries and communities and explicates the shifts in global motherhood in the twenty-first century.

Globalized ART and Gestational Surrogacy

> Surrogate contracts have created a … traffic in women – a system in which women are movable property, objects of exchange, brokered by go-betweens mainly serving the buyer. A surrogate contract is not simply an arrangement between a woman and a supposedly desperate couple – it is the procurement of women for breeding. (Raymond May/June 1991, 30)

Globalization has not only changed women's lives in developing countries through their recruitment into new forms of labor, but also through the transmission of medical information and technologies that flow from global North to South. These technologies, including the globalization of assisted reproductive technologies (ART), have profoundly transformed women's reproductive lives and perhaps motherhood itself

(DasGupta and Dasgupta 2010, Pande 2009b). By bringing not only pregnancy and delivery, but also conception under the purview of medical control, sexuality and maternity become separated and motherhood becomes fragmented into genetic, gestating, and nurturing segments (Balsamo 1999).

The global manifestations of ARTs are varied. Consumers of ARTs as reproductive aid range from infertile couples to couples who want children with special characteristics (Asch 2003, Binham 30 March 2003, Celizic 3 March 2009, Dorsey 2002, Halweil and Bell 2002, Mooney 2002) and of a particular sex (Gokhale 30 June 2006, Malpani, Malpani and Modi 2002, Medindia 16 March 2008, Nagi 22 August 2006, Oaklander 10 September 2007, Patole 26 December 2001, Pereira 3 September 2006, Puri 2005, 17 March 2006, Singh 17 June 2006, Swift 7 January 2009, Thayil 7 September 2001, The Asian Pacific Post 11 August 2005) to same sex couples (Lehner 14 August 2010, Spar 2005) and women beyond their reproductive ages (Nolen 13 February 2009, Schaefer 12 December 2007). However, the playing field of ARTs remains distinctly uneven in correspondence with the political power that different nations wield in the global market. Thus, while the West remains the consummate consumer, the global South continues to be the source of raw materials and supplier of services. Moreover, due to the stark inconsistency of ART regulations in various countries, the lucrative global infertility industry has become "the last great market" (Moore 1999, 81), such that couples from countries where ART is more legally restricted, or more expensive, can obtain desired interventions by traveling to less restrictive or less expensive countries. A case in point is India, where the cost of gestational surrogacy might be $22,000 or less while in the U.S. it might run to $100,000 (Fontanella-Khan 23 August 2010).[12]

The pioneer in India's gestational surrogacy trade is Dr. Nayna H. Patel,[13] whose career in surrogacy began when she enabled a local woman to become her British daughter's gestational surrogate in 2003 (Mukherjee 12 February 2007, Smerdon 2008, Spring 12 April 2006). Dr. Patel's infertility clinic in Gujarat, Akanksha (literally meaning 'desire'), has since continued to facilitate the realization of numerous childless women's (and men's) desires of motherhood via local gestation facility providers (Fontanella-Khan 23 August 2010, Haworth August 2007, Mukherjee 12 February 2007, Thakur 21 March 2008, Winfrey and Ling October 11 2007, Zakaria 25 June 2010).[14] The industry overall is marked by a drastic lack of regulations, practice guidelines, and transparency, allowing for opportunities for exploitation of the surrogates to creep in (DasGupta and Dasgupta 2010, Haimowitz and Sinha 2008, Pande 2009a; Subramanian 2

July 2007). Even as The Assisted Reproductive Technologies (Regulation) Bill-2010 proposed by the Government of India's Ministry of Health and Family Welfare is awaiting legislative review (2010), the industry keeps growing in response to the demands in the West (Pande 2009b). Every major city in India such as Mumbai (formerly Bombay), Delhi, Chennai (formerly Madras), Bengaluru (formerly Bangalore), and Kolkata (formerly Calcutta) have joined in the surrogacy trade and offer gestational surrogacy services to all who can afford the fees (Bhatia 20 May 2009, Bhattacharya 12 January 2008a, Haimowitz and Sinha 2008, Mukherjee12 February 2007, Nolen 13 February 2009, Wade 31 January 2009a, 31 January 2009b), including both foreign (mostly Western) clients and wealthy Indians.

Regardless of the 'benefits' it provides to women (financial advancement for one and children for the other), Western feminists have long characterized surrogacy as “international traffic in women” (Corea 1985, 245). As long ago as 1985, Gena Corea predicted the expansion of surrogacy to international markets, where couples from developed countries could either ‘import’ women or travel to the ‘Orient’ in search of surrogate mothers. “They come from underdeveloped countries “where food is a serious issue.” These countries do not have an industrial base, but they have a human base…” [T]hey know how to take care of children,” Since that’s missing here…,” obviously it’s a perfect match.”” (Corea 1985, 245). Corea’s dire predictions have clearly come to fruition in the context of twenty-first century India, which, after surrogacy was legalized in 2002, has become the world capital of commercial gestational surrogacy (Bhatia 20 May 2009, Carney March/April 2010, Fontanella-Khan 23 August 2010, Subramanian 2 July 2007).

However, unadulterated condemnations of surrogacy are not without complexity. The belief that poor women in the global South are not 'free' to make choices due to the compulsion of their poverty denies their agency outright and consequently, reduces them to uncomplicated 'victims' who deserve our pity and protection. Contrastingly, the same latitude is not necessarily offered to surrogates of the global North, who are assumed to exert their 'free-will' and thereby 'choose' to earn money by surrogacy, and thus, perhaps less deserving of social protection. While it might be true that some surrogates in the global South are forced into the work (DasGupta and Dasgupta 2010, Pande 2009a), not all are (Pande 2009b, Zakaria 25 June 2010). Not unlike their counterparts in the global North, the majority of these women utilize their bodies for economic advancement of their families and themselves (DasGupta and Dasgupta 2010, National Public Radio 15 June 2010, Pande 2009a, 2009b).

Surrogate Identity, Sisterhood, and Gift Economy

Ethnographic research with Indian surrogates suggests that these women are formulating their identities in fascinating, and perhaps subversive ways. Based on her interviews with surrogates at Akanksha, Amrita Pande (2009b) theorizes that Indian surrogates are constructing surrogacy in ways that subtly undermine patrilineal and genetically based family structures. By emphasizing relational bonds between themselves and the fetuses they carry, and between themselves and their female clients, Indian surrogates are replacing traditional familial ties founded on patrilineage and inheritance with attachments created by women's shared labor and transnational sisterhood - blood and sweat. In the words of Raveena, one of Pande's interviewees, "...[S]he [the IM] just gave the eggs, but the blood, all the sweat, all the effort is mine" (2009b, 379).

This construction of a sisterly connection between surrogates and IMs – what Pande calls "everyday forms of kinship" and "labored ties across borders" (2009b, 380), is apparent in other interviews of Indian surrogates and IMs alike. Consider the words of thirty-year-old Rubina Mondal, who says of the woman whose embryo she carried and whose surrogacy fees helped pay for expensive surgery to repair her 8-year-old son's cardiac defect, "Karen became like my sister" (Haworth 2007). Underlying this construction of surrogacy as a 'sisterly' exchange based on altruistic feelings on the part of the surrogate is the notion of the surrogacy exchange as 'gift economy' (DasGupta and Dasgupta, 2010). In the words of Pushpa Pandya, a twenty-seven year old mother of two, who dreams that the approximately $500 per month she earns as a surrogate will help send her children to college: "The joy of giving someone a child is a very different feeling." She stresses, "It's more than money. I will always remember that child and think how happy the real parents must be" (Mann and Bindra 17 October 2006). Similarly, on being asked by TV journalist Lisa Ling if she thought gestational surrogacy was exploitative, intended mother Jennifer West, "tearfully and indignantly" responded, "Sangeeta and I give each other a life that neither of us could achieve on our own" ('Journey to parenthood' 1 January 2006).

We have argued (DasGupta and Dasgupta 2010) that this language of altruism (Markens 2007) around Indian surrogacy serves to obfuscate the commercial and exploitative aspects of this industry. Pande also (2009a) found that Indian surrogates did not discuss surrogacy as a 'choice', rather as an economic 'compulsion'. Yet, such explicit discussions of surrogacy as economic necessity/exploitation are frequently downplayed in favor of the rhetoric of techno-biologic sisterhood based on 'gift exchange'. Such language is similar to that used in Western surrogacy, and in the realm of organ donation, where organs are 'gifted' from living or deceased donors and pseudo-familial bonds formed between donor families and organ recipients (Sharp 2007). In the rhetoric of Western organ transplantation, a victim of a car accident who is subsequently a heart donor, does not only give an organ of blood and tissue, muscle and vessels, but the very 'gift of life'. These notions, as anthropologist Leslie Sharp asserts, are steeped in Christian values regarding spiritual rebirth and the value of non-reciprocal giving, even to a needy stranger (Sharp 2007). Interestingly, studies of organ donation in South Asia suggest that in that context, donation is not usually framed in the language of altruism or gifting, as such rhetoric has little cultural resonance in non-Christian societies which value relationships over autonomy, interdependence over self-governance, and group identity over individualism (Moazam 2006). In these contexts, one's body is usually not one's own but the responsibility of the collective. A contravention of this practice means not only breaking the laws of the family and society but also divine directives.[15] Thus, the adoption of ideas regarding gifting and altruism in Indian surrogacy discourse, even by surrogates themselves, suggests that the locus of rhetorical control in this transnational exchange lies entirely with the Western clients. Indeed, central to the language of surrogacy as 'gift economy' are Western cultural notions about bodily 'ownership'. But one cannot 'gift' something that one does not 'own'.

Cyber-Community Building

How, then, do Western intended mothers frame their relationships with Indian surrogacy beyond altruism and sisterhood? Prominent in the blogs we surveyed was the bond *between* Western IPs rather than the one between IMs and their Indian surrogates. Sociologists Gywn Kirk and Margo Okazawa-Rey suggest, "Our identity is a specific marker of how we define ourselves at any particular moment in life" (2001, 49). Thus, 'self' (our personhood) or the idea of 'who am I' is narrated and negotiated through an individual's lived realities in particular social contexts (Rose 1996). From this perception of personal identity, we develop social identities that connect us to others who, we believe, are similar to us (Hogg and Vaughan 2002, Tajfel and Turner 1986). One's social identity is then based on membership in a group and not in another. Individuals sharing a social identity develop rhetoric and behavior that distinguish them as in-group in contrast to 'others'. In its turn, social identity creates a basis for the development of national identity where nation is a group of people with similar background, culture, and perhaps a historical narrative.

Motherhood has historically been a core identity for women, and their social realities dominated by the activities related to child bearing and rearing. Despite feminist efforts to demythologize the role and identity, motherhood still occupies a central position in women's identities. Whether choosing to enter motherhood or being coerced into it, whether embracing or deliberately rejecting it, motherhood still wields strong influences on women regardless of class; a perception that fundamentally transforms their lives (Atkinson 2006, Ireland 1993, McMahon 1995).

Motherhood has often been considered a lonely enterprise, particularly in the West; from pregnancy to childrearing, historically, middle and upper class mothers were frequently confined to restricted spaces and activities. Western cyber-communities of mothers organized by politics,[16] profession,[17] and even musical taste[18] undoubtedly help break that isolation. Similarly, IMs using Indian surrogates are creating an active cyber-community that challenges isolation in addition to sharing information, offering emotional support, and ultimately engaging its members in advocacy for and around transnational surrogacy in India. This burgeoning community bears the characteristics of a type of cross-border nationhood that not only shares a common identity, but also (1) 'others' surrogates, (2) 'others' India itself, while simultaneously defending Indian surrogacy, and (3) re-enacts a 19th century imperialist rhetoric of 'saving'/ 'empowering' brown women, as well as a commercially-based colonialism.

As we surveyed blogs from the U.S., Australia, and U.K., what began to emerge was a pattern of cross-border cyber-nation, a nation of IPs defined by the 'space' of their individual blogs, but more importantly, the spaces in between. As we have discussed above, the bloggers of the 'Indian surrogacy community' self-identify in several ways: first, through their blog titles, which often reference India or have recognizable Indian symbols (e.g., Million Rupee Baby, Chai Baby, and Baby Masala), or alternately, with a post-title blog description (e.g., the blog "+ 1 (make that 2) will make us a family"'s 'subtitle' reads "The story of our Journey to start a family with the help of an Indian Surrogate). A second way in which these blogs identify their common cultural space is through their blogrolls; that is, the identification of similar blogs in the 'cyber-nation'. Not only do these bloggers follow each others' blogs, and recommend others do the same, but they actively participate in populating the spaces *in between* the blogs. These bloggers comment on each others' postings and pictures, post public congratulations (for another blogger's new baby) and sympathy (for another blogger's baby loss), and send out calls to mobilize what many bloggers refer to as 'the Indian surrogacy community'. For example, on 16 July 2009, Amani and Bob's Indian surrogacy blog posted the following note, explicitly connecting their personal family life with the lives of other families in the community (Amani 21 July 2010):

> **Calling out to the Indian surrogacy community**
> Our little boy got daddy's cold and has been quite restless, snotty and generally unwell…This worried me greatly, being my first-ever child, and being so little, it is emotionally wrenching to see such a tiny little lamb so distressed ...which leads me to the title of this blog. Toby having a cold is nothing compared to the agony and ecstasy of our new bloggers Sam and Phil. I can only imagine how rough things are for them. Ben and his twin brother Zac were born on July 4 at 27 weeks. Tragically Zac has passed away and Ben is in Delhi Newborn Centre (Level 5 NICU) where he is stable and improving day by day…Can our beautiful surrogacy friends from all over the world please head over to Sam, Phil and little Ben at http://samandphilblog.blogspot.com/ Please add this new family to your blog lists and support them with your love and prayers.[19]

Bloggers continue to feel a part of the Indian surrogacy community even after their children are born, and nurture newer members of the community by sharing not only emotional support, but doctor and hotel recommendations, wisdom regarding Indian travel, and even outgrown baby clothes. In the words of Baby Masala,

> I'm so excited to see this year's "crop" of surrogacy babies. ...I remembered that this time last year, we were anxiously finishing our packing and planning for our trip to pick up our baby. In fact, I ...was having my last minute panic, writing tigerlilycat [the blogger at Made in India] so that she could re-assure me that this pregnancy in India thing wasn't just a huge hoax and that there really would be a baby arriving for us. (19 June 2010)

In parallel to this sort of OL community consolidation, is a RL community creation. Indian surrogacy bloggers often meet and seek to meet other Western IPs like themselves, both while in India, and in their home countries. The blogger at Million Rupee Baby posted the following while she was in Gujarat for ova harvesting:

> A few more (talkative) couples have arrived. It has been really lonely here, and seeing other people that want to socialize is like being freed from solitary confinement! We all chatted in Dr. Hitesh's office yesterday and today. Then B and I went to Cafe Coffee Day (think Starbucks with Britney Spears music), and we met up with another couple from Germany. They are both surgeons and this is their second time here. (15 July 2008)

Whether European, Australian, or American, IPs feel a cross-border bond with others in their community (read: other IPs). They consolidate this connection by rhetorically defending its borders against Western nay-sayers, Indian surrogates, and the country of India itself.

Othering Mothers

By Kirk and Okazawa-Rey's formulation, the cyber-community of IMs defines itself both by who they are and who they are not (2001). This task of defining 'self' as different from 'other' is accomplished both explicitly and implicitly. Here, we will examine two cyber-practices common to IM bloggers that effectively accomplish these tasks by differentiating themselves from 'their surrogates': (1) the posted ultrasound photo; and (2) the posted surrogate 'belly shot'.

It is quite common in the Indian surrogacy blogosphere, as it is in the 'mommy blogosphere' as a whole, for IPs to post 3- and 4-D ultrasonographic images of 'their' fetuses – either as still images, or even, as clickable videotapes. The important difference, of course, is that the images of surrogate fetuses are several-times mediated: taken by Indian physicians examining Indian surrogate mothers, sent via email from India to the West, and only then posted by IPs on their blogs. Interestingly, however, the goal of these posted images is to *decrease* the distance between IP/IM and the fetus by effectively erasing the surrogate from the picture. Indeed, scholars have argued that fetal ultrasonography has transformed modern motherhood altogether such that mothers are no longer relied upon as sources of accurate information regarding their pregnancies (e.g., through reports of fetal movement or quickening, and the like); rather, they are encouraged to seek a mediated knowledge of their own bodies and a view of their own fetuses via the technology of the ultrasound and the specialized knowledge of the physician/technologist (Martin 1992, Stabile 1993, Taylor, 2000). In the words of Paul Brodwin,

> Laparoscopy and fetal photography [...] furnish ever more invasive and naturalized depictions of the fetus, which performs the crucial ideological work (in the context of American new Right politics) of visually separating mother and fetus, asserting fetal autonomy, and reducing women to passive reproducing machines." (2000, 4)

In the case of surrogacy, this ideological work has the additional layer of not only "reducing" surrogates "to passive reproducing machines" (Brodwin 2000, 4) but creating a consumer class for this 'mechanized' reproductive product – the fetus. Indeed, Taylor (2008) argues that fetal ultrasonography has commodified the fetus in a way so as to transform mothers from embodied agents regarding their own pregnancies into consumers – of medical information, health care services, and ultimately, of the fetus itself. In the case of Indians surrogacy, then, posted ultrasound images serve to separate gestating maternal embodiment from fetal embodiment, affiliating the fetus with the intended mother (consumer) and placing her on an essentially level playing field with any other gestating (non-surrogate) mother posting ultrasonographic images online.

In seeming contradiction to the practice of posting ultrasound images is that of posting 'belly shots' of the surrogates at various stages of pregnancy. Such images have the potential to counteract the cultural work of the ultrasound in erasing the embodied surrogate from the space of the cyber-nation. And indeed, while some blogs, such as Made in India, include photographs of the pregnant surrogate's body and face, most 'belly shots' are so called because they are limited to the surrogates' midsections only, leaving their heads out of the picture. Although such a framing is undoubtedly to preserve some vexed sense of anonymity, it is both haunting and reductive. Such an image accompanied the highly publicized 2007 *Marie Claire* article on Indian surrogacy that featured a photograph of protuberantly expecting, sari clad, headless brown bellies. We have argued elsewhere (DasGupta and Dasgupta 2010) that such images encourage in the viewer a gaze pregnant with Orientalist[20] possibilities,[21] in which the faceless body of the pregnant surrogate is very literally unable to look back. One can also understand these images in light of Foucault's construction of the docile body frozen in time and space, removed of subjectivity (Foucault 1995), as well as Jonathan Beller's notion of 'visual economy' and 'sensual labor' (2006). For instance, Amani and Bob posted the following text after a 'belly shot' of 'their' surrogate swathed in a sparkling white, silver and pink sari:

> INTRODUCING ... OUR FRONT BUMP!
>
> Our bump! Don't look side on as I did, and think "what a lovely slim pregnant lady" the pic is taken from front on, so belly is poking out the front. Our SMR was very shy and squirmy and ran away from the camera. Bless her. A bump is a bump, I see a bump and I am loving that bump! I have a gift for SMR that I have had tucked away for ages. Dr Shivani doesn't encourage gift-giving until after baby is born. I am busting to send it and to write SMR a card and tell her how wonderful I think she is, and what an amazing job she is doing. But we have to wait. (Thursday, 1 April 2010)

The comments to this posting reinforce an Orientalist gaze indeed; commenter "George," a single father of two babies by Indian surrogacy – Elektra and Eros, remarks "beautiful!/can i rub her belly for good luck?/ looks like she dressed in all her finest for the pic, and she said she is shy? lol" [sic]. Other commenters use the pronoun "your" instead of "her" when referring to the "bump," as does the blogger herself ("Our bump!") cementing the idea that the headless belly 'belongs' to the blogger IM, not the surrogate. Or perhaps, even more disturbingly, that the surrogate herself 'belongs' to the IM ("Our SMR…"), and thereby, so does the surrogate's pregnant uterus. The cultural capital of the 'belly shot'- almost as ubiquitous on these blogs as ultrasound images, is clear. Johnny and Darren, a gay Australian couple who had their babies by Indian surrogacy, remark on Amani and Bob's pregnancy "bump" photo by noting "Great picture, you both must be happy to have this. I know when we received ours it took pride of place on the fridge door."[22]

Yet, the problematic nature of the "belly shot" is articulated even by bloggers themselves. The blogger at Chai Baby noted,

> Today we received some beautiful photos of our surrogate. We didn't ask for them and as it turns out it is something that SCI are trying to do more of, so we can see the progress of our surrogacy. ...Before i received our photos, i felt that the 'belly shot' was a bit exploitative and felt generally uncomfortable about it all. It seemed to reduce our surrogate to the bits that carried our babies. Now i have these wonderful shots of our smiling surrogate, with a tentative wave to the camera and it's different. She is smiling and looks content and clearly pregnant, with our babies [sic]. (19 October 2010)[23]

Although the blogger notes that the surrogate is smiling at her, the image she posts is a classic side "belly shot" without a head. Chai Baby's blogger also testifies to the particular difficulty of the 'belly shot' for the IM, who cannot herself become pregnant.

> Another blog recently posed the question "how does it feel to be pregnant" and there were perspectives shared. As a women [sic], when you tell people you're pregnant, they immediate look at your belly and then i have to explain that i am not carrying our babies and with that goes the ache that i am not able to carry our babies. Some days i can say it in quickly and the feeling rushes past so quickly that i can almost ignore it, other days it is like a lead weight pushing down me down in the place that should be able to carry our babies. (Ibid)

Clearly, these dual gestures of posting images of both fetal ultrasounds and headless pregnant surrogate bodies are enacting a tension between the gestating mother, IM, and the fetus. By locating the fetal image in the space of the blogosphere, the blogger reinscribes fetal autonomy, while implanting the fetus in the IM cyber-nation. Simultaneously, the headless gestating belly provides a nod to the presence of the surrogate, while disallowing any real agency, any literal or figurative 'face.'

Othering India

> There is no race. There is no gender. There is no age. There are no infirmities. There are only minds. Utopia? No, Internet. (MCI commercial "Anthem" quoted in Nakamura 2002, 255).

The above "Anthem" is now a classic example of early assertions that cyberspace somehow signaled a freedom from embodiment. Work by postcolonial critics of digital spaces have taken such simplistic conceptions of the cybernetic world as post-ethnic, post-gender, post-disability, and post-human entity to task. "[T]he Internet as a medium of communication exhibits a fascinating paradoxical nature—the RL body of speakers is simultaneously unimportant and vitally meaningful. ...While cyberspace may cloak people from each other, the prejudices of society are still carried into the system" (Chambers 2004, 387, 397). Far from being a disembodied or "out of body" space, cyberspace is extraordinarily corporeal. As Helen Kennedy (2003) has asserted in her discussion of "technobiographies," there can be no discussion of on-line lives without an understanding of off-line contexts. Indeed, as both a subjective and an intersubjective location, cyberspace affords bodies "an invariably public dimension; constituted as a socially bound up power phenomenon in the public sphere, my body is and is not mine" (Butler 2004, 21).

Thus, it is critical to examine the role of race and xenophobia in transnational surrogacy exchanges. We have already contended elsewhere that race is a way in which Indian gestational surrogates are made 'other' from the fetuses they bear (DasGupta and Dasgupta 2010). The rhetoric, espoused even by surrogates themselves, appears to be that a brown-skinned woman will have an easier time in relinquishing a white skinned baby. For instance, Najima Vorha, who was carrying a child for New Jersey yoga school proprietor Jessica Ordenes, is reported as saying, "It won't have the same skin color as me… so it won't be hard to think of it as Jessica's… If I do feel sad after the birth, I won't show it" (Haworth August 2007, 127).

Helena Ragoné's work on inter-ethnic surrogacy suggests that phenotypic dissimilarity is used by surrogates and intended parents alike to de-emphasize the specter of 'relatedness' between surrogates and the babies they deliver (Ragoné 1998). Seline Szkupinski Quiroga notes that the U.S. fertility industry is fond of saying that their aim is to "create families," yet, "what remains unspoken is the desire to create a certain type of family, one that closely matches, and thus reproduces, the heteropatriarchal model of a white nuclear family" (Quiroga 2007, 144).[24]

Indeed, the Indian surrogacy blogosphere carries many stories of traveling to India that are steeped in a sort of racist and xenophobic discourse consistent with the image of 'ugly American' or 'my vacation in a Third World hell'[25] narrative. Below, two seemingly innocuous posts from Million Rupee Baby reflect this sort of narrative:

> We left Hong Kong on Monday morning for Delhi. We arrived in Delhi at 1:15 PM and then began our 9 1/2 hour layover. The only way I can describe this airport is to say that it is worse than a Greyhound bus station, and I would rather get a bladder infection than use the toilets there.
>
> (11 March2009)[26]

> Our Laundry REEKS!
>
> We had our laundry done by the hotel twice while we were here. The first time it smelled fine. This past time it smelled like a dirty jock strap. F'ing disgusting. In my "can't hold onto any food state" I made B stay far away from me because of his shirts' aroma. He too is so disgusted by it that he has been wearing fragranced lotion on his upper lip. (15 July 2008)[27]

Bloggers frequently post photographs of Indian traffic congestion, complete with grazing or lounging goats, dogs, or cattle. In addition, bloggers have posted Youtube videos of bumpy auto-rickshaw rides, cautioning "if you tend to suffer from motion sickness, don't watch this video."[28]

Complicating this sort of discourse of India as a congested, smelly, dirty, 'Other' place are *anti*-xenophobic, *anti*-racist, and *anti*-queerphobic arguments put forth on many of these sites. Bloggers often find themselves *defending* India and Indians against the racist comments of their friends and family. For example, Million Rupee Baby posted:

> STOOPID FAQS
>
> Here are a few of the less intelligent questions that we have gotten from close friends and family members regarding our pregnancy via a surrogate in India.
>
> Q. Are you going to feed baby Raj Indian food?

A. Maybe when our baby is older he or she will like Indian food. Also, you are a racist a$$hole.
Q. Will your baby be born with a dot on it's [sic] forehead?
A. Seriously? You may need to be checked out for brain rot.
Q. Did B have sex with M (our surrogate) to get her pregnant?
A. No. We did a cycle of IVF and then transferred *our* embryo to M. (27 September 2008)[29]

In the comments section to this post, Amani of Amani and Bob's Indian Surrogacy Blog responded, "Egad. Unbelievable. How about this one:/The baby will come out smelling of curry/or this:/You could call the baby poppadum./Yea, right."

The need for IMs of Indian surrogates to defend Indian surrogacy becomes clear when one looks at the discourse on broader surrogacy discussion boards. On 17 June 2010, in response to a television documentary called "Google Baby" (Bellfante 15 June 2010), American surrogates and IMs alike suggested that surrogacy in India was "dirty," "hurtful to the surrogates," and "almost like prostitution…push(ing) surrogacy more into the realm of human exploitation, being all about the money, making Caucasian babies…instead of …making families, giving a gift of life to another women who cannot" (HopefulMommy2B, Comment #1).[30] On that same thread, Norwegian surrogate 'Starfish' suggested, "India is on the fast track to becoming a baby farming country" ("Renate: Momx3, TSx2, Looking for IPs," Comment #15). Other posters were "saddened," "disgusted," and "horrified," while a few others took this evaluation of Indian surrogacy into a critique of India itself: "It really, really saddens me that other countries live the way they do," ("Lynn: Wife, Mom, GS," Comment #18). Similarly, an IM who tried Indian surrogacy posted the following comment regarding the practice of housing surrogates in a 'dorm' at Akanksha:

> …[T]rust me when I say these [surrogates] were living like royalty for where they are from. They have cooks, maids and a psychologist there at all times to help take care of them. …It is so sad to see how these woman [sic] live at home, they live in little make shift huts with tarps as the roofs and have dogs and cows, yes cows sleeping in the same quarters. I saw babies laying under bridges with only their very young siblings tending to them. Also many children are crippled, blinded and many other horrific things to up their value as beggars. (drgnfly, Comment #55)

The response to these sorts of sentiments – that Indian surrogates are exploited and oppressed, that India is backward and oppressive – is exemplified by the following 'open letter' by the blogger Amani to an

Australian congressperson proposing a bill curtailing transnational surrogacy to India:

> I am the mother of a beautiful little baby boy ...who was born through a commercial surrogacy agreement in Delhi, India. I am SO GRATEFUL!!! I [was] supported by our wonderful surrogate mother, Rani, who was, or is, neither impoverished nor exploited. My husband and I never once exploited, denigrated, abused nor took advantage of our Rani, nor her husband, nor her children. At no stage did our Rani ever feel exploited, denigrated, or taken advantage of. Only the people party to our very private agreement get to decide who is exploited. ...I will also never allow my son, nor any child, born through commercial surrogacy abroad, be it USA, Ukraine, India - where ever - to become Australia's latest "stolen generation" - abused, disenfranchised and discriminated against because of how they came into the world. ...I will also fight for any Australian single person or couple - be they same-sex, heterosexual, de facto, green, black, orange or blue - to have this amazingly life-enriching opportunity taken from them - enriching not only for the parents but also the women who help us all to become parents... (Nov. 11, 2010)[31]

Interesting is Amani's willingness to make connections between babies born by Indian surrogacy and Australia's "lost generation"[32] and her connection of Indian surrogacy to the struggles of LGBT and other marginalized people everywhere. Indeed, due to the predominance of gay male partners using Indian surrogacy services, much IM rhetoric supporting surrogacy is often also supportive of LGBT issues.

Interestingly, other similar comments sometimes seek to diminish the role of India in Indian surrogacy, erasing the import of the surrogate altogether. When Amani re-posted an August 2010 blogpost entitled "inside baby factory farms" that was critical of Indian surrogacy,[33] a commenter ".jon" suggested the need for "better language" than the "buzzword" of "Indian surrogacy." The commenter went on,

> When I look at my babies I don't see a label on their forehead that reads "Product of Indian surrogate". Actually that is the last thing I see. The surrogate, bless her heart and soul, was a conduit for bringing them into this world. Plain and simple... By continuing to use this term [Indian surrogacy] we... narrowly focuses on the venue (India) and one player on the team (surrogate).[34]

IM Cyber-Nationhood

Our understanding of the Indian surrogacy blogosphere-as-nation is framed by Wendy Hui Kyong Chun's (2007) formulation of cyberspace as a Foucaultian heterotopia – an electronic frontier structure that, for all of its futuristic imaginings, replicates 19th-century ideas of the colonizing subject. "Like all explorations," writes Chun, "charting cyberspace entailed uncovering what was already there and declaring it 'new'. It entailed obscuring already existing geographies and structures so that space becomes vacuous yet chartable, unknown yet populated and populatable" (2007, 243). Similarly, Jonathan Beller states,

> Territories are still dominated, but in addition to the traditional and military methods, they are also dominated by a deterritorialization that renders them effectively 'global,'...the vanguard methods of the postmodern conquistadors are computers, televisions, fax machines, cell phones, and film – technologies that work by inserting the spatial and temporal exigencies of the First World into Third World bodies and organizations. (2006, 74)

Keeping Chun's and Beller's assertions in mind, we see that the practices of 'othering' both surrogates and India itself, functions as a sort of cybernetic imperialist discourse, seeking to erase, as .jon suggests, the term "Indian surrogacy" altogether, and position the Indian surrogate as but one minor player in the process of cross-border, cyber-mediated baby making. Indeed, in that same comment on Amani and Bob's blog, .jon also suggested that to "create life" you need not only a surrogate, an egg, a sperm, a clinic, a doctor etc. but that "You also need other intangible players as well. You need capital...You need internet technology. You need an understanding and appreciation for globalization and its impact on more personal areas of our lives. You need cooperative home governments."

If Western IMs of Indian surrogates are involved in forms of OL and RL imperialism, these acts are mediated by a commercial and capitalist sensibility. Note below that in a post called "Golden Arches," a seemingly simple craving for McDonalds food by the blogger at Million Rupee Baby ends with a nationalistic chant:

> I can't wait to get home and eat meat. I have been planning my first meal back (which is common for most prisoners and hostages), and it is either going to be McDonalds or Chipotle.... I am so over mango juice, curry, naan, rice and anything spicy. I just want the tastes and comfort of home, which for me is McDonalds. USA! USA! USA![35]

This post brings to mind the notion of 'Coca-Colonization', or colonialism through capitalism (Iyer 1989). Indeed, in addition to the common surrogacy discourse of 'gifting' motherhood are actual gifts from IPs to surrogates, which become integral to masking surrogacy's commercial buying and selling of reproductive potential. In the language of the LA Times, "Many of the surrogate mothers are showered with gifts of food and medicine and monitored with solicitous attention by the waiting parents, usually educated, sophisticated people who want to ensure that their investment yields its much-hoped-for fruit" (Chu 2006). This language of "showering with gifts" by "educated, sophisticated people" clearly constructs a dualism whereby the Indian recipient of this beneficence is poor, unsophisticated, and (assuredly) grateful. At the same time, gifts become a sort of "investment" assurance/insurance. A discussion thread on the (now defunct) Surrogacy India Online Support Group puzzles over this thorny issue of appropriate "gifts for surro." Lisa B., an Australian woman posts,

> Both trips we took dried fruit and chocolate (remember Indian's LOVE incredibly sweet things) as well as toy cars for our surro's sons and dolls (with blonde hair) for her daughter. NB - we've used the same surro twice. We also took fabric as we were aware our surro's husband was a tailor. I thought a new outfit or two would have been made, but they used the materials to make cushion covers and curtains etc to decorate their house instead. Don't think they'll ever forget us now!!! (19 October 2008)[36]

Significant here are Lisa B.'s helpful tips to her fellow IPs regarding Indian dietary preferences as well as her choice to perpetuate, or perhaps impose, Western standards of beauty by bringing dolls "with blonde hair" for her Indian surrogate's daughter. This is apparent as well in a comment by Michelle, a 38-year-old woman from Florida,

> I was recently at Disney World with my family and got our surro a collectors snowglobe / music box that depicts Mickey Mouse and all of the Disney parks. For her children I got (what else) Mickey Mouse and Minnie Mouse dolls. Not sure how many kids she has, boy/girl, etc, but I figure everyone knows who Mickey and Minnie are. (20 October 2008)[37]

Despite this cross-border commercialism, there is a great deal of anxiety among the Indian surrogacy 'nation' about the liminal status of babies born. Laws are often unclear and volatile, as policy makers in the U.S., Europe, Australia, and Asia struggle to catch up with the shifting ground realities of rapidly changing reproductive technologies. Indeed, the IM 'nation' is rife with discussion about citizenship problems and the 'import' of babies; for instance, undergoing DNA testing to document that one at least one IP is genetically related to the child. The issues are so complex, one blogger, Amani, posted a link to a lengthy Google document outlining the various forms and procedures necessary to "get [a baby] out of Dodge [India]."[38]

These issues took traction in the community after the case of "Baby Manji" in 2008 – when a baby born via an Indian surrogate, a Japanese IF's sperm and an Indian egg donor suddenly found herself between countries (*BBC News* 6 August 2008, *Biopolitical Times* 18 September 2009, *The Telegraph* 18 October 2008). Due to the IP's divorce, and the IM's refusal to take the baby, IF Ikufumi Yamada found himself without legal recourse, as a single man is unable to adopt a girl child according to Indian law. This law, created to prevent child trafficking, resulted in "Baby Manji" being unable to leave India for months, and highlighted the tenuous, equivocal citizenship status of babies born by Indian surrogacy. The discourse at the time on surrogacy message boards, reflected complicated tensions.[39] Many posters' comments were along the lines of "you get what you pay for," but some went further, pointing to the oppressions that "Indian women face" including "honor killings" (zoocrew, Comment #46). A Virgina-based surrogate posted, "Personally, were I an IP, I would be uncomfortable using an [sic] surrogate in a country so well known for poverty and extremely poor womens' [sic] rights" (unspecified42, comment #50). Retorts to these comments suggested that perhaps U.S. based surrogates were "jealous" of Indian surrogacy "taking off" and that U.S. surrogates had "superiority complexes" to Indian surrogates.

Critical to remember is that this sort of discourse takes place without voices of Indian surrogates visible or present. Indeed, embedded in these conversations about exploited and oppressed Indian women is a re-enactment of post colonial critic Gayatri Chakravorty Spivak's notion of "white men saving brown women from brown men" (2007, 33). Spivak's analysis of British imperialist concern over issues such as sati and widow remarriage in India suggests that the trope of "rescuing women" becomes a way to legitimize colonial violence, while, of course, keeping brown women's voices silent.[40] Although Western IMs often find themselves defending India and Indian surrogates against charges of being backward or exploited, we contend that such a discourse of a global sisterhood mediated by money manifests a post-globalization, post-feminist reconstitution of the "white man's burden," as now, the "white woman's burden." The IM "nation" exerts its imperialism in both commerce and a complex discourse in which Indian women are both defended as agents of their own destinies, and simultaneously silenced in the dialogue about their lives, virtually obliterated.

This inability to hear Indian surrogates' voices, or register moments of protest, was the most distressing aspect of this project. However, there are flickers of resistance to this imperialist rhetoric that can be seen if one takes a closer look. In a photo posted by Baby Masala, the surrogate mother is seen swathed in the colors of the Indian flag.[41] Although the bloggers do not comment on it (it is possible they did not realize the gesture), the image of an Indian surrogate draped in a sari that gestures to Indian nationalism is powerful. Notably, the Indian flag had particular symbolic potency in the context of Indian independence from two hundred years of British rule, a mere 60+ years ago. A bit more vexed is a photo posted at Million Rupee Baby, featuring the IF with his child Lila, and another father-child pair, all dwarfed by a giant statue of Mohandas K. Gandhi, father of the Indian revolution.[42] Such gestures perhaps underscore the tensions of Western 'multiculturalism' whereby 'globalization' is embraced by the global North while the global South remains marked by 'ethnicity'.

There are, of course, no fixed answers to the question of motherhood by transnational surrogacy, no facile solutions. However, we must recognize that online motherhood by surrogacy is creating spaces for support and community while simultaneously reinforcing imperialist patterns of colonialism and commercialism, enacting rhetorical and representational violence that may mirror the actual violence of transnational surrogacy itself.

Works Cited

Asch, Adrienne. 2003. "Disability equality and prenatal testing: Contradictory or compatible?" *Florida State University Law Review,* 30: 315-42.

Atkinson, B. 2006. "Gaining motherhood, losing identity?" *MIDIRS Midwifery Digest,* 16: 170-174.

Balsamo, Anne. 1999. "Notes Toward a reproductive theory of technology." *Playing Dolly: Technocultural Formations, Fantasies and Fictions of Assisted Reproduction*, edited by E. Anne Kaplan and Susan Squier. 87-97. Piscataway, NJ: Rutgers University Press.

BBC News. 2008. "India-Japan baby in legal wrangle," 6 August. Online. Accessed 26 April 2009. (http://news.bbc.co.uk/2/hi/south_asia/7544430.stm).

Bellafante, Ginia. 2010. *Google baby: Surrogate Pregnancy Goes Global,* 15 June. Online. Accessed 3 November 2010 (http://www.nytimes.com/2010/06/16/arts/television/16google.html?_r=1&r=3).

Beller, Jonathan. 2006. *The Cinematic Mode of Production: Attention Economy and The Society of the Spectacle.* Hanover, NH: Dartmouth.

Bhatia, Shekhar. 2009. "Investigation: Surrogate baby delivered every 48 hours." *London Evening Standard,* May 20. Online. Accessed 9 November 2010 (http://www.thisislondon.co.uk/standard/article-23695609-investigation-surrogate-baby-delivered-every-48-hours.do).

Bhattacharya, Kajari. 2008a. "Surrogate motherhood emerges as a job option." *The Statesman* (Kolkata, India), 12 January: 1.

—. 2008b. "Surrogacy coloured by white bias." *The Statesman* (Kolkata, India), 13 January: 1.

Binham, Caroline. 2003. "What makes an egg Jewish?" *NYU Arthur L. Carter Journalism Institute Portfolio.* 30 March. Online. Accessed 20 April 2009 (http://journalism.nyu.edu/portfolio/binham/eggs_jewish.html).

Biopolitical Times. 2009. "Complications of surrogacy: The case of baby Manji." 18 September. Online. Accessed 2 November 2010 (http://www.biopoliticaltimes.org/article.php?id=4923).

Brodwin, Paul P. 2000. "Introduction." *Biotechnology and Culture: Bodies, Anxieties, Ethics (Theories of Contemporary Culture),* edited by Paul P. Brodwin. 1-23. Bloomington: Indiana University Press.

Butler, Judith. 2004. *Undoing Gender.* New York: Routledge.

Carney, Scott. 2010. "Inside India's rent-a-womb business." *Mother Jones,* March/April. Online. Accessed 15 November 2010 (http://motherjones.com/politics/2010/02/surrogacy-tourism-india-nayna-patel).

Celizic, Mike. 2009. "Special deliveries: Are designer babies coming?" *Today,* 3 March. Online. Accessed 13 April 2009 (www.msnbc.msn.com/id/29478274/).

Chambers, Tod. 2004. "Virtual Disability: On the internet, nobody knows you're not a sick puppy." *Cultural Sutures: Medicine and Media,* edited by Lester D. Friedman. 386-98. Durham, NC: Duke University Press.

Chun, Wendy Hui Kyong. 2007. "Othering space." *Visual Culture Reader,* (2nd edition), edited by Nicholas Mirzoeff. 243-254. New York: Routledge.

Corea, Gena. 1985. *The Mother Machine: Reproductive Technologies from Artificial Insemination to Artificial Wombs.* New York: Harper Collins.

DasGupta, Sayantani and Shamita Das Dasgupta. 2010. "Motherhood jeopardized: Reproductive technologies in Indian communities." *The Globalization of Motherhood: Deconstructions and Reconstructions of Biology and Care*, edited by JaneMaree Maher and Wendy Chavkin. 131-153. NY: Routledge.

Dorsey, Michael. 2002. "The new eugenics." *World Watch*, 15: 21-23.

Enloe, Cynthia. 1990. *Bananas, Beaches and Bases: Making Feminist Sense of International Politics*. Berkeley & Los Angeles: University of California Press.

Fontanella-Khan, Amana. 2010. "India, the rent-a-womb capital of the world." *Slate*. 23 August. Online. Accessed 30 October 2010 (http://www.slate.com/id/2263136/).

Foucault, Michel. 1995. *Discipine and Punish: The Birth of the Clinic*. New York: Vintage.

Gokhale, Ketaki. 2006. "Indian couples seek out U.S. sex selection clinics." *India West*, 30 June. Online. Accessed 25 April 2009 (http://news.newamericamedia.org/news/view_article.html?article_id=54a58cce914f335cb8fb6e722aa1028d).

Government of India. 2010. "The assisted reproductive technologies (regulation) bill-2010." *Ministry of Health and Family Welfare*. Online. Accessed 9 November 9 2010 (http://www.scribd.com/doc/33533932/Art-Regulation-Draft-Bill1-India).

Haimowitz, Rebecca and Vaishali Sinha (Co-directors & Co-producers). 2008. *Made in India* (Documentary film) (http://www.madeinindiamovie.com/index.html).

Halweil, Brian and Dick Bell. 2002. "Beyond cloning: The larger agenda of human engineering." *World Watch*, 15: 8-10.

Harlow, Harry. 1958. "The nature of love." *American Psychologist,* 13: 73-85.

Haworth, Abigail 2007. "Womb for rent." *Marie Claire*, 27 August: 125-29.

Hogg, Michael A. and Graham M. Vaughan, 2002. *Social Psychology,* 3rd edition. London: Prentice Hall.

Ireland, Mardy S. 1993. *Reconceiving Women: Separating Motherhood from Female Identity*. New York: Guilford Press.

Iyer, Pico. 1989. *Video Night in Kathmandu: And Other Reports from the Not-So-Far East*. New York: Vintage.

"Journey to parenthood." 2006. *The Oprah Winfrey Show*, 1 January. Online. Accessed 20 April 2009 (http://www.oprah.com/world/Wombs-for-Rent/1).

Kennedy, Helen. 2003. "Technobiography: Researching lives online and off." *Biography,* 26: 120-39.

Kirk, Gwyn and Margo Okazawa-Rey. 2001. "Identities and social locations: Who am I? Who are my people?" *Women's Lives: Multicultural Perspectives* (2nd edition). Mountain View, CA: Mayfield.

Kung, Michelle. 2010. "Google baby documentary sheds light on outsourcing surrogacy." *Speakeasy (The Wall Street Journal),* 16 June. Online. Accessed 3 November 2010 (http://blogs.wsj.com/speakeasy/2010/06/16/google-baby-documentary-sheds-light-on-outsourcing-surrogacy/).

Lehner, Marla. 2010. "Neil Patrick Harris to be a dad-to twins." *People*, 14 August. Online. Accessed 3 November 2010 (http://www.people.com/people/article/0,,20413182,00.html).

Malpani, A., A. Malpani. and D. Modi. 2002. "Preimplantation sex selection for family balancing in India." *Human Reproduction*, 17: 11-12.

Mann, Jonathan and Satinder Bindra. 2006. "Outsourcing to Indian surrogate mothers." *CNN.com*, 17 October. Online. Accessed 20 April 2009 (http://transcripts.cnn.com/TRANSCRIPTS/0610/17/i_ins.01.html).

Markens, Susan. 2007. *Surrogate Motherhood and the Politics of Reproduction.* Berkeley: University of California Press.

Martin, Emily. 1992. *The Woman in the Body: A Cultural Analysis of Reproduction.* Boston: Beacon Press.

Medindia. 2008. "Govt.'s concern with sale of gender identification kits in India." 16 March. Online. Accessed 29 July 2009 (www.medindia.net/news/Govts-Concern-With-Sale-of-Gener-Identification-Kits-in-India-34231-1.htm).

McLean's. 2007. "Outsourcing life itself: What India teaches us." 2 July: 4.

McMahon, Martha. 1995. *Engendering Motherhood: Identity and Self-transformations in Women's Lives.* NY: Guilford Press.

McNeil, Laurie. 2003. "Teaching an old genre new tricks: The diary on the Internet." *Biography,* 26: 24-47.

Moazam, Farhat. 2006. *Bioethics and Organ Transplantation in a Muslim Society.* Bloomington: Indiana University Press.

Mooney, Pat. 2002. "Making well people "better"." *World Watch*, 15: 13-16.

Moore, Pamela L. 1999. "Selling reproduction." *Playing Dolly: Technocultural Formations, Fantasies and Fictions of Assisted Reproduction,* edited by E. Anne Kaplan and Susan Squier. 80-6, Piscataway: Rutgers U Press.

Mukherjee, Krittivas. 2007. "Rent-a-womb in India fuels surrogate mother debate." *Reuters Report Posted on Center for Genetics and Society Website*, 12 February. Online. Accessed 20 April 2009 (http://www.geneticsandsociety.org/article.php?id=3386).

Nakamura, Lisa. 2007. ""Where do you want to go today?" Cybernetic tourism, the Internet, and transnationality." *The Visual Culture Reader,*" 2nd edition, edited by Nicholas Mirzoeff. 255-263. New York: Routledge.

Nagi, Milon. 2006. ""Not how a second-generation should bond" - Sex selection in US South Asian communities." *The Women's Media Center,* 22 August. Online. Accessed 3 September 2006 (www.womensmediacenter.com/ex/082206_main.html).

National Public Radio. 2010. "Google baby follows birth outsourced to India" (host: Neal Conan). 15 June. Online. Accessed 15 October 2010 (http://www.npr.org/player/v2/mediaPlayer.html?action=1&t=1&islist =false&id=127860111&m=127860104).

Nolen, Stephanie. 2009. "Desperate mothers fuel India's 'baby factories'." *Toronto Globe and Mail*, 13 February. Online. Accessed 20 April 2009 (http://www.geneticsandsociety.org/article.php?id=4526).

Oaklander, Mandy. 2007. "No girls please, we're Indian: Sex selection ads land ethnic media in hot water." *New America Media*, 10 September. Online. accessed 25 April 2009 (http://news.newamericamedia.org/news/view_article.html?article_id= 3c7ed640212a030bc2f3163dfdcc8bcb).

Pande, Amrita. 2009a. "Not an 'angel', not a 'whore': Surrogates as 'dirty' workers in India." *Indian Journal of Gender Studies*, 16: 141-73.

—. 2009b. ""It may have her eggs but it's my blood": Surrogates and everyday forms of kinship in India." *Qualitative Sociology*, 32: 379-397.

Patole, Geetanjali. 2001. "Say no to Gen-Select, urge doctors, chemists, doctors, chemists reject Gen-Select." *The Times of India*, 26 December. Online. Accessed 27 April 2009 (http://timesofindia.indiatimes.com/).

Pereira, Maxwell. 2006. "Sex selection in India dodges existing laws." *Indo-Asian News Service*, 3 September. Online. Accessed 25 April 2009 (http://news.newamericamedia.org/news/view_article.html?article_id= 74832773372eba82348c055505376c87).

Puri, Sunita. 2005. "Boy or girl? Choosing the sex of a child prior to conception." *Student Journal.* Online. Accessed 3 September 2006 (http://berkeley.edu/news/students/2005/gender/gender-about.shtml).

—. 2006. "Sex selection alive and well in South Asian immigrant communities in the US." *India Currents, New America Media*, 17 March. Online. Accessed 25 April 2009 (http://news.newamericamedia.org/news/view_article.html?article_id=77ccb8095412ea46e40184e503787025).

Quiroga, Seline S. 2007. "Blood is thicker than water: Policing donor insemination and the reproduction of whiteness." *Hypatia,* 22: 143-61.

Ragoné, Helena. 1998. "Incontestable motivations." *Reproducing Reproduction: Kinship, Power and Technological Innovation,* edited by Sarah Franklin and Helena Ragoné. 118-131. Pennsylvania: University of Pennsylvania Press.

Raymond, Janice G. 1991. "Women as wombs: International traffic in reproduction." *Ms. Magazine*, May/June, 29-30.

Rudrappa, Sharmila. Forthcoming. "Making India the "mother destination": Outsourcing labor to Indian surrogates."

Said, Edward. 1979. *Orientalism.* New York: Vintage.

Schaefer, Louisa. 2007. "Children and families: Germany's egg donation prohibition is outdated, experts say." *Deutsche Welle, DW-World.De*, 12 December. Online. Accessed 20 April 2009 (http://www.dw-world.de/dw/article/0,2144,2999675,00.html).

Sharp, Lesley A. 2007. *Bodies, Commodities, and Biotechnologies: Death, Mourning and Scientific Desire in the Realm of Human Organ Transfer* (Leonard Hastings Schoff Lectures). New York: Columbia U Press.

Singh, Khushwant. 2006. "US sex-determination kit spells fears." *The Times of India Online*, 17 June. Online. Accessed June 17 2006 (http://timesofindia.indiatimes.com/NEWS/India/US-sex-determination-kit-spells-fears/articleshow/1655667.cms).

Smerdon, Usha R. 2008. "Crossing bodies, crossing borders: International surrogacy between the United States and India." *Cumberland Law Review*, 39: 15-85.

Spar, Debora. 2005. "Reproductive tourism and the regulatory map." *The New England Journal of Medicine,*(Health Policy and Reform), 352, 6: 531-533.

Spivak, Gayatri C. 2007. "Can the subaltern speak?" *The Post-Colonial Studies Reader*, edited by Bill Ashcroft, Gareth Griffiths, and Helen Tiffin. 28-37. New York: Routledge.

Stabile, Carol. 1998. "Shooting the mother: Fetal photography and the politics of disappearance." *The Visible Woman: Imaging Technologies, Gender, and Science,* edited by Paula A. Treichler, Lisa Cartwright, and Constance Penley. 171-197. New York: New York University Press.

Subramanian, Sarmishta. 2007. "Wombs for rent." *Maclean's*, July 2, 120: 40-47.

Tajfel, Henri and John C. Turner. 1986. "The social identity theory of inter-group behavior." *Psychology of Intergroup Relations*, 2nd edition, edited by Stephen Worchel and William G. Austin. 7-24. Chicago: Nclson-Hall.

Taneja, Poonam. 2008. "Baby Tourism." *BBC Radio – Asian Network*, 13 October (Producer: P. Khatkar). Online. Accessed 20 April 2009 (http://www.bbc.co.uk/asiannetwork/documentaries/babytourism.shtml).

Thakur, Sunita. 2008. "Mother for only nine months." *BBC News*, 21 March. Online. Accessed 20 April 2009 (http://news.bbc.co.uk/2/hi/south_asia/7202043.stm).

Thayil, Jeet. 2001. "Sex determination tests worry Indian Americans." *India Abroad*, 7 September: 32.

The Asian Pacific Post. 2005. "New pregnancy kit makes Asia jittery." 11 August. Online. accessed 5 September 2005 (www.asianpacificpost.com/apnews/news/).

The Telegraph. 2008. "Japan gate-pass for Baby Manji." 18 October. Online. Accessed 3 November 2010 (http://www.telegraphindia.com/1081018/jsp/nation/story_9984517.jsp).

Wade, Matt. 2009a. "Cheap wombs for rent…nine month contracts only and no bond." *The Sydney Morning Herald (smh.com.au)*. 31 January. Online. Accessed 20 April 2009 (http://www.smh.com.au/news/world/the-takeaway-baby-boom/2009/01/30/1232818725697.html?page=fullpage#contentSwap1).

—. 2009b. "The takeaway baby boom." *The Sydney Morning Herald (smh.com.au)*. 31 January. Online. Accessed 20 April 2009 (http://www.smh.com.au/news/world/the-takeaway-baby-boom/2009/01/30/1232818725697.html?page=fullpage#contentSwap1).

Winfrey, Oprah and Lisa Ling. 2007. "Lisa Ling investigates Wombs for Rent." *youtube*. 11 October. Online. Accessed 20 April 2009 (http://www.youtube.com/watch?v=gjEWlOl5Vnc&eurl=http%3A%2F%2Fmillionrupeebaby%2Eblogspot%2Ecom%2Fsearch%3Fupdated%2Dmax%3D2008%2D09%2D01T20%253A00%253A00%2D07%253A00%26max%2Dresults%3D7&feature=player_embedded).

World Vision Report. 2009. "Surrogates for hire." (Radio podcast). Online. Accessed 20 April 2009 (http://www.worldvision.org/worldvision/radio.nsf/stable/ED1E72059 D09300888257179005D0FBF?OpenDocument).

Zakaria, Rafia. 2010. "The cheapest wombs: India's surrogate mothers." *Ms. Blog*, 25 June. Online. Accessed 3 November 2010 (http://msmagazine.com/blog/blog/2010/06/25/the-cheapest-womb-indias-surrogate-mothers/).

Notes

[1] Most frequently the fertilized egg carries genetic material of both the intended parents. However, it might include ova donation from someone other than the intended mother, sperm donation from other than the intended father, or both.

[2] Media reports dubbing gestational surrogacy the 'outsourcing of pregnancy' are too numerous to name here (a few examples are: Kung 16 June 2010; Maclean's 2 July 2007).

[3] Surrogacy may well be more akin to sex work, which does not require technical skills, but only the mere corporeality of the female body. As opposed to sex work, however, surrogacy is not solely a service industry, rather, it does create a 'product' – a baby, who, when viewed through a Marxist lens, is irrevocably separated from the worker who produced her. Ultimately, surrogates, often poor, are motivated by desperate economic necessity.

[4] The term Assisted Reproductive Technologies or ART is being used here to refer to the spectrum of medically mediated procedures used to achieve pregnancy, including but not limited to: (1) Artificial Insemination (AI), which can involve intrauterine insemination (IUI) or intracervical insemination (ICI); (2) In vitro fertilization (IVF), which can involve transvaginal ovum retrieval (OCR), assisted zona hatching (AZH), intracytoplasmic sperm injection (ICSI), zygote intrafallopian transfer (ZIFT), ovum donation, and gestational surrogacy; (3) pre-implantation genetic diagnosis (PGD); and (4) surgical sperm retrieval (SSR). Pre-implantation methods of sex selection can involve either PGD or sperm sorting.

[5] It is often difficult to disentangle the intended mothers (IMs) from intended fathers (IFs); thus, we frequently refer to the group as intended parents (IPs).

[6] E.g., Amani and Bob's Indian Surrogacy (http://amaniandbobsurrogacy.blogspot.com/), Made in India (http://152am.blogspot.com/), Million Rupee Baby (http://millionrupeebaby.blogspot.com), The Switzer's (http://theswitzers.us/), Baby Masala (http://babymasala.blogspot.com/), Cocoa Masala (http://cocoamasala.blogspot.com/) , +1 (Make that Two) Will Make Us a Family (http://plus1makesusafamily.blogspot.com/), and Chai Baby (http://havingababyinindia.blogspot.com).

[7] www.surromomsonline.com, as well as the now defunct message board run by surrogacy india (www.surrogacyindia.com)

[8] E.g., Spawn of Mike and Mike (http://spawnofmikeandmike.blogspot.com/), Two Afro Dads (http://2afrodads.blogspot.com/), Orea Zoi

(http://orea-zoi.blogspot.com/), From India with Love (http://johnnyanddarren.blogspot.com/).

[9] At least one surrogate lost one of a twin pregnancy, and another family, the Schwitzers, had one of their live born twin girls later die in infancy. Furthermore, several of the bloggers were dissatisfied with their surrogacy experiences – one family switched physicians and hospitals mid-way through the process, and another became embroiled in a public, heated struggle with their surrogacy broker (Surrogacy India, or SI) evident in several angry posts regarding threatened law suits, reprints of letters to the brokerage, etc.

[10] Most message boarders included with their comments a personal "tag" that often had personal information such as "Mother to…" (names and ages of their children, often with the tag "by surrogacy"). Gestational surrogates were identifiable by tags such as "GSx3" or "GS seeking IPs." Information about stillbirths/miscarriages was also included through comments like "GS to 1 Angel Baby."

[11] Shamita is mother to Sayantani and grandmother to Sayantani's two children.

[12] Amrita Pande reports slightly lower numbers such as $50,000 to $80,000 in the U.S. and Canada and between $5,000 and $12,000 in Akanksha clinic in Anand, Gujarat (2009b).

[13] See, http://www.ivfcharotar.com/meet_dr_patel.php.

[14] We are using the terms 'mother' and 'motherhood' not so much as tied to a particular gender but as Harry Harlow referred to it in his study of infant attachment (1958), as indication of primary caregiver; that is, of (loving) parenthood regardless of gender.

[15] In India and perhaps all of Asia, deliberate removal of organs that are given to one at birth signifies the flouting of god's order. For example in ancient China, men who were castrated to become imperial guards were given back their severed genitalia in a jar to be kept by them and interred with them at death. The individual was to return to his heavenly abode as he came to this world – intact (Wikipedia 2009).

[16] Moms Rising (http://www.momsrising.org/)

[17] Mothers in Medicine (http://www.mothersinmedicine.com/)

[18] Mamapalooza: woman-empowered, mom branded entertainment education and business (http://mamapalooza.com/)

[19] See, http://amaniandbobsurrogacy.blogspot.com/2010/07/calling-out-to-indian-surrogacy.html.

[20] Here, we are using the concept of Orientalism as discussed by Edward Said (1979), as a process by which the 'the Orient' is constructed as a cultural, political, and social entity.

[21] Notably, an Australian gestational surrogacy support site (http://www.australiaindiasurrogacyadvocates.org/) predominantly features both a (presumably) white baby and vibrant photos of bejeweled Indian women dancing at a wedding (presumably not surrogates, but providing local color). A link to "photos" enthuses, "We love India!" and shows beautiful photos of Indians and India labeled "New friends," "Joyful dancing," "Incredible dancing." The site emphasizes an Orientalist gaze, a type of reproductive tourism that focuses equally

on reproduction and tourism. This is quite different from other sites, particularly the U.S. ones, which tend to make the brown woman and the country of India comparatively invisible, creating a narrative of "tech support" as opposed to tourism.

[22] See, http://amaniandbobsurrogacy.blogspot.com/2010/04/introducing-our-front-bump.html.

[23] See, http://havingababyinindia.blogspot.com/2010/10/our-surrogate-our-babies.html.

[24] Complicating these dynamics, however, are new articles (July 21, 2009 Hindustan Times, posted by Amani and Bob:
http://mixedchild.com/NEWS/July2009/Indian_Egg_Donor.htm)
which assert that, in fact more Western IPs may be seeking Indian egg donors because of the perception that "mixed race babies are brighter and healthier."

[25] P. J. O'Rourke's travel writings including his book *Holidays in Hell* are examples of a xenophobic discourse wrapped in humor and sarcasm.

[26] See, http://millionrupeebaby.blogspot.com/2009/03/sorry-for-long-post_11.html

[27] See, http://millionrupeebaby.blogspot.com/2008/07/potpourri.html

[28] See, http://millionrupeebaby.blogspot.com/2008/07/keep-your-hands-inside-vehicle-kids.html

[29] See, http://millionrupeebaby.blogspot.com/2008/09/faq.html

[30] See, http://www.surromomsonline.com/support/showthread.php?t=165623

[31] See, www.amaniandbobsurrogacy.blogspot.com. This letter was removed from the site by the time of essay publication.

[32] Australian aboriginal children who were forcibly removed from their families and communities and placed with white families as domestic servants, or alternately, housed in boarding schools where they were educated in English, and forbidden to leave, contact their families or even speak their native languages.

[33] See,
http://fourtimesthefun.blogspot.com/2010/08/inside-baby-factory-farms.html

[34] See,
https://www.blogger.com/comment.g?blogID=4540368213787806270&postID=2747922085542005221

[35] See, http://millionrupeebaby.blogspot.com/2008/07/golden-arches.html

[36] See, SurrogacyIndia's Online Support Group
(http://surrogacyindia.forum5.com/login.php?mforum=surrogacyindia), which has gone offline to nonregistered visitors now.

[37] Ibid.

[38] See, http://amaniandbobsurrogacy.blogspot.com/2010/08/finally-idiots-guide-to-getting-out-of.html

[39] See, http://www.surromomsonline.com/support/showthread.php?t=128199

[40] Feminist academics including Sylvia Federici have used Spivak's analysis to critique U.S. and British justifications for the recent wars in Afghanistan and Iraq, whereby, for instance, public acceptance of war was tied to their investment in the 'unveiling' of Muslim women. Federici and others have suggested that this concern about veiling is not so much about the freedom of women as the inhibition

of the misogynist and colonial proprietary gaze. For a commentary on Federici's visit to New York, see http://www.barnard.edu/sfonline/reverb/runions5.htm.

[41] See, http://babymasala.blogspot.com/2009/07/few-more-photos.html

[42] See, http://millionrupeebaby.blogspot.com/2010/11/20-months.html

CONTRIBUTORS

Lorin Basden Arnold (Ph.D. Purdue University) is currently Dean of the College of Communication at Rowan University. She is author of *Family Communication: Theory and Research.* Her research primarily focuses on the intersection of family communication and gender. This is the fourth study she has completed regarding mothering in online communities.

Denise Barnum Burgess is an English Instructor at Arizona State University and a PhD candidate at the University of Arizona. Her scholarship and political advocacy work focus on reshaping educational spaces to be inclusive of all students, including those on the autism spectrum.

Peter Buzzi (pbuzzi@asenseofself.org) is an author, researcher, mentor, consultant, and lecturer with various research and publication interests in social psychology, psychotherapy, management and behavioural economics. He is the Managing Director of 'A Sense Of Self'; an organisation that offers services, programmes and trainings dedicated to mental health and empowering individuals to transform their lives and overcome challenges.

After receiving her Ph.D. in Sociology from Duke University in 2007, **Jennifer Moren Cross** was a Research Associate at the University of Alabama at Birmingham School of Medicine. Presently, she stays home with her three young children, participating in a private online community of mothers and occasional scholarly projects.

Shamita Das Dasgupta is a cofounder of Manavi, an organization focusing on violence against South Asian immigrant women. She teaches at NYU Law School. Shamita is the author of four books, *The Demon Slayers and Other Stories:* (1995), *A Patchwork Shawl* (1998), *Body Evidence* (2007), and *Mothers for Sale* (2009).

Sayantani DasGupta, MD MPH is a teacher, physician, writer, and parent who publishes and speaks nationally on issues of embodiment, feminist science studies, narrative, health and social justice. She is the author of several books including an award winning collection of women's illness narratives. Learn more at www.sayantanidasgupta.com

Patricia Drentea, Ph.D. is an Associate Professor in Sociology at the University of Alabama at Birmingham. Her interests include gender, work and family, as well as how the Internet shapes our parenting experiences. When not at work, she enjoys time with her two young daughters and husband.

Marceline Thompson-Hayes is an associate professor of Communication Studies at Arkansas State University. Her research interests include communication in families of children with autism, as she is the parent of a child with autism herself. She has also co-authored several manuscripts dealing with family and mediated communication as well.

Venetia Kantsa teaches anthropology at the University of the Aegean, Greece. She is author of *Potentially Friends, Potentially Lovers* (Polychromos Planitis 2010), co-editor of *Gender and Social Sciences in Modern Greece* (Aleksándreia, 2010), *Language and Sexuality (through and) beyond gender* (Cambridge Scholars Publishing 2010), *Studies on Gender in Anthropology and History* (Aleksándreia 2011), and editor of *Motherhood in the Forefront. Recent Research in Greek Ethnography* (Aleksándreia 2011).

Sarah Leavitt is a curator at the National Building Museum in Washington, D.C. Her book, *From Catharine Beecher to Martha Stewart: A Cultural History of Domestic Advice*, was published in 2002; other publications include an article on the history of the pregnancy test. Leavitt holds a Ph.D. from Brown University.

Barbara L. Ley is an associate professor in the Department of Journalism and Mass Communication at the University of Wisconsin-Milwaukee. She teaches and researches topics related to health, science, media, and digital culture. She is the author of *From Pink to Green: Disease Prevention and the Environmental Breast Cancer Movement* (2009) and has published in journals such as *Public Understanding of Science*, *Science Communication*, *Journal of Computer-Mediated Communication*, and *Medical Anthropology*.

Todd Lindley is Visiting Lecturer in the International Studies Program at Indiana University, where he also received his PhD in Geography in 2010. He teaches courses on Global Integration and Development, Introduction to International Studies, Research Methods, World Regional Geography, and Population/Demography. His research areas include migration, transnationalism, globalization, and intercountry adoption with a focus on Southeast Asia and the Philippines.

Curtis B. Livesay is a graduate student in Communication Studies at the University of Iowa. His research interests include family communication and social media. He is currently writing his dissertation on nonresidential fathers' performances of their fathering identity via social media.

Brittney D. Lee (BA, 2009, Ouachita Baptist University) is Graduate Teaching Assistant and M.A. student in Communication, University of Arkansas. Her research examines gender and on-line communication, especially blogging.

Michelle L. McGowan is an Assistant Professor of Bioethics at Case Western Reserve University School of Medicine. Her research encompasses the social and ethical implications of reproductive and genetic technologies in the United States, and is focused specifically on preimplantation genetic diagnosis, egg donation and personal genome scanning.

Claudia Megele is an author, researcher, practitioner, consultant and lecturer. She is the Service Director of "A Sense Of Self." She is a member of the editorial board of the Race/Ethnicity Journal and a member of the advisory board of the Journal of Sociological Imagination.

Michelle Moravec (Ph.D. UCLA), Associate Professor of History, Rosemont College, researches the intersections of gender, culture and history. Her work on motherhood has appeared in *The M Word: Real Mothers in Contemporary Art*, *Journal of the Association for Research on Mothering*, *Journal of the Motherhood Initiative,* as well as art exhibition catalogs.

Jenna Vinson is a doctoral candidate in the Rhetoric, Composition, and the Teaching of English program at the University of Arizona. She teaches writing and rhetoric to beginning and advanced college students. Her research interests include the rhetorical construction of motherhood, feminist theories, and visual rhetoric.

Lynne M. Webb (PhD, 1980, University of Oregon) is Professor of Communication, University of Arkansas. Her research examines interpersonal communication in romantic and family contexts. Her research appears in over 50 essays published in scholarly journals and edited volumes. She is co-editor of Computer-Mediated Communication in Personal Relationships.

Originally trained as a journalist in The Netherlands, **Liesbeth Wiering** received a Masters degree in Communication from San Diego State University in 2007. Her research efforts focused on the communication of health and culture. Today, she works as a communication instructor at various community colleges in San Diego, CA.

Yahui Zhang is Assistant Professor of Communication at Wayland Baptist University in Texas. She received her doctoral degree in Communication from Bowling Green State University in Ohio. She has been actively engaged in conducting research in women's empowerment online, communication pedagogy, and agency in Chinese mothers' blogs.